# ANTI-AMERICAN

# TERRORISM AND

# THE MIDDLE EAST

A DOCUMENTARY READER | EDITED BY

BARRY RUBIN AND JUDITH COLP RUBIN

# ANTI-AMERICAN

# TERRORISM AND

# THE MIDDLE EAST

OXFORD
UNIVERSITY PRESS
2002

# OXFORD
### UNIVERSITY PRESS

Oxford   New York
Auckland   Bangkok   Buenos Aires   Cape Town   Chennai
Dar es Salaam   Delhi   Hong Kong   Istanbul   Karachi   Kolkata
Kuala Lumpur   Madrid   Melbourne   Mexico City   Mumbai   Nairobi
São Paulo   Shanghai   Singapore   Taipei   Tokyo   Toronto

and an associated company in Berlin

Copyright © 2002 by Oxford University Press, Inc.

Published by Oxford University Press, Inc.
198 Madison Avenue, New York, New York 10016

www.oup.com

Oxford is a registered trademark of Oxford University Press

Library of Congress Cataloging-in-Publication Data
Anti-American terrorism and the Middle East : a documentary reader / edited by Barry
Rubin and Judith Colp Rubin.
p. cm.
Includes index.
ISBN 978-0-19-517659-9
1. Terrorism—History—Sources.   2. Terrorism—United States—History—Sources.   3.
Terrorism—Middle East—History—Sources.   I. Rubin, Barry.   II. Rubin, Judith Colp.
HV6431 .A566 2002
303.6'25'0973—dc21      2002022462

9  8  7  6  5  4  3  2

Printed in the United States of America
on acid-free paper

*To Gabriella and Daniel,*
*our co-authored children*

# ACKNOWLEDGMENTS

We wish to acknowledge the help of the staff of the Global Research in International Affairs (GLORIA) Center in this project: Cameron Brown, Lawrence Joffe, Joy Pincus, and Caroline Taillandier. We also wish to thank Benjamin Orbach, Rafael Perl, Josh Pollack, and David Zeidan. This book was made possible through the efforts of Joe Spieler, our literary agent, and Dedi Felman, our editor. We warmly thank them both.

# CONTENTS

## 4  USAMA BIN LADIN AND HIS MOVEMENT    135

## 7    MIDDLE EAST REACTION TO SEPTEMBER 11

## 8  SEPTEMBER 11 AND THE WAR AGAINST TERRORISM    317

# ANTI-AMERICAN

# TERRORISM AND

# THE MIDDLE EAST

# INTRODUCTION

The attacks of September 11, 2001, concentrated the attention of the American people and the world as a whole on the threat and consequences of anti-American terrorism from the Middle East. Yet despite the unique and extraordinary nature of those events, this issue had repeatedly caused crises over the previous thirty years as well. Indeed, the issue of Middle East terrorism directed against Americans can accurately be described as one of the main causes of international conflicts involving the United States even before September 11.

During the 1970s, events relating to this issue included airplane hijackings by Palestinian groups, the holding of American diplomats as hostages in Iran from 1979 to 1981, attacks on U.S. installations in Lebanon and elsewhere, and the assassination of U.S. diplomats by Palestinian and Lebanese groups. The Iran hostage issue became the main crisis faced by the administration of President Jimmy Carter.

During the 1980s Americans were held hostage and murdered in Lebanon, where the U.S. Marine peacekeeping force and the U.S. embassy were also bombed in 1983. In an attempt to free hostages, President Ronald Reagan became involved in a secret arms deal with Iran in 1986 that turned into one of his administration's main crises. There were more airplane hijackings and also bombings—most notably that of a Pan American plane over Lockerbie, Scotland, in 1988—with large losses of life. A bomb attack on a Berlin nightclub in 1986, intended to kill American soldiers, brought a U.S. retaliatory attack on Libya. The Lockerbie attack was also attributed to Libya.

During the 1990s a series of escalating attacks took place on Americans, of which the deadliest were those against the Khobar Towers, a residential building in Saudi Arabia for U.S. soldiers, in 1996; the bomb attack on the U.S. embassies in Kenya and Tanzania in 1998; and the attack on the destroyer USS Cole in Yemen in 2000. The embassy and Cole operations were carried out by the al-Qa'ida group headed by Usama bin Ladin.

Even in the United States itself, which had hitherto been virtually immune to Middle East–related terrorist attacks, there had been gradually escalating efforts to launch operations. The year 1993 saw a sniper attack on Central Intelligence Agency employees in Virginia and the first bomb attack on the World Trade Center. In 1999 attempts to hit public targets were made to coincide with the millennium celebrations.

An interesting question is why terrorism within the United States developed only gradually. One logical explanation is that the United States is so far from the Middle East. After all, Middle East–related terror had long been a problem in Europe. In addition, social and political conditions in the United States were quite alien to those in the Middle East, and it seems that terrorist groups did not understand—since they viewed the United States in such hostile terms—how open a society it was and how easy it was to operate there. This situation was changed by several factors. The growth of Middle Eastern and especially Muslim communities in the United States provided more contacts and confidence. At first cells were developed and fund-raising operations were carried out. These activities developed into some operations on American soil, though the number of actual attacks was very small.

Beyond this, of course, is the question of why Middle Eastern groups wanted to target America and Americans at all. Of course, the importance of the United States as a superpower—and after around 1990 the world's only superpower—is an important part of the picture. The United States has also been deeply involved in the Middle East over many decades.

One simple and apparent reason for the use and growth of terrorism against America is the existence of grievances resulting from U.S. policies in the region. Yet this response is both inadequate and inaccurate for a number of reasons. First, many other groups, countries, and regions of the world harbor grievances against the United States but do not resort to terrorism. The Middle East is a clear exception. (Of course, grievances are always a major factor in international conflicts. Nazi Germany held grievances because of its defeat in World War I and the international sanctions and reparations imposed on it thereafter. Japan attacked Pearl Harbor in 1941 in part because it objected to U.S. support for China, which it was then trying to conquer, and to economic sanctions imposed on it to deter its aggression.)

For some Middle East countries, then, sponsoring or engaging in terrorism against the United States was a way of addressing political conflicts that they could not resolve by direct military means.

Second, U.S. policies have always helped some countries in the Middle

East—usually moderate and often Arab states with largely Muslim popula- tions—to defend themselves against radical neighbors. The U.S.-led liberation of Kuwait after it was annexed by Iraq in 1990 is only one example of this pattern. Militant, aggressive regimes—most notably Iran, Iraq, Syria, and Libya—view the United States as blocking their ambitions and have sponsored terrorism against it.

Third, most governments in the region have failed to deliver better lives, democracy, civil liberties, productive economies, or honest administration for their citizens. They have found it useful to direct their people's anger and hatred outward, blaming their problems on foreigners—especially the United States—and demanding that everyone support the rulers in this struggle.

Fourth, a particular ideological intersection of Middle East doctrines gen- erally rejected liberalism and Western thought, preferring a variety of more authoritarian interpretations of the world. These included elements of Marxism, extreme nationalism, third world radicalism, and radical Islamism. Extremist ideologies are often a disease of the development process—a response to the difficulties, slowness, or blockage of progress. In the Middle East, radical Is- lamism sometimes won a dominant position for its reinterpretation of Islam, while radical Arab nationalism often became the main form of nationalism— just as in certain European countries communism hijacked liberalism and so- cialism, and fascism hijacked conservatism and nationalism.

Fifth, revolutionary forces that failed to overthrow a local regime attributed their defeat not to having a wrong or unpopular doctrine, nor to the cleverness of the regime that had beaten them, but to American intervention. While this view had some merit in other parts of the world, the United States rarely played an important role in the internal affairs of any Middle Eastern countries. In their first stage, revolutionary Islamist movements were unable to take power in Arab states. This gave rise to a second phase—in which Usama bin Ladin, who had failed to overthrow the Saudi government, played an important role— that tried to internationalize the battle and turn it into an anti-American *jihad*.

Sixth, a range of specific issues sparked antagonism toward the United States. The two most frequently mentioned were the Arab-Israeli dispute and the sanctions against Iraq. In both cases the issues were very much exaggerated and inflamed. A dozen other conflicts were also cited—and distorted—to prove America's enmity, ranging from Indonesia and the Philippines in the east to Kosovo and Bosnia in the west.

Seventh, there was an element of cultural conflict and antagonism toward Western society as represented by the United States. Globalization, Westerni- zation, modernization, and Americanization were all seen as spreading values and institutions that threatened the Arab and Muslim ways of life. Jealousy over American power and success was also a factor.

Finally, there is also an aspect of happenstance and accident. Without bin

Ladin, his charisma and extraordinary personal wealth, the history of anti-American terrorism would have been different. Even given this situation, a lucky break in intelligence or a mistake by the al-Qa'ida group might have prevented September 11 from happening.

This book tries to deal with these issues and events through first-hand accounts of participants and historical documents. Chapter 1 presents some of those thinkers and activists who challenged traditional Islamic thinking to produce radical Islamist movements. Chapter 2 shows how these ideas were turned into programs for overthrowing the region's existing order.

Chapter 3 discusses both U.S. policy in the area and the critique of the United States produced by both secular and Islamist radicals there. In chapter 4 the specific ideology of bin Ladin and his allies is presented. Among their innovations was to argue that the United States was not only the main enemy but should also be the main and direct target of revolutionary violence.

Chapter 5 analyzes the operations and structure of bin Ladin's movement in launching attacks on the United States. It also shows the American reaction against both bin Ladin's al-Qa'ida group and its host, the Taliban government in Afghanistan. In chapter 6 the background and aftermath of the attacks on September 11, 2001, are presented from the standpoint of al-Qa'ida.

In contrast, chapter 7 examines the reactions to the events of September 11, 2001, throughout the Middle East, showing a variety of attitudes and conclusions. Finally, chapter 8 chronicles the U.S. government's reaction to September 11 and its war against terrorism, which brought down the Taliban government in Afghanistan and retaliated against al-Qa'ida.

Obviously, any selection of materials is by its nature incomplete. It would always have been possible to find particular documents to drop or others to add. Restrictions of space and availability must also, however, be taken into account.

Ensuring a systematic transliteration from Arabic to English always involves imperfect choices. We have standardized certain key spellings, such as al-Qa'ida and Usama bin Ladin, but have otherwise generally left alone the versions used in court documents, for example, where names are rendered as the people involved actually wrote them in English. We have opted for a minimalist approach, employing familiar spellings to make it easier for the reader to recognize names, places, and concepts.

Material in brackets has been placed to ensure the clarity of Arabic words, religious concepts, and the identification of names where needed. Two glossaries at the end of the book, one for names and one for terms, provide further explanation.

# 1

# THE RADICAL

# CRITIQUE OF ISLAM

Islam has existed for almost fourteen hundred years, but the radical Islamist political philosophy is a modern creation. While the Islamists can cite specific Koranic statements, sayings of Muhammad, actions taken during the early years of Islam, and different Islamic thinkers of later centuries, theirs is a highly selective reading that is often at variance with Islam as it was practiced over the centuries.

Indeed, Islamist political thought is a reaction to the dislocations of modern times, the impact of Western ideas, and the perceived failure of other political philosophies in places Muslims live, especially the Arab world and Iran. In "The Islamist View of Life as a Perennial Battle," written for this volume, David Zeidan analyzes the development of Islamist thinking, its arguments with traditional mainstream Islam, and its internal debates.

The Egyptian political leader Hasan al-Banna was a key figure in the development of contemporary Islamist thought and the founder of the Muslim Brotherhood, which became the first large movement of that type. In his essay "On the Doctrine of the Muslim Brothers," written in the 1940s, he lays down the basic principles that have characterized many of its successors. While the Muslim Brotherhood became a mass movement in Egypt during the 1940s and 1950s—and established branches in other countries—it was also involved in terrorist violence. Banna was assassinated by political enemies, and his movement was suppressed by the Egyptian president Gamal Abdel Nasser's regime in the 1950s after an assassination attempt against him by members of the brotherhood. This fate symbolized the defeat of incipient Islamist movements by Arab nationalists during this period.

Iran was another place of origin for modern Islamism, though this became clear only in the 1970s. The key thinker there was Ayatollah Ruhollah Khomeini, a cleric whose essay "Islam Is Not a Religion of Pacifists" showed the lines along which he was thinking as early as 1942. Khomeini conceived of Islam as a revolutionary religion, in contrast to mainstream Islam, which was politically passive and usually supported rulers who were Muslims. The fact that Khomeini was a Persian and a Shia limited his direct influence among Arabs who were Sunni Muslims. Nevertheless, many of his ideas either paralleled or had an effect on Islamism throughout the region.

Although Banna was the main political leader of the Egyptian Islamists, who were in the vanguard of the movement's first generation throughout the Middle East, Sayyid Qutb was the Egyptian Islamists' most important theorist. Like many of Usama bin Ladin's followers decades later, Qutb had been very much affected by his own encounter with the West during several years spent in the United States. His article "Paving the Way," written about 1955, shows his view of *jihad* as an offensive to gain world domination. Qutb also developed the idea that contemporary society, even in Muslim countries, was comparable to the pre-Islamic era of *jahiliyya*. In this sense, *jihad* was not so much a struggle in defense of Islam but also a revolutionary movement against all existing Islamic societies. Representative of the triumph of Arab nationalism in that era was Qutb's own execution by the Nasser government in 1966.

Although Islamist movements were gradually developing during the 1970s, the great impetus for their rapid growth was the victory of a radical Islamist revolution in Iran. Just as the Russian Revolution shaped the Left for decades thereafter and led to the creation of communist parties, the upheaval in Iran had a similar effect on Islamist movements throughout the Middle East. Many of these groups were independent of Iranian control, but their ideas closely parallel Khomeini's thought. His speech at Feyziyeh Theological School on August 24, 1979, and his talk on the nature of the Islamic state on September 8, 1979, created a sort of Leninism for the Islamist movement. According to him, there is a worldwide struggle between the forces of Islam and those of corrupt materialism, a struggle in which everyone must take sides. The Muslim masses must be mobilized to fight the West, and Western conceptions of freedom must be rejected.

The fact that similar themes continue to dominate Iran, despite the development of a moderate pro–democracy movement there in the 1990s, is demonstrated by the speech by Khomeini's hand-picked successor, Ali al-Husseini al-Khamene'i, to the meeting of the Organization of Islamic Countries held in Tehran on December 9, 1997. Disagreeing with his rival, President Muhammad Khatami, Khamene'i tried to persuade the summit meeting of the world's most important Islamic political organization to follow an Islamist line.

In contrast to these figures, Sheikh Muhammad Sayyed Tantawi, leader of al-Azhar Islamic university in Cairo, is one of the most powerful voices of non-Islamist Islam. He was a strong supporter of the Egyptian government and a critic of the Islamists who tried to use violence to seize power in Egypt. Nevertheless, his talk "Suicide Operations Are Legitimate Defense," given on April 8, 1997, shows how difficult it was for mainstream Islamic clerics to remain independent of the ideas introduced by the Islamists. While Tantawi qualifies the use of suicide bombing, he goes further toward accepting it than anyone would have done ten or twenty years earlier.

A statement by an important Saudi cleric supporting the Taliban, who ruled Afghanistan at the time, shows the penetration of these types of ideas into Saudi Arabia. The senior Saudi clerics, who supported the Saudi government, did not accept the opinion of Sheikh Hammoud al-Uqlaa in his November 2000 *fatwa* on the Taliban, but the sheikh's statement does show the type of argument used to argue that this regime was following the right path.

This material only provides a small sampling on the background of radical Islamist ideology that laid a basis for bin Ladin's thought. Later chapters show how this was actually deployed by bin Ladin and other revolutionary movements in the Middle East.

# The Islamist View of Life as a Perennial Battle

DAVID ZEIDAN*

The Islamist political movement (Islamic fundamentalism or Islamism) is a fairly modern phenomenon that started in the 1920s in Egypt with the founding of the Muslim Brotherhood. It is partly a reaction to the severe crises of modernity converging with the rise of charismatic prophetic leaders. It is both a religious reform movement and a political ideology that includes a social element of protest by have-nots against an oppressive order, as well as a counter-attack on secularism, which had reduced the power of religion in recent decades.[1]

As a result, a wide variety of fundamentalist movements and views have arisen to offer Islam as a total way of life and a viable alternative to Western secular ideologies. They aim at bringing all contemporary society under God's sovereignty, rule, and law. The restoration of Islamic glory would be achieved by purifying society from un-Islamic teachings and practices, by a return to Islam's original pure sources, the Koran (God's written revelation through Muhammad) and *hadith* (the divinely inspired traditions of Muhammad's sayings and deeds) as the only authority, and by the establishment of an ideal Islamic state modeled on that of Muhammad and his Companions in the seventh century. The state to be created would be based on *Sharia* (the all-encompassing law ordained by God for humans and based on the Koran and *hadith*).

The differences between movements stem from arguments on how best to achieve these goals and on whether to emphasize an internationalist program or focus on achieving power in a specific state as a first step. The debate is between moderate gradualists, who are willing to work within the constraints of a local political system, and the radical revolutionaries, who are willing to use force to achieve their aims.

Islamists contrast sharply with Muslim traditionalists in many areas, but

* A longer version of this article was published in *Middle East Review of International Affairs* (*MERIA*) 5, no. 4 (December 2001): 26–53.

1. Ameer Ali, "Islamism: Emancipation, Protest, and Identity," *Journal of Muslim Minority Affairs* 20, no. 1 (2000): 11–28. For a very thorough discussion of fundamentalisms across various religions, the reader is directed to *The Fundamentalist Project*, ed. Martin E. Marty and Scott Appleby, 5 vols. (Chicago: University of Chicago Press, 1991–95).

especially in their ideological emphasis on the state. Islamists view the state as the main instrument for implementing their vision of a God-pleasing society under *Sharia*. They concentrate on capturing the state and its centers of power—either legally within the democratic framework, or violently by revolution or coup d'état.[2]

While Islamists are a minority in most Muslim societies and states, their vehement discourse has had much effect on the Muslim world, filling the vacuum left by the failure of secular regimes. This discourse has redefined orthodoxy, reconstituted the boundaries of political power relations and limited the borders of the permissible. It has resonated in the hearts of the impoverished masses and has had a particular appeal to a new strata of literate people with a modern technical education.[3]

Islamists view history as a cosmic struggle between good and evil.[4] This battle is fought in the realms of personal spiritual and moral development, as well as in the sphere of ideas, worldviews, and ideologies.[5] This battle is seen as part of a great cosmic and spiritual confrontation between God's forces of good (true Islam, i.e., the Islamists), and Satan's forces of evil (Western secularism, Christianity, etc.), which have infiltrated and entirely taken over many countries and cultures.

Sayyid Qutb (1906–66) was the ideologue of the Egyptian Muslim Brotherhood in the 1950s and 1960s whose reinterpretation of traditional Islamic concepts catalyzed the rise of radical Islamist groups. He was tortured and executed under the regime of Egypt's president, Gamal Abdel Nasser, the most revered Arab nationalist leader. Qutb's book *Milestones* (*Ma'alim fil tariq*) reinterpreted traditional Islamic concepts to justify a violent takeover of the state. While believers do not always win and often suffer defeat and martyrdom, there is no cause for despair, as God comforts them and the final victory is assured.[6]

Islamists emphasize the battle against *jahiliyya*, traditionally understood as the pagan state of ignorance in pre-Islamic Arabia but reinterpreted by Qutb to mean any contemporary system not based on the original holy sources of Koran and *hadith* and not operating under *Sharia*. Qutb also reinterpreted *jihad*

2. Laura Guazzone, "Islamism and Islamists in the Contemporary Arab World," in *The Islamist Dilemma: The Political Role of Islamist Movements in the Contemporary Arab World*, ed. Laura Guazzone (Reading, Pa.: Ithaca Press, 1995), 10–12.

3. Salwa Isma'il, "Discourse and Ideology in Contemporary Egypt" (Ph.D. diss., McGill University, 1992), 1–2, 89–92, 112–16.

4. Lionel Caplan, in *Studies in Religious Fundamentalisms*, ed. Lionel Caplan (Albany, N.Y.: State University of New York Press, 1987), 18–19.

5. Mark Juergensmeyer, *The New Cold War? Religious Nationalism Confronts the Secular State* (Berkeley, Calif.: University of California Press, 1993), 156–60.

6. Sayyid Qutb, *Milestones* (Indianapolis: American Trust Publications, 1990), 130–37; originally published in Arabic as *Ma'alim fil tariq*.

to mean not just specific wars against unbelievers, but the permanent conflict between the Islamic system and all contemporary *jahili* paradigms. The concepts of the two systems are totally incompatible, so there is no possibility of compromise or coexistence with them. Islam is God's truth, and all that opposes it is inevitably false. Islam means total submission to God and his law, while *jahili* systems are "a deviation from the worship of One God and the divinely ordained way of life."[7]

Abul A'la Mawdudi (1903–79), a Pakistani who was one of the greatest founding figures and ideologues of the Islamist movement, pictured true Islam and its leaders as a modern-style revolutionary party engaged in a revolutionary struggle (*jihad*) "which seeks to alter the social order of the entire world and rebuild it in conformity with its own tenets and ideals. 'Muslims' is the title of that 'International Revolutionary Party' organized by Islam to carry out its revolutionary program. 'Jihad' refers to that revolutionary struggle and utmost exertion which the Islamic Nation/Party brings into play in order to achieve this objective. . . . There is no doubt that all the Prophets of Allah, without exception, were Revolutionary Leaders, and the illustrious Prophet Muhammad was the greatest Revolutionary Leader of all."[8]

Mawdudi had a dichotomous view of the world. He argued that as *islam* means "submission to God," *kufr* means "disobedience toward God." God loves Muslims but dislikes *kafirs*. Muslims find God's forgiveness; *kafirs* do not. Muslims will go to *janna* (paradise), *kafirs* to *jahannum* (hell). Both camps consist of human beings, but Muslims recognize and obey their Lord, while *kafirs* neither recognize him nor obey him. That is the basic difference.[9]

Qutb also divides the world into two camps: God's party versus Satan's. Each individual must either submit to God's law in *Sharia* or be God's enemy. There is only one God, one truth, one law—all else is error, and all other law is mere human caprice: "Islam cannot accept any compromise with *jahiliyya*. . . . Either Islam will remain, or *jahiliyya*; Islam cannot accept or agree to a situation which is half-Islam and half-*jahiliyya*. In this respect Islam's stand is very clear. It says that truth is one and cannot be divided; if it is not the truth, than it must be falsehood. The mixing and coexistence of the truth and falsehood is impossible. Command belongs to Allah, or else to *jahiliyya*. The *Sharia* of Allah will prevail, or else people's desires."[10]

These concepts are foundational in the thought of Usama bin Ladin (1956–),

---

7. Qutb, *Milestones*.
8. Abul A'la Mawdudi, *Jihad in Islam*, trans. Khurshid Ahmad (Birmingham: UK Islamic Dawah Centre, 1997), 3, 8–9; originally published in Arabic as *Jihad fi sabilillah*.
9. Abul A'la Mawdudi, *Let Us Be Muslims*, ed. Khurram Murad (Leicester: Islamic Foundation, 1982), 53–54.
10. Qutb, *Milestones*, 101–2, 112.

the Saudi leader of al-Qa'ida, the radical Islamist group that carried out such anti-American terrorist acts as the bombing of the U.S. embassies in Nairobi and Dar es Salaam in 1998 and the September 11, 2001, attacks on the World Trade Center in New York City and the Pentagon in Washington, D.C. He also sees the world as divided into two camps, "one of faith, where there is no hypocrisy, and one of infidelity, from which we hope God will protect us." The camp of faith is the Muslim camp, and the camp of unbelief is led by the United States under the banner of Christianity.[11]

For most Islamists, the fight to defeat the evil lower self entails separation from improper elements in the world. This struggle and separation are a preparatory stage in the political quest for the establishment of the Islamic state modeled on Muhammad's practice. Qutb started this contemporary debate by his reinterpretation of separation (*mufassala*) and migration (*hijra*). He argued that the first Muslim community developed in clearly defined stages that must be emulated today. First was the proclamation of the message (*da'wa*), then the separation from unbelievers, and finally the fight to implement God's new society on earth (*jihad*). In the Islamic golden age, when a person became a Muslim he made a clean break with his past, separating himself totally from the *jahili* environment and starting a new life with the Koran as his only guide. Qutb concludes that this stage is necessary for any modern renewal, and he understands it as a spiritual separation one makes while staying in society to proclaim and recruit.[12] The radical Egyptian Islamist group al-Jihad, for example, accepted and implemented Qutb's concept of separation as purely spiritual and moral at the same time they penetrated *jahili* society and structures in order to bring about a radical change as soon as possible. Thus, al-Jihad tried to infiltrate the military, security services, and government institutions so as to wage immediate *jihad*, which it initiated by assassinating Egypt's president Anwar al-Sadat in 1981.[13]

Abd al-Salam Faraj (1952–82), the founder and theorist of al-Jihad, in his popular booklet "The Neglected Duty" raised violent *jihad* to the status of a sixth pillar of Islam.[14] Several leaders of this group (especially Ayman al-Zawahiri) became close allies of bin Ladin and participated in attacks on U.S. targets.

---

11. Usama bin-Ladin, "Bin Ladin's Warning: Full Text," full text of a recorded statement broadcast on al-Jazira television. BBC News, South Asia, Sunday, October 7, 2001, <http://1585636.stmnewsid_1585000 w.th_asia english hi news.bbc.co.uk>.

12. Qutb, *Milestones*, 14–16, 113–14, 120.

13. Nabeel T. Jabbour, *The Rumbling Volcano: Islamic Fundamentalism in Egypt* (Pasadena, Calif.: William Carey Library, 1993), 143–57; see also Gilles Kepel, *The Prophet and The Pharaoh: Muslim Extremism in Egypt* (London: al-Saqi, 1985), 95–96, 150.

14. Walid M. Abdelnasser, *The Islamic Movement in Egypt* (London: Kegan Paul International, 1994), 216. See also Derek Hopwood, *Egypt: Politics and Society, 1945–1990* (London: Harper Collins Academic, 1991), 118.

Radical Islamists define the enemy against whom *jihad* should be waged as secularism, the Christian West, Judaism (especially Zionism), and Freemasonry. While bin Ladin was especially explicit in calling for battle against a Christian-Jewish conspiracy against Islam, this basic view is a common one among radical Islamists. Islamic conspiracy theories are rooted in frustration arising out of several centuries of colonialism and dependency.

Against the views held by traditionalists of Jews and Christians as protected *dhimmis* and "people of the Book" (*ahl al-kitab*), Islamists link contemporary Western supremacy to the historic opposition of Jews and Christians to Muhammad in the seventh century, and to texts in the Koran and *hadith* with anti-Christian and anti-Jewish implications. They have developed a modern concept of uninterrupted Christian and Jewish hatred for Islam since its inception, expressed in continual efforts throughout history to divide, weaken, and destroy Islam. Muslims who are also secularists are viewed as being anti-Islamic foreign agents. Rulers in Muslim states are viewed as puppets of these forces who betray their countries into dependence on the West and secularization.[15]

Qutb believed there was a worldwide conspiracy of the crusading Christian West, Marxist communism, and world Jewry against true Islam. Modern imperialism was a masked crusade by the Christian West aided by the Jews for the purpose of attaining world domination. Secular Europe inherited the contempt for all things Islamic from religious Europe, and in spite of its rationalism, these irrational prejudices survive, strengthened by Western imperialism, which saw Islam as the main obstacle to its achieving world domination. This anti-Islamic spirit unites all Western states and cultures.[16]

Khomeini, too, had much to say about the conspiracies of Jews and Christians against Islam:

> Since its inception, Islam was afflicted with the Jews who distorted the reputation of Islam by assaulting and slandering it, and this has continued to our present day. The Crusades made the Christian West realize that Islam with its laws and beliefs was the biggest obstacle to their control and domination of the world. That is why they harbored resentment and treated it unjustly. Then more than three centuries ago, came the evil colonists who found in the Muslim world their long-sought object. To achieve their ambitions they labored to create the conditions that would lead to the annihilation of Islam. Missionaries, Orientalists, the information media— all are in the service of the colonialist countries and all are guilty of distorting Islam in a way that has caused many Muslims to steer away from it and not find their way back to it. While Islam is the religion of struggle for right, justice, freedom and independence, those enemies have portrayed it in a distorted manner, even in the academic world, aiming at extinguishing its flame and robbing it of its revolu-

15. Kate Zebiri, "Muslim Anti-Secularist Discourse in the Context of Muslim-Christian Relations," *Islam and Christian-Muslim Relations* 9, no. 1 (1998): 3.

16. Qutb, *Milestones*, 94–96.

tionary character. They teach that Islam has no relevance to society and government and is only concerned with private rituals. These enemies have implanted their falsehoods in the minds of the Muslim people with the help of their agents, and have managed to eliminate Islam's judiciary and political laws from the sphere of application, replacing them by European laws. The colonialists and their lackeys claim there is a separation between state and religion, so they can isolate Islam from the affairs of society and keep the ulama' away from the people. When they have separated and isolated us they can take away our resources and rule us.[17]

Ayatollah Ali al-Husseini al-Khamene'i (1939–), Khomeini's successor as Iran's supreme guide, makes the same arguments, portraying America as leader of the world's evil forces and Iran as champion of the Islamic camp. The United States, he says, fully deserves the title "The Great Satan" because "it engages in evil, in treachery, in murder and because it is arrogant." America is also "the greatest supporter of the Zionist regime which has thrown out an Islamic nation from its homeland."[18]

Bin Ladin argues in similar terms, although with his own group rather than Iran as the proper leader for all Muslims. America, he and his allies claimed in February 1998, had made "a clear declaration of war on God . . . and Muslims."[19] For bin Ladin, an infidel crusader-Jewish alliance under the cover of the United Nations is said to have spilt Muslim blood in massacres perpetrated in Palestine, Iraq, Lebanon, Tajikistan, Burma, Kashmir, Assam, the Philippines, Somalia, Eritrea, Chechnya, and Bosnia.[20] The United States has also invaded Saudi Arabia, the center of Islam, in alliance with the puppet Saudi government and is plotting to divide that country into three separate states.[21]

Compared to Christian Europe, traditional Islam had a good record of treating Jews with tolerance as protected *dhimmis* and "people of the book" (*ahl al kitab*). In contrast, modern Islamists, reacting to the Israeli-Palestinian conflict, have developed a virulent new form of anti-Semitism that propagates the view of all Jews everywhere and at all times as the enemies of God and as conspirators against Islam.[22]

---

17. Ruhollah Khomeini, "Islamic Government," in *Islam in Transition: Muslim Perspectives*, ed. John Donohue and John Esposito (New York: Oxford University Press, 1982), 314–15.
18. Ali Khamene'i, "No Need for Iran-US Negotiations," excerpts from a *khutbah* addressed to Tehran's Friday worshippers on January 16, 1998. *MSANEWS* 27 (January 1998).
19. "Usama bin Ladin: The Destruction of the Base," interview by Jamal Isma'il, aired on al-Jazira television June 10, 1999. Published by the Terrorism Research Centre, <http://www.terrorism.com/terrorism/BinLadinTranscript.shtml>.
20. Usama bin Ladin, "Declaration of War against the Americans Occupying the Land of the Two Holy Places" (1996). For the complete text of this statement see chapter 4 of this volume.
21. Bin Ladin, "Declaration of War against the Americans."
22. Martin Kramer, "The Salience of Islamic Antisemitism," lecture delivered at the Institute of

Qutb used classic works of Western anti-Semitism such as the *Protocols of the Elders of Zion*.[23] For Qutb, modern-day Jews are identical to the Jews of Arabia at the time of Muhammad, who opposed the prophet and plotted against the early Muslim community. Since then, all Jews have always been wicked enemies of Islam and continue to attack it today.[24]

Qutb accuses the Jews of poisoning Islam by inserting falsehoods into it in order to confuse Muslims.[25] Jews are inherently evil because all through the ages they have rebelled against God. As a result, "From such creatures who kill, massacre and defame prophets one can only expect the spilling of human blood and dirty means which would further their machinations and evilness." They are characterized by ingratitude, selfishness, fanaticism, isolationism, and hatred for all others, always fomenting dissension in their host societies, and exploiting all disasters to profit from the misery of others. They utilize usury to accumulate wealth, infiltrate societies, and dominate the world.[26]

Qutb stated that Jews have been behind every misfortune that has befallen the Muslims through the ages, Zionism being but the latest. Modern secularism is a trap laid by Jews to enable them to penetrate every country with their "satanic usurious activity," which will finally "deliver the proceeds of all human toil into the hands of the great usurious Jewish financial institutions."[27] Jews have poisoned Western academic studies of Islam and have even infiltrated Muslim states by bribing political leaders to betray their own people: "Therefore the struggle between Islam and the Jews continues in force and will continue, because the Jews will be satisfied only with the destruction of this religion (Islam)."[28]

Bin Ladin's views reveal a mixture of traditional and modern anti-Jewish sentiments. He states that the Jews want to divide the Muslim world, enslave it, and loot its wealth, and that they use Western powers to achieve these aims. The Jews in the past attacked the prophets and accused Mary, the mother of Jesus, who is revered in Muslim tradition, of a great sin. They believe that all other humans were created to be exploited by Jews; that they engage in killing, raping, and stealing; and that they have managed to install governments in

---

Jewish Affairs in London; published in *Institute of Jewish Affairs Reports* 2 (October 1995). For the article see http://www.ict.org.il/articles/articledet.cfm?articleid=32.

23. Sayyid Qutb, "Our Struggle with the Jews," in *Past Trials and Present Tribulations: A Muslim Fundamentalist's View of the Jews*, ed. Ronald Nettler (Oxford: Pergamon Press, 1987), foreword, x, 72, 81.

24. Qutb, "Our Struggle with the Jews," 81.

25. Qutb, "Our Struggle with the Jews," 72.

26. Qutb, "Our Struggle with the Jews," 94–96.

27. Sayyid Qutb, "Social Justice in Islam," in *Sayyid Qutb and Islamic Activism: A Translation and Critical Analysis of "Social Justice in Islam,"* ed. W. Shepard (Leiden: E.J. Brill, 1996), p. 303.

28. Qutb, "Our Struggles with the Jews," 75–85.

America that serve as their agents and do their bidding.[29] Similar ideas are expressed by many other Islamist ideologues and pervade Internet sites established by such people and groups.[30]

Azzam Tamimi, director of the Institute of Islamic Political Thought in London, represents a more moderate Islamist viewpoint. He recognizes the traditional Muslim perception of Jews as protected people of the Book who are accorded a safe haven in Muslim lands from Christian persecution and allowed to participate in the Islamic state. It was Christians, not Muslims, who regularly blamed Jews for every catastrophe and crisis. Tamimi argues that it was modern Zionism and the creation of the state of Israel that changed this perception, turning Jews into enemies of Muslims. Tamimi warns against this shift to a view that sees all Jews everywhere as always corrupt and scheming against Islam. He recognizes the contribution of modern Western anti-Jewish writings to the emerging Islamist anti-Semitism. Hostility to the Zionist project has blurred the traditional distinction between the Koranic condemnation of some Jews for their bad conduct, and the Koranic injunction to give Jews covenant (*dhimmi*) rights, the violation of which is a grave sin.[31]

Tamimi warns against failing to distinguish between Zionist and anti-Zionist Jews, and he calls for a restoration of the contextual interpretation of Koranic texts that clearly distinguish between evil and righteous Jews and will prepare the Muslim world for the post-Israel period when, owing to the Muslim political revival, the state of Israel will disappear—but Jews will remain.[32]

As bearers of a revolutionary ideology, fundamentalists are actively engaged in recruiting, mobilizing, and organizing for the showdown with the hostile systems. Radical fundamentalists see militancy as a defense against modern secularizing tendencies threatening to destroy religion, and ultimately they are willing to break state laws in the name of a higher sacred law.[33]

In traditional Islam the term *jahiliyya* denotes the historic condition of immoral paganism and crude ignorance in pre-Islamic Arabia. For most Muslims, traditional and fundamentalist, real history began with Islam—anything before it is *jahiliyya* and therefore of no value except as a counterpoint to Islamic

29. Usama bin Ladin, "Conversation with Terror" [Interview], *Time*, January 11, 1999, 34–35. On antisemitic Web sites see also Al-Bayan Homepage, <http://albayan www.ummah.net.pk; and Ahmad Rami, "Ahmad Rami's Idealism," interview by *Pravda*, broadcast on Radio Islam, July 15, 1997.

30. See, e.g., Al-Bayan Homepage, <http://www.ummah.net.pk/albayan>; also Jessie, "Right On!" Radio Islam, <http://www.radioislam.net/letters/chrtmus.htm>.

31. Azzam Tamimi, "Jews and Muslims in Post-Israel Middle East," *MSANEWS*, June 30, 1999.

32. Tamimi, "Jews and Muslims in Post-Israel Middle East."

33. David Rapoport, "Comparing Militant Fundamentalist Groups," in Marty and Appleby, *The Fundamentalist Project*, 439–40, 446–47.

greatness.[34] Islamists have reinterpreted *jahiliyya*, applying it to present-day societies, rulers, and regimes.

Radical and mainline movements differ over the application of *jahiliyya* to Muslim society and states. Does it apply to society as a whole or only to the regime? Does it include the bureaucracy and the military? The *ulama* [Muslim clerics] establishment? If the entire society, not just the government, is *jahili*, then this legitimizes attacks on civilians, who are effectively apostates—there is no neutral ground.[35] For extreme Muslim fundamentalists, *jahiliyya* is the present condition of a society that by its non-implementation of full *Sharia* reveals its rebellion against God's sovereignty. All Western society and the international organizations dominated by it are *jahili*, as are all Muslim regimes.

Since the violent seventh-century Khariji rebellions (the Khariji were radical Muslims whom some see as ancestors of today's radical Islamists), the *ulama* have recognized the dangers of *takfir* (official labeling as apostate), ruling that it cannot be used against professing Muslims.[36] The Wahhabis of Arabia were the first to reintroduce the Khariji concept of *takfir* into their doctrinal worldview. Muhammad Ibn Abd al-Wahhab (1691–1787), founder of the Wahhabi movement, which later gave birth to the Saudi Arabian state, used *takfir* both against non-Muslims and against Muslims he defined as hypocrites or infidels. He was also the first to expand the concept of *jahiliyya* to include Muslim societies of his time that had diverted from the pure path of Koran and Sunna by their sins of *shirk* (the great sin of associating others with God), especially in the veneration of saints and their tombs.[37] Designating Muslims as *jahilis* and *kafirs* opened the way for proclaiming *jihad* against them.[38] Early Wahhabism influenced contemporary fundamentalist movements in Egypt via Rashid Rida (1865–1935), who accepted many of their ideas.

The Saudi government, while battling a homegrown radical Islamist opposition that included bin Ladin, has encouraged and financed modern Wahhabi

---

34. As'ad Abu-Khalil, "The Incoherence of Islamic Fundamentalism: Arab Islamic Thought at the End of the Twentieth Century," *Middle East Journal* 48, no. 4 (Autumn 1994).

35. John Strawson, "Encountering Islamic Law," paper presented at the Critical Legal Conference, New College, Oxford, September 9–12, 1993. World Wide Web Virtual Library: Islamic and Middle Eastern Law, <http://jsrps.html law socsci faculties www.uel.ac.uk>, p. 11; Abu-Khalil, "The Incoherence of Islamic Fundamentalism."

36. The Kharijis seceded from 'Ali's camp in 659 A.D. because of his compromise with Mu'awiya. They judged Muslims who committed sins to have become non-Muslim apostates worthy of death and instigated many rebellions in the first centuries of Islam until they were cruelly suppressed.

37. Werner Ende and Udo Steinbach, eds., *Der Islam in der Gegenwart* (München: C.H. Beck, 1984), 96–98.

38. Amam al-Yasini, *Religion and State in the Kingdom of Saudia* (Boulder, Colo.: Westview Press, 1985), 28–29.

movements across the Muslim world as well as every variety of radical Islamist movement abroad, thus spreading these concepts in contemporary Muslim societies. Since the 1950s, when Saudi Arabia supported Egyptian Islamists against the Arab nationalist regime of Nasser and granted asylum to many of them, there has been a process of cross-fertilization and integration between Wahhabism and contemporary Islamism. Radical Saudi opposition figures such as bin Ladin carry this integrated Wahhabi-fundamentalist legacy.[39] The Afghan *jihad* against the Soviets led to these concepts' radicalizing Pakistani and Afghan traditional reform movements of the Deobandi school, such as Jamiat-e Ulema-i Islam, which eventually gave birth to the Taliban movement.[40]

Although the large mainline fundamentalist movements such as the Muslim Brotherhood use the *jahili* concept in their discourse, they follow the tradition of not pronouncing *takfir* on any Muslim, accepting claims of belonging to the faith at face value while leaving the judgment of intentions to God. In contrast, however, Qutb claimed that the first step toward Islamic renewal is to judge all societies, institutions, and regimes. All Western societies, be they Christian, Jewish, or Communist, and all contemporary Muslim societies are denounced as *jahili*, and no truly Islamic state exists in the world today. This pronouncement of individuals and communities as apostate (*takfir*) made them legitimate targets for active *jihad*, thus paving the way for indiscriminate terror as practiced by al-Jama'a al-Islamiyya in Egypt or by the Armed Islamic Group (GIA) in Algeria.[41]

Following Qutb's reinterpretations, radical movements use the concepts of *jahiliyya* and *takfir* to legitimize their actions. They are willing to denounce as *kufr* whole societies, including Muslim ones, and regimes as well as individuals. According to the radicals, a state's failure to implement *Sharia* makes that state a *jahili* state under *takfir*, and all true Muslims are duty-bound to wage *jihad* against its regime. Radical movements, such as al-Jama'a al-Islamiyya and al-Jihad in Egypt, claim that gradualist attempts at reform are un-Koranic and view most regimes in Muslim countries as being in a state of *jahiliyya* resembling the Arabs in pre-Islamic times. However, for contemporary radicals modern *jahiliyya* is far worse, for it includes the rejection of the message of Islam: "It is not a *jahiliyya* of ignorance, but a *jahiliyya* of conscious rejection."[42]

39. Joseph Kostiner, "State, Islam and Opposition in Saudi Arabia," in *Religious Radicalism in the Greater Middle East*, ed. Bruce Maddy-Weizman and Efraim Inbar (London: Frank Cass, 1997), 75–89. Kostiner characterizes some opposition figures as Wahabbis who are modern-educated and influenced by ideas of the Muslim Brotherhood and radical revivalist groups in Egypt (81).
40. On the rise of the Taliban, and on whether they are traditionalists or fundamentalists, see William Maley, "Interpreting the Taliban," in *Fundamentalism Reborn? Afghanistan and the Taliban*, ed. William Maley (London: Hurst), 1–28.
41. Qutb, *Milestones*, 5–10, 15–17, 45–50, 66–67, 101, 123.
42. Strawson, "Encountering Islamic Law," 11.

While accepting that the individual's internal struggle is important, many fundamentalists see *jihad* mainly as an external struggle against evil and as a strategy for spreading Islam and for establishing a true Islamic system based on *Sharia*. The only question is whether the goal is to be achieved by a peaceful struggle or by a violent effort. Radicals go beyond the concept accepted by mainline movements of a gradual struggle to improve society (reserving the use of force for defense against aggressors) to include aggressive violent action aimed at taking over power in the state. Some use it to justify attacks on other Muslim and non-Muslim *jahili* states, seen as *dar al-harb* (the house of war), in order to impose the Islamic system and *Sharia* on the whole world.

Hasan al-Banna (1906–49), founder of the mainline Muslim Brotherhood in Egypt, saw *jihad* as a God-ordained defensive strategy, stating that most Islamic scholars "[a]gree unanimously that *jihad* is a communal defensive obligation imposed upon the Islamic ummah in order to broadcast the summons [to embrace Islam] and that it is an individual obligation to repulse the attack of unbelievers upon it." However, as a result of unbelievers ruling Muslim lands and humbling Muslim honor, "[i]t has become an individual obligation, which there is no evading, on every Muslim to prepare his equipment, to make up his mind to engage in *jihad*, and to get ready for it until the opportunity is ripe and God decrees a matter that is sure to be accomplished."[43]

Banna does not accept as sound the *hadith* about the internal *jihad* being the greater *jihad*, and he glorifies active defensive *jihad*: "The supreme martyrdom is only conferred on those who slay or are slain in the way of God. As death is inevitable and can happen only once, partaking in *jihad* is profitable in this world and the next."[44]

Qutb views *jihad* as both defensive and offensive, stating that *jahiliyya* is always evil in whatever form it manifests itself and that *jihad* by force (*bil saif*) must be used to annihilate all *jahili* regimes, replacing them with Islamic systems. He argues that the motto "There is no compulsion in religion" defines Islam's attitude to individuals, not societies. However, to guarantee individuals the free choice of accepting true Islam, they must live in a Muslim environment where no impediment is placed on the implementation of *Sharia*. The goal of *jihad* is to free people from enslavement to other men so that they might serve God alone in a society where all can see Islam operating as God intended: all are free, all are equally slaves to God, legal and social justice is practiced, and greed and usury are eliminated.

As there is no such freedom today, it is incumbent upon Muslims to launch

---

43. Hasan al-Banna, *Five Tracts of Hasan al-Banna (1906–1949): A Selection from the Majmu'at Rasa'il al-Imam al-Shahid* (Berkeley: University of California Press, 1978), 150–51.
44. Al-Banna, *Five Tracts of Hasan al-Banna*, 155–56.

a struggle that is committed to destroying the regimes that deny people the freedom to listen to the message of Islam and force them to bow to their own sovereignty rather than to that of Allah. Having annihilated tyranny, Islam will then establish a new social, economic, and political system in which all enjoy real freedom.[45]

Mawdudi seems to go a step further, explaining *jihad* as the revolutionary struggle to eliminate all evil and establish God's just order on earth: "To bring about a revolution and establish a new order in conformity with the ideology of Islam." This struggle is undertaken to earn God's pleasure, to establish a "just and equitable social order among human beings." Mawdudi explains that it is the duty of true believers to "wipe out oppression, wrongdoing, strife, immorality, arrogance, and unlawful exploitation from the world by force of arms. It is their objective to shatter the myth of the divinity of 'demi-gods' and false deities, and to reinstate good in the place of evil." Under an evil government, evil systems take root and flourish, and no pious order can ever be established. This is why the Islamic party has no option but to wrest the authority of government from wicked hands and transfer it to the hands of true Muslims.[46]

Faraj of al-Jihad declared both Egypt's regime and its employees as *jahili* and under *takfir*; therefore *jihad* against them is justified and imperative. Active *jihad* was God's way of dealing with apostate rulers. Faraj taught that violent *jihad* against all unbelievers is the suppressed sixth pillar of Islam, the main religious duty of true Muslims, and must be given top priority. True Islam means immediate and continuous *jihad* against atheist rulers and states. Focusing on the achievement of political power, Faraj gave priority to an immediate coup against the Egyptian regime, seizure of political power, and the assassination of the nation's leader. After the enemy at home was destroyed, the movement could deal with external enemies.[47]

Abdullah Azzam (1941–89), a prominent Palestinian *jihad* fighter in Afghanistan considered by many to be bin Ladin's mentor, also saw *jihad* as the greatest religious obligation after faith. It is God's ordained method for establishing Islam in the world, a "battle . . . for the reformation of mankind, that the truth may be made dominant and good propagated." Only the ill, the crippled, children, women, and the aged are excused from this duty.[48] Like Faraj,

45. Qutb, *Milestones*, 43–50.
46. Mawdudi, *Jihad fi sabilallah*, 4–6, 10–11.
47. Muhammad Abdessalam Faraj, *al-Farida al-Gha'ibah*, translated in G.H. Jansen, *The Neglected Duty: The Creed of Sadat's Assassins and Islamic Resurgence in the Middle East* (New York: Macmillan, 1986), 159–79, 186–89, 192–93, 207–13; see also Hamid Ansari, "The Islamic Militants in Egyptian Politics," *International Journal of Middle Eastern Studies* 16 (1984): 136–37; see also John Esposito, *The Islamic Threat: Myth or Reality?* (New York: Oxford University Press, 1999), 134–35.
48. Abdullah Azzam, *Defence of the Muslim Lands* (Ahle Sunnah Wal Jama'at, n.d.), 4–17.

Azzam claims that this obligation has been forgotten and that its neglect is the cause of contemporary Muslim humiliation. When not under direct attack by unbelievers, *jihad* is a communal obligation (*fard kifaya*); however, as some Muslim lands are now under infidel occupation (Palestine, Afghanistan in the 1980s, Kashmir, etc.), it becomes a personal duty (*fard 'ayn*) on every Muslim. Azzam recommends concentrating first on Afghanistan and Palestine "because they have become our foremost problems."[49]

Azzam also calls for Muslims to give up narrow nationalism and let their vision extend beyond national borders "that have been drawn up for us by the Kuffar." He repudiates all arguments against the immediate prosecution of *jihad*, such as the lack of a qualified *emir* (princely leader), internal squabbles among Muslims, and the lack of manpower. Nothing annuls the obligation of fighting in the defense of Muslim lands. Indeed, conducting *jihad* is part of the process of uniting Muslims and establishing a real caliphate.[50]

Active martyrdom is another area of reinterpretation and implementation for Islamists. Martyrdom (*istishad*) is being actively encouraged and glorified by fundamentalists, and its rewards in the afterlife have been stressed to induce many to court it. Extreme fundamentalists have revived the Khariji and assassin (Isma'ili) traditions of suicide killings as a legitimate weapon in their contemporary *jihad*.[51] This was especially true of Shia fundamentalists[52] but has now spread to Sunni groups, motivating their members to acts of violent martyrdom.[53]

Ali Shariati (1933–77), the main ideologue of the Iranian revolution, laid great stress on martyrdom as a revolutionary weapon. The martyrdom of Hussein, Muhammad's grandson and a role model for Shia Muslims, is the great paradigm, a protest against tyranny and a witness to the true values of Islam, guaranteeing that faith would survive. Martyrdom is a legitimate, deliberate choice that will strengthen future generations whilst shaming the evil powers of the enemy. It is a true *jihad* that guarantees honor, faith, and the future of the powerless. It transforms Shi'ites from passive "guardians of the cemeteries" to fighters for truth on every front. Referring to the place and date of Hussein's

49. Abdullah Azzam, *Join the Caravan* (London: Azzam, 1996), 36–38.
50. Azzam, *Defence of the Muslim Lands*, 7–17.
51. Ziauddin Sardar, "Clinton Provokes a Jihad: Bin Laden vs. Hasan-e Sabah," *New Statesman*, August 28, 1998. The assassins were an extreme Shia group of Nizari Ismailis who used suicide missions and political assassinations to further their goals of establishing a worldwide Ismaili state.
52. For a good introduction to contemporary Shia thought on martyrdom, see Ali Shariati, *Martyrdom: Arise and Bear Witness* (Teheran: Ministry of Islamic Guidance, 1981), in which Shariati stresses the importance of martyrdom as a revolutionary weapon.
53. Olivier Roy, *The Failure of Political Islam* (London: I.B. Tauris, 1994), 65–67; see also Gabriel Ben-Dor, "The Uniqueness of Islamic Fundamentalism," in *Religious Radicalism in the Greater Middle East*, ed. Bruce Maddy-Weizman and Efraim Inbar (London: Frank Cass, 1997), 246–47.

death, Shariati states: "In the permanent battle of history—everywhere and everyplace, all fields are Karbala, all months are Moharram, all days are Ashura." Shariati argues that when false religion is established, when all avenues of protest are closed, when potential revolutionaries are bribed, co-opted, or killed, then Hussein's model teaches man to be a martyr and by his death to become a witness to the truth and a shaker of the evil empire: "It is an invitation to all ages and generations that if you cannot kill, die."[54] This concept was adopted by Sunni radicals and became an important component in their arsenal of weapons, as demonstrated by Palestinian suicide bombers and by the recent suicide attacks on the Twin Towers in New York.

Traditional Islam forbids suicide (*intihar*), stressing that it is not part of the *jihad* discourse in *Sharia* and that it is a major sin.[55] Most radicals agree that suicide is a major sin forbidden in Islam. However, they use Koranic verses, *hadith*, and cases from the early history of Islam to prove that the voluntary sacrifice of oneself in the cause of Islam (including blowing oneself up as a living bomb) with the objective of defending Muslims and hurting their enemies is not considered suicide but is a legitimate fight to the death.[56] Other approaches are to claim that it is martyrdom, which is different from suicide and legitimate in Islam, or simply to affirm that suicide bombings are permissible as a form of fulfilling the individual duty (*fard 'ayn*) of *jihad*.

Sheikh Yusuf al-Qaradawi (1926–), a prominent Egyptian cleric who is head of the Department of Sunna Studies at the University of Qatar and considered a moderate Muslim Brotherhood member, argued that suicide bombings are "heroic operations of martyrdom," have nothing to do with suicide, and "are the supreme form of *Jihad* for the sake of Allah, and a type of terrorism that is allowed by the *Shari'a*."[57] All agree that someone attempting to end his life for personal reasons is committing a forbidden act of suicide. Muhammad Sayyed Tantawi, sheikh of al-Azhar, argues that suicide operations are to be regarded as martyrdom if the intention is to kill enemy soldiers, but not if they kill women or children. Qaradawi argued that they are legal against Israel even

54. Shia martyrdom has a long pedigree beginning with the martyrdoms of 'Ali and Hussein, which are annually commemorated in the 'Ashura. Martyrdom as a political and military tool has been especially cultivated by Shia groups in Iran (Fedayin-i-Islam) and Lebanon (Hizballah), and the Palestinian Hamas and Islamic Jihad groups, though it appears also in other arenas of Islamic struggle against perceived enemies as in Afghanistan, Chechnya, etc.

55. On the discussions between *ulama* on the question of suicide bombings in the context of the Palestinian uprising, see Yotam Feldner, "Debating the Religious, Political, and Moral Legitimacy of Suicide Bombings," *Middle East Media and Research Institute Inquiry and Analysis* 53 (May 2, 2001), <http://www.memri.org/1A5301.html>.

56. Abu Ruqaiyah. "The Islamic Legitimacy of the 'Martyrdom Operations,' " *Nida'ul Islam* (December–January 1996–97), <http://articles martyrdom.htm 16 www.islam.org.au>.

57. Yotam Feldner, "Debating the Legitimacy of Suicide Bombings"; see also *Middle East Media and Research Institute Inquiry and Analysis* 65 (July 26, 2001).

if women and children are killed because Israeli society is militaristic by nature and women serve in its army. Children and the elderly elsewhere should not be targeted, though if they are killed accidentally this can be excused by the principle of necessity, which justifies the forbidden. A group of al-Azhar scholars published a *fatwa* supporting suicide attacks in which people sacrifice themselves to protect the rights, honor, and land of Muslims.[58]

Following the September 11, 2001, attack on New York, the grand mufti of Saudi Arabia, Sheikh Abdul Aziz ibn-Abdullah ibn-Muhammed al-Sheikh, issued a statement condemning the act as criminal on the grounds that Islam forbids hijacking of planes, terrorizing innocent people, and shedding blood. This is representative of many statements issued by regime-appointed scholars justifying their government's support of the United States. However, he did not touch on the question of martyrdom or suicide—a significant omission.[59]

In the 1970s and 1980s, most radical Islamist groups tended to focus their violent activities on destabilizing and destroying the infidel regimes in their own states, following the injunction of fighting the enemies at hand before dealing with those further afield. The 1990s saw a shift owing to the Afghan war against the Soviets, when thousands of volunteers from across the Muslim world joined the *jihad* and forged a cooperative alliance, helping to internationalize the movement.

Many veterans of the Afghan war returned home after the Soviet withdrawal and worked to radicalize their Islamist groups. There was a marked increase in violence in their home countries, especially in Algeria and Egypt. Others found new sponsors and moved to such flashpoints as Kashmir, Bosnia, Chechnya, Kosovo, and the Philippines. They were also instrumental in intensifying the militancy of Islamist movements in Indonesia and in sub-Saharan Africa.[60]

Another interesting development of the 1990s was the relocation of the centers of many extremist movements from their countries of origin to the West because of repression in their home countries. Many leaders and activists went

58. Feldner, "Debating the Legitimacy of Suicide Bombings"; see also *Middle East Media and Research Institute Inquiry and Analysis* 65 (July 26, 2001); <http://www.memri.org/ia/IA6501.html>.
59. Ain-al-Yaqeen (September 21, 2001), <http://www.ain-al-yaqeen.com/issues/20010921/feat6en.htm>.
60. Richard Engel, "Inside Al-Qaeda: A Window into the World of Militant Islam and the Afghani Alumni," *Jane's International Security News* (September 28, 2001), <http://janes010928_1_n.shtml misc news inter.ity security www.janes.com; see also Simon Reeve, *The New Jackals: Ramzi Yousef, Osama bin Laden, and the Future of Terrorism* (London: Andre Deutsch, 2000), 172–89; and Shaul Shay and Yoram Schweitzer, "The 'Afghan Alumni' Terrorism: Islamic Militants against the Rest of the World," *International Policy Institute for Counter Terrorism* (November 6, 2000), <http://www.ict.org.il/articledet.cfm?articleid=140>.

to Western Europe, the United States, and Canada, where they utilized the relative freedom of operation granted them in the secular-liberal democracies to set up bases and networks. From the West they could more effectively link up with each other and propagate their doctrines back into their home countries using fax, e-mail, and the Internet while recruiting new members in the Western Muslim communities and raising money for increased activities.[61]

The 1991 Gulf War further radicalized these groups by endorsing their perception of the West as aiming to recolonize Muslim states. They were especially enraged by the stationing of U.S. troops in Saudi Arabia. The presence of *kafir* soldiers polluting the Land of the Two Holy Places was perceived as an aggressive act of infidels aimed at dominating the Muslim heartland.

The United States thus became an enemy near at hand and the major focus of attention for groups such as the Egyptian al-Jihad and al-Jama'a al-Islamiyya groups. Usama bin Ladin's al-Qa'ida was in the forefront of those preparing assaults that would really hurt and humiliate America. Petty squabbles and enmity to regimes in Muslim lands became secondary in light of this *jihad* against the greater *kufr*. The results of this shift were seen in the bombings of the American embassies in Nairobi and Dar es Salaam and in the dramatic attacks on the World Trade Center in New York City using hijacked civilian planes.

What characterizes bin Ladin is his pan-Islamic stance, which does not recognize internal divisions in the *umma*, his sense of grievance over its weakness and its continued humiliation at the hands of the West. His capabilities in administration and technical matters, as well as his charisma, motivating power, and ability to form alliances across a wide spectrum of ideologies, have placed him in the forefront of radical Islamists who use terror to further their cause. He is not a shadowy, secretive figure like other leaders of radical groups, but rather courts publicity, giving interviews and appearing on videos and television programs. The staggering magnitude of his exploits in terms of victims and destruction and his gift for public relations have made him the darling of Muslim masses worldwide. He appeals to their popular views of *jihad*, articulating their sense of wounded pride and wish for revenge and identifying a highly visible scapegoat, the United States, as the root of all evil and corruption.

The concept of battle seems to have come full circle. Beginning with the desire to reform Islam itself in an activist spiritual and intellectual struggle to remove inherent internal causes of the *umma*'s weakness and decadence, Islamism has developed an escapist version of searching for scapegoats, which were first defined as corrupt regimes and institutions in Muslim states and societies and later identified as Western powers and especially the United States and

61. Reeve, *The New Jackals*, 232.

Israel. Reformist energies are being subverted and dissipated by venting all the frustrations of the past few centuries of dependency and humiliation on an attempt to injure non-Muslims. This appeals to the populist notion that shame, wounded pride, and loss of honor are redeemable only by the shedding of blood. Yet such activities do not change anything in the Middle East or bring any actual benefits to Muslims themselves.

# On the Doctrine of the Muslim Brothers (1940s)

### HASAN AL-BANNA*

1. We believe that the doctrines and teachings of Islam are all-comprehensive and govern the affairs of men in this world and the next. Those who believe that these doctrines and teachings apply only to spiritual matters and to religious worship are mistaken, for Islam is at once . . . religion and state, spirit and work, holy book and sword. . . .

2. The [Muslim] Brothers believe, moreover, that the basis and source of Islam are the book of Allah [Koran] (may it be blessed and elevated) and the *Sunna* of the prophet (may Allah's blessings and peace be on him); if the nation holds on to them it will never lose its way. . . .

3. The Muslim Brothers also believe that Islam as a universal religion regulates all the affairs of man's life, that it applies to all nations and all people, and that it is for all ages and for all times. . . .

This is why Islam has never failed to benefit from any order or system that does not contradict its fundamental principles or its basic laws. . . .

Many people ask: is it the intention of the Muslim Brothers to use force in achieving their purpose and reaching their goals? Do the Muslim Brothers think of a general revolution against the political or social order in Egypt? . . .

I say to these questioners that the Muslim Brothers will use physical force only when nothing else will do, and then only when they are convinced they have perfected the faith and unity. [But] when they [decide to] use force they will be honorable and frank and will give advance warning. . . . As for revolu-

---

* Hasan al-Banna is leader of the Egyptian Muslim Brotherhood.

tion, the Muslim Brothers do not think of it or depend on it or believe in its benefits and results. Nevertheless, they have been frank in telling every government that has taken over power in Egypt that if conditions remained as they were and if those responsible failed to find speedy solutions to these problems, this would inevitably lead to a revolution, which would not be the making of the Muslim Brothers or the response to their call. . . .

Another group of people ask: Is it part of the program of the Muslim Brothers to take over the government . . . ? The Muslim Brothers do not demand power for themselves; if they find anyone capable of carrying this burden and of fulfilling the trust of government in accordance with a program based on Islam and the Koran, then they will be his soldiers, supporters, and helpers. But if they do not find such a man, then power is included in their program, and they would strive to seize it from the hands of any government that does not fulfill Allah's commands. . . .

The Muslim Brothers love their country and are anxious to preserve its unity; they find nothing [against] any man in being loyal to his country, dying for the sake of his people, and wishing for his fatherland every glory and every honor, and every pride. All this is from the particular standpoint of nationalism. . . .

The Arabs are the core and guardians of Islam. . . . Arab unity is an essential prerequisite for the restoration of Islam's glory, the reestablishment of the Muslim state, and the consolidation of Muslim power. This is why it is the duty of every Muslim to work for the revival and support of Arab unity. . . .

The truth is that just as Islam is a religious faith and a system of worship, it is also patriotism and nationality. . . . As such, Islam does not recognize geographic frontiers nor the distinctions of nationality or race, but considers all Muslims as one single nation and the Islamic homeland as one single territory, no matter how far-flung or remote the countries of which it is composed may be. . . . It should thus be evident that the Muslim Brothers owe respect to their own particular nationalism, Egyptian nationalism, which constitutes the primary basis of the revival that they seek. After that they support Arab unity, which constitutes the second link in the movement of revival; and finally they strive for the Islamic League, which constitutes the perfect [framework] for the larger Islamic homeland. It is only left to say that the Brothers desire the good of the whole world and indeed call for world unity, which is the purpose and final goal of Islam. . . .

# Islam Is Not a Religion of Pacifists (1942)

AYATOLLAH RUHOLLAH KHOMEINI*

Islam's *jihad* is a struggle against idolatry, sexual deviation, plunder, repression, and cruelty. The war waged by [non-Islamic] conquerors, however, aims at promoting lust and animal pleasures. They care not if whole countries are wiped out and many families left homeless. But those who study *jihad* will understand why Islam wants to conquer the whole world. All the countries conquered by Islam or to be conquered in the future will be marked for everlasting salvation. For they shall live under [God's law]. . . .

Those who know nothing of Islam pretend that Islam counsels against war. Those [who say this] are witless. Islam says: Kill all the unbelievers just as they would kill you all! Does this mean that Muslim should sit back until they are devoured by [the unbelievers]? Islam says: Kill them [the non-Muslims], put them to the sword and scatter [their armies]. Does this mean sitting back until [non-Muslims] overcome us? Islam says: Kill in the service of Allah those who may want to kill you! Does this mean that we should surrender [to the enemy]? Islam says: Whatever good there is exists thanks to the sword and in the shadow of the sword! People cannot be made obedient except with the sword! The sword is the key to paradise, which can be opened only for holy warriors!

There are hundreds of other [Koranic] psalms and *hadiths* [sayings of the prophet] urging Muslims to value war and to fight. Does all that mean that Islam is a religion that prevents men from waging war? I spit upon those foolish souls who make such a claim.

# Paving the Way (1955)

SAYYID QUTB**

Those who say that Islamic *jihad* was merely for the defense of the "home land of Islam" diminish the greatness of the Islamic way of life. . . . This is not the

* Ayatollah Ruhollah Khomeini was an Iranian Islamist leader. This translation of "Islam Is Not a Religion of Pacifists," from *Holy Terror*, by Amir Taheri, published by Century Hutchinson, is reprinted by permission of the Random House Group Ltd.
** Sayyid Qutb is an Egyptian Islamist theorist. This essay is from his book *Milestones* (Indianapolis, Ind.: American Trust Publications, 1993).

Islamic point of view, and ... [it] is a creation of [the] modern age and is completely alien to Islamic consciousness. What is acceptable to Islamic consciousness is its belief, the way of life which this belief prescribes, and the society which lives according to this way of life. The soil of the homeland has, in itself, no value or weight. From the Islamic point of view, the only value which the soil can achieve is because on that soil Allah's authority is established and Allah's guidance is followed; and thus it becomes a fortress for the belief, a place for its way of life to be entitled the "homeland of Islam," a center for the movement for the total freedom of man.

Of course, in that case the defense of the "homeland of Islam" is the defense of the Islamic beliefs, the Islamic way of life, and the Islamic community. However, its defense is not the ultimate objective of the Islamic movement of *jihad* but it is a means of establishing the Divine authority within it so that it becomes the headquarters for the movement of Islam, which is then to be carried throughout the earth to the whole of mankind, as the object of this religion is all humanity and its sphere of action is the whole earth. . . .

There are many practical obstacles in the establishing of Allah's rule on earth, such as the power of state, the social system and traditions and, in general, the whole human environment. Islam uses force only to remove these obstacles so that there may not remain any wall between Islam and individual human beings, and so that it may address their hearts and minds after releasing them from these material obstacles, and then leave them free to choose to accept or reject it. . . .

Today, too, we are surrounded by *jahiliyya*. Its nature is the same as during the first period of Islam and it is perhaps a little more deeply entrenched. Our whole environment, people's beliefs and ideas, habits and art, rules and laws is *jahiliyya*, even to the extent that what we consider to be Islamic culture, Islamic sources, Islamic philosophy, and Islamic thought are also constructs of *jahiliyya!* This is why the true Islamic values never enter our hearts, why our minds are never illuminated by Islamic concepts, and why no group of people arises among us equal to the caliber of the first generation of Islam.

This is why in the early stages of our training and education for the Islamic movement we must remove ourselves from all influences of the *jahiliyya* in which we live and from which we derive benefits. We must return to that pure source from which the first generation derived its guidance, free from any mixing or pollution. Only from it can we reliably derive our concepts of the nature of the universe, the nature of human existence, and the relationship of these two with the Perfect, the Real Being, Allah Most High. From the Koran we must also derive our concepts of life, and our principles of government, politics, economics, and all other aspects of life. . . .

We must also free ourselves from the clutches of the *jahili* society, *jahili* concepts, *jahili* traditions, and *jahili* leadership. Our mission is not to compromise with the practices of *jahili* society, nor can we be loyal to it. *Jahili* society, because of its *jahili* characteristics, is not a worthy partner for compromise. Our aim is first to change ourselves so that we may later change the society.

Our foremost objective is to change the practices of the society. Our aim is to change the *jahili* system at its very roots—this system which is fundamentally at variance with Islam and which, with the help of force and oppression, is keeping us from living the sort of life demanded by our Creator.

Our first step will be to raise ourselves above the *jahili* society and all its values and concepts. We will never change our own values and concepts in the slightest order to make a bargain with this *jahili* society! We and *jahiliyya* are on different roads, and if we take even one step in its company, we will lose our goal entirely and lose our way as well. . . .

*Jahiliyya* wants to find an excuse to reject the Divine system and to perpetuate the slavery of one man to another. It wants to divert the power of Muslims from the work of establishing the Divinely ordained way of life so they will not go beyond the stage of belief to the stage of a dynamic movement. It wants to distort the very nature of this method—the method in which Islamic belief matures through the struggle of the Islamic movement to develop the details of the Islamic system through practical implementation and to promulgate laws designed to address practical problems and actual difficulties. . . .

The purpose of *jihad* in Islam is to secure complete freedom for every man throughout the world by releasing him from servitude to other human beings so that he may serve Allah, who is one and who has no associates. This is what motivated the early Muslims to fight the cause of Allah. If they had been asked, "Why are you fighting?" none would have answered, "My country is in danger; I am fighting for its defense," or "The Persians and the Romans have attacked us," or "We want to extend our dominion and want more spoils." They would have answered the same as Raba'i ibn Amer, Huzaifa ibn Muhsin, and Mughira ibn Sh'uba answered when the Persian general Rustum asked them one by one during three successive days before the battle of Qadisiyya [when the Arab Muslims destroyed the Persian empire]: "For what purpose have you come?" Their answer was the same: "Allah has sent us to bring anyone who wishes from servitude to men into the service of Allah alone, from the narrowness of this world into the vastness of the hereafter, and from the tyranny of religions into the justice of Islam. Allah raised a messenger for this purpose to teach his creatures his way. If anyone accepts this way of life, we turn back and give his country back to him, and we fight with those who rebel until we are martyred or become victorious."

No doubt Islam must defend itself against aggressors. Islam's very existence as a general declaration of the universal lordship of Allah and of the freedom of man from servitude to any being other than Allah, its commitment to organize a movement with a new leadership after removing the present *jahili* leadership, and its efforts to create a distinct and permanent community based on divine authority and submission to the One God, Allah, are sufficient cause for the surrounding *jahili* society, which is based on human authority in some form or another, to rise against it in order to preserve itself by suppressing Islam. Clearly, under these conditions, the newly organized Islamic community will have to prepare itself for defense. The question of Islam liking or disliking such a situation is irrelevant, for it is imposed upon Islam. This is quite natural for two systems that cannot co-exist for long. Islam has no choice but to defend itself against aggression.

But still there is another more important fact. By its very nature Islam liberates human beings everywhere from servitude to anyone other than Allah. It cannot be restricted within any geographic or racial confines, because this would leave mankind in evil, chaos, and servitude to lords other than Allah.

Some enemies of Islam may consider it expedient not to take any action against Islam, if Islam leaves them alone in their geographical boundaries with some men lords over others and does not propagate its message of universal freedom within their domain. But Islam cannot agree to this unless they submit to its authority by paying *jizya* [tax paid only by non-Muslims], which will be a guarantee that they have opened their doors for Islam and will not put any obstacles in its propagation through the power of the state. . . .

There is a great difference between this concept of Islam and the view that Islam is confined to geographical and racial boundaries and does not take any action except out of fear of aggression. In the latter, all its inherent dynamism is lost.

# Speech at Feyziyeh Theological School (August 24, 1979)

### AYATOLLAH RUHOLLAH KHOMEINI*

Islam grew with blood. The great religions of the preceding prophets and the momentous religion of Islam, while clutching divine books for the guidance of the people in one hand, carried arms in the other. Abraham . . . in one hand carried the books of the prophets; in the other, an ax to crush the infidels.

---

* Translation in U.S. Department of Commerce, Foreign Broadcast Information Service (FBIS), August 27, 1979.

Moses, the interlocutor of God . . . in one hand carried the Pentateuch and in the other a staff, which reduced the pharoahs to the dust of ignominy, a staff that was like a dragon swallowing up the traitors.

The great prophet of Islam in one hand carried the Koran and in the other a sword; the sword for crushing the traitors and the Koran for guidance. For those who could be guided, the Koran was their means of guidance, while as for those who could not be guided and were plotters, the sword descended on their heads. . . . Islam is a religion of blood for the infidels but a religion of guidance for other people.

We have sacrificed much blood and many martyrs. Islam has sacrificed blood and martyrs.

We do not fear giving martyrs. . . . Whatever we give for Islam is not enough and is too little. Our lives are not worthy. Let those who wish us ill not imagine that our youths are afraid of death or of martyrdom. Martyrdom is a legacy which we have received from our prophets. Those should fear death who consider the aftermath of death to be obliteration. We, who consider the aftermath of death a life more sublime than this one, what fear have we? The traitors should be afraid. The servants of God have no fear. Our army, our gendarmerie, our police, our guards have no fear. Our guards who were [killed] . . . have achieved eternal life. . . .

These people who want freedom, who want our youth to be free, write effusively about the freedom of our youth. What freedom do they want? . . . They want the gambling casinos to remain freely open, the bars to be freely open, they want the fleshpots to remain freely open, they want heroin addicts to be free, opium addicts to be free. They want the seas [reference to mixed bathing] to be free everywhere for the youth.

Our youth should be free to do whatever they want. To be dragged into any form of prostitution they want. This is something dictated by the West. This is something by which they want to emasculate our youth, who could stand up to them. We want to take our youth from the bars to the battlefield. . . .

We want to take our young people from these [movie theaters] that were designed and made to drag them to corruption, and to take them by the hand to places where they will be of some use to the nation. This freedom that these people want is a freedom that the powerful have dictated, and our writers are either unaware of this or are traitors. . . .

The safeguarding of the realm cannot be effected with the freedom that you proclaim. This freedom fragments and ruins the realm. This freedom that you want is a freedom dictated by others so that they can devour the realm and deprive us of young people who could administer a rebuff; this is how we have seen them act, and we have seen the consequences. Calamities have been inflicted on our realm because they dragged our youth into corruption.

We want to release our youths from the opium pipe and place machine guns in their hands. We want to release our youths from the opium pipe and dispatch them to the battlefield. You want us to let things be free and easy so that our youth may become corrupt and so that your masters may reap the profits.

Yes, we are reactionaries, and you are enlightened intellectuals: You intellectuals do not want us to go back 1,400 years. You are afraid lest we bring up our youth in the same way as 1,400 years ago, when just a small number of them were able to relegate to oblivion two great empires. We are reactionaries! You who want to drag our youth into Western teachings and not the teachings that they possess, the teachings of the Islamic countries, you are intellectuals! You, who want freedom, freedom for everything, the freedom of parties, you who want all the freedoms, you intellectuals: freedom that will corrupt our youth, freedom that will pave the way to the oppressor, freedom that will drag our nation to the bottom. This is the freedom that you want; and this is a dictate from abroad that you have imposed. You do not believe in any limits to freedom. You deem license to be freedom. . . .

In the name of democracy, in the name of liberalism, in the name of intellectualism—in various names—the traitors in this realm embarked on their activities and machinations with a free hand. . . . Of course, a freedom that will culminate in corruption, that will result in the fragmentation of the nation, the dissolution of the state, we cannot grant such a freedom, this freedom that you want, this freedom whereby you wish to bring up our youth to indifference, whereby everything could happen anywhere and whereby everyone will do what he wants, whereby the great powers will take away all our revenues and will enjoy life. . . .

Those who saved our realm are none other than the masses of the people. . . . It was these youths, these workers, these farmers who saved our realm; and now the likes of you, entertaining the thought of freedom, liberalism, democracy, and similar things, now want to return them to their former condition. . . . Let these people be free to do whatever they want, so that in another generation not a single committed man may be found—this is the freedom you want, and this is the same freedom that inspires you from abroad.

We do not accept this imported freedom. We must safeguard this nation. We must safeguard these youths. We must take these young people away by the hand from dissolution and render them powerful. We need a militant man. . . . We do not need intellectuals, those intellectuals. Of course, there are a great many good people among the intellectuals, among the educated. But these people who are using their pens so effusively against the nation and are now taking steps against the nation and are threatening the people, shall be crushed. [*Cheers*]. . . .

# On the Nature of the Islamic State
# (September 8, 1979)

AYATOLLAH RUHOLLAH KHOMEINI*

. . . I would like to see everyone believe that our movement . . . for which considerable efforts were made, sacrifices given, young people killed and families ruined . . . was only for Islam. I cannot believe, I do not accept that any prudent individual can believe that the purpose of all these sacrifices was to have less expensive melons, that we sacrificed our young men to have less expensive housing. No one in his right mind would lose young men simply to acquire less expensive housing. There is a false logic promoted perhaps by some self-seeking individuals, that, as it were, the aim of our sacrifices is to improve agriculture. No one would give his life for better agriculture. . . .

Liberals and intellectuals keep complaining that there is no freedom. Indeed, what happened when this freedom was lost? The taverns have been destroyed, houses of disrepute have been closed—actually, I am not sure whether all of them have been closed. We no longer allow boys and girls to undress and go bathing in the sea. To these people this is a freedom they want—a freedom designed for us by the West, rather than a freedom planned by us. This freedom has been dictated by colonialist countries. These freedoms are imported. Now these unfair and so-called supporters of human rights, these unfair so-called writers—not all of them, of course—these unfair liberals are making propaganda in support of this type of freedom. This is a freedom that would lead our country to destruction. A country depends on its young men, on its manpower. What wastes the manpower destroys the country. Any country without manpower will fail.

The point is that those who plan to plunder our wealth wish to do so without obstacles. They say to themselves: . . . The thing to do is to facilitate ways of revelry for these young men . . . while we are busy plundering their resources. This is what has been happening during the past fifty years. They were encouraging our men to corruption, to indifference.

Islam has put an end to means that lead our young men to corruption. Islam wants fighters to stand up to the unbelievers, to those attacking our country. Islam wants to create *mujahid;* it has no intention of making revelers, so that while they are engaged in having a good time, others denigrate and dishonor them. Islam is a serious religion. There is no debauchery in Islam. . . . The only games allowed by Islam are shooting and horse racing, and only for fighting. . . .

---

* Tehran radio, September 8, 1979. Translation in FBIS, September 10, 1979.

However, the West wants to keep us as before. . . . We must try to implement the true nature of the Islamic Republic, adhere to Islam. Certain drastic and profound changes have taken place that give rise to hopefulness. . . .

# Suicide Operations Are Legitimate Defense (April 8, 1997)

## SHEIKH MUHAMMAD SAYYED TANTAWI*

[Tantawi said that the fact that Palestinians are forced into suicide bombing confirms the gravity of the injustice inflicted on them.] What can a man do when injustice becomes heavy and he finds none to ward it off from him? In that case he is forced into legitimate defense of soul, honor and land. . . . [He has] "no option but to urge our brothers in Palestine to defend themselves, their rights, their land and their honor. I tell them: Defend all these in the legitimate means accepted by Islam and noble ethics without aggression or wronging anybody."

[Divine laws do not approve the killing of children, old people, and peaceful citizens, but those doing suicide operations are] in a state of legitimate self-defense against those who attack them and do not show mercy to old people, children, or women. . . . Those who say that this act is *haram* [forbidden by the *Sharia*] should first ask what motivated it.

Why must young people sacrifice themselves? What can we expect from the Palestinians when the Israeli premier repeats with every new dawn that Jerusalem is the eternal capital of Israel, which is something that no reason or religion or law can accept? Injustice breeds an explosion and a person who is severely wronged may sacrifice himself. Honorable people prefer to die than to live in humiliation. . . .

I tell [Israelis] you are the cause of all that is happening. When land is usurped and injustice intensified, fury spreads and explosions happen in self-defense. I also see Jewish rabbis inciting to injustice. Shall I then stand silent? I tell the Palestinians: Defend your land and your sanctities through legitimate

---

* Sheikh Muhammad Sayyed Tantawi is head of Al-Azhar Islamic University and is often considered the most important moderate Islamic cleric in the Arab world. *Al-Hayat*, April 8, 1997.

means. I say to the Jewish rabbis: Speak the truth and demand that your government abide by justice and refrain from racism and bigotry. The divine religions were revealed by God for the happiness of humanity. They preach peace and security and the handing of rights to the deserving parties. They abhor injustice, terrorism, and the destruction of life.

# Speech to Organization of Islamic Countries Meeting (December 9, 1997)

ALI AL-HUSSEINI AL-KHAMENE'I*

Dear Guests, our gathering is not one of friends who get together in pursuit of certain interests. . . . We are brothers who have been eternally linked by our belief in the Koran and who have all become a united body, namely the Islamic *umma* [the community of Muslims], irrespective of any historical, geographical, and political diversity.

We have inevitably accepted this link through our submission to Islam. Complaints, differences, and even tensions cast a pall on this fact, but these can always be washed away by recourse to wisdom, reason, and forbearance. . . .

During the early days after its advent and even at present, Islam has been—and still is—a pathway toward a new world, warranting a prosperous life, moral soundness, and salvation for mankind. At the time of the advent of Islam, previously and even today, the major sufferings and grievances of man—which Islam is bent on eradicating—have permanently been the same: poverty, ignorance, discrimination, war, insecurity, and finally man's incarceration in the prison of materialism and captivity by his evil tendencies. . . .

Today, too, contrary to life's colorful and pleasant surface appearance, mankind suffers from the same pains and sufferings that have beset humanity in the course of history: The majority of people of the world are poor, while a small number hold the major part of assets and wealth on earth. Most nations are deprived of scientific progress, while a group have used their science and knowledge as a means to mete out oppression on others. Wars flare in nooks

---

* Ali al-Husseini al-Khamene'i is Iran's spiritual guide. This speech was delivered at the opening ceremony of the Eighth OIC Summit Meeting, Tehran.

and corners of the world, while others not affected by war are constantly in fear of the eruption of war. All over the world, there is discrimination among the countries, while there are class differences in most states. The Western materialistic civilization is directing everyone toward materialism, while money, gluttony, and carnal desires are made the greatest aspirations. Finally, sincerity, truthfulness, altruism, and self-sacrifice have been replaced in many parts of the world by deception, conspiracy, avarice, jealousy, and other indecent features.

Science, technology, equipment, speed, and facility have dramatically changed the world as compared with the past, but the chronic and age-old pains and chagrin of humanity still remain unchanged. The major problems of today are the same that existed in the past.

Western liberalism, communism, socialism, and all other -isms have gone through their tests and proved their debility. As in the past, today Islam is the only remedial, curative, and savior angel. . . .

The important consideration is the observation and recognition of the true visage of Islam (devoid of any embellishments). The illuminated visage of Islam has been defaced and defiled in the course of several centuries by the foes and in the course of longer spans of time by the ignorant and heedless friends. They have deliberately or ignorantly made additions or deletions in Islam.

At present, too, incorrect understanding and quest for interests are still at work by the inner circles to tarnish the image of Islam. But without a shade of doubt, enemy publicity in this regard is by far more effective, by trying to embark upon this move through subtle and sly ways.

One instance of the enemies' incessant efforts to this end is the massive bulk of publicity against the Islamic Iran after the establishment of the Islamic government in Iran. They felt that leveling accusations and furnishing false news would be the most conclusive ways to stave off the impacts of this grand revolution. They have uttered such falsities about us and ascribed such things to us that their words have become repetitive and completely monotonous and boring for the listeners. The Zionists, the notorious global Zionist media, and arrogant agents, in particular the Americans—namely those who have sustained the greatest losses due to the revolution—have been and are most active and vocal in this area. . . .

In our culture, arrogance refers to a power clique that relies on its political, military, scientific, and economic power and gets inspiration from a discriminatory outlook toward mankind to exert pressure on and exploit large groups of human beings, namely nations, governments, and countries with bullying and contemptuous domination, to interfere and intervene in their affairs, to plunder their assets and wealth, to bully the governments, to oppress the nations, and to insult their cultures and traditions. Salient examples are colonialism, neo-colonialism, and recently the extensive and all-out political, economic, publicity, and even military invasion of the previous colonizers and their heirs. All of these are carried out in front of the eyes of our nations, which are tasting their bitter fruits.

In this effective invasion, the Western powers have reaped the benefit of their academic and technological advancement and of some of their national and indigenous features. We do not reprimand the enemy. Those who pave the ground for the victory of their enemies and their own defeat through short-sightedness search for ease and comfort, and egotism deserve to be rebuked.

The West, in its all-rounded invasion, has also targeted our Islamic faith and character. In the light of its store of science, needed by all, the West intensely and persistently exported to our countries the culture of laxness and disregard for religion and ethics, a culture with which it is gripped.

Indubitably, this ethical quagmire will, on a not-too-distant day, engulf the present Western civilization and wipe it out.

At the present juncture, the world of Islam is in a calamitous condition due to hostile invasions, coupled with the inner factors affecting the past generations. Poverty, ignorance, academic backwardness, moral laxness, and worst yet, the cultural and at times political domination of its enemies, on the one hand, and great problems such as those of Palestine, Afghanistan, Lebanon, Iraq, Kashmir, Bosnia-Herzegovina, the Caucasus, and others, on the other hand, offer a long list of divine and human responsibilities to the governments, political dignitaries, and leaders of the Islamic world.

Today, we should take the initiative. So far, the enemy has always held the initiative, and we have, at most, complained. . . .

If we regulate our ties and make them brotherly . . . what can the United States do vis-à-vis the united front of the Islamic countries, ranging from Indonesia to North Africa? Today, global arrogance gains hope and strength through creating discord and disunity in this front. Is it not time to bolster and strengthen this rank in our own favor?

Perhaps the existence of an enemy such as Israel in the heart of the Islamic lands could have brought us closer. . . . But the covert hands of arrogance effaced even this peril from along its way: It did something to us [such] that right now we fear each other more than we fear the enemy! The temptations, falsehoods, and sly publicity have made the Islamic countries erroneously and unduly intimidated by one another.

For eighteen years now, the political designers of arrogance are breathing their poisonous breath to make our neighbors in the Persian Gulf fearful of Islamic Iran, which holds the banner of unity and brotherhood. I declare that Islamic Iran poses no threat to any Islamic country.

Blessed by the Koranic injunctions, Islamic Iran is today more than ever for the unity, dignity, and might of the world of Islam. Thanks to the Islamic faith and notwithstanding the enemies' publicity ploys, we Iranians have upheld and preserved our national unity in an unprecedented way and enhanced public involvement in the affairs, contrary to the claims and innate wishes of our enemies. The brilliant presidential election this year was an example of this daily increasing public involvement.

The government is united and uniform and all officials are cordial with one another. Confidence and self-reliance are the major decisive factors in all our academic, political, economic, and cultural endeavors. Possessed of this belief in our selves, which Imam Khomeini taught us, we have been able to reconstruct and rehabilitate a ruined and backward country left from the Pahlavi era and made even more ruined during the eight-year-long imposed war. We witness the same endeavor in some other brotherly countries as well.

But political dignity and power are of greatest importance. Our nation and government have eradicated the influence and intervention of the foreigners in their country by recourse to Islam. Nowadays, the Islamic *umma* is avid for that self-confidence and for this dignity and independence. And all of us should muster efforts to this end. This is a historical responsibility. Today, the ground is paved for fulfillment of this duty and for acquisition of dignity, power, and full independence of the world of Islam. . . .

# Fatwa on the Taliban (November 29, 2000)

SHEIKH HAMMOUD AL-UQLAA*

To determine the implementation or rejection of *Sharia* by a country depends on a number of factors:

Firstly, it is legislation by the book of Allah and the *Sunna* [teachings] of his messenger [Muhammad] in all the branches of ruling and . . . in other worldly dealings.

Secondly, indeed one of the most important components of a country is its control of land. It is well known that the Taliban government has over 95 percent of Afghanistan under its control. [This was not accurate, for much of the country was controlled by the Northern Alliance and by Iranian-backed Shia groups.—*Eds.*]

---

* Sheikh Hammoud al-Uqlaa is a Saudi cleric.

Thirdly, that its relations and dealings with other countries are established on [a proper Islamic basis].

The Taliban regime in Afghanistan has been proven to fulfill these factors, so it is the only country in the world in which there are no man-made laws and legislations. Rather, its legislation is indeed established on the *Sharia* of Allah and his messenger in the courts of law, in the ministries, in the governmental circles, and in other establishments. . . .

Amongst the evidence that the Taliban government is a *Sharia* government is the fact that the disbelieving countries who are enemies of Islam and the Muslims are hostile toward it, have imposed an economic boycott on it, isolated it, and tightened their grip on it for no reason other than its adherence to the *deen* [beliefs] of Islam.

Furthermore, military strikes are about to be carried out on Afghanistan just like America attacked it with cruise missiles in 1998. At the same time, these same disbelieving countries continue to support the opposition Northern Alliance with funds, weapons, and advisors. This itself is clear evidence of the Taliban government's implementation of *Sharia* and that they have truth on their side in their fight against the Northern Alliance. In addition, the failure of the disbelieving nations to recognize the Taliban regime as a nation and a government further removes any doubt in the *Sharia* implementation of the Taliban government. . . .

And from the greatest qualities further proving the validity of the Muslim Taliban government are:

1. Its efforts to support the *mujahidin* and defend them against their enemies. This has been witnessed in this government.
2. It does not contain any forms of media that are forbidden in the *Sharia*.
3. Indeed it is adamant, sincere, and honest in its efforts to implement *Sharia* from its establishment of the Islamic penal code to forbidding open acts of disobedience to Allah and his messenger, meting out suitable punishments for them and Islamicizing education and media.
4. Indeed, it is the only country in the world that is striving for women's rights according to the *Sharia* and not according to the ways of the secularists who encourage the women to display their beauty, cast off their *hijabs* [headscarves], mix freely with men, drive cars alone, and other things like that.
5. It is the only country in the world that has a separate ministry by the name of the Ministry to Encourage Good and Forbid Evil.

[In October 2001, the Council of Senior Scholars of Saudi Arabia rejected this *fatwa* and said that Uqlaa had no right to make it.—*Eds.*]

# 2

# THE

# REVOLUTIONARIES

Building on the philosophy of earlier Islamists and the success of Iran's revolution, a number of radical Islamist movements developed. Some were influenced by those who had fought in Afghanistan against the Soviets, but most were developed locally. By the mid-1980s the most significant opposition groups throughout the Arab world were Islamists. In several countries—notably Algeria, Egypt, Iraq, and Syria—they launched ill-fated efforts to seize power. In other places, such as Lebanon and among the Palestinians, they tried to take the leadership in fighting against Israel in order to gain control of their communities and show that they were the fiercest warriors in the cause of "national liberation."

In his book smuggled out of Afghanistan, *Knights under the Prophet's Banner: Meditations on the Jihadist Movement*, Ayman al-Zawahiri, an Egyptian leader of al-Qa'ida, graphically describes the personal and political importance of the Afghan struggle against the Soviets as a crucible for his movement. Afghanistan was the place where these groups gained military experience, ideological certainty, and organizational cohesion. Especially interesting is his point on how involvement in Afghanistan allowed the radical Islamists to distance themselves from the influence of Arab nationalism, both as a doctrine and as a factor dividing the Islamists into movements seeking revolution in specific Arab states.

Hizballah in Lebanon was one such movement. Its program was based on the idea of using the battle against Israel to build a mass base that would then let them take over Lebanon itself and turn it into an Islamic republic. Its 1985 program shows its ideology and strategy. Despite enjoying Iran's backing, Syria's toleration, and patriotic credentials for attacking Israel and its presence in south Lebanon, the movement came nowhere close to seizing power in Lebanon. There were too many other religious forces in the country and even competition within Hizballah's own Shi'ite community. While Hizballah claimed credit for Israel's withdrawal from southern Lebanon in 2000, its loss of that target within Lebanon also eroded much of its appeal.

Hamas tried a similar approach to Hizballah. Its 1988 charter shows its attitudes toward key issues. Israel was to be wiped off the map, and its analysis of that country was riddled with anti-Semitism. Palestinian nationalism was treated as both a brother and as a less worthy rival. The struggle against non-Muslims was to be a stepping-stone toward mobilizing Muslims, winning their support, taking over leadership of the movement, and eventually becoming the leadership of an Islamist state. Terrorism was a key element in the military strategy. But while Hamas also did build a solid base of support and carry out many terrorist attacks, including suicide bombings, it could never displace the Palestinian nationalist movement or defeat Israel.

The main group of Islamists in Saudi Arabia, which was already defined by its government as an Islamic state, took a different course. In 1992 they presented a petition to the king signed by a number of Islamic clerics and others who had been discussing this project for a year since the end of the war over Kuwait. Called "The Letter of Demands," the petition was phrased in democratic-sounding language, but the goal of the signers was to turn the country into an Islamist state. The government ignored it, and bin Ladin later characterized this refusal as justifying the Islamist revolutionary movement to overthrow the Saudi regime.

One of the key influences in the second generation of Islamist movements, as well as a direct personal influence on bin Ladin, was Abdullah Azzam. Azzam was a Palestinian educator who worked in Jordan and eventually played an important part in the building of the Arab Islamist forces fighting in Afghanistan, where he was killed. As can be seen in this article about his life by Abdullah bin Omar, "Abdullah Azzam, the Struggling Sheikh," Azzam became a role model for Islamist revolutionaries. He is presented here as an exemplary human being whose example should be emulated.

To some extent, Umar Abd al-Rahman has been an Egyptian equivalent of Azzam as well as a pioneer in conducting Islamist agitation and armed struggle within America. A leading figure in the opposition to the Egyptian government, Rahman was permitted to emigrate to the United States, where he became a focal point in Islamist movements. The blind sheikh was convicted of being a key figure in the first terror attack on the World Trade Center and imprisoned. Demanding his release was an important priority for radical Islamists. In an interview he talks about his life and battles.

Rifa'ey Ahmad Taha, another Egyptian Islamist leader, exemplifies the strategic misperceptions and outlandish claims of success that so often fill Islamist speeches and propaganda. In a 1997 interview, he claims that "[t]he Islamic State in Egypt is approaching," while actually his and other groups had been defeated by the government by then. He paints a picture of an unpopular regime that functions as a U.S. puppet and is on the verge of collapse.

Zawahiri depicts the Islamist revolution in Egypt, in which he participated as a leader of the al-Jihad group before joining al-Qa'ida, as a succession of heroic battles by courageous warriors whom the masses would soon join. In fact, though, his account in *Knights under the Prophet's Banner* is a series of total defeats and almost total failures punctuated by factional splits and quarrels. His description of the movement's greatest moment and crushed uprising—after its assassination of President Anwar al-Sadat in 1981—is typical in this regard. The suppression of the movement by Egypt's government in the 1980s, the failure of the masses to respond, and the decision of some of his colleagues to accept a cease-fire all pushed Zawahiri to shift his own focus to the Islamist internationalism of al-Qa'ida and to focusing on fighting America rather than the Egyptian regime.

A young Jordanian Islamist, Sheikh Abu Muhammad al-Maqdissy, provides an interesting account of his conversion to radical Islamism, his attempts to organize against the government there—a key goal was opposition to an elected parliament—and his capture and imprisonment. The December 1997 interview reprinted here gives a sense of the Islamist struggle on a more practical and grassroots level.

Finally, the Taliban—former rulers of Afghanistan, which was the only Sunni Muslim Islamist state—is represented by an interview with one of its more dynamic young leaders, Mullah Ma'soum Afghani, its spokesman and ambassador to Pakistan. He presents the Taliban as a combination of a good-government movement and a broad Islamic front, playing down its problems and the degree of opposition in the country.

# The Importance of Afghanistan for the Islamist Revolution (January 2002)

AYMAN AL-ZAWAHIRI*

My connection with Afghanistan began in the summer of 1980 by a twist of fate, when I was temporarily filling in for one of my colleagues at al-Sayyida Zaynab Clinic, which was administered by the Muslim Brotherhood's Islamic Medical Society. One night the clinic director, a Muslim Brother, asked me if I would like to travel to Pakistan to contribute, through my work as a surgeon, to the medical relief effort among the Afghan refugees. I immediately agreed because I saw this as an opportunity to get to know one of the arenas of *jihad* that might be a tributary and a base for *jihad* in Egypt and the Arab region, the heart of the Islamic world, where the basic battle of Islam was being fought. . . .

The problem of finding a secure base for *jihad* activity in Egypt used to occupy me a lot, in view of the [activity against us] by the security forces and because of Egypt's flat terrain, which made government control easy, for the River Nile runs in its narrow valley between two deserts that have no vegetation or water. Such a terrain made guerrilla warfare in Egypt impossible. . . .

For this reason this invitation [to participate in medical assistance to the Afghan refugees] came as a predestined event. I accepted the invitation out of an earnest wish to get to know the suitable arenas where I could establish a secure base for *jihadist* action in Egypt, particularly during the term of Anwar al-Sadat, when the signs of a new crusade became apparent to everyone who had perspicacity and were obvious to everyone concerned about his nation's affairs.

And so I actually left for Peshawar in Pakistan in the company of a colleague who was an anesthetist. We were soon followed by another colleague who specialized in plastic surgery. We were the first three Arabs to arrive there to participate in relief work among the Afghan refugees. . . .

[The importance of Afghanistan for the radical Islamists:]

1. A *jihadist* movement needs an arena that would act like an incubator

---

* Ayman al-Zawahiri is an al-Qa'ida leader. The essay is from *Knights under the Prophet's Banner: Meditations on the Jihadist Movement*, published in *al-Sharq al-Awsat* newspaper in eleven installments in January 2002. Translated by U.S. Department of Commerce, Foreign Broadcast Information Service (FBIS).

where its seeds would grow and where it can acquire practical experience in combat, politics, and organizational matters. . . . Abu Ubaydah al-Banshiri [an al-Qa'ida official] . . . used to say: "It is as if 100 years have been added to my life in Afghanistan."

2. The Muslim youths in Afghanistan waged the war to liberate Muslim land under purely Islamic slogans, a very vital matter, for many of the liberation battles in our Muslim world had used composite slogans that mixed nationalism with Islam and, indeed, sometimes caused Islam to intermingle with leftist, communist slogans. This produced a schism in the thinking of the Muslim young men between their Islamic *jihadist* ideology that should rest on pure loyalty to God's religion, and its practical implementation.

The Palestine issue is the best example of these intermingled slogans and beliefs under the influence of the idea of allying oneself with the devil [i.e., the Arab regimes] for the sake of liberating Palestine. They allied themselves with the devil, but lost Palestine.

Another important issue is the fact that these battles that were waged under non-Muslim banners or under mixed banners caused the dividing lines between friends and enemies to become blurred. The Muslim youths began to have doubts about who was the enemy. Was it the foreign enemy that occupied Muslim territory, or was it the domestic enemy that prohibited government by Islamic *Sharia*, repressed the Muslims, and disseminated immorality under the slogans of progressiveness, liberty, nationalism, and liberation? This situation led the homeland to the brink of the abyss of domestic ruin and surrender to the foreign enemy, exactly like the current situation of the majority of our [Arab] countries under the aegis of the new world order. . . .

In Afghanistan the picture was perfectly clear: A Muslim nation carrying out *jihad* under the banner of Islam, versus a foreign enemy that was an infidel aggressor backed by a corrupt, apostatic regime at home. In the case of this war, the application of theory to the facts was manifestly clear. This clarity was also beneficial in refuting the ambiguities raised by many people [who were] professing to carry out Islamist work but who escaped from the arena of *jihad* on the pretext that there was no arena in which the distinction between Muslims and their enemies was obvious.

3. Furthermore, the Afghan arena, especially after the Russians withdrew, became a practical example of *jihad* against the renegade rulers who allied themselves with the foreign enemies of Islam. Najibullah in Afghanistan was an example that we had seen before. He prayed, fasted, and performed pilgrimage. At the same time he prohibited government by Islam and allied himself with the enemies of Islam, allowed them to enter his country, and brutally oppressed the Muslims and the *mujahidin*.

4. A further significant point was that the *jihad* battles in Afghanistan destroyed the myth of a [superpower] in the minds of the Muslim *mujahidin*

young men. The USSR, a superpower with the largest land army in the world, was destroyed, and the remnants of its troops fled Afghanistan before the eyes of the Muslim youths and as a result of their actions.

That *jihad* was a training course of the utmost importance to prepare Muslim *mujahidin* to wage their awaited battle against the superpower that now has sole dominance over the globe, namely, the United States.

It also gave young Muslim *mujahidin*—Arabs, Pakistanis, Turks, and Muslims from Central and East Asia—a great opportunity to get acquainted with each other on the land of Afghan *jihad* through their comradeship-at-arms against the enemies of Islam.

In this way the *mujahidin* young men and the *jihadist* movements came to know each other closely, exchanged expertise, and learned to understand their brethren's problems.

While the United States backed Pakistan and the *mujahidin* factions with money and equipment, the young Arab *mujahidins'* relationship with the United States was totally different.

Indeed, the presence of those young Arab Afghans in Afghanistan and their increasing numbers represented a failure of U.S. policy and new proof of the famous U.S. political stupidity. The financing of the activities of the Arab *mujahidin* in Afghanistan came from aid sent to Afghanistan by popular organizations. It was substantial aid.

The Arab *mujahidin* did not confine themselves to financing their own *jihad* but also carried Muslim donations to the Afghan *mujahidin* themselves. Usama bin Ladin has apprised me of the size of the popular Arab support for the Afghan *mujahidin* that amounted, according to his sources, to $200 million in the form of military aid alone in ten years. [Zawahiri implies this was aid raised from the masses, but ironically, much of this money comes from the Saudi government he and bin Ladin said was un-Islamic and wanted to overthrow.—*Eds.*] Imagine how much aid was sent by popular Arab organizations in the non-military fields such as medicine and health, education and vocational training, food, and social assistance (including sponsorship of orphans, widows, and the war handicapped). Add to all this the donations that were sent on special occasions such as Id al-Fitr and Id al-Adha feasts and during the month of Ramadan.

Through this unofficial popular support, the Arab *mujahidin* established training centers and centers for the call to the faith. They formed fronts that trained and equipped thousands of Arab *mujahidin* and provided them with living expenses, housing, travel, and organization.

# Program (February 1985)

## HIZBALLAH*

## Our Identity

We are often asked: Who are we, the Hizballah, and what is our identity? We are the sons of the *umma* (Muslim community), the party of God (Hizb Allah) the vanguard of which was made victorious by God in Iran. There the vanguard succeeded in laying down the bases of a Muslim state that plays a central role in the world. We obey the orders of one leader, wise and just, that of our tutor and *faqih* [jurist] who fulfills all the necessary conditions: Ruhollah Musawi Khomeini. God save him!

By virtue of the above, we do not constitute an organized and closed party in Lebanon, nor are we a tight political cadre. We are an *umma* linked to the Muslims of the whole world by the solid doctrinal and religious connection of Islam, whose message God wanted to be fulfilled by the Seal [i.e., the last] of the prophets, that is, Muhammad. This is why whatever touches or strikes the Muslims in Afghanistan, Iraq, the Philippines, and elsewhere reverberates throughout the whole Muslim *umma* of which we are an integral part. Our behavior is dictated to us by legal principles laid down by the light of an overall political conception defined by the leading jurist [*wilayat al-faqih*].

As for our culture, it is based on the Holy Koran, the Sunna, and the legal rulings of the *faqih*, who is our source of imitation [*marja' al-taqlid*]. Our culture is crystal clear. It is not complicated and is accessible to all.

No one can imagine the importance of our military potential, as our military apparatus is not separate from our overall social fabric. Each of us is a fighting soldier. And when it becomes necessary to carry out the Holy War, each of us takes up his assignment in the fight in accordance with the injunctions of the Law, and that in the framework of the mission carried out under the tutelage of the Commanding Jurist.

## Our Fight

The United States has tried, through its local agents, to persuade the people that those who crushed their arrogance in Lebanon and frustrated their con-spiracy against the oppressed were nothing but a bunch of fanatic terrorists whose sole aim is to dynamite bars and destroy slot machines. Such suggestions cannot and will not mislead our *umma*, for the whole world knows that whoever wishes to oppose the United States, that arrogant superpower, cannot indulge

---

* *Al-Safir*, February 16, 1985

in marginal acts that may make it deviate from its major objective. We combat abomination, and we shall tear out its very roots, its primary roots, which are the United States. All attempts made to drive us into marginal actions will fail, especially as our determination to fight the United States is solid.

We declare openly and loudly that we are an *umma* that fears God only and is by no means ready to tolerate injustice, aggression, and humiliation. America, its Atlantic Pact allies [NATO], and the Zionist entity in the holy land of Palestine attacked us and continue to do so without respite. Their aim is to make us eat dust continually. This is why we are, more and more, in a state of permanent alert in order to repel aggression and defend our religion, our existence, our dignity. They invaded our country, destroyed our villages, slit the throats of our children, violated our sanctuaries, and appointed masters over our people who committed the worst massacres against our *umma*. They do not cease to give support to these allies of Israel, and do not enable us to decide our future according to our own wishes.

In a single night the Israelis and the Phalangists [the main Christian militia] executed thousands of our sons, women, and children in Sabra and Shatilla. [Actually, the massacres were carried out by Christian forces in Lebanon who, at the time this charter was written, were—like Hizballah—also clients of Syria. The death toll was in the hundreds, not thousands. There is no mention in this document of Syria's occupation in much of Lebanon.—*Eds.*] No international organization protested or denounced this ferocious massacre in an effective manner, a massacre perpetrated with the tacit accord of America's European allies, which had retreated a few days, maybe even a few hours, earlier from the Palestinian camps. The Lebanese defeatists accepted putting the camps under the protection of that crafty fox, the U.S. envoy Philip Habib.

We have no alternative but to confront aggression by sacrifice. The coordination between the Phalangists and Israel continues and develops. A hundred thousand victims—this is the approximate balance sheet of crimes committed by them and by the United States against us. Almost half a million Muslims were forced to leave their homes. Their quarters were virtually totally destroyed in Nab'a, my own Beirut suburb [The person referred to here, and clearly a major—if not the sole—author of this document, is believed to have been Sheikh Hussein Fadlallah, Hizballah's spiritual guide—*Eds.*], as well as in Burj Hammud, Dekonaneh, Tel Zaatar, Sinbay, Ghawarina, and Jubeil. . . . The Zionist occupation then launched its usurpatory invasion of Lebanon in full and open collusion with the Phalanges [a Lebanese Christian party]. The latter condemned all attempts to resist the invading forces. They participated in the implementation of certain Israeli plans in order to accomplish its [i.e., Israel's] Lebanese dream and acceded to all Israeli requests in order to gain power. . . .

Our people could not bear any more treachery. It decided to oppose infidelity—be it French, American or Israeli—by striking at their headquarters and launching a veritable war of resistance against the occupation forces. Finally, the enemy had to decide to retreat by stages.

## Our Objectives

Let us put it truthfully: the sons of Hizballah know who are their major enemies in the Middle East—the Phalanges, Israel, France, and the United States. The sons of our *umma* are now in a state of growing confrontation with them and will remain so until the realization of the following three objectives:

> (a) to expel the Americans, the French, and their allies definitely from Lebanon, putting an end to any colonialist entity on our land;
> (b) to submit the Phalanges to a just power and bring them all to justice for the crimes they have perpetrated against Muslims and Christians;
> (c) to permit all the sons of our people to determine their future and to choose in all liberty the form of government they desire. We call upon all of them to pick the option of Islamic government, which alone is capable of guaranteeing justice and liberty for all. Only an Islamic regime can stop any further tentative attempts at imperialistic infiltration into our country.

These are Lebanon's objectives; those are its enemies. As for our friends, they are all the world's oppressed peoples. Our friends are also those who combat our enemies and who defend us from their evil. . . .

We are an *umma* that adheres to the message of Islam. We want all the oppressed to be able to study the divine message in order to bring justice, peace, and tranquility to the world. This is why we don't want to impose Islam upon anybody, as much as . . . others impose upon us their convictions and their political systems. . . .

In the light of our conceptions, our opposition to the present system is the function of two factors: (1) the present regime, which is the product of an arrogance so unjust that no reform or modification can remedy it. It should be changed radically; and (2) world imperialism, which is hostile to Islam.

We consider that all opposition in Lebanon voiced in the name of reform ultimately can only profit the present system. All such opposition that operates within the framework of the conservation and safeguarding of the present constitution without demanding changes at the level of the very foundation of the regime is, hence, an opposition of pure formality, which cannot satisfy the interests of the oppressed masses. . . . We could not care less about the creation of this or that governmental coalition or about the participation of this or that political personality in some ministerial post, which is but a part of this unjust regime. . . .

If you, Christians, cannot tolerate that Muslims share with you certain domains of government, Allah has also made it intolerable for Muslims to participate in an unjust regime, unjust for you and for us, in a regime not predicated upon the prescriptions of religion and upon the basis of the *Sharia* as laid down by Muhammad. . . . If you search for justice, who is more just than Allah? It is he who sent down from the sky the message of Islam through his successive prophets in order that they judge the people and give everyone his rights. If you were deceived and misled into believing that we anticipate vengeance against you, your fears are unjustified. For those of you who are peaceful, continue to live in our midst without anybody even thinking to trouble you.

We don't wish you evil. We call upon you to embrace Islam so that you can be happy in this world and the next. If you refuse to adhere to Islam, maintain your ties with the Muslims and don't take part in any activity against them. . . . Banish from your hearts all fanaticism and parochialism. Open your hearts to our Call [to join Islam, *al-da'wa*], which we address to you. Open yourselves up to Islam, where you'll find salvation and happiness upon earth and in the hereafter. We extend this invitation also to all the oppressed among the non-Muslims. As for those who belong to Islam only formally, we exhort them to adhere to Islam in religious practice and to renounce all fanaticisms, which are rejected by our religion.

We reject both the USSR and the United States, both capitalism and communism, for both are incapable of laying the foundations for a just society.

With special vehemence we reject UNIFIL [the UN peacekeeping forces on the Lebanese-Israeli border], as it was sent by world arrogance to occupy areas evacuated by Israel and to serve for the latter as a buffer zone. They should be treated much like the Zionists. . . .

## The Necessity for the Destruction of Israel

We see in Israel the vanguard of the United States in our Islamic world. It is the hated enemy that must be fought until the hated ones get what they deserve. This enemy is the greatest danger to our future generations and to the destiny of our lands, particularly as it glorifies the ideas of settlement and expansion, initiated in Palestine, and yearning outward to the extension of Israel, from the Euphrates to the Nile.

Our primary assumption in our fight against Israel states that the Zionist entity has been aggressive from its inception, and built on lands wrested from their owners, at the expense of the rights of the Muslim people. Therefore our struggle will end only when this entity is obliterated. We recognize no treaty with it, no cease-fire, and no peace agreements, whether separate or consolidated.

We vigorously condemn all plans for negotiation with Israel, and regard all negotiators as enemies, for the reason that such negotiation is nothing but the recognition of the legitimacy of the Zionist occupation of Palestine. Therefore we oppose and reject the Camp David agreements, the proposals of King Fahd, the Fez and Reagan plan, Brezhnev's and the French-Egyptian proposals, and all other programs that include the recognition (even the implied recognition) of the Zionist entity.

# Charter (August 1988)

HAMAS

. . . Article Six: The Islamic Resistance Movement is a distinct Palestinian movement which owes its loyalty to Allah, derives from Islam its way of life and strives to raise the banner of Allah over every inch of Palestine. Only under the shadow of Islam could the members of all religions coexist in safety and security for their lives, properties and rights. In the absence of Islam, conflict arises, oppression reigns, corruption is rampant, and struggles and wars prevail. . . .

Article Nine: Hamas finds itself at a period of time when Islam has waned away from the reality of life. For this reason, the checks and balances have been upset, concepts have become confused, and values have been transformed; evil has prevailed, oppression and obscurity have reigned; cowards have turned tigers, homelands have been usurped, people have been uprooted and are wandering all over the globe. The state of truth has disappeared and was replaced by the state of evil. Nothing has remained in its right place, for when Islam is removed from the scene, everything changes. These are the motives. As to the objectives: discarding the evil, crushing it and defeating it, so that truth may prevail, homelands revert [to their owners], calls for prayer be heard from their mosques, announcing the reinstitution of the Muslim state. Thus, people and things will revert to their true place. . . .

Article Eleven: The Islamic Resistance Movement believes that the land of Palestine has been an Islamic *waqf* [foundation] throughout the generations and until the Day of Resurrection, no one can renounce it or part of it, or abandon it or part of it. No Arab country nor the aggregate of all Arab countries, and no Arab king or president nor all of them in the aggregate, have that right, nor has that right any organization or the aggregate of all organizations, be they Palestinian or Arab. . . .

Article Twelve: Hamas regards nationalism as part and parcel of the religious faith. Nothing is loftier or deeper in nationalism than waging *jihad* against the enemy and confronting him when he sets foot on the land of the Muslims. And this becomes an individual duty binding on every Muslim man and woman; a woman must go out and fight the enemy even without her husband's authorization, and a slave without his masters' permission. This [principle] does not exist under any other regime, and it is a truth not to be questioned. While other nationalisms consist of material, human, and territorial considerations, the nationality of Hamas also carries, in addition to all those, the all-important divine factors that lend to it its spirit and life; so much so that it connects with the origin of the spirit and the source of life and raises in the skies of the homeland the banner of the Lord, thus inexorably connecting earth with heaven. . . .

Article Thirteen: [Peace] initiatives, the so-called peaceful solutions, and the international conferences to resolve the Palestinian problem are all contrary to the beliefs of Hamas. For renouncing any part of Palestine means renouncing part of the religion; the nationalism of Hamas is part of its faith, [and] the movement educates its members to adhere to its principles and to raise the banner of Allah over their homeland as they fight their *jihad*: "Allah is the all-powerful, but most people are not aware. . . ." Those conferences are no more than a means to appoint the nonbelievers as arbitrators in the lands of Islam. Since when did the unbelievers do justice to the believers? "And the Jews will not be pleased with thee, nor will the Christians, till thou follow their creed. Say: Lo! the guidance of Allah [himself] is the Guidance. And if you should follow their desires after the knowledge which has come unto thee, then you would have from Allah no protecting friend nor helper" [Koranic citation]. There is no solution to the Palestinian problem except by *jihad*. The initiatives, proposals, and international conferences are but a waste of time, an exercise in futility. The Palestinian people are too noble to have their future, their right, and their destiny submitted to a vain game. . . .

Article Fourteen: The problem of the liberation of Palestine relates to three circles: the Palestinian, the Arab, and the Islamic. Each one of these circles has a role to play in the struggle against Zionism, and it has duties to fulfill. It would be an enormous mistake and an abysmal act of ignorance to disregard anyone of these circles. For Palestine is an Islamic land where the First *Qibla* [first direction of prayer chosen by Muhammad but later abandoned by him] and the third holiest site [the al-Aqsa mosque] are located. That is also the place whence the prophet, be Allah's prayer and peace upon him, ascended to heaven. "Glorified be He who carried his servant by night from the Inviolable Place of worship to the Far Distant Place of Worship, the neighborhood whereof we have blessed, that we might show him of our tokens! Lo! He, only He, is the Hearer, the Seer" [Koranic citation]. In consequence of this state of affairs, the liberation of that land is an individual duty binding on all Muslims every-where. This is the base on which all Muslims have to regard the problem; this has to be understood by all Muslims. When the problem is dealt with on this basis, where the full potential of the three circles is mobilized, then the current circumstances will change and the day of liberation will come closer. . . .

Article Twenty: Islamic society is one of solidarity. The Messenger of Allah, be Allah's prayer and peace upon him, said: What a wonderful tribe were the Ash'aris! When they were overtaxed, either in their location or during their journeys, they would collect all their possessions and then would divide them equally among themselves. This is the Islamic spirit, which ought to prevail in any Muslim society. A society that confronts a vicious, Nazilike enemy who does not differentiate between men and women [or between] elder and young ought to be the first to adorn itself with this Islamic spirit. Our enemy pursues the style of collective punishment of usurping people's countries and properties, of pursuing them into their exiles and places of assembly. It has resorted to breaking bones, opening fire on women and children and the old, with or with-out reason, and to setting up detention camps where thousands upon thousands are interned in inhuman conditions. In addition, it destroys houses, renders children orphans, and issues oppressive judgments against thousands of young people who spend the best years of their youth in the darkness of prisons. The Nazism of the Jews does not skip women and children; it scares everyone. They make war against people's livelihood, plunder their moneys, and threaten their honor. In their horrible actions they mistreat people like the most horrendous war criminals. Exiling people from their country is another way of killing them. As we face this misconduct, we have no escape from establishing social solidarity among the people, from confronting the enemy as one solid body, so that if one organ is hurt the rest of the body will respond with alertness and fervor. . . .

Article Twenty-Two: The enemies have been scheming for a long time, and they have consolidated their schemes, in order to achieve what they have achieved. They took advantage of key elements in unfolding events and accu-mulated a huge and influential [amount of] material wealth, which they put to the service of implementing their dream. This wealth [permitted them to] take over control of the world media such as news agencies, the press, publishing houses, broadcasting [networks], and the like. [They also used this] wealth to stir revolutions in various parts of the globe in order to fulfill their interests and pick the fruits. They stood behind the French and the Communist Revo-lutions and behind most of the revolutions we hear about here and there. They also used the money to establish clandestine organizations that are spreading around the world in order to destroy societies and carry out Zionist interests. Such organizations are: the Freemasons, Rotary Clubs, Lions' Clubs, B'nai B'rith, and the like. All of them are destructive spying organizations. They also used the money to take over control of the imperialist states and made them colonize many countries in order to exploit the wealth of those countries and spread their corruption therein. As regards local and world wars, it has come to pass and no one objected that they stood behind World War I, so as to wipe out the Islamic caliphate. They collected material gains and took control of many sources of wealth. They obtained the Balfour Declaration and established the League of Nations in order to rule the world by means of that organization. They also stood behind World War II, during which they collected immense benefits from trading with war materials and prepared for the establishment of their state. They inspired the establishment of the United Nations and the Security Council to replace the League of Nations in order to rule the world by their intermediary. There was no war that broke out anywhere without their fingerprints on it: "As often as they light a fire for war, Allah extinguishes it. Their effort is for corruption in the land and Allah loves not corrupters" (Sura V, verse 64). The forces of imperialism in both the capitalist West and the communist East support the enemy with all their might, in material and human terms, taking turns between themselves. When Islam appears, all the forces of unbelief unite to confront it, because the community of unbelief is one. "Oh ye who believe! Take not for intimates others than your own folk, who would spare no pain to ruin you. Hatred is revealed by [the utterance of] their mouth, but that which their breasts hide is greater. We have made plain for you the revelations if you will understand" [quote from Koran]. It is not in vain that the verse ends with God's saying: "If you will understand. . . ."

Article Twenty-Six: The Hamas, while it views positively the Palestinian national movements which do not owe their loyalty to the East or to the West, does not refrain from debating unfolding events regarding the Palestinian problem, on the local and international scenes. These debates are realistic and expose the extent to which [these developments] go along with, or contradict, national interests as viewed from the Islamic vantage point.

Article Twenty-Seven: The PLO [Palestine Liberation Organization] is among the closest to the Hamas, for it constitutes a father, a brother, a relative, [and] a friend. Can a Muslim turn away from his father, his brother, his relative, or his friend? Our homeland is one, our calamity is one, our destiny is one, and our enemy is common to both of us. Under the influence of the circumstances that surrounded the founding of the PLO, and the ideological confusion that prevails in the Arab world as a result of the ideological invasion which has swept the Arab world since the rout of the Crusades, and which has been reinforced by orientalism and the Christian mission, the PLO has adopted the idea of a secular state, . . . secular thought is diametrically opposed to religious thought. . . . Therefore, in spite of our appreciation for the PLO and its possible transformation in the future, and despite the fact that we do not denigrate its role in the Arab-Israeli conflict, we cannot substitute it for the Islamic nature of Palestine by adopting secular thought. For the Islamic nature of Palestine is part of our religion, and anyone who neglects his religion is bound to lose. "And who forsakes the religion of Abraham, save him who befools himself?" [quote from Koran]. When the PLO adopts Islam as the guideline for life, then we shall become its soldiers, the fuel of its fire, which will burn the enemies. And until that happens, and we pray to Allah that it will happen soon, the position of the Hamas toward the PLO is one of a son toward his father, a brother toward his brother, and a relative toward his relative who suffers the other's pain when a thorn stabs him, who supports the other in the confrontation with the enemies and who wishes him divine guidance and integrity of conduct. . . .

Article Twenty-Eight: The Zionist invasion is a mischievous one. It does not hesitate to take any road, or to pursue all despicable and repulsive means to fulfill its desires. It relies to a great extent, for its meddling and spying activities, on the clandestine organizations which it has established, such as the Freemasons, Rotary Clubs, Lions, and other spying associations. All those secret organizations, some which are overt, act for the interests of Zionism and under its directions strive to demolish societies, to destroy values, to wreck answerableness, to [overthrow] virtues and to wipe out Islam. It stands behind the diffusion of drugs and poisons of all kinds in order to facilitate its control and expansion. The Arab states surrounding Israel are required to open their borders to the *jihad* fighters, the sons of the Arab and Islamic peoples, to enable them to play their role and to join their efforts to those of their brothers among the Muslim Brothers in Palestine. The other Arab and Islamic states are required, at the very least, to facilitate the movement of the *jihad* fighters from and to them. We cannot fail to remind every Muslim that when the Jews occupied Holy Jerusalem in 1967 and stood at the doorstep of the blessed al-Aqsa mosque, they shouted with joy: "Muhammad is dead, he left daughters behind." Israel, by virtue of its being Jewish and of having a Jewish population, defies Islam and the Muslims. . . .

Article Thirty-One: Hamas is a humane movement, which cares for human rights and is committed to the tolerance inherent in Islam regarding attitudes toward other religions. It is only hostile to those who are hostile toward it, or who stand in its way in order to disturb its moves or to frustrate its efforts. Under the shadow of Islam it is possible for the members of the three religions, Islam, Christianity, and Judaism, to coexist in safety and security. Safety and security can prevail only under the shadow of Islam, and recent and ancient history is the best witness to that effect. The members of other religions must desist from struggling against Islam over sovereignty in this region. For if they were to gain the upper hand, fighting, torture and uprooting would follow; they would be fed up with each other, to say nothing of members of other religions. The past and the present are full of evidence to that effect. "They will not fight you in body [except] in fortified villages or from behind wells. Their adversity among themselves is very great. Ye think of them as a whole whereas their hearts are diverse. That is because they are a folk who have no sense" (Sura 59, verse 14). Islam accords his rights to everyone who has rights and averts aggression against the rights of others. The Nazi Zionist practices against our people will not last the lifetime of their invasion, for "States built upon oppression last only one hour, states based upon justice will last until the hour of Resurrection." . . .

## The Attempts to Isolate the Palestinian People

Article Thirty-Two: World Zionism and imperialist forces have been attempting, with smart moves and considered planning, to push the Arab countries, one after another, out of the circle of conflict with Zionism, in order ultimately to isolate the Palestinian people. Egypt has already been cast out of the conflict, to a very great extent through the treacherous Camp David accords, and she has been trying to drag other countries into similar agreements in order to push them out of the circle of conflict. Hamas is calling upon the Arab and Islamic peoples to act seriously and tirelessly in order to frustrate that dreadful scheme and to make the masses aware of the danger of [leaving] the struggle with Zionism. Today it is Palestine and tomorrow it may be another country or other countries. For Zionist scheming has no end, and after Palestine they will covet expansion from the Nile to the Euphrates. Only when they have completed digesting the area on which they will have laid their hand they will look forward to more expansion, and so on. Their scheme has been laid out in the *Protocols of the Elders of Zion* [anti-Semitic forgery produced in Czarist Russia.—*Eds.*], and their present [conduct] is the best proof of what is said there. Leaving the circle of conflict with Israel is a major act of treason and it will bring curses on its perpetrators. "Who so on that day turns his back to them, unless maneuvering for battle or intent to join a company, he truly has incurred wrath from Allah, and his habitation will be hell, a hapless journey's end" (Sura 8, verse 16). We have no escape from pooling together all the forces and energies to face this despicable Nazi-Tartar invasion. Otherwise we shall witness the loss of [our] countries, the uprooting of their inhabitants, the spreading of corruption on earth, and the destruction of all religious values. Let everyone realize that he is accountable to Allah. . . . "Whoever does a speck of good will see [the consequences] and whoever does a speck of evil will see [the consequences]." Within the circle of the conflict with world Zionism, the Hamas regards itself the spearhead and the avant-garde. It joins its efforts to all those who are active on the Palestinian scene, but more steps need to be taken by the Arab and Islamic peoples and Islamic associations throughout the Arab and Islamic world in order to make possible the next round with the Jews, the merchants of war. . . . The greedy have coveted Palestine more than once and they raided it with armies in order to fulfill their covetousness. Multitudes of Crusaders descended on it, carrying their faith with them and waving their cross. They were able to defeat the Muslims for a long time, and the Muslims were not able to redeem it until they sought the protection of their religious banner; then they unified their forces, sang the praises of their God, and set out for *jihad* under the command of Saladin al-Ayyubi for nearly two decades, and then the obvious conquest took place when the Crusaders were defeated and Palestine was liberated. "Say (Oh Muhammad) unto those who disbelieve: ye shall be overcome and gathered unto hell, an evil resting place" [quote from Koran]. This is the only way to liberation; there is no doubt in the testimony of history. That is one of the rules of the universe and one of the laws of existence. Only iron can blunt iron, only the true faith of Islam can vanquish their false and falsified faith. Faith can only be fought by faith. Ultimately, victory is reserved to the truth, and truth is victorious. . . .

# The Letter of Demands to the King of Saudi Arabia (April 1992)

SAUDI ISLAMISTS

To the Custodian of the Two Holy Mosques, May God Guide his steps. . . .

This state has distinguished itself by announcing its adherence to Islamic *Sharia*, and the *ulama* and those capable of offering guidance have always fulfilled their divine obligation in offering sound advice to those in power. We therefore find that the most pressing task, at this critical juncture and at a time when all have realized the necessity of change, is to direct our energies to reforming the situation that put us in our present predicament. For this reason, we request the ruler to look into the matters that need to be addressed by reform in the following areas:

- Establishing a consultative council to decide on internal and external affairs. The members of this body should be selected so as to include individuals of diverse specializations, and who must be known for their sincerity and upright conduct. The council must be fully independent and free from any pressures that could affect the discharging of its full responsibilities.

- Examining all political, economic, and administrative laws and regulations to ascertain their conformity to *Sharia*. This task should be conducted by fully mandated, competent, and trustworthy *Sharia* committees. All laws not conforming to *Sharia* should then be abrogated.
- Ensuring that all state officials and its representatives internally and abroad must be competent and suitably specialized. They must also be dedicated, upright, and honest. Failure to fulfill any of these requirements must be deemed a betrayal of trust and a major threat to the country's interest and its reputation.
- Achieving justice and equality for all individuals in society, safeguarding full rights and exacting duties without preferment to the privileged or condescension toward the disadvantaged. It should also be realized that taking advantage of one's influence to shirk one's duties or usurp the rights of others could cause the disintegration of society and lead to the dire fate against which the prophet (peace be upon him) has warned.
- Subjecting all officials without exception, and especially those in key posts, to rigorous accountability, and removing anyone found to be corrupt or incompetent, no matter who he may be.
- Ensuring fairness in the distribution of pubic wealth between all classes and groups within society. All taxes should be canceled, and all levies that became a burden to the people should be reduced, while the resources of the state must be protected from wastage and exploitation. Priority should be given to expenditure in areas where need is more pressing, while illegal monopolies must be ended and improperly acquired assets reclaimed. The ban on Islamic banks must be ended, and all private and public banking institutions must be purged from usury, which is equivalent to waging war on God and his prophet, and is a cause for the loss of God's favor and blessing.
- Building a strong and integrated armed forces, fully equipped from diverse sources. Special attention should be paid to the development of military industries. The aim of the army should be to protect the country and its sacred values.
- Reconstructing the media to bring them in line with the kingdom's policy of serving Islam. The media should reflect the values of society and enhance and advance its culture, and they must be purified from all that contradicts the above goals. Freedom of the media to educate and inform through the propagation of true stories and constructive criticism must be safeguarded in accordance with legitimate safeguards.
- Directing foreign policy to safeguard the interests of the nation away from illegitimate alliances. The state must champion Muslim causes,

while the status of our embassies abroad must be rectified to reflect the Islamic character of this country.

- Developing the religious and missionary institutions in this country and providing them with all the necessary human and material resources. All obstacles preventing them from fulfilling their tasks properly must be removed.
- Unifying judicial organs, according them full and real independence, and ensuring that the authority of the judiciary extends to all. An independent body must be set up to follow up the implementation of judicial decisions.
- Safeguarding the rights of individuals and society, and removing any trace of restrictions on the will of the people and their rights, [and] safeguarding human dignity in accordance with the proper legitimate safeguards.

[This petition was signed by a number of clerics as well as retired officials and businessmen. The government ignored it.—*Eds.*]

# Abdullah Azzam, the Struggling Sheikh (July 1996)

### ABDULLAH BIN UMAR*

Despite the fact that Sheikh Abdullah Azzam is buried in the Pakistani city of Peshawar on the borders of Afghanistan, he was born in the village of Assba'ah al-Hartiyeh, province of Jenin, in the occupied sacred land of Palestine in 1941. Brought up in a humble house where he was taught Islam he was fed with the love of Allah, his messenger, those striving, the righteous people, and the desire for the hereafter.

In 1966 he graduated from the University of Damascus with a bachelor's degree in *Sharia*. In 1969 he graduated from al-Azhar University in Cairo, with

* *Nida'ul Islam* magazine, July–September 1996. Translated by Muhammad Saeed. Abdullah Azzam was a major influence on bin Ladin, and *Nida'ul Islam* is an Islamist magazine based in Australia.

a master's degree, and in 1979 he obtained his Ph.D. in the principles of jurisprudence. The late sheikh . . . held the essential belief that the concept of the oneness of Allah's names and attributes would be defective and incomplete unless it were reinforced with the doctrine of loyalty toward the believers and to be distinct from and immune to the disbelievers. Allah says: "Whoever takes them [disbelievers] as protectors then he surely is one of them." . . .

The sheikh's life revolved around a single goal, namely the establishment of Allah's rule on earth, this being the clear responsibility of each and every Muslim. So in order to accomplish his life's noble mission of restoring the *khalifa*, the sheikh focused on *jihad*.

He believed *jihad* must be carried out until the *khalifa* is established so the light of Islam may shine on the whole world.

From his pulpit, Sheikh Azzam was always reiterating his conviction that "*jihad* must not be abandoned until Allah alone is worshipped. *Jihad* continues until Allah's word is raised high. *Jihad* until all the oppressed peoples are freed. *Jihad* to protect our dignity and restore our occupied lands. *Jihad* is the way of everlasting glory."

When Azzam realized that only by means of an organized force would the *umma* ever be able to gain victory, then *jihad* and the gun became his preoccupation and recreation. "*Jihad* and the rifle alone: no negotiations, no conferences, and no dialogues," he would say.

By practicing what he was preaching, Azzam became one of the first Arabs to join the Afghani *jihad* against the communist USSR. Prior to this, he did his share of *jihad* in his own country: Palestine. His heroic deeds in the al-Sheikh refugee camps in Jordan spoke loudly for him and rightly justified his long experience with *jihad*.

In the early 1980s Azzam came to experience the *jihad* in Afghanistan. In this *jihad* he found satisfaction of his longing for and untold love of fighting in the path of Allah. Allah's prophet once said, "A few moments spent fighting in the path of Allah is worth more than seventy years spent in praying at home" [a *hadith*].

Inspired by this *hadith*, Azzam asked to be transferred from the University of Jordan, where he taught, to Islamabad, in Pakistan. He immigrated with his family to Pakistan in order to be closer to the field of *jihad*. . . .

In Peshawar [Pakistan, near the Afghan border] Azzam founded the Mujahidin Services Bureau with the aim of offering all possible assistance to the Afghani *jihad* and the *mujahidin* through establishing and managing projects that supported the cause. The bureau also received and trained volunteers pouring into Pakistan to participate in *jihad* and allocating them to the front lines.

Unsurprisingly, this was not enough to satisfy Sheikh Azzam's burning desire for *jihad*. That desire drove him finally to go to the frontline. On the battlefield, the sheikh gracefully played his destined role in that generous epic of heroism. In Afghanistan he hardly ever settled in one place. He traveled throughout the country, visiting most of its provinces. . . .

These travels allowed Azzam to witness firsthand the heroic deeds of these . . . people who had sacrificed all that they possessed—including their own lives—for the supremacy of the religion of Islam.

In Peshawar, upon his return from these travels, Azzam spoke about *jihad* constantly. He prayed to restore unity to the divided *mujahidin* commanders; [and he] called upon those who had not yet joined the fighting to take up arms and follow him to the front before it was too late. . . .

On every occasion Azzam reminded all Muslims that "Muslims cannot be defeated by others. We Muslims are not defeated by our enemies, instead, we are defeated by our own selves." . . .

When Allah willed that Azzam should leave this world to be in His closest company, the sheikh departed in a glorious manner. This great martyr of Islam was assassinated when a land mine exploded beneath the car he was driving [as he was] on his way with his two sons to the local mosque for Friday prayers.

That fateful blast indeed ended the worldly journey of Azzam, which had been spent well in struggling, striving, and fighting in the path of Allah. It also secured his more real and eternal life in the gardens of paradise. . . .

# Interview with Umar Abd al-Rahman (April 1997)*

I have tried to speak the word of truth in Egypt and to face idols or dictatorship of a single ruler, which existed, and still [does], in Egypt, through seminars, lectures and lessons. Al-Jamaa al-Islamayya [the Islamic Group] put forth a great effort to let people better know their religion. I have been arrested several times. . . . Allah, however, gave us victory over the regime in those court cases.

* Umar Abd al-Rahman is an Egyptian Islamist cleric and revolutionary who had immigrated to the United States. He was convicted of being the leader of the first bomb attack in 1993 on New York's World Trade Center. The interview appeared in *Nida'ul Islam* magazine, April–May 1997.

I traveled to Europe, passing through Britain, Denmark, Sweden, and many other countries. I met with sincere brothers and sisters [and] gave numerous lectures and talks to make Muslims aware of their obligation to struggle for their religion and to face their enemies. We ended in America, where I visited many states, talking about the duties of Muslims toward their religion [and] how to make Islam their first priority all the time and to struggle for the sake of Allah. No single year should pass from the life of a Muslim without [his] living the struggle. I then went to many countries in the world, but ended with being framed with this fraudulent case and with a prison sentence. We ask Allah to let us stay firm along the truth and to benefit us with the blessings and rewards he gives his imprisoned servants. There are many rewards and blessings in being imprisoned, and we ask him to let us benefit from it. . . .

The confrontation between crusaders and Islam is an old one. In the early years of Islam there were two super empires, the Persian and the Roman. It took only a few battles, ending with Qadisiyya, to demolish the Persian empire for good. The Roman empire, however, has had many strands across the centuries. When one strand is destroyed, another strand comes in another century, as illustrated in the *hadith* of Allah's messenger. . . . The Roman empire means an international crusade and international Zionism. War with the crusades is ongoing until the Day of Judgment. . . . This is a ferocious and ongoing war. Whenever the Muslims hold on to their religion, they manage to defeat their enemies. But when they are fragmented and disunited, as they are now, their enemies manage to defeat them. . . .

The disbelievers spend their money to keep people away from the way of Allah. They will spend it, yet will deeply regret it and will finally be defeated. The disbelievers shall be assembled into hell. Allah also says: "Tell the disbelievers: you shall be defeated and thrown into hell." What a miserable end! . . .

They sent missionaries to Africa and said that Africa will be Christianized in centuries or even decades. Decades and centuries have passed, however, [and] Africa is even better, from the point of view of the Islamic religion, than ever before. Why? Their money has been lost, their efforts have been wasted, and their missionaries have achieved very little, if at all. They manage to Christianize one, but ten new embrace Islam. They Christianize ten, and one hundred new [converts] embrace Islam. . . .

Let me remind you, in the nineteenth and twentieth centuries, when Muslims were fragmented and powerless, when Western British and French colonialism was in command and Islam had no power, who preserved Islam? And who preserved Muslims? Allah says: "Today, the disbelievers gave up on your religion, so do not fear them.". . . . Gave up. . . . Gave up fourteen centuries ago. . . . Gave up in the fourteenth century, gave up in the thirteenth century, the twelfth century. . . . And so on. . . . The disbelievers gave up on your religion, so do not fear them, fear me [Allah]. Despair is an ongoing phenomenon. Despair of changing or altering Islam. They have allocated huge amounts of money in the [UN] conference on [population held] in Egypt to come out with resolutions allowing adultery, abortion, and homosexuality, resolutions encouraging girls to give their honor and chastity, resolutions to weaken the authority and influence of parents over children. . . . That does not scare us. What really scares us is being split from within. We cannot be defeated from [the outside]; we are not concerned from the numbers of our enemies nor by their resources. We are only concerned with being defeated from within, with some of us to being our enemies, declaring war against each other. We, the Muslims, have to hold on to our religion and be steadfast and united around our faith. . . .

[The West] took those words "extremism," "terrorism," and "fundamentalism" to mean every committed Muslim. . . . Allah says: "and prepare for them whatever you can of power and horses to terrorize the enemy of Allah and your enemy." . . . Everyone who is steadfast to his religion, everyone who holds on to his religion, everyone who defends his religion became a terrorist, and he is the extremist and he is the fundamentalist!

Fundamentalism is taken from the Christian use of the word. But here we find their media attacking Muslims who do not let go of their religion, who hold on to that religion, who work for that religion, and who preserve that religion. The West and the so-called Islamic governments hit the fundamentalist movements and extremist movements hard. What is the meaning of "extremist movements"? The Islamic movements that preserve their religion and hold the book of their Lord and the teachings of their prophet. These are the target of Western media and those behind it. . . .

If I say that the central African countries have more freedom than the United States, I shall not be wrong. . . . Those are hollow words, because they have freedom for themselves, but they do not allow any freedom to others. It is democracy for them to enjoy, but they do not allow others to have an opinion or separate thoughts. I came running away from prison to the country of freedom, but I was imprisoned. I came running away from lack of freedom and from being prevented from making statements, but I was shocked by the fact that it is even worse in America. Those words are only for a specific race or specific groups to enjoy, but others are denied them. . . .

The responsibilities of Muslims in the West toward their religion are to unite and develop themselves financially. They must have money. Money is the element for life, the mainstay of life. A strong Muslim is better and more beloved by Allah than a weak Muslim. Muslims must get the strength of money [in order] to have their media outlets, to have strong productivity, and to unite in industrial and agricultural organizations. They have to preserve their religion [and] their families and not mix in a way that will make them let go of their religion. . . .

# The Islamic State in Egypt Is Approaching (April 1997)

SHEIKH RIFA'EY AHMAD TAHA*

The Jama'a [al-Islamiyya group] . . . [aims] to establish an Islamic caliphate in accordance with prophetic guidance, and to seek the pleasure of Allah, the Lord of the worlds. . . .

[One] of our most important achievements is the major role we played alongside the Islamic tide, the Islamic revival, that raised the awareness of the Muslims with respect to contemporary issues and situations . . . after being absent or not noticeable due to the forced Westernization and various oppressions from the non-religious governments that had governed Egypt.

Many of the important and potent religious and intellectual issues were not known, such as the issues of sovereignty, *jihad*, and the Islamic government. Today they have become the talk of the man in the street, and of the issues keeping public opinion busy. . . . From a practical aspect, we regard the Islamic movement and the al-Jama'a al-Islamiyya from its inception to have broken the negative attitude and the apathy, and it was able to let loose the "change" energies in our Muslim people. . . .

The reality is that the Egyptian regime did not just participate in the destruction which took place in Egypt—the Egyptian regime is destruction itself. . . .

On the economic front: the regime has completely surrendered to international bodies such as the World Bank, the [International Monetary Fund], and so on, and promoted the systems of the West despite the obviousness of their failure and the clarity of their goals, which aim at realizing the interests

---

* Sheikh Rifa'ey Ahmad Taha is an Egyptian leader. This essay appeared in *Nida'ul Islam*, April–May 1997.

of the international powers by increasing in the siphoning of our wealth and at the expense of our people, who live below the poverty line. . . .

As for the moral front: the spread of fornication, the popularizing of decadence, the spread of corruption becoming government policy. . . .

Corruption also spread, as did patronage, and bribery became a common governing practice in all dealings. . . .

As for the political front: Egypt has not known in all its history, a policy that has failed as bad as that during the [President Husni] Mubarak period, for he is the one who took the leadership of the Arabs to their downfall. While he responded, day and night, to the calls for "peace" with Israel, he practiced hostile policies against the peoples of Iraq and Sudan. This is not so strange as the person who has alienated, degraded, and humiliated his own people, and practiced against his nation the ugliest of the tortures of the old colonialists . . . in obedience to the orders of the White House, and who has accepted the policy of being subjugated, which has become a habit for him, . . . as long as it pleased his masters, who work to maintain his regime with all their energies.

It is not important that Egypt may lose its position in the region, or that Israel continues to fulfill its greedy designs, or that our people starve in the names of the international bodies, or that the Americans control our resources. All that is unimportant, for keeping Mubarak in government is the great national goal, and the grand national victory, because he is the man! . . .

We recognize that the future Islamic state will inherit the accumulated ruins of *jahili* regimes; however, Allah Most High says: "Had the people of the towns believed, and became pious, we would have opened for them blessings from the sky and the earth; however, they lied, so we took them with what they did earn." This blessing is only understood by the people of faith. This talk is not accepted by the secularists and the materialists, those who ignore that some of this blessing is the secret of the progress of the Muslims when their will is freed. Indeed, when the Muslims take the reins of science and progress, they will achieve many times over what others have achieved.

The nation we seek is not a nationalistic, materialistic one that worships the world. It is a nation that, if it were to face a calamity, its people would be patient and rely on Allah, because they embraced Islam because it is the religion from Allah, before it became a solution to their problems.

# On the Islamist Revolution in Egypt (January 2002)

AYMAN AL-ZAWAHIRI*

[In the 1981 uprising against the Egyptian government there were two fronts.] The first front was the attack on Sadat and the upper echelons of his regime during the military parade on October 6 and the attempt to kill the largest number of officials and seize the radio building [in Cairo]. Activity on this front succeeded in killing Anwar al-Sadat, but the upper echelons of the regime escaped, and the attempt to seize the radio [station] did not succeed.

The second front was the armed uprising in Asyut and the attempt to seize the city. The uprising started two days after the assassination of Sadat—in other words, after the army succeeded in controlling the country and securing the regime. This attempt succeeded in seizing some police centers. But the government summoned the Special Forces, which started pounding the resistance positions of the brotherly young *mujhahidin*, who were forced to leave these centers after running out of ammunition.

The armed rebellion in Asyut was doomed to fail. It was an "emotional" uprising that was poorly planned. The rebellion occurred two days after the assassination of Sadat and was based on an unrealistic plan to seize Asyut and then advance northward toward Cairo, disregarding any figures about the enemy's strength and matériel. . . .

However, the issue must not be viewed from the angle of these small events. That uprising must be viewed from the angle of the aftereffects of these events and the facts that they proved. It is obvious that the uprising proved several facts:

1. The events showed the courage of the fundamentalists, who attacked forces that were more experienced and larger in number and equipment.

2. The events showed the offensive nature of the fundamentalist movement, which decided to attack the regime in an attempt to kill its upper echelons among a huge crowd of spectators.

3. The events showed that changing the regime, which had departed from Islam, became the central idea that preoccupied the Islamists, who rejected partial reform programs, patch-up jobs, and attempts to beautify the ugly face of the regime with some reformatory measures.

---

* From *Knights under the Prophet's Banner: Meditations on the Jihadist Movement*. Published in *Al-Sharq al-Awsat* in eleven installments in January 2002. Translated by FBIS.

4. The events proved that the phase of the unilateralism of the regime in attacking the Islamic movement had ended and that the enemies of Islam in the White House and Tel Aviv and their agents in Cairo must expect a violent response to every repression campaign they carried out.

5. The events proved that the idea of work through martial law, submission to the secular constitution imposed by referendums, and recognition of the legitimacy of the government had become worn-out ideas in the minds of the Islamists. Those Islamists decided to carry arms to defend the absented creed, the banned *Sharia*, their violated honor, their homeland, which was occupied by new international imperialism, and their sanctities, which were sold in the agreements of surrender with Israel.

6. The events also showed the utter failure of the security services, which did not know that the country was charged with the *jihadi* current. This current was able to infiltrate the armed forces and to take from them some weapons, and [it] was able to join the military parade forces, despite the tight security measures that were adopted to secure the parade.

I say that the youth of the 1981 uprising were "pure" and vigilant, avoiding and even rejecting blandishments. They carried arms in defense of their religion, creed, sanctities, nation, and homeland. . . .

After this brief and quick review of the history of the Islamic movement in Egypt, we could pause here to examine the harvest of this recent past and era, which continued from 1966 until approximately 2000. . . .

1. Spreading: There is no doubt that the struggling Islamic movement has gained much ground during that period, particularly among the youths, and that it continues to grow and spread.

2. Collision: The Islamic movement has been on the offensive against the enemies of Islam. It demonstrated a sense of resistance until the last breath. The major events, beginning with the [rebellion] at the Technical Military College in 1974 [and going] up to the Luxor incident [the massacre of tourists] in 1997, provide the best proof of this.

3. Continued dedication: The Islamic movement has offered tens of thousands of detainees and wounded and tortured people and thousands of dead in its continuing struggle. This proved two things:

First, that its roots are strong and deeply established in the ground. Despite all these strikes and sacrifices, which no other political force in Egypt could have endured, this *mujahid* Islamic movement continues to operate for the sake of God.

[Second, the movement poses the main threat to the government's

security. It must use emergency laws and military tribunals and imprison an alleged 60,000 Muslim youths.] . . .

4. The international alliance and international pursuit: The regime had
   no choice but to turn the battle against the *mujahid* Islamic movement
   into an international battle, particularly when the United States became
   convinced that the regime could not survive alone in the face of this
   fundamentalist campaign. It was also convinced that this spirit of *jihad*
   would most likely turn things upside down in the region and force the
   United States out of it. This would be followed by the earth-shattering
   event that the West trembles at the mere thought of, which is the
   establishment of an Islamic caliphate in Egypt. If God wills it, such a
   state in Egypt, with all its weight in the heart of the Islamic world,
   could lead the Islamic world in a *jihad* against the West.

   It could also rally the world's Muslims around it. Then history
   would make a new turn, God willing, in the opposite direction against
   the empire of the United States and the world's Jewish government.

5. The continuation of the battle: Any observer of the progress of the
   Islamic movement will realize that its battle with the regime continues
   to this very day. The battle has not stopped in the past thirty-six years.
   The fundamentalist movement is either on the attack or in the process
   of preparing for an attack. . . .

6. . . . The Islamic movement has largely succeeded in clarifying the
   main elements of its ideology, relying on strong evidence from the
   Koran, the prophet's tradition, and the respected scholars. This provided it with a solid base on which it hoisted its banner, which every
   day attracts new advocates, God willing.

7. . . . We must admit that good planning and preparations have been
   missing in many of the acts of violence. . . . Shortcomings in planning
   were evident. . . .

8. The weakness of the message to the people: The fundamentalist movement's message continues to be mostly geared toward the elite and the
   specialists. The public and the masses do not understand this message.
   This is a gap that the *jihad* movement must strive to fill. . . . If we add
   to Najibullah [the communist president who was overthrown and hung]
   the media siege imposed on the message of the *jihad* movement as well
   as the campaign of deception mounted by the government[-controlled]
   media, we should realize the extent of the gap in understanding between the *jihad* movement and the common people.

9. Failure of some leaders to continue the confrontation: The best proof
   of this is the initiative made by the Islamic Group leaders in Turah
   Prison to suspend military action [against the Egyptian govern-
   ment]. . . .

10. Conclusion: Has the *jihad* movement failed or succeeded in the past thirty-six years? The answer is:

   A. We must admit that the fundamentalist movement's goal of establishing an Islamic government in Egypt is yet to be achieved.

   B. The *jihad* Islamic movement, however, has not set a specific date for achieving this goal. More importantly, this is a goal that could take several generations to achieve. The Crusaders in Palestine and Syria left after two centuries of continued *jihad*. The Islamic nation at the time had *jihad* rulers and regular and disciplined armies. . . . It was led by prominent scholars. . . . Despite this, the Crusaders did not leave in 30 or 50 years. . . . The British occupied Egypt for 70 years. The French occupied Algeria for 120 years.

   C. What I see clearly is that the *jihad* Islamic movement has gone a long way on the road to victory.

      (1) It possesses a clear-cut ideology based on firm *Sharia* foundations and tangible and realistic facts.

      (2) It has succeeded in outlining to the youths issues that were absent from the minds of the Muslim masses, such as the supremacy of the *Sharia*, the apostasy of the rulers who do not rule according to God's words, and the necessity of going against rulers who are affiliated with the enemies of Islam.

      (3) The *jihad* movement has exposed the close links between the international regime and the Egyptian regime.

      (4) The *jihad* movement has not confined itself to a theoretical debate of these issues. It has put them into practice with an offensive that has shaken the pillars of the regime several times. It also succeeded in assassinating [President Sadat].

      (5) Based on the above, [we must conclude that] the *jihad* movement has strongly influenced Muslim youth in theory and in practice. This has led to the spread of the fundamentalist spirit among large segments of the Egyptian youths. In addition, the fundamentalist movement has influenced broad sectors of the Egyptian people. . . . Any observer of the *jihad* Islamic movement could see the clear difference in the strength, clarity of ideology, and activity at the time it started and at the present time.

11. Thus, we could affirm that the *jihad* movement is growing and making progress in general. It may retreat or relax for a while, but this happens because of campaigns of brutality or during periods of siege.

Therefore, the *jihad* Islamic movement must not stop the resistance and must get the entire nation to participate with it in its battle.

# Interview with Sheikh Abu Muhammad al-Maqdissy (December 1997)*

I was born in 1959 in . . . Nablus, Palestine, and I left the city with my family when I was about three or four years old and settled in Kuwait, where I completed my high school studies. My ambition then was to study *Sharia* at the Islamic University in Medina. However, to please my parents, I went to study science at al-Mausel University in northern Iraq.

It was during this period that I found my Islamic orientation, and I came into contact with many groups. . . . I traveled about Kuwait and Hijaz [western Saudi Arabia], where I had good affiliations with students . . . and sheikhs who taught me the keys to understanding Islamic knowledge. However, they did not quench my thirst about the answers Muslim youth demand, such as insight into the true state of affairs, how to implement correct legal rulings on the state of things as they are, what our true stance is regarding the rulers of our time, the clear vision of the path that will change the reality of the *umma*, and so on. Thereupon I devoted myself to study the books of Ibn Taymiyya [a favorite theologian of radical Islamists] . . . Furthermore, during my visits to Medina, I was attracted to the books of Sheikh Muhammad Ibn Abd al-Wahhab [founder of the Wahhabi school, which dominates Saudi Islam]. . . . I traveled several times to Pakistan and Afghanistan, and there I met many brothers and Islamic groups who came from various regions of the Islamic world. . . .

I finally settled in Jordan in 1992, two years before my arrest. I found the country swarming with [hypocritical Muslims] who wander about it in joy. I began . . . teaching in three places. . . . These lessons happened to be during the elections of the legislative council. Consequently, discussions . . . flared up between my students and the supporters of democracy and elections. This issue needed clarification, and accordingly I took the initiative to write an essay relating to this issue and refuting . . . those people. I entitled the hastily prepared essay "Democracy Is a Religion, and Whoever Has a Religion Other than Islam, It Will Never Be Accepted of Him."

We printed this essay and distributed it. Furthermore, . . . I openly invited the people to denounce man-made laws [and] to disbelieve in the legislative council and not take part in it.

I was keen to spread the scope of our [religious propaganda], so my brothers and I embarked on a number of travels to the north and south of the country. We visited some of our brothers who participated in the Afghani *jihad*. . . .

---

* Sheikh Abu Muhammad al-Maqdissy is a Jordanian Islamist. This interview appeared in *Nida'ul Islam*, December 1997–January 1998. Translation by Abu al-Waleed al-Hamwi.

[These efforts] caught the attention of the security officials. . . . The intelligence then began to search for and arrest our brothers one by one. . . . The enemies of Allah . . . used to ask some of our arrested brothers: "Why don't you seek your learning [with well-known mainstream scholars]? You forsake these sheikhs for a terrorist?" . . .

[One *hadith* explains:] "No [prophet] has conveyed without being opposed and treated as an enemy." Hence, he who is not opposed by the enemies of Allah has not conveyed the message and must have certain deficiencies, aberrations, or deviations in him. . . .

My brothers and I decided not to surrender ourselves. At the same time, we dismissed the confrontation alternative as an unmeasured reaction that we could be drawn into and time-fixed by the enemy.

My house was broken into seven times seeking my arrest; they broke down the door and searched my house, confiscating many books, documents, writings, and whatever belongings appealed to them. In every raid, they demanded that I turn myself in.

Finally, I was arrested along with a group of brothers, some of whom had previously asked me for a *fatwa* regarding their going across the river to Palestine for a covert operation using some explosives that I had saved. Even though I did not mind such operations, I still say that . . . at this stage . . . maintaining patience and striving for its cause is more important in this country. The reason is that there are many supporters of such operations against the Jews, especially in this country, owing to its geographical location relative to Palestine. Whereas there are few supporters of the [proper Islamist line] who are getting ready with arms to fight the imams of *kufr* [i.e., the Jordanian government]. These traitors are in reality the guards of "Israel" and those who implanted it in the heart of the Muslim world and made it possible for the [nonbelievers] of the East and West to drain our wealth and fortune.

Verily, Allah has said the truth: "And they wanted to harm him, but we made them the worst losers." . . .

They sometimes used intimidation by saying that I would spend my jail sentence, which is fifteen years, in this prison, and that they would not return me to the central jail. At other times they would offer to release me if I denounced my books and cautioned the youth about my [movement]! I was not sure whether they were serious about their offer or were just testing my reaction. In any case, by Allah's bounty we were steadfast and rejected their offer. . . . I was returned to the central jail after spending fifty days there [in prison]. Less than a month later, my brothers and I were surprised at being transferred to a small jail in the suburb of al-Balqaa; hence, all of those indicted for Islamic cases were isolated from the rest of the prisoners. . . .

# Interview with Mullah Ma'soum Afghani
# (April 1997)*

[After the Soviet withdrawal] the *jihad* leaders [in the anti–Soviet struggle] failed to achieve the goals and objectives of *jihad* and were unable to establish an Islamic regime and state. Anarchy and lack of security and stability resulted. This increased with time in Kabul and [other] Afghani cities. The Afghani people were subjected to the injustice of the Islamic leaders. The people had to face those actions, try to form the Islamic state, and restore stability and peace in the country. It is clear, then, that Taliban was supported and financed by the Afghani people and merchants. The movement now controls twenty-two of the thirty Afghani provinces. It collects customs fees in those provinces, which provides a reasonable source of income to the movement and its activities. Our goal is to restore peace and establish a pure and clean Islamic state in this country, which is the goal of every Muslim and religious student. Mullah Umar Muhammad was publicly elected as the chief and *amir-ul-mu'mineen* (commander of the believers) and is now, with the grace of Allah, supported by the Afghani people. . . .

During the *jihad* period, the scholars and students played a role in *jihad* and in conveying the message of Islam. We do not have any ties with the Pakistani army because we aim for peace and implementation of *Sharia* in our country. However, we want a good relationship with Pakistan and with every Muslim country within the Islamic system and law. . . .

The political principles of the movement are stability in Afghanistan, implementation of *Sharia*, and collecting weapons and ammunition and transferring them to major military bases. These weapons will be submitted to a responsible body. When collection of the weapons and ammunition in Afghanistan is complete, peace and stability will be restored. That is why there is no priority for negotiations under the threat of weapons. The Taliban now controls 80 percent of the land in Afghanistan and implements *Sharia* in it, and peace prevails there. Weapons and ammunition must be collected from those militias. When other groups failed in the past in achieving this goal, the need for their existence became unjustified. Those other groups must therefore submit what they have to the Taliban and save their country from killing and destruction. They should not give [other countries] a chance for external interference in Afghanistan. . . .

Islam is a comprehensive way of life. It has [basic answers] for every social,

---

* Mullah Ma'soum Afghani was the spokesman of the Taliban movement. This interview appeared in *Nida'ul Islam*, April–May 1997. Translation by Sayed Qandil.

political, economical, and military event. As far as women are concerned, they also must abide by Islamic teachings, and they will get all their rights granted by Islam. Under current circumstances, it is hard for us to provide education for women, owing to our economic condition. . . .

We seek good relationships with every Islamic country. We want Iran to stop interfering in Afghanistan. If it does this, our relations will be good. We are working to establish good relationships with the others irrespective of their rulers.

# 3

## AMERICAN POLICY AND

## ANTI-AMERICANISM

 Two critical issues about U.S. policy and its relationship with anti-American terror are the extent to which American actions provoked this enmity and the actual roots of hostility to the United States. Barry Rubin, in "The Truth about U.S. Middle East Policy," argues that U.S. policy in the Middle East was quite different than the Islamists and other critics claimed. The real issue is that dictatorial regimes and radical opposition groups often tried to portray the United States as the enemy of Arabs or Muslims to garner support for themselves, to block moderate rulers from obtaining U.S. help in defending themselves, and to cover up shortcomings of their own governments and movements.

Ayatollah Ruhollah Khomeini, in his November 7, 1979, speech, assured his supporters that the United States would not intervene against them after they had seized the American embassy in Tehran and taken U.S. diplomats hostage. Five days later, Radio Tehran broadcast an analysis, "No Room for Leniency," of why America would not act. This is another important theme in attitudes toward the United States: America is said to be an imperialist bully, but at the same time the revolutionary claims he possesses the secret of defeating the United States. In fact, the claim is extremely ironic: the main reason U.S. policy did not intervene unless pushed too far was precisely because it was not as Khomeini described it. It did not seek to control Middle Eastern countries and wanted to avoid being considered hostile by them.

Actually, this combination made anti-Americanism a perfect rationale for the movement: people should hate the United States as the entity responsible for all local problems and overthrow any government friendly with it. Yet this all-powerful America can be defeated if one obeys the leader. Khomeini said the secret weapon was mass mobilization around an Islamist movement. Saddam Hussein would say the secret was Arab unity. In later years, as with bin Ladin, the secret was said to be terrorist attacks that proved America's helplessness.

The United States did deal decisively regarding another event in 1979 that was to become critical to the future of Islamist movements: the Soviet invasion of Afghanistan. U.S. leaders saw this as a dangerous move they were determined to counter. The national security advisor under President Jimmy Carter, Zbigniew Brzezinski, in a December 26 memo to the president described the idea that would eventually lead to U.S. support for anti-Soviet guerrillas in Afghanistan, some of whom later supported anti-American terror groups.

Carter also spoke about both the Iranian hostage and the Afghanistan issues in his State of the Union Address of January 23, 1980. The focus of the speech is on the Cold War aspect of the problem, and he calls for persuading Iranian leaders to view the USSR as the main danger. It is notable that on this as on other occasions he did not try to stir any hostility or threaten Iran.

In addition to attacking U.S. policy toward Israel, President Hafiz al-Asad of Syria, in his speech of October 1, 1981, also portrays the United States as an imperialist power with ambitions to destroy the Arabs, making them puppets, slaves, and indeed part of its directly controlled empire. These themes are repeated in a February 16, 1985, Syrian radio analysis entitled "U.S. Policy Views Mideast as 'U.S. Possession.' " The disagreement with the United States was not about specific policies but concerned the whole conception of America's goals in the world and the advantage of using America as an enemy for mobilizing the Arab masses.

During the 1980s Lebanon became a major front in the struggle against America. On many occasions Americans were taken as hostages, held for a long time, and sometimes killed. Terrorist attacks were also launched against the U.S. embassy and the brief military presence that tried to restore stability during the Lebanese civil war and following Israel's military offensive there in 1982. Hizballah leaders such as the group's spiritual guide, Muhammad Hussein Fadlallah, and Subhi al-Tufayli, a Hizballah official, in three February 1987 interviews spoke about and justified hostage taking.

With the Soviet Union's collapse and the Cold War's end, America became the world's sole superpower. In a major speech to an Arab summit meeting in February 1990, President Saddam Hussein of Iraq analyzed this situation and proposed a joint Arab effort, presumably under his leadership, to counter the United States. Six months later he tried to begin implementing this strategy by invading and annexing Kuwait. In response, though, a U.S.-led coalition defeated Iraq and restored Kuwait's independence during the opening months of 1991. American influence in the region reached an all-time high for several years.

Despite, or perhaps because of, U.S. efforts to weaken Iraq's threat to its neighbors, promote stability in the Persian Gulf area, and broker an Arab–Israeli peace agreement, anti-Americanism developed in new ways during the 1990s. New groups began to organize terror attacks against American citizens and interests. The U.S. Department of Justice's indictment of those who bombed the Khobar Towers, a residence for American military personnel in Saudi Arabia, in June 1996 shows the development of one such Iranian-backed operation.

On the ideological front, radical regimes and groups kept up their view of America as the principal enemy of Arabs and Muslims. An example from Ali al-Husseini al-Khamene'i, Iran's spiritual guide, speaking to the Organization of Islamic Countries meeting on December 9, 1997, is included here, along with three short attacks by Palestinian Islamists: Saqr Abu Fakhr (December 2, 1998); Atallah Abu al-Subh (December 3, 1998), and Ahmad Abu Halabiya (October 2000). The Palestinian Islamists' complaint regarded the kind of peace that the United States was trying to mediate between the Palestinians and Israelis—or, more accurately, the fact that it was seeking to make peace at all.

Writing just before the September 11, 2001, attack on the United States, Ayman al-Zawahiri explained the need for such tactics in his book *Knights under the Prophet's Banner*. He argues that the radical Islamists cannot seize power in Muslim countries and then attack the United States because America will prevent the success of such revolutions. Thus, it is necessary to strike directly at America, preferably on its own soil, using suicide bombing as a tactic. Only by frightening and damaging the United States to an extraordinary degree could it be forced to change its policies, or at least be made unable to implement them. Such a strategy would also inspire the Muslim masses, making them see the movement as strong and ultimately victorious, while the United States would be perceived as weak and vulnerable.

# The Truth about U.S. Middle East Policy

BARRY RUBIN

After the September 11, 2001, terrorist attack that killed almost 3,000 people in the United States, there was much discussion about what role U.S. policy in the Middle East had played in motivating the terrorists and those who supported them or at least sought to justify their deeds. American policy was said to be responsible for profound grievances on the part of Arabs and Muslims that required an apology for past behavior and a change of course for future U.S. policy and that somehow justified or explained the attack.

But this argument misrepresented the history and nature of U.S. Middle East policy to the point where it became a caricature of reality. Equally, such distortions made it far harder to understand the terrorists' true motives and the reasons many Arabs and Muslims seemed to support or sympathize with them.

Obviously, the United States, like all countries, seeks to make a foreign policy in accord with its interests. The important question, however, is how U.S. policymakers interpret those interests. If the United States saved Kuwait from annexation by a radical secularist regime in Iraq in 1991 because of oil, for example, its policy was still in practice pro–Kuwait, pro–Muslim, and pro–Arab. After all, the United States could as easily have tried to seize oil assets for itself or demanded lower petroleum prices or benefits for American companies. What is important is that U.S. leaders usually defined American interests and set policies in a way that sought support from the largest possible group of Arabs and Muslims.

In fact, the main external influence on U.S. Middle East policy has been the conflicts among Arab and Muslim states and factions, which usually pit radical Arab regimes and forces (often themselves militantly secularist and anti-Islam) and radical Islamist regimes and groups (which most Muslims hold to be deviant if not heretical) against their moderate counterparts. The same factor played a key role in the background of the September 2001 attacks, another case of radical groups wishing to seize power by defining themselves as the only legitimate Muslims, against whom any resistance is opposition to Islam itself.

During the 1940s and early 1950s, U.S. leaders wanted to play an anti-imperialist role in the Middle East. They tended to oppose continued British and French rule in the region and to voice support for reform movements.[1] When Gamal Abdel Nasser took power in Egypt in 1952, American policymakers welcomed his coup. The same year, the United States also opposed British proposals to overthrow the nationalist government in Iran.[2]

The Cold War—the global U.S.-Soviet conflict that shaped all U.S. foreign policy for many decades—altered this strategy. By the mid-1950s U.S. leaders believed with good reason that this conflict was being extended into the Middle East, where local governments were also taking sides. The United States saw that Nasser had decided to align with the Soviets. Some states, such as Lebanon and Jordan, saw a wave of radical nationalist subversion; in others, such as Syria and Iraq, this turmoil led to coups whose new regimes also became friendly to Moscow. Fearing that the government of the Iranian prime minister Muhammad Mossadegh was being taken over by communist forces, the United States helped overthrow it and returned the shah to power in 1953.

Even so, there was one last service the United States rendered to radical Arab nationalism. In 1956, in an unusual break in its close relationship to England and France, the United States opposed their plot to overthrow Nasser during the Suez crisis because it thought this action would antagonize the Arab world and increase Soviet influence. It threatened Britain and pressured Israel to withdraw from Egyptian territory. Thus, the United States saved Nasser, its biggest enemy in the region.

Basically, what U.S. policy did was to take sides in an inter-Arab conflict— Malcolm Kerr aptly called this the "Arab Cold War"—that had taken on global implications. Far from being anti-Arab, between the 1950s and 1980s the United States backed some Arab countries that were under assault by others that happened to be allied with the Soviet Union. This same fundamental policy of backing moderates against radicals was the pattern that prevailed in many circumstances down to the Kuwait crisis of 1990–91, as well as in U.S.-Israel relations.

During most of this period, the United States was the political patron of Islam in the Middle East. After all, traditional Islam was a major bulwark against communism and radical Arab nationalism. Saudi Arabia, the stronghold for the doctrine of using Islam against radicalism, sought U.S. help to ensure its survival under the Nasserist and Ba'athist threat. Even in Iran, the U.S.-organized 1953 coup against the nationalists and in support of the shah met with the approval of most Muslim clerics.

---

1. Regarding U.S. anti-imperialism, see Barry Rubin, *The Great Powers in the Middle East, 1941–1947: The Road to the Cold War* (London: Frank Cass, 1981).
2. On U.S. relations with Nasser's coup and regime, see Barry Rubin, *The Arab States and the Palestine Conflict* (Syracuse, N.Y.: Syracuse University Press, 1982). For a detailed account of these events, see Barry Rubin, *Paved with Good Intentions: The American Experience and Iran* (New York: Oxford University Press, 1980).

Understandably, militant nationalists portrayed themselves as representing the only legitimate Arabs and claimed that moderate regimes—such as Morocco, Jordan, Saudi Arabia, Lebanon, and also post-Nasser Egypt—were merely stooges of the West, a claim later adapted by Islamists, who insisted that Muslims who opposed them were not proper Muslims. Yet while the moderate Arab regimes were not models of democracy or human rights, the radical states—such as Libya, Syria, Iraq, and Islamist Iran—were always far worse in these categories.

Consider a Cold War analogy. Soviet propaganda claimed that by opposing the triumph of communism in Western Europe, the United States foiled the wishes of the European masses. Equally, the United States fought Germany (which proposed a new order of a united Europe) in coalition with other European states and Japan, which promised to unite all Asia in prosperity.

Actually, the Cold War's centrality in American strategy deterred the United States from taking tougher stands against Arab radical forces. American policymakers reasoned that Arab regimes or groups too alienated by American actions might side with the Soviet Union. Thus, the United States pursued a careful course, always on the lookout for winning away those Arabs aligned with the Soviets and avoiding the loss of those who did not. Thus, when the United States successfully wooed Egypt in the late 1970s, that country therefore became the second-largest recipient of U.S. aid in the world (with Israel in first place). The United States also did not attack or act too directly to counter Syria, whose control over Lebanon it accepted, or Iraq.

Even with the existence of an Arab-Israeli conflict and despite the myth of Arab and Muslim unity, much of the region's turbulence as well as U.S. involvement resulted from conflicts among Muslim and Arab groups or states. America was dragged into crises when Muslim Iraq attacked Muslim Iran, when Arab Muslim Iraq seized Arab Muslim Kuwait, and when Arab Muslim but secularist Egypt threatened Arab Muslim Jordan and Saudi Arabia. Usama bin Ladin's anger was most provoked by the presence of U.S. troops in Saudi Arabia starting in 1990. Yet this action not only protected Saudi Arabia and freed Kuwait from an Iraqi threat but was sanctioned by the Arab League. The grievance most closely associated with bin Ladin's turn to an anti-American strategy and the September 11 attacks was clearly based on a U.S. action that was pro-Arab and pro-Muslim.

This situation also posed an insoluble dilemma for U.S. policy common to all great powers. If the United States supports and aids a government such as Egypt or Saudi Arabia, it can be accused of sabotaging revolutionary movements that seek to overthrow that regime. But if the United States opposes any given Arab government or presses it to be more democratic or tolerant of human rights, it can be accused of meddling in domestic affairs and thus of acting in an imperialist manner.

In fact, the United States played a very limited role in the internal conflicts pitting radical Islamist revolutionaries against Middle Eastern regimes in the 1980s and 1990s. Equally, during Iran's Islamist revolution in 1978, the United States decided not to intervene and therefore in effect restrained the shah from taking tougher action to save his throne. Certainly the U.S. government hoped the shah would survive or that a moderate regime would emerge, but it nonetheless did little to prevent Ayatollah Ruhollah Khomeini's triumph.[3]

Once the revolution succeeded, President Jimmy Carter sought to conciliate the Islamist regime. It was indeed the growing contacts between the United States and moderate elements in the new government that led to the seizure of the U.S. embassy in November 1979. The United States was such an immediate threat not because it tried to bring down Khomeini, but because it might influence the revolution to be less radical. While the United States did not want Iran to spread its revolution, it preferred to have the best possible relations with Tehran in order to minimize that country's cooperation with the USSR. During the mid-1980s the administration of President Ronald Reagan was even ready to sell arms to Tehran in order to build an alliance with the Islamist regime there.

American "counterrevolutionary" involvement in the Arab world was also limited. Arab regimes neither wanted nor needed U.S. help to fight and defeat Islamist insurgents. Even if the United States had totally ignored the Middle East during the 1980s or 1990s, it is doubtful that a single additional Islamist revolution would have succeeded. In Algeria the United States maintained a neutral stance, despite the Algerian government's attempt to get its help. Similarly, the United States never took sides in Lebanon's civil war. At the same time, the most ruthless suppression of Islamist revolutions took place not with U.S. involvement but at the hands of two anti-American countries—Syria and Iraq.[4]

Ironically, the deepest and only real direct U.S. involvement in a battle between a regime and Islamists took place in Afghanistan, where the United States took the side of Islamist forces battling the Soviets. Bin Ladin, who would later claim the victory proved the viability of radical Islamist revolution,

---

3. Rubin, *The Arab States and the Palestine Conflict*; Rubin, *Paved with Good Intentions*.
4. Compared to Europe, Latin America, and Asia, U.S. involvement in Middle Eastern domestic conflicts to preserve existing regimes was positively minuscule. In Europe the Marshall Plan and other policies did help defeat communism in the late 1940s. In Latin America there were periodic interventions and massive support for the local militaries, focusing on internal security efforts. In Asia there were the Korean and Vietnam wars plus other direct and active counterinsurgency efforts, as well as the long-term presence of huge U.S. bases. Yet none of these activities ever inspired very much anti-American terrorism, except for a few limited acts in South America.

forgot that U.S. arms, training, and financial help had played a central role in that triumph. Elsewhere, blaming the United States was an excuse for radical Islamists as it had been earlier for militant Arab nationalists, a way to explain away their own ineffective tactics and inability to win the support of the Muslim (or Arab) masses.

As Fawaz Gerges accurately wrote, "Radical Islamists blame the United States for their defeat at the hands of the pro-U.S. Arab regimes. They claim that the West, particularly the United States, tipped the balance of power in favor of secular regimes by providing them with decisive political and logistical support."[5] The Islamists' claim was untrue, but it became a central rationale for their decision to turn their guns against the American people.

Taken as a whole, then, U.S. policy in the Middle East was usually intended to win support from the great majority of Arabs and Muslims who were opposed to radical forces seeking to take power in the region through coup, revolution, or aggression. On many other occasions, the United States tried to win over enemies by proving its goodwill or ability to help them. For example:

- The United States saved Yasir Arafat in Beirut in 1982 by arranging safe passage for him out of Lebanon, where he was besieged by the Israeli army. It initiated a dialogue with the Palestine Liberation Organization in 1988 and turned a blind eye to terrorism by PLO member groups until a blatant attack and the PLO's refusal to renounce it made this policy unsustainable in 1990. The United States became the Palestinians' patron between 1993 and 2000. It forgave Arafat for his past involvement in murdering American citizens, including U.S. diplomats. The United States worked hard to mobilize financial aid to the Palestinian Authority. Arafat was frequently invited to the White House. The United States almost always refrained from criticizing the Palestinian Authority. President Bill Clinton went to Gaza and made a sympathetic speech to an audience of Palestinian leaders. Finally, the United States tried to broker a peace agreement producing an independent Palestinian state with its capital in East Jerusalem. After Arafat rejected the U.S. peace attempts and did not implement cease-fires he promised to the United States, American leaders did not criticize him. Despite this, Arabs and Muslims supported or justified bin Ladin's attack by blaming Palestinian suffering on the United States.
- The United States proposed numerous détente efforts with Islamic Iran by Carter in 1979 and by Reagan in the mid-1980s, as well as sev-

5. Fawaz Gerges, "The Tragedy of Arab-American Relations," *Christian Science Monitor*, September 18, 2001.

eral initiatives by the Clinton administration. The United States did maintain sanctions on Iran to try to change three specific Iranian policies (sponsoring terrorism, developing weapons of mass destruction, and opposing Arab-Israeli peace), but it also sought to find ways to end those sanctions through diplomatic compromise and never waged a serious campaign to overthrow that regime.

- The United States saved Afghanistan from the Soviets; Kuwait and Saudi Arabia from Iraq; and Bosnia and Kosovo from Yugoslavia. In the first case the United States used covert means and in the other two instances actually sent U.S. troops into combat situations. In short, the United States risked American lives to help Muslims. Despite this fact, bin Ladin and his apologists blamed the United States for Muslim suffering in Bosnia and Kosovo, while labeling it an aggressor and defiler of Islam because it deployed troops in Saudi Arabia.

- Year after year, administration after administration, U.S. governments were careful not to hurt Muslim sensibilities in any speech or policy. In every statement, distinctions were made between radical Islamist movements and Islam itself.

- The U.S. government supported Muslim Pakistan against India, though Congress put some sanctions on Pakistan because of its nuclear weapons program. The United States ignored Pakistan's sponsorship of terrorism against India.

- The U.S. government supported Turkey, a country with a Muslim population, against Greece over the Cyprus conflict.

- In Somalia, where no vital U.S. interests were at stake, the United States engaged in a humanitarian effort to help a Muslim people suffering from anarchy, civil war, and murderous warlords. When it became clear that the mission could not succeed, U.S. forces left. Bin Ladin and others portrayed U.S. involvement in Somalia as yet another grievance justifying the attacks, as an imperialist anti-Islamic aggression defeated by Islamist Somalis.

- The United States supported Arab Iraq against Iran during the latter part of the Iran-Iraq war, a step it took at the urging of such Arab allies as Saudi Arabia and Kuwait.

- When President Saddam Hussein of Iraq began to seek Arab leadership in 1989 and repeatedly denounced the United States, U.S. policy did not respond in a tough enough manner in order to avoid offending Arabs. The United States continued to provide Iraq with credits and other trade benefits even when it had evidence that the money Iraq obtained was being used illegally to buy arms. When Saddam Hussein directly threatened Kuwait, the United States hurried to assure him, through the U.S. ambassador, April Glaspie, that America was not his enemy and was neutral in this dispute. Convinced America would not intervene, Saddam then invaded Kuwait.

• When Saddam Hussein hid weapons of mass destruction and refused to cooperate with UN inspectors, the United States supported continued sanctions against the Iraqi regime. Had the Baghdad government kept its commitments, the sanctions would have ended years earlier. Moreover, Iraq's government incurred suffering on its own people as a propaganda tool and continued to threaten its Arab and Muslim neighbors. Bin Ladin and his apologists portrayed American policy as a deliberate attempt to injure and kill the Iraqi people.

• For many years the United States kept its military forces out of the Persian Gulf to avoid offending the Arab and Muslim peoples there. It went in only when requested, first to reflag Arab oil tankers and later to intervene against Iraq's invasion of Kuwait. Its forces never went where they were not invited and left whenever they were asked to do so by the local states. American forces also stayed away from Mecca and Medina to avoid offense to Islam. Once Kuwait was liberated, the United States even advocated the concept of the Damascus agreement, in which Egypt and Syria would have played a primary role in protecting the Gulf. It was the Gulf Arab states that rejected implementation of this idea. Nevertheless, bin Ladin, other Arabs, and Iran's government portrayed the U.S. presence as an imperialist plot to dominate the area and subjugate its people.

• The United States rescued Egypt at the end of the 1973 war by pressing Israel to stop advancing and by insisting on a cease-fire. The United States became Egypt's patron in the 1980s, after the Camp David peace agreement, providing large-scale arms supplies and other military and financial assistance while asking little in return. Indeed, none of this help gave the United States any leverage over Egyptian policies, or even goodwill in the state-controlled Egyptian media and in the statements of that country's leaders. Bin Ladin and his allies, however, portrayed Egypt as a puppet of the United States.

Indeed, in twelve major issues where Muslims had a conflict with non-Muslims or secular forces, or Arabs had a conflict with non-Arabs, the United States sided with the former groups in eleven out of twelve cases.

The United States backed Muslim versus non-Muslim states in six of seven conflicts: It supported Turkey over Greece; Bosnia and later Kosovo against Yugoslavia; Pakistan against India; the Afghans fighting the Soviets; and Azerbaijan against Armenia. The only exception to this pattern was U.S. support for Israel in the Arab–Israeli conflict.

When Muslims came into conflict with secular forces, the United States helped moderate Islamic-oriented states against both Egyptian Nasserism and the Ba'athist regimes in Iraq and Syria; and it assisted Kuwait and Saudi Arabia in resisting Iraq. The only apparent exception to this rule was U.S. help for Iraq against Iran, but even this effort was an attempt to help conservative Islamist Gulf Arab regimes threatened by militant Islamist Iran. Given this aspect of the Iran-Iraq war, the United States helped Muslim against secularist governments in three of three conflicts.

If one considers Arab versus non-Arab conflicts, the United States supported Arab Iraq against non-Arab Iran; and both the Arabs and Iran against the Soviet Union.[6]

Remarkably, then, the U.S. backing for Israel was the only significant case in which the United States did not follow this pattern. No matter how much Arabs and Muslims are aggrieved at that particular U.S. policy—an issue discussed at greater length later—it is strange that this single complaint should so overwhelm all the points raised above. Indeed, for reasons also discussed later, virtually none of these events is even mentioned in Arab or Muslim discussions about the United States.

This pattern of U.S. attempts to maintain good relations with Arabs and Muslims is so strong that even after several thousand Americans were murdered in a massive terrorist attack, U.S. leaders spent much of their time urging that there be no retaliation against Muslims or Arabs in the United States. American policymakers repeated at every opportunity that they did not see Islam as the enemy and tried everything possible to gain Arab and Muslim support or sympathy for the U.S. effort.

Rather than seek revenge against Afghanistan, whose safe haven for bin Ladin had helped make the attacks on New York and Washington possible, President George W. Bush even asked American schoolchildren to send donations to help the children of Afghanistan. The United States dropped food to the Afghan people, waged war to overthrow the Taliban while trying to minimize Afghan civilian casualties, eliminated the ferocious dictatorship ruling the country, turned power over to a broad-based new government, and organized large-scale aid for reconstruction there.

Again, the fact that many or even most Arabs and Muslims in the Middle East did not recognize that consistent thread in U.S. policy does not mean it did not exist. But what it does demonstrate is that there were forces and factors within the region that had a stake in distorting American policy for their own purposes.

Just as the United States took many steps to help Arabs and Muslims—

---

6. U.S. support for Israel is only counted once in this list. I have put this issue in the first category, but it could just as well be placed in the last one.

or at least moderate against radical ones—it is equally revealing to analyze what the United States did not do. This tally also undercuts the notion of overwhelming and justified Arab and Muslim grievances based on American misdeeds in the Middle East. If the United States wanted to carry out "anti-Arab" or "anti-Muslim" policies, as is charged, or even if it wanted to act as a traditional great power, it could have taken dozens of actions justified by events there. The fact that the United States did not do so relates to its goals, including a serious desire to win support from Arabs and Muslims for reasons ranging from the Cold War to wanting good trade relations to avoiding conflict.

Clearly, a large part of the Arab and Muslim critique of U.S. policy is based on an expectation of what America wants and how it might behave. Whatever the failure of America and Americans in understanding the Middle East, the inability of Middle Easterners to understand the United States seems to exceed it. Many in the Middle East view the United States as a projection of what their own leaders or movements would do if they were in control of the world's most powerful country. They would seek global hegemony and control over the Middle East, using force to do so and wiping out enemies without mercy or tolerance. Consequently, the United States is accused of thinking the same way—as intending to subordinate the Arab world and defeat or destroy Islam.

Consider what the United States did not do in past decades:

- It did not embark on an all-out effort to overthrow the Islamist regimes in Iran, Afghanistan, or Sudan, even though these regimes sponsored terrorism against the United States and unilaterally declared it to be an enemy. Nor did it attack Iran for its involvement in holding American hostages in Lebanon or sponsoring terrorist attacks that cost American lives. The United States merely invoked economic sanctions to change certain specific policies of these states.
- Even when Iran held American diplomats as hostages, the United States publicly declared it would avoid using force and sought diplomatic means to resolve the situation.
- It did not try to overthrow Saddam Hussein in 1991, partly because it accepted the argument that to do so would make the United States unpopular in the Arab world. Even when Kurdish and Shi'ite Iraqis rose up against the regime, the United States did not help them bring down its most hated enemy in the Middle East.
- It did not pressure or seek to subvert Syria even when Damascus was involved in anti-American terrorism. It courted Syria during the Kuwait war and in the subsequent peace process but put no serious pressure on Damascus even when the Syrians walked out of the peace pro-

cess. Rather than act as an imperialist power, the United States flattered and courted Damascus.

- It did not try to destroy Arafat and the PLO even when they were responsible for anti-American terrorism and aligned with the USSR. It usually did not criticize or pressure them when they broke agreements (rejecting Clinton's two peace initiatives in 2000) and broke cease-fires promised to the United States in 2000 and 2001. The United States did not have an "anti-Palestinian" policy except in the sense that it opposed Palestinian efforts to destroy Israel's existence, while supporting efforts to find a compromise solution to the conflict that would help satisfy moderate Palestinian goals.

- It did not try to punish Egypt for rapprochement with Iraq or secret purchases of missiles from North Korea. It did not threaten Egypt with a cut-off of aid even when Cairo refused to cooperate with the war against terrorism in 2001.

- It did not bully King Hussein of Jordan after he decided to follow the domestic radical forces' demand that he support Iraq, a country at war with America, during the Kuwait crisis. Afterward, Jordan suffered no U.S. retaliation. Indeed, it was Saudi Arabia and Kuwait that denied Jordan aid, while the United States tried to persuade these states to forgive and help Amman.

- It dropped sanctions on Libya when Libya turned over two intelligence officers and took no further actions, even though a court case showed Libyan involvement in the bombing of a U.S. airliner with the deaths of many Americans. It bombed Libya on one occasion for its involvement in terrorism aimed at killing Americans—a bombing in West Berlin—but never used military force against Libya at any other time.

- When two U.S. embassies in east Africa were blown up, with immense loss of life, by Usama bin Ladin's group in 1998, it responded only with one cruise missile attack on a specific factory in Sudan allegedly owned by bin Ladin and being used to make chemical weapons, and one similar attack on a terrorist training base in Afghanistan. If the United States was so bullying, imperialistic, and eager to hurt Islamist forces, it could have justifiably launched full-scale military assaults and other punishments on those hosting or helping bin Ladin.

- It did not go all out in supporting Israel even when the peace process collapsed in 2000, but instead maintained a studious position of neutrality, probably spending more time criticizing Israel than it did the Palestinians, at least during the conflict's first twelve months.

- It did not use all its assets and resources to force Arab states to support the peace process with Israel, but employed only very limited ef-

forts at persuasion. When these efforts were rebuffed, as happened almost every time, the United States did not retaliate.

- It did not use the occasion of an Iraqi attempt to assassinate former
President George Bush to go to war with Iraq, sending only a one-day
cruise missile attack on Iraqi intelligence headquarters, and even that
was done at night in order to minimize casualties.
- While the United States did bomb Iraq and fight to retain sanctions
when Iraq broke commitments on eliminating weapons of mass destruction, the United States also made compromises to ease sanctions,
tried to improve the humanitarian situation in Iraq, limited its use of
force, and resisted proposals to go all out in using the Iraqi opposition
to try to overthrow Saddam.
- When U.S. oil companies' holdings were nationalized and oil prices
were raised steeply, the United States did not try to overthrow regimes
or force or threaten them to lower prices.
- The United States did not try to dominate the Persian Gulf after 1990,
despite its position of overwhelming military strength there; it did not
overthrow or dominate the local governments; and it did not demand a
huge payment for its help (unlike Iraq did after the Iran-Iraq war) or
threaten to punish Gulf states unless they changed their policies to be
more to America's liking (unlike the behavior of the radical Arab states
and Iran) or insist that they transform their systems (unlike Iran and
radical movements had done).
- The United States did not at any time launch an anti-Islamist campaign in the region. It did not send forces or special counterinsurgency
aid, or demand that Islamist groups be repressed, or do a host of other
things it could have done in this regard.
- It did not take advantage of the USSR's disappearance as a superpower
to impose anything on anybody and certainly not to establish American
domination in the region. Despite having won the Cold War, the
United States did not seek to take revenge on regimes that had supported the losing side.

This list is far from complete, but it gives a sample of how the United
States chose options that reflected the fact that it did not seek to dominate the
region, destroy Islam, undermine Arabism, or take other actions of which it has
been accused. Whatever America has done or done wrong in the Middle East,
it used a small portion of its potential power, stopped far short of what it could
have done, and avoided intervention whenever possible. If, for whatever reason,
the United States limited its actions in the region, then the alleged grievances
against this restrained superpower should also be smaller.

How has the real U.S. record come to be so disregarded in the Middle East, and why?

Four techniques are being used to distort this history. The first is simply to ignore the truth about U.S. policy. For reasons discussed later, Arab and Iranian media hardly ever say anything positive about the United States. Arab and Iranian leaders—even those who benefit from U.S. help—rarely praise America. Shut off from contrary information and constantly fed antagonistic views, it is hardly surprising that the masses are hostile to the United States. Those who would present a different view are discouraged by peer pressure, censorship, and fear of being labeled U.S. agents.

The second technique is to distort the record. For example, bin Ladin himself charges that the suffering of Muslims in Kosovo and Bosnia (whom the United States actually protected) or in places like East Timor, the Philippines, and Algeria (where the United States played no role) are America's fault. In other areas, American motives can be misrepresented. For instance, U.S. humanitarian efforts in Somalia are portrayed as an imperialistic, anti-Muslim campaign defeated by heroic local resistance. Again, the Arab media and leaders are complicit in this approach, having laid a foundation for it by their own presentation of issues.

A third method is to ignore other threats to the region. An outstanding example here is the whitewashing of Saddam Hussein. After all, the Iraqi leader began two wars, killing hundreds of thousands of Muslims and Arabs; looted and vandalized Kuwait; threatened all his neighbors and thus the holy cities of Mecca and Medina as well; tortured and repressed his own people, against some of whom he also used chemical weapons; fired missiles at Iran, Saudi Arabia, and Israel; and has been working to develop nuclear arms with which he could seize power in the Persian Gulf region.

Yet now the Arab peoples are told that it is the United States, not Iraq, that threatens to dominate the Gulf and enslave its people. American-backed international sanctions against Iraq and the use of sporadic force to make Iraq less dangerous are cited as major reasons justifying the assault on America. The strange implicit alliance between bin Ladin and Saddam Hussein, a secularist who has killed many Muslim clerics (albeit Shia ones mainly), is one of the more bizarre elements of the situation.

Fourth, there has been an attempt to reduce all of American policy to a single issue, defined as "U.S. support for Israel," while also distorting the nature and policies of Israel itself. This point is discussed later. For the moment, though, it can be said that to try to negate all the United States has done for the Arab and Muslim world—and all that it has not done *to* the Arab and Muslim world—on the sole basis of U.S.-Israel relations shows the flimsiness of the case against America.

Just because the United States has been accused of pursing a policy hostile to Arabs and Muslims does not mean that these accusations are true and certainly does not mean that American policy should be changed. Indeed, the reasons for this claim have far more to do with Middle East politics than with U.S. policy. And when the purposes of this campaign are thoroughly examined, it reflects credit on American motives, choices, and strategies.

Before considering the real roots of anti-American views and behavior, however, the issue of the relationship between the United States and Israel requires some separate consideration. Clearly, the United States has been Israel's main ally since the 1970s. But what does the concept that "the United States supports Israel" mean in the overall context of U.S. policy and the current spate of anti-Americanism?

Part of the problem is how the Arab world and Islamists conceive of Israel itself. It is not surprising that those whose starting point of analysis is that Israel is some evil force seeking to dominate the Middle East, kill Arabs, and despoil Islam view any U.S. help to Israel as a terrible deed. More accurately, though, the United States helped Israel survive efforts from Arab neighbors to remove it from the map. In addition, during that entire period the U.S. goal was to achieve a mutually acceptable compromise peace agreement between the Arabs and Israel that would ensure good American relations with both sides in the conflict. In addition, the U.S.-Israel alliance was also created and reinforced owing to the fact that Arab states took certain hostile steps, including aligning with the USSR and using such tactics as sponsoring anti-American terrorism.

Radical forces in the Arab world objected to all aspects of the U.S. policy toward Israel because of their own objectives and interests. They wanted to eliminate Israel and saw U.S. policy as blocking their success. At the same time, they did not want a peaceful solution to the conflict, since they rejected any outcome in which Israel survived. Equally, a successful peace process would deny them the benefits of using the conflict to foment support for revolution and justify their rule. Finally, American success in achieving a resolution of the conflict would strengthen U.S. leverage in the region, making it better able to counter radical forces there.

From the 1970s on, the United States repeatedly tried to seize opportunities to advance a negotiated solution of the Arab-Israeli conflict. In the 1993–2000 Oslo process, the United States tried to facilitate a deal on the Israeli-Palestinian and Israeli-Syrian fronts. While it is possible to critique the details and timing of specific American efforts, the overall goal was quite clear. The United States put such peacemaking efforts at the head of its international agenda, and top U.S. officials devoted a considerable portion of their time to this issue. Over time, when it was convinced that forces on the Arab side were ready to make peace, the United States moved considerably closer to the Arab-

Palestinian standpoint and urged Israel to do so as well. When the United States doubted the readiness of Arab leaders to resolve the issue, however, U.S. policy moved in the opposite direction.

Negotiating a compromise agreement was always in the U.S. interest precisely because it did want good relations with the Arab world. By resolving this passionate issue, the United States would be better able to promote regional stability, reduce the possibility of war, and ensure its own regional position. For these same reasons, Islamist radicals opposed this U.S. policy. U.S. efforts at peacemaking were more antithetical to their revolutionary goals than if the United States had refrained from such activities. This is the reason radical Islamist forces opposed the peace process altogether and staged many terrorist attacks to try to destroy it.

Their complaint was not that the diplomatic process moved too slowly but that it might succeed at all. Peace would make it hard for Hamas and Islamic Jihad, the Palestinian Islamist groups, peace to gain power and continue their armed struggle. Ironically, if one Middle Eastern leader benefited from U.S. efforts to strengthen him against Islamist forces in the 1990s, it was Yasir Arafat. The fact that Arafat and the Palestinian Authority became virtual U.S. clients in that era only further dismayed the Islamist radicals.

Events demonstrate the accuracy of the foregoing analysis. Israel's withdrawal from Lebanon, urged and supported by the United States, was not seen as a step toward "ending occupation" or achieving peace but as a sign that Israel was weak and a signal to escalate violence against it. Bin Ladin's ideological framework was laid down and the September 11 attacks were being planned at a time when the peace process seemed closest to success, even though the actual attack took place at a time when it had clearly failed.

It is strange that the height of anti-Americanism in the Middle East came at the height of U.S. proposals to support an independent Palestinian state with its capital in East Jerusalem. And even if the specific offers are judged inadequate by various Arabs because of their details or presentation (and often on the basis of misleading information about what was offered), this hardly explains or justifies claims that U.S. policy was brutal and hostile.

The attempt to reduce all of U.S. Middle East policy to the phrase "support for Israel"—and then to misrepresent what that stance actually entailed—was really an attempt to exploit xenophobia as a tool justifying radical groups and dictatorial regimes. The real complaint was that the United States helped Israel survive, then sought a diplomatic solution that would undermine both the case for Islamist revolution and the justification for the regimes' dictatorial rule. It was not "U.S. support for Israel" as such that created anti-Americanism, but rather the distortion of what the United States was actually doing and the goals of various forces within the region.

Obviously this is not necessarily the way most Arabs and Muslims see—

or at least publicly professed to see—America and its Middle East policy. "For many Arabs, regardless of their politics, the United States has replaced colonial Europe as the embodiment of evil," Gerges wrote. "In their eyes, the United States is the source of the ills and misfortunes that befell their world in the second part of the past century. Today, to be politically conscious in the Arab world is to be highly suspicious of America, its policies, and its motives."[7] Why, then, is the perception so different?

Obviously, differences of opinion in viewing events are rooted in a whole set of cultural and historical factors and questions of language, familiarity, interests, and politics. Nevertheless, to attribute this outcome to simple misunderstandings or honest disagreements over the facts is insufficient. Only by examining such issues further can the reason for anti-Americanism and especially its timing be better understood.

The real basis of anti-Americanism in the Arab world is that this is a strategy that offers something for everyone there, and at no significant cost.

*For radical oppositionists*, anti-Americanism is a way to muster mass support after they failed to do so for an antigovernment revolutionary strategy. Given the inability of revolutionary Islamist movements to overthrow any Arab government using a variety of strategies, they desperately sought some new tactic. The masses overwhelmingly rejected the radical Islamists' claims that they represent true Islam, noting the many ways their views deviated from Islam as it was always practiced. But this objection can be swept aside by clothing the Islamist cause in the attractive garments of xenophobia. It is an old trick of totalitarian movements and one that works very well. An added benefit for radical opposition movements is that anti-Americanism is a relatively safe strategy. Arab regimes that will quickly and brutally repress a challenge to themselves will do nothing against militants who attack only the United States. Indeed, it is precisely because the image of a bullying and anti-Arab America is a myth that verbally bashing the United States is such a profitable and secure enterprise. The extremists' real goal is to delegitimize the moderate forces; to mobilize the masses using the existing hatred for America and stirring up more; and to maintain the myth of Arab or Islamist unity against a foreign foe. Our enemy, they argue, cannot come from our own ranks but must be external and alien to our religion and culture. The cause of our problems and suffering is not in any way due to our own actions or decisions but purely to the meddling of evil foreigners and their local agents.

*For the regimes*, anti-Americanism is a way to distract attention from numerous failings. Instead of pressing for democracy, human rights, higher living standards, less corruption and incompetence, a change of leadership, or any of

---

7. Gerges, "The Tragedy of Arab-American Relations."

numerous other demands that would damage the interests of governments and rulers, the focus of attention is turned to shouting at the United States. This strategy defuses opposition and takes the pressure off the rulers.

By seizing control of the anti-Americanism issue, regimes also defuse its use by the opposition and make it into a factor that strengthens their own power. The Egyptian government can accept billions of dollars in U.S. aid, obtain American arms, use the United States to protect them from an aggressive Iraq, and even carry out joint military maneuvers with U.S. forces. It can then push anti-Americanism in its own state-controlled media and officials' statements. Such a strategy appeases radicals, distracts the citizens, and maintains the state's legitimacy as a politically correct Arab and Muslim power. Governments can even demand national unity (i.e., insist no one criticize them or demand domestic change) in the face of this American "threat." They can simultaneously deflect Islamist anger from themselves, distance themselves from bin Ladin, and glean the benefits of alliance with the United States. Even if the Arab or Iranian governments do nothing, they know that the United States will eliminate the threat of bin Ladin for them.

*For Iraq,* anti-Americanism becomes a useful tool in its battle to escape sanctions and rebuild its military might. With America being charged with murdering defenseless Iraqis through sanctions, who can remember Iraq's seizure of Kuwait? Even the 1991 war is transformed from a U.S.-led liberation struggle to an example of anti-Muslim, anti-Arab American aggression.

*For Iran,* putting the emphasis on anti-Americanism provides an opportunity to get U.S. forces out of the Gulf and to make a trans-Muslim appeal that negates Iran's regional handicaps of being Shia, not Sunni, and Persian, not Arab. At the same time, the United States eliminated Iran's troublesome neighbor, the Taliban government in Afghanistan, though Tehran does not want Afghanistan to become a U.S. client either.

*For Syria,* anti-Americanism is a substitute for the reform that President Bashar al-Asad promised and quickly squelched. For Palestinian leaders, anti-Americanism erases their own rejection of compromise peace offers and resort to violence while providing a good weapon with which to mobilize the Arab world and a lever with which to undermine Israel's international support and demand more concessions. Claiming that U.S. support for Israel is the cause of anti-Americanism, Palestinians can even demand new American concessions.

Egypt can once again show itself to be the leading champion of Arab interests, with some additional Islamic credentials added to the government's credit. Cairo can expect that a refusal to cooperate with the American war against terrorism and the anti-American hostility of the state-controlled Egyptian media will in no way jeopardize its $2 billion in annual U.S. aid.

Arab governments can also use the crisis to demand more concessions from the West and hence material gains for themselves. They argue they can do nothing because their hands are tied by the passion of public opinion (a factor that never stops them from taking tough action when this same factor threatens their own interests). They insist that the United States must pressure on Israel for unilateral concessions, end sanctions against Iraq, and meet their other demands—without any reciprocal action on their part—as the only way of defusing the problem.

None of this means that any Arab government likes bin Ladin, endorses his specific brand of Islamist ideology, or wants him to succeed. But they will exploit aspects of his ideas and deeds, adapting them to their own needs, and they will attack his forces directly only if they are deemed a threat to internal stability. Contrary to bin Ladin, they seek no real confrontation with the West or war with Christianity. They do not want to lose the trade, economic aid, or military defense arrangements they have with the United States. But they will play the militancy game at home for domestic benefit, reinforcing their own people's antagonism to the West and the United States and making a peaceful resolution of the Arab-Israeli dispute more difficult.

*For intellectuals and opinion makers*, anti-Americanism permits them to vent their anger against a government-approved target rather than risk their positions as the rulers' privileged courtiers by taking courageous stands against their own societies' injustices. They also do not have to consider changing their own traditional militant ideologies. Anyone who differs from the prevailing view can be intimidated into silence by accusations of being anti-Arab, anti-Muslim, and agents of America. Those who talk of domestic reform, democratization, privatization, and other changes can be shut up.

*For the masses*, anti-Americanism falls in line with what they have been taught in school, told by the state-controlled media, heard preached at the mosque, and seen purveyed by their leaders, whether they be the nation's rulers or the Islamist oppositionists. Holding America responsible for everything wrong in their lives makes them feel better and provides an explanation of how the world works. The anti-American struggle makes them feel strong, giving them hope for a better future. It validates their pride in being virtuous Arabs and Muslims superior to their evil enemies.

Consider, for example, how Egypt—America's greatest ally in the Arab world—handled the Egypt Air crash of 1999. Official statements and the state-controlled media claimed this tragedy was caused by a U.S.- or Israeli-orchestrated conspiracy. Suggestions that an Egyptian co-pilot might have deliberately caused the crash for political or personal reasons were rejected as a slander on Egypt and its people. In short, even the investigation of a plane crash was presented to the masses in inflammatory anti-American terms.[8]

Are there legitimate Arab and Muslim grievances against America? Of

8. See "Egypt Air Crash: The Hidden Hand behind Disaster," *al-Aharm* (Egypt), April 2, 2000, <http://www.albalagh.net/current_affairs/egypt_crsh.html>.

course there are. But there are also legitimate American grievances against Arab states and Islamist opposition movements that are equally impressive. Moreover, one must assess the overall level of legitimate grievances and the legitimacy of a terrorist response to them. A good way to do so is to compare them to the grievances and responses of people in other countries and regions.

If one wants to assess relative grievances against America based on past U.S. policies, the Arabs and Muslims of the Middle East would be relatively far down on the list. After all, one could far more easily find, justify, and see as more serious the grievances of Native Americans and African Americans; of the Japanese and Germans, defeated and occupied after the Second World War; of Latin Americans, who faced U.S.-supported coups and military regimes that really did depend on U.S. backing, along with a high level of American economic dominations; of Filipinos and Puerto Ricans, who were ruled by the United States for decades; of Cubans, subject to U.S. sanctions; of Russians and other ex–Soviet bloc citizens defeated in the Cold War; of the Vietnamese and other people in Southeast Asia who suffered hundreds of thousands of casualties through American carpet bombing, napalm, and deforestation; of the Chinese, who dislike U.S. support for Taiwan; or of sub-Saharan Africans, who deplored U.S. support for South Africa. Yet virtually none of these peoples evince significant anti-American sentiments, nor do they carry out or justify anti-American terrorism.

One grievance that, while paramount in other regions, has relatively little objective basis in the Middle East is the issue of economic exploitation. The oil-producing states have a great deal of economic power and wealth and boss around U.S. companies as they wish. Unlike in Latin America and Asia, there is little American investment in the Middle East. There is no U.S. control of the economy as there is in Latin America, sweatshops as there are Asia, or ownership of raw materials as there is in Africa. In this respect, the Middle East has far less reason for grievances than other regions. It is hard to argue that Arabs are poor because Americans are rich. And it cannot be claimed that Arab raw materials are sold at low prices in exchange for high-priced Western industrial goods, a situation quite different from that of countries having only cacao or tin to sell.

Another grievance for which the Middle East, compared to other areas, has little or no foundation is the complaint that the United States makes or breaks governments there. Since the pro–shah Iranian coup of 1953, there has not been a single case in which U.S. covert intervention can be credibly charged, much less proven, to have changed a Middle Eastern regime. In recent memory, only regarding Iraq has the United States been even halfheartedly involved in trying to overthrow the government.

One can argue that everyone in the world—including Europeans—has an equal or better case for grievances against the United States than people in the

Middle East. Yet only in that part of the world does this hatred take such an intense and popular form. Nowhere else is there popular and governmental support for terrorist attacks against the United States. Something is very peculiar in this situation, and clearly the problem does not stem from the extent of America's misdeeds. Instead, the problem emerges from the use of America by local forces as an excuse and as a tool for political manipulation and control.

In the Middle East, the case against America is often an attempt to justify the use of the United States as a handy target, employing the same technique that Nazi Germany, the Communist USSR, and other dictatorships did in their time. It is a way to mobilize masses, to excuse the shortcomings of local governments, and to carry ideological movements to victory. It is also a way to disparage a whole set of otherwise attractive ideas—political freedom, modernization, and so on—that are linked to America by slandering the perceived exemplar and sponsor of that way of life. "The United States exports evil, in terms of corruption and criminality," says Saddam Hussein, "not only to any place to which its armies travel, but also to any place where its movies go."[9]

Traditional Islam and aspects of Arab society are under assault by Westernization or Americanization, modernization, and globalization. But the same applies also to every other part of the world, including Europe. In many places this challenge is met by rejecting some aspects of these things and adapting others. Nowhere else in the world, however, is resistance as uncompromising and thoroughgoing as it is (at least in rhetorical terms) in the Arab and Muslim world. Anti-Americanism is also a specific element in this response.

A subtlety of labeling is very revealing on this point. Starting with the Iranian revolutionary leader Ayatollah Ruhollah Khomeini in the 1970s, it has become commonplace to label the United States as the "great Satan" (and Israel as the "little Satan"). But Satan, in both Christian and Muslim theology, is not an imperialist bully; rather, he is a tempter. He makes his wares seem so attractive that people willingly and voluntarily sell their souls to him.

Many of the extremist Islamists, including most of the September 11 suicide terrorists, had a great deal of personal contact with the West, as did many of the militant Iranian students who supported Khomeini and seized the U.S. embassy in Tehran in 1979. They were people who came close to yielding to the "temptation," who came to define their Islam not as most normal Muslims do—as a body of belief in which their faith is secure—but as a way of maintaining personal identity against America and the West precisely because they fear their own desire to join Western society. This basic attitude is to a greater or lesser extent common among Arabs, especially the class of people who govern

---

9. Saddam Hussein, Republic of Iraq Television, September 12, 2001; translation in U.S. Department of Commerce, Foreign Broadcast Information Service (hereafter cited as FBIS).

and who dominate the media. In short, anti-Americanism in this respect arises not from the ugliness of U.S. policy but from the attractiveness of American society.

Samuel Johnson once said that extreme patriotism is the last refuge of scoundrels. In a real sense, anti-Americanism is the last refuge of failed political systems and movements in the Middle East. Hatred of America justifies a great deal that is bad in the Arab world and helps keep it politically dominated by dictatorships, socially unfree, and economically underdeveloped. Blaming national shortcomings on America means that the Arab debate does not deal with the internal problems and weaknesses that are the real and main cause of these countries' problems. It justifies the view that the only barrier to complete success, prosperity, and justice for the Arab (and Islamic) world is the United States.

Instead of dealing with privatization, women's equality, democracy, civil society, freedom of speech, due process of law, and twenty other issues the Arab world needs to address, attention can be focused on—or rather, diverted to—the conjuring of American conspiracy. Fixing blame for the Arab world's problems on Israel's existence is a regional staple. Yet no matter how emotional the charge against Israel is, its salience is truly overwhelming only for the Palestinians. The advantage of anti-Americanism is that there is something to everyone's advantage in this argument, and any Arab or Muslim can adapt it to his own list of priorities. The solution for the dilemma of the Arab world and of the hard-liners in Iran was not peace but the stirring up of a new wave of hysteria against external enemies.

While bin Ladin's function is particularly important in helping to kill the best chance in modern history that Arab and Muslim societies had to rethink their past mistakes and change course, the role he is playing is hardly new. Islamic thought holds the idea of a "century reformer," a charismatic individual who appears at the end of each century to revitalize Islam. But bin Ladin might more accurately be called a "decade challenger."

In every decade, a leader has arisen to issue a call for the Arab or Islamic world to rise up against the West. This was the function of Nasser in the 1950s and 1960s, of Palestinian and other revolutionary movements in the 1970s, of Khomeini in the 1980s, and of Saddam Hussein in the 1990s. Each has mustered a broad range of support and for a historical moment held center stage. Each promised to be the savior who would solve the Arabs' problems, defeating their enemies and ushering in a new age when the Arabs (or Muslims, or Iranians) would be powerful, happy, rich, and restored to their rightful place of world leadership.

Each also failed. But after a period of disappointment, a new hero and magic idea has been grasped. Islam rejects the use of alcohol, but the ideology of utopian expectation has proven to be an equally dangerous intoxicant.

Enter bin Ladin. After so many defeats, the September 11 attacks on America could be judged a great success. Anti-Americanism was the new and badly needed doctrine. It made sense. What was being rejected, after all, was an "American" paradigm for modernization and change, so why not hit directly at the source of the despised program of moderation, peace, democracy, compromise, private enterprise, secularization, Westernization, rule of law, open media, pragmatism, and so on? If America is the example you do not want to follow and want to discourage people from accepting, then it must be bad, all bad. If America is the temptation that seems so appealing, it must be made repugnant. Anyone who likes that paradigm and the paradigm itself must be discredited. Bin Ladin's ideas will not lead Islamists to victory over either their own governments or America. But they are very useful in stopping the kinds of rethinking and change that would most benefit the Arab and Middle East Muslim worlds.

One of the most fascinating aspects of anti-Americanism is the contradiction between seeing the United States as an arrogant bully whose mistreatment of the Arabs and Muslims merits punishment and regarding it as a cowardly weakling that is impotent to punish those who criticize or even attack it. There are two slight variations on how this problem is addressed, though the difference between them is not important. It could be claimed that America was always cowardly, and the heroic revolutionaries are only exposing that fact, or that the United States is made cowardly by the revolutionaries' own heroism and clever strategy of attacking America directly.

While the radicals must portray America as a bully to provoke outrage against it, they must also portray America as weak to encourage Arabs and Muslims to fight it and believe they can win. After all, the revolutionaries and radical states are frustrated by the fact that too many Arabs and Muslims are already afraid of the United States, or at least see its friendship as an asset they do not want to lose. The revolutionaries have an uphill battle in solving this problem. How can they explain why people listen to them and rise up against their rulers and U.S. influence? Why don't regimes all go to war against Israel at once, and why don't Muslims by the thousands become suicide bombers? Why aren't U.S. interests attacked everywhere and American "ideas" rejected outright?

An obvious reason is that various people and governments are afraid they will lose this war because they are afraid of the United States. Of course, one by-product of building up America as the "Great Satan" is to make it seem even more frightening, giving it even more leverage in the region. As has often been shown in Middle Eastern history, whatever they say loudly in public, many politicians and others want such a powerful force on their side.

So the revolutionaries must persuade the masses and leaders that America is simultaneously horrible and helpless: that the United States cannot do anything if it is attacked, ridiculed, and disregarded. Powerless against their own dictators, against defeats, against corruption of the regime, against restrictions on their religion or the restrictions of their religion, and against poverty, any Arab or Muslim may feel it possible at least to spit on the United States and get away with it.

Consequently, the truth is the exact opposite of the complaint. Anti-Americanism is encouraged not by a real belief that the United States is too tough but by the notion that it is too weak and meek not to be defeated. Far from attacking America because it is really a big bully, extremists past and present launched assaults to prove their belief that the United States was a paper tiger. Such sentiments were voiced by Khomeini, Saddam Hussein, and many others. An Egyptian Islamist writes that the Americans are cowards while the Muslims are brave: "The believers do not fear the enemy. . . . Yet their enemies protect [their] lives like a miser protects his money. They . . . do not enter into battles seeking martyrdom. . . . This is the secret of the believers' victory over their enemies."[10] Bin Ladin himself explained, "[Those] God guides will never lose. . . . America [is] filled with fear from the north to south and east to west. . . . [Now there will be] two camps: the camp of belief and of disbelief. So every Muslim shall . . . support his religion."[11]

Middle East leaders who complained of America's alleged hostility always made it clear in their own statements that power—not popularity—was the most important factor for having influence and gaining success for one's interests. Bashar al-Asad noted that "it is important to gain respect, rather than sympathy."[12] The deputy foreign minister of Iraq at the time, Nizar Hamdoon, wrote in similar terms: "Aggressors thrive on appeasement. The world learned that at tremendous cost from the Munich agreement of 1938. . . . How could the German generals oppose Hitler once he had proven himself successful? Indeed, aggressors are usually clever at putting their demands in a way that seems reasonable."[13]

Rather than having been guilty of bullying, the United States was too soft to merit respect. After the United States did not respond toughly to so many terrorist attacks against its citizens, stood by impotently while Americans were seized as hostages in Iran and Lebanon, let Saddam Hussein think he could invade Kuwait without American opposition but let him stay in power while

10. Abdallah al-Najjar, *al-Gumhuriya*, October 7, 2001. Translation in Middle East Media Research Institute report no. 289 (October 19, 2001).
11. Usama bin Ladin, al-Jazira television, October 7, 2001.
12. Interview in *al-Safir*, July 16, 2001. Translation in Middle East Media Research Institute report no. 244 (July 20, 2001).
13. Nizar Hamdoon [Iraqi deputy foreign minister], "The U.S.-Iran Arms Deal: An Iraqi Critique," *Middle East Review* (Summer 1982).

letting the shah fall, pressured its friends and courted its enemies, allowed its prized peace process to be trashed without a word of criticism for those responsible, and acted so often in this same pattern, why should others respect its interests or fear its wrath?

Many Iranians were fearful of pushing the revolution too far in 1978 and 1979, convinced that America would step in and destroy them. This was in tune with a classic part of the Iranian worldview that saw their country as a pawn of stronger foreigners and their conspiracies. Now Khomeini proclaimed that everything would be different. If the United States, with all its power and satanic determination, could not free its own diplomats who had been taken as hostages, how could it destroy Iran's revolution? "Our youth should be confident that America cannot do a damn thing," Khomeini said repeatedly. The United States was too impotent to interfere by direct military force, and if necessary, Iran could defeat such a move by mobilizing its own people, who were willing to become martyrs.[14]

Iranian leaders continued to stress this theme. Almost a decade later Iran's minister of planning and budget, Mas'ud Zanjani, ridiculing U.S. intervention to defend Persian Gulf shipping from Iranian attacks in 1987, explained that the United States would never fight in the Gulf because its forces were so vulnerable; the American people and their European allies would oppose intervention, and the Americans would quickly retreat if they suffered casualties.[15]

In 1998, after another decade, Ali al-Husseini al-Khamene'i, Khomeini's successor as supreme guardian of the Islamic republic of Iran and leader of the hard-line faction, insisted there was no need to negotiate with the United States. After all, he proclaimed, Iran had demolished the American superpower's myth of invincibility by standing up to its threats and not bowing to its demands. Following Iran's example, Muslims all over the world had started fighting and expressing their Islamic feelings. Khamene'i posits a struggle during the last twenty years between two competitive camps on the world political scene—the camp of arrogance, led by America, and the Islamic camp, led by the Islamic Republic of Iran. The Islamic camp had advanced and gained victories, with Islamic movements coming to power in various states.

Saddam Hussein did not agree with Khomeini about much, but he did agree that the man who would lead the Middle East in attacking America must convince Arabs and Muslims that America was weak. And, like Khomeini, he was assisted by U.S. policies that seemed to prove his point. In response to Saddam's actions and threats in the late 1980s, Washington sent signals of weakness to Baghdad. Saddam interpreted attempts to avoid conflict as proof that

---

14. For example, his speech of November 7, 1979. Text in FBIS, November 8, 1979.
15. *Kayhan*, October 20, 1987. Text in FBIS, November 4, 1987, 54.

America feared confrontation with him. Each act of appeasement only increased Iraq's boldness without persuading it that the United States wanted to be its friend. The Americans "are out to hurt Iraq," one of that country's top leaders claimed. The problem was not that U.S. actions alienated Iraq, but that the nature of Iraq's regime inevitably made it antagonistic to the United States.

After evincing no strong reaction to Iraq's use of chemical weapons against the Kurds, threats against Israel, outspoken anti-Americanism, or ultimatum to Kuwait, the United States had helped convince Saddam that he could get away with occupying and annexing his neighbor. By seeking to avoid any trouble with Iraq, U.S. policy helped precipitate a much bigger crisis in August 1990.

Saddam told the visiting assistant secretary of state, John Kelly, in February 1990 that America was the only outside power that counted in the Middle East. He assumed the United States would use its overwhelming power as he would in its place: to eliminate the radical regimes and seize control of the region. If the United States would not act, Saddam would fill the vacuum. But the Iraqi leader knew that America was objectively strong and could presumably dictate changes in policy and behavior for Arab regimes. What could the Arabs do to save themselves from America? Two weeks after meeting Kelly, Saddam openly launched Iraq's new radical phase in one of the most important speeches of his career, on February 24, 1990.[16]

Saddam suggested that the Arabs had three choices. They could wait until a new balance of power would be restored—perhaps allowing them to play off Europe against the Americans—but by then it could be too late. Or the Arabs could give up, arguing that there was "no choice but to submit" to America. This second alternative would require the Arabs give up forever the hope of destroying Israel or of uniting themselves.

There was, however, a third possibility. Rather than revising their own thinking, the Arabs might change the situation. Saddam claimed that Arab pessimism, not Arab nationalism, was the delusion. If Arabs united behind a strong leader, they could still defeat the United States and Israel, or at least hold their ground against the alleged U.S. and Zionist conspiracies to destroy them. Saddam's unconventional weapons would make Iraq the Arab super-power, replacing the lost Soviet nuclear umbrella.

The United States, he insisted, was far weaker than it seemed because it feared military confrontation and losses. America had shown "signs of fatigue, frustration, and hesitation" in Vietnam and Iran and had quickly run away from Lebanon "when some Marines were killed" by terrorist suicide bombers there in 1983. He believed that if Iraq acted boldly, America would not dare confront

---

16. Speech at Arab Cooperation Council, Royal Cultural Center in Amman, February 24, 1990. Text in FBIS, February 27, 1990, 1–5. Extracts from this speech are in this chapter.

him. Had not this been his experience with the United States during the last two years?

These declarations were not merely a challenge to the United States, they were also a dare to the Arab world. Would the Arab leaders and peoples remember the unpleasant lessons or recent history—the cycle of war, failure, and wasted resources—or would the old ideas and patterns of behavior overwhelm common sense and carry them into another adventure?

The result was just as Saddam had hoped: the Arab masses cheered, and the Arab governments—whatever their private contempt and fear of Iraq—jumped on his bandwagon. The United States stayed out of his way. Of course, Saddam was wrong in thinking that he could take over Kuwait while America stood by and did nothing. But he was right enough about the United States to be in power many years after making that miscalculation.

Bin Ladin himself, and Islamist writers such as the Egyptian al-Najjar, both quoted above, similarly concluded that America would not fight effectively after the September 11 attacks. A Hizballah leader in Lebanon, Sheikh Nabil Qaook, remarked that America had been loud and dominating in the past, but now, "when the balance of power leans the other way, we hear them scream."[17]

A member of Hamas exulted over anthrax: "You have entered the . . . White House and they left it like horrified mice. . . . The Pentagon was a monster before you entered its corridors. . . . And behold, it now transpires that its men are of paper and its commanders are of cardboard, and they hasten to flee as soon as they see . . . chalk dust! . . . You make the United States appease us, and hint to us at a rosy future and a life of ease." He suggested that terrorism was a good way to obtain concessions from the United States without giving anything in return, though he made clear that even such surrender would be insufficient.[18]

In arguing that striking against America was a reasonable, practical, and successful way of getting what they wanted, these anti-Americans attributed U.S. behavior to cowardice. They were wrong in their reading of U.S. motives. But if America acted in this same manner instead out of a desire to prove to Arabs and Muslims that America was a friend and to win their support through niceness, the result could be the same. The exercise of American good intentions could be just as costly to the United States in the Middle East as would have been the wrongly alleged sins of bullying and cowardice.

By this same token, the United States will not persuade its adversaries and critics that anti-Americanism is a mistake or misunderstanding. Even if the

---

17. *New York Times*, November 8, 2001.
18. Atallah Abu al-Subh, in *al-Risala*, November 1, 2001. Translated in Middle East Media Research Institute report no. 297 (November 7, 2001). Extracts from this article can be found in chapter 7.

United States were to pressure Israel, end sanctions on Iraq, pull its troops out of the Persian Gulf, and take other such steps, the Arab media, opposition, and even regimes would not praise it as a wonderful friend and noble example. Instead, these acts could well be taken as signals of fear and weakness that encouraged even more contempt and could make a campaign of anti-American terrorism seem irresistible. And if the root cause of this wave of anti-Americanism was internal, it is dependent on those needs and forces rather than anything the United States actually does. Indeed, the quick U.S. defeat of the Taliban in Afghanistan in December 2001 did more to silence sympathy for bin Ladin than any words might have achieved.

Finally, the ferocity of anti-Americanism, in word or deed, will leave the longest-term, most lasting damage on the Arab world itself. Blaming external forces blocks any serious effort Arabs might make to deal with their own very serious internal problems and shortcomings, which are the real causes of continuing dictatorship, violence and instability, relatively slow economic and social development, and other problems.

Like so many totalitarians of earlier times—past dictators in Japan, Germany, and the USSR; and current dictators in Iran, Iraq, and elsewhere—those who have declared war on America are playing the dangerous game of exaggerating outside menaces to justify their incompetence at home and aggressiveness abroad. They deliberately misunderstand American policy and society, successfully soiling them also in the eyes of others. At least, though, one might hope that the United States would not join in this slander. That would be a betrayal not only of American interests and ideals, but also of those in the Arab world and Iran who have been fighting against the decadent order there and for a truly better and freer life for their peoples.

# The United States Will Not Intervene Militarily (November 7, 1979)

## AYATOLLAH RUHOLLAH KHOMEINI*

. . . You know that right now our youth have occupied America's seat of corruption [the U.S. embassy in Tehran] and they have detained the Americans

---

* From 1979 to 1988, Ayatollah Ruhollah Khomeini was the leader of Iran. This translation is from U.S. Department of Commerce, Foreign Broadcast Information Service (FBIS), November 8, 1979.

who were in that hive of corruption. Our youth should be confident that America cannot do a damn thing. Talk about what will happen if America interferes in a military way is wrong. Can America interfere in this country? It is impossible. The whole world is [watching] Iran. Can America stand up to the whole world and interfere militarily? She doesn't have the temerity to do so. If they want to interfere militarily I, myself, will move and you the dear nation will move. Don't be frightened and don't frighten other people. . . . America is far too impotent to interfere in a military way here. If they could have interfered, they would have retained the shah. They tried with all their powers—even their power of propaganda—to keep him here, but our nation paid no heed and since the nation wanted something, they were not able to stand up against the nation.

They always undertake mischievous interference. The interference is to hatch plots. If they want to do something, they incite our youth to take part in demonstrations, and their agents take part in the demonstrations and cause clashes and create turmoil so that we cannot have a free and calm environment. They send Satans to my very pure and dear youth to carry out propaganda and write [slogans or propaganda] and paste them on walls.

# No Room for Leniency (November 12, 1979)

RADIO TEHRAN*

What will happen if the occupation of the U.S. embassy by the students who are following Ayatollah Khomeini's path continues for a long time? . . . This is a question brought up by enemies to weaken the students' will. We are confident that the United States is unable to do anything . . . for the following reasons:

1. It relies on a policy of formulas. The United States and all Western policies are based on calculations and computer formulas. They do not embark on any venture until they know the results. For them politics is nothing but a mathematical process: two plus two equals four or four is two plus two. If the results are not known . . . they do not do anything. . . . A confrontation between the United States and Iran would result in unknown factors at the Pentagon's

* Radio Tehran analysis. Translation in FBIS, November 13, 1979.

military operations center. It goes without saying that the United States will not do anything if the results are not known in advance.

2. The ABC's understood by the United States since the beginning of the revolution is that all oppressed people will unite in solidarity with the Iranian people. The confrontation with the Iranian people means confrontation with all the peoples of the world.

3. The United States understands that any stupid action taken will be at the expense of the lives of its agents being held inside the embassy. They will receive just punishment, not only because they are hostages but because they are guilty conspirators who turned the U.S. embassy into a spying center.

Let us assume that the United States moves against Iran. What will happen? Ayatollah Khomeini answered this question. He said: If the United States embarks on a military action, the 35 million people, the Iranian Muslim people, are ready to go to war. . . .

# Memo to President Jimmy Carter on Soviet Intervention in Afghanistan (December 26, 1979)

ZBIGNIEW BRZEZINSKI*

. . . We are now facing a regional crisis. Both Iran and Afghanistan are in turmoil, and Pakistan is both unstable internally and extremely apprehensive externally. . . .

Accordingly, the Soviet intervention in Afghanistan poses for us an extremely grave challenge, both internationally and domestically. While it could become a Soviet Vietnam, the initial effects of the intervention are likely to be adverse for us for the following domestic and international reasons.

### Domestic

A. The Soviet intervention is likely to stimulate calls for more immediate U.S. military action in Iran. Soviet "decisiveness" will be contrasted with our restraint, which will no longer be labeled as prudent but increasingly as timid;

---

* Zbigniew Brzezinski was National Security Advisor during the Carter administration.

B. At the same time, regional instability may make a resolution of the Iranian problem more difficult for us, and it could bring us into a head-to-head confrontation with the Soviets;

C. SALT [Strategic Arms Limitations Talks] are likely to be damaged, perhaps irreparably, because Soviet military aggressiveness will have been so naked;

D. More generally, our handling of Soviet affairs will be attacked by both the Right and the Left.

## International

A. Pakistan, unless we somehow manage to project both confidence and power into the region, [blacked out; presumably, "will be weakened or worse"];

B. With Iran destabilized, there will be no firm bulwark in Southwest Asia against the Soviet drive to the Indian Ocean;

C. The Chinese will certainly note that Soviet assertiveness in Afghanistan and in Cambodia is not effectively restrained by the United States.

## Compensating Factors

There will be, to be sure, some compensating factors:

A. World public opinion may be outraged at the Soviet intervention. Certainly, Muslim countries will be concerned, and we might be in a position to exploit this.

B. There are already 300,000 refugees from Afghanistan in Pakistan, and we will be in a position to indict the Soviets for causing massive human suffering. That figure will certainly grow, and Soviet-sponsored actions in Cambodia have already taken their toll as well.

C. There will be greater awareness among our allies for the need to do more for their own defense.

## A Soviet Vietnam?

However, we should not be too sanguine about Afghanistan becoming a Soviet Vietnam:

A. The guerrillas are badly organized and poorly led;

B. They have no sanctuary, no organized army, and no central government—all of which North Vietnam had;

C. They have limited foreign support, in contrast to the enormous amount of arms that flowed to the Vietnamese from both the Soviet Union and China;

D. The Soviets are likely to act decisively, unlike the U.S., which pursued in Vietnam a policy of inoculating the enemy. As a consequence, the Soviets might be able to assert themselves effectively, and [in] world politics nothing succeeds like success, whatever the moral aspects.

## What Is to Be Done?

What follows are some preliminary thoughts, which need to be discussed more fully:

A. It is essential that Afghan resistance continue. This means more money as well as arms shipments to the rebels, and some technical advice;

B. To make the above possible we must both reassure Pakistan and encourage it to help the rebels. This will require a review of our policy toward Pakistan, more guarantees to it, more arms aid.

C. We should encourage the Chinese to help the rebels also.

D. We should concert with Islamic countries both [in] a propaganda campaign and in a covert action campaign to help the rebels;

E. We should inform the Soviets that their actions are placing SALT in jeopardy. . . . Unless we tell the Soviets [they] will not take our "expressions of concern" very seriously, with the effect that our relations will suffer, without the Soviets ever having been confronted with the need to ask the question whether such local adventurism is worth the long-term damage to the U.S.-Soviet relationship;

F. Finally, we should consider taking Soviet actions in Afghanistan to the UN as a threat to peace.

# State of the Union Address (January 23, 1980)

### PRESIDENT JIMMY CARTER

. . . In Iran, fifty Americans are still held captive, innocent victims of terrorism and anarchy. Also at this moment, massive Soviet troops are attempting to subjugate the fiercely independent and deeply religious people of Afghanistan.

These two acts—one of international terrorism and one of military aggression—present a serious challenge to the United States of America and indeed to all the nations of the world. . . . Three basic developments have helped to shape our challenges: the steady growth and increased projection of Soviet military power beyond its own borders; the overwhelming dependence of the Western democracies on oil supplies from the Middle East; and the press of social and religious and economic and political change in the many nations of the developing world, exemplified by the revolution in Iran. Each of these factors is important in its own right. Each interacts with the others. All must be faced together, squarely and courageously. . . .

In response to the abhorrent act in Iran, our nation has never been aroused and unified so greatly in peacetime. Our position is clear. The United States will not yield to blackmail. We continue to pursue these specific goals: first, to protect the present and long-range interests of the United States; secondly, to preserve the lives of the American hostages and to secure, as quickly as possible, their safe release, if possible, to avoid bloodshed which might further endanger the lives of our fellow citizens; [thirdly,] to enlist the help of other nations in condemning this act of violence, which is shocking and violates the moral and the legal standards of a civilized world; and [finally,] also to convince and to persuade the Iranian leaders that the real danger to their nation lies in the north, in the Soviet Union and from the Soviet troops now in Afghanistan, and that the unwarranted Iranian quarrel with the United States hampers their response to this far greater danger to them. If the American hostages are harmed, a severe price will be paid. We will never rest until every one of the American hostages [is] released.

But now we face a broader and more fundamental challenge in this region because of the recent military action of the Soviet Union. . . . The implications of the Soviet invasion of Afghanistan could pose the most serious threat to the peace since the Second World War. The vast majority of nations on earth have condemned this latest Soviet attempt to extend its colonial domination of others and have demanded the immediate withdrawal of Soviet troops. The Muslim world is especially and justifiably outraged by this aggression against an Islamic people. No action of a world power has ever been so quickly and so overwhelmingly condemned. But verbal condemnation is not enough.

The Soviet Union must pay a concrete price for [its] aggression. While this invasion continues, we and the other nations of the world cannot conduct business as usual with the Soviet Union. . . . The region which is now threatened by Soviet troops in Afghanistan is of great strategic importance: It contains more than two-thirds of the world's exportable oil. The Soviet effort to dominate Afghanistan has brought Soviet military forces to within 300 miles of the Indian Ocean and close to the Straits of Hormuz, a waterway through which most of the world's oil must flow. . . .

Let our position be absolutely clear: An attempt by any outside force to gain control of the Persian Gulf region will be regarded as an assault on the vital interests of the United States of America, and such an assault will be repelled by any means necessary, including military force. . . .

# Speech to Syrian Soldiers (October 1, 1981)

SYRIAN PRESIDENT HAFIZ AL-ASAD*

... We must remain alert and ready to sacrifice effort, sweat, and blood. We must be ready to proceed strongly toward the honor of martyrdom when this is required. You are the owners of a cause in which you believe, that is, the cause of the people. . . . With such an understanding of life, man, the nation's cause, and martyrdom, we will not fear Israel's reaction and plotting. . . . We will not fear the U.S. plotting, which is escalating day by day. . . . We will defeat this plotting and defeat all the agents of this plotting in the region, in Israel, in Egypt, and in others of the Camp David [the U.S.-brokered Egypt-Israeli peace agreement of 1978] group.

The United States was not content, comrades, with all it had offered Israel throughout the years. Israel has been established on the land of Palestine. [The United States] is offering Israel the most modern weapons and hardware. It is offering Israel a complete and unlimited political guarantee. . . . The United States agreed with Israel to bring the U.S. forces to occupied Palestine to be stationed there. They also agreed to establish U.S. arms warehouses in occupied Palestine so that under certain circumstances, as happened in the October [1973] war, the United States would not need to resort to an air bridge. The U.S. Army weapons would be in warehouses in Israel. After a short while we would see near us the U.S. soldier in person. . . . They reiterate that this deal is aimed at fighting the Soviet Union. But where is the Soviet Union? Is the Soviet Union in Palestine, Jordan, or Syria? The Soviet borders are not here. . . .

Comrades, people in Israel are taught, and they teach their children, that the land of the Israelis, the country of the sons of Zion, is Greater Israel from the Nile to the Euphrates. You can imagine what it means to say from the Nile to the Euphrates. The area between the Nile and the Euphrates comprises all the Arabian Peninsula. . . . The Israelis dream that they will occupy the Holy Kaba [the main Muslim shrine in Mecca] just as they occupied Holy Jerusalem. Have those agents who raise the slogan of Islam and falsely claim to be defenders of Islam and upholders of its banner thought of this? They are agents who have sold themselves since they rose as a movement, a gang, the gang of the Muslim Brotherhood.

A few days ago, the U.S. administration made several statements which

---

* Damascus Radio. Speech at graduation ceremony for paratroopers in Katakia, Syria. Translation in BBC Survey of World Broadcasts, October 3, 1981.

insulted our intelligence and belittled us by asserting that the strength of Israel was necessary for peace. Comrades, Arab citizens, does this not mean that the weakness of the Arabs is necessary for peace as understood by the United States? Why did they not once say that the strength of the Arabs was necessary for peace? Why did they not once say that military balance between the Arabs and Israel was necessary for peace? They say only that Israel's strength is necessary for the achievement of peace.

U.S. intentions are clear. U.S. and Zionist objectives are clear. The United States wants us to be puppets so it can manipulate us the way it wants. It wants us to be slaves so it can exploit us the way it wants. It wants to occupy our territory and exploit our masses. . . . It wants us to be parrots repeating what is said to us.

This explains the fumbling of agent [Egyptian President Anwar al-Sadat], who has split from his nation and betrayed its cause, creed, and principles. You have heard him, after he has unmasked himself and fallen into the swamp of imperialism, bragging, fumbling, and contradicting his opinions and statements from day to day. You have heard his demagoguery and noted his shallow mind when he thought, like his masters in U.S. intelligence, that he could mislead the people, our Arab masses.

One day he says: "I am against foreign bases." One day he says that Egypt is against foreign bases, and the same day he states over and over again: "Come, Americans; come, Europeans, Egyptian territory is open to you. Take bases. . . . Place your weapons in them in defense against the Soviet Union."

Sadat turns his back on the Arab nation, betrays the Arabs, and says: "Come, Americans, station your forces in Egypt so as to defend the Arab [Persian] Gulf." Nobody in the Arab Gulf wants the Americans to defend him. Who trusts the wolf to defend him? Whom do we fear, we the Arabs here in the Gulf? We fear only the United States, which is dominated by world Zionism.

Sadat misleads the Egyptian people and tells them: We are giving bases to the United States so it can defend the Arabs. Does he think they are so simple and naive as he wants them to be? The Egyptian people know that if the other Arab countries wanted the United States to defend them or to establish any form of cooperation with it, they would have gone directly to the United States. They would not have asked Sadat to play this dishonorable role. The Egyptian citizen knows that the Arab states can deal directly with the United States and in the manner they deem appropriate. . . .

Young men and women, the United States, Israel, and their agents in the region will fail. Our people, all of us, we the people, will remain proud and courageous until we achieve victory and defeat of the enemies.

# U.S. Policy Views Mideast as "U.S. Possession" (February 16, 1985)

SYRIAN GOVERNMENT RADIO*

Washington reports say that U.S. President Ronald Reagan has rejected the idea of holding an international conference on the Middle East under UN sponsorship and in which all concerned parties, including the USSR and the PLO, would participate. These reports add that Reagan pointed out that the United States wanted to tackle the Middle East issue through direct negotiations among the parties that are close to the dispute. Reagan was more specific when he named Jordan as a candidate for attending these direct negotiations, representing itself as well as the Palestinians.

Reagan's remarks on the Middle East and its problems show that U.S. rulers believe that this important area of the world is a U.S. possession and an extension of closed U.S. zones of influence. The United States runs the affairs of the region and decides its fate; it keeps the United Nations away or allows its presence whenever it wants; and it accepts or rejects the convening of an international conference whenever it wishes. The United States has been unilaterally dealing with the problems in the region since 1974, depending on Anwar al-Sadat's deviation from the Arabs and his claim that 99 percent of the cards for a solution are in U.S. hands—thus depriving the United Nations of its role and keeping the USSR away from participating in the search for and contributing to the implementation of a just and permanent solution.

What was the result of this unilateral policy? The region's crisis became more complicated and difficult, possibilities for peaceful solution diminished, wars occurred, Israel occupied more Arab lands, and neither peace nor security was achieved. It was proven that the cards for a solution are not in U.S. hands, and that the cards which are in U.S. hands are played against Arab interests and rights, as well as against the United Nations and its resolutions. The question is: Who allowed the United States to own the region? Who gave the United States the right to be in charge of the region's affairs? Who gave the United States the right to object to the United Nations [and] its charter and resolutions? If the United States believes that the Israeli war machine, which is under U.S. command and which depends on U.S. aid, gives it such right, it is mistaken. If the United States believes that its very special relations with Israel and its cordial relations with some Arab countries give it an excellent position in the region, it is mistaken in this too.

It is correct that the United States is one of the two superpowers in the

---

* FBIS 5, no. 34 (February 20, 1985).

world, a permanent member of the Security Council, and a country that has a presence in the region, special relations with Israel, and a variety of relations with many countries in the region. This situation gives it a role and makes it shoulder responsibilities. However, all this will not place it above the United Nations, nor will it remove the concern of the other countries, particularly countries, such as the USSR, that border the region. The U.S. position cannot remove the region's people, weaken their role, disavow their rights, or cancel their ability to chart history and geography in this region.

The U.S. stands, which were defined and renewed by President Reagan, show fundamental contradictions between the U.S. stand and the minimum level that is acceptable to the Arabs. The United States wants to unilaterally tackle the region's problems, while Arab interests call for a UN role and effective participation [of all concerned parties]. The United States rejects the international conference, while Arab interests call for holding an international conference with the participation of the United Nations and the USSR so that the United States will not use the conference to impose conditions of capitulation on the Arabs. The United States rejects the PLO's participation in any conference or talks on the Middle East and the Palestine cause, while the Arabs adhere to the PLO's right to represent the Arab Palestinian people and to their right to self-determination. The United States rejects UN resolutions on the Middle East and Palestine, particularly the resolutions on the Israeli withdrawal from all Arab occupied territory and the Palestinian people's right to self-determination, while the Arabs call for respecting the UN resolutions and the UN Charter. As preaching and sweet talk have not succeeded in changing U.S. stands in the past, these stands will not be changed now or in the future by seeking U.S. sympathy or making concessions to them.

# On U.S. Hostages (February 1987)

MUHAMMAD HUSSEIN FADLALLAH*

This issue [Americans who were taken hostage in Lebanon] has become a political card manipulated by the United States for its political and security in-

---

* Muhammad Hussein Fadlallah is Hizballah's spiritual guide. The article appeared in *al-Nahar al-Arabi wa al-Duwali*, February 9–15, 1987. Translation in FBIS, February 19, 1987.

terests. Thus, it is willing to distribute the problems of the issue to more than one country. The United States has discovered that it can play the hostage card in more than one political or security position and use it to exert pressure on many political positions, whether these are negative or positive in its views. Hence, the issue of the hostages is not a humanitarian one any more, as we wanted it to be; it has turned into a political issue in all the meanings of this word. The human aspect in it has merely become a factor of excitement that feeds the political issue, exactly like all our problems in Lebanon and in the East. . . .

We find that the United States, France, Iran, maybe Syria, and the PLO have benefited in more than one way. We can see that the continuation of the issue, despite the tragic humanitarian dimension, is aimed at achieving more than one political advantage for more than one of the countries I have mentioned. If the media are trying to imply that Iran stands to benefit, then I claim that the United States, France, and other regional circles have done so. The benefit does not derive from the release of their hostages, but from the fact that they have been able to activate their policies, while saving face, to break through the impasse that had been reached, and to solve a complicated problem. I believe that these issues were not simple and are not that simple now.

If we look at similar problems in the world, we find that the prices that have to be paid to solve them might differ according to the deal proposed in the international political market. . . .

The policy of the United States is a devious one. It reflects the U.S. fondness for fads. Thus the United States is working to feed the imagination of the American people on the problems and emotions it stirs up, in addition to studying the movement of its strategic interests in the world. Despite the clamor that the United States is now raising against Iran, it still aspires to use the question of the hostages as a door to enter the Iranian arena to normalize its relations with Iran. This is what we have observed in its recent many-sided and complicated actions in the Gulf war. One cannot but think that the United States is jealous of its weapons and does not want them to fall into the hands of a regime that is hostile to it. After all, Iran does overlook the strategic areas that surround the Soviet Union. This gives the issue its political dimension, which might not be immediately apparent. . . .

I do not believe any U.S. or Western military attack could cause this exciting movement in the region to collapse, but it might make the situation more complicated. . . . I do not believe that the atmosphere in the region allows military action over the hostage issue, because it would not be politically logical. It is possible that the hostages' question will provide a bridgehead for the United States to enter into more than one war in the area and to shuffle the cards. . . .

# On U.S. Policy (February 17, 1987)

MUHAMMAD HUSSEIN FADLALLAH*

. . . We are studying the possibility of U.S. military intervention on the basis of two premises: first, the release of the hostages by force, and second, the subjugation of opposition forces. Regarding the first alternative, no military operation can pinpoint the exact location of the hostages; therefore it will be a failure. If they are able to pinpoint their location and an attack is launched at the place where they are held, then the hostages' lives will be in danger.

Regarding the second alternative, to make the opposition forces serve U.S. interests in the area, the broad masses cannot allow the fall of the political positions of the opposition forces. There is a great difference between U.S. aircraft bombing Libyan cities and military action in Lebanon. Even if we assume there is cooperation among the United States, Israel, and some forces in Lebanon carrying out such an operation, the matter is not simple as some people believe. There are numerous forces in Lebanon, and the situation will become more complex and dangerous. Perhaps that will lead to the outbreak of a general war in Lebanon, which could have greater and more serious consequences on both Arab and international levels. Some people outside Lebanon may think Washington might do something to foil many of the plans that it perceives as hostile. However, these people must realize we do not forget or disregard the Soviet Union's role in Lebanon's politics, for the Soviet Union plays an effective role in the region.

Nevertheless, we do not believe the United States will carry out wide-scale military action. Let us suppose it does decide to carry out a military action similar to the French military action against the Lebanese city of Ba'labak; then Washington will face enormous difficulties. President Reagan will face another scandal, "Lebanongate," which will be more serious than Irangate. The question is more political than military. If it is military, it will be limited. However, if Israel should intervene on a large scale, then Syrian-Israeli war will immediately break out. However, it appears that such a development is unlikely at present in view of its seriousness. Nevertheless, we do not rule out a limited Israeli attack on a smaller scale than the 1978 and 1982 incursions. Moreover, any military action against Lebanon will not change anything in the present extremely complex situation. If such an action should take place, it will bring about completely opposite results, for the parties hostile to the United States will become even more hostile and will reject its presence at whatever cost.

---

* *Al-Bayan*, February 17, 1987. Muhammad Hussein Fadlallah is the spiritual guide of the Lebanese terrorist group Hizballah.

# On U.S. Hostages (February 1987)

SUBHI AL-TUFAYLI*

Islam seeks to build a society on the basis of God and justice. At the same time, it does not permit man to make himself a beast of prey. It compels him to defend himself; otherwise, he will be a partner with his oppressors in the injustice done to him. Hence, the Muslim has the duty to defend himself. As you know, our Muslim people in Lebanon have been subjected to all sorts of oppression and tragedies at the hands of the United States, some European countries, and Israel. It is the duty of our people to defend themselves with what they have. We do not consider the use of kidnapping and the detention of hostages as a tool for self-defense in the face of cruelty from our enemies. Apparently, however, some of them consider it a useful tool. . . .

The United States has sent its fleets to the eastern Mediterranean Sea and to the northern part of the [Persian] Gulf to flex its muscles in front of the Muslims so they will be frightened. This method has scared and frightened others, but we like to tell the United States that we will be very happy when the war between us and them starts face to face. We boast and are proud of ourselves when we are the head of the Muslim spear in the chest of the U.S. authority. Thus, we welcome any U.S. return because this will give us the opportunity to fight it more effectively.

Some people try to tie this issue to Lebanon's calamities, but aside from the question of kidnappings and such, did the enemies leave Lebanon healthy enough that the kidnappings affected it negatively? I am not in the position of defending kidnappings, but in the position of telling the facts. Lebanon is a torn and dead body. The Israeli invasion, what preceded it, the U.S. occupation that followed it, and the subsequent internal plots have not left anything healthy to be damaged. The exit of U.S. nationals from Lebanon is a good omen because it will reduce the country's calamities.

---

* Subhi al-Tufayli is a Hizballah official. This article appeared in *al-Nahar al-Arabi wa al-Duwali*, February 9–15, 1987. Translation in FBIS.

# A Strategy for the Arab World
# (February 24, 1990)

IRAQI PRESIDENT SADDAM HUSSEIN*

. . . Among the most important developments since the international conflict in
the Second World War has been the fact that some countries that used to enjoy
broad international influence, such as France and Britain, have declined, while
the influence and impact of two countries expanded until they became the two
superpowers among the countries of the world—I mean the United States and
the Soviet Union. Of course, with these results, two axis have developed: the
Western axis under the leadership of the United States, with its known capitalist
approach and its imperialist policy; and the Eastern bloc under the leadership
of the Soviet Union and its communist philosophy. . . .

The Eastern bloc, led by the USSR, supported the Arabs' basic rights,
including their rights in the Arab–Zionist conflict. The global policy continued
on the basis of the existence of two poles that were balanced in term of force.
They are the two superpowers, the United States and the USSR.

And suddenly, the situation changed in a dramatic way. The USSR turned
to tackle its domestic problems after relinquishing the process of continuous
conflict. . . . The USSR went to nurse the wounds that were inflicted on it as
a result of the principles and the mistaken policy it followed for such a long
time, and as a result of the wave of change it embarked on, which began to
depart from the charted course. It has become clear to everyone that the United
States has emerged in a superior position in international politics. This superiority will be demonstrated in the U.S. readiness to play such a role more than
in the predicted guarantees for its continuation.

We believe that the world can fill the vacuum resulting from the recent
changes and find a new balance in the global arena . . . which we expect will be
in Europe and Japan. America will lose its power just as quickly as it gained it
by frightening Europe, Japan, and other countries through continuously hinting
at the danger of the USSR and communism. The United States will lose its
power as the fierce competition for gaining the upper hand between the two
superpowers and their allies recedes.

However, we believe that the U.S. will continue to depart from the restrictions that govern the rest of world throughout the next five years until new
forces of balance are formed. Moreover, the [United States'] undisciplined and

---

* This speech to the Arab Cooperation Council Summit in Amman, Jordan, was broadcast on
Amman television, February 24, 1990. Translation in FBIS, February 27, 1990.

irresponsible behavior will engender hostility and grudges if it embarks on rejected stupidities.

Given the relative erosion of the role of the Soviet Union as the key champion of the Arabs in the context of the Arab-Zionist conflict and globally, and
given that the influence of the Zionist lobby on U.S. policies is as powerful as
ever, the Arabs must take into account that there is a real possibility that Israel
might embark on new stupidities within the five-year span I have mentioned.
This might take place as a result of direct or tacit U.S. encouragement. On the
other hand, the Arabs have a plus, and that is Arab solidarity, which will be
effective if the Arabs work out a well-defined plan of action and devise regional
policies vis-à-vis neighboring foreign countries, and if they forge fruitful cooperation based on strong foundations oriented toward clear goals. The cooperation will have to encompass culture, politics, economics, and other areas.
Recent American utterances and behavior as far as pan-Arab security and Palestinian Arab rights to their homeland are concerned inevitably cause alarm and
warrant Arab vigilance, or are supposed to evoke such a reaction on our part.
One may cite recurrent statements by U.S. officials about their intention to
keep their fleets in the [Persian] Gulf for an unlimited period of time, and their
support for an unprecedented exodus of Soviet Jews to Palestinian territory,
neither of which would have been possible solely under the cover of the slogan
of human rights had not the Americans put pressure on the Soviets, exploiting
the latter's special circumstances so as to incorporate the issue into their bilateral
agreements with the Soviets. Add to that the increasing support for the Zionist
entity's strategic arms stockpiles and [the Americans'] giving it license to deploy
them when necessary, the judgment on when to use them being left up to Israel.
This is above and beyond U.S. assistance to Israel in other areas.

We all remember, as does the whole world, the circumstances under which
the United States deployed and bolstered its fleets in the Gulf. Most important
of these circumstances: the war that was raging between Iraq and Iran. Iranian
aggression had extended to other Arabian Gulf countries, most notably the
sisterly state of Kuwait. At the time, beyond the conflicting views regarding
the presence of foreign fleets in Arab territorial waters and foreign bases on
their territory and their repercussions for pan-Arab security, that excessive de-
ployment was somehow comprehensible. But now, and against the background
of the recent world developments and the cessation of hostilities between Iraq
and Iran, and with Kuwait no longer the target of Iranian aggression, the Arabian Gulf states, including Iraq, and even all Arabs would have liked the Americans to state their intention to withdraw their fleets.

Had they said that under the same circumstances and causes they would
have returned to the Gulf, it might have been understandable also. But U.S.
officials are making such statements as if to show that their immediate and
longer-term presence in Gulf waters and, maybe, on some of its territory is not

bound to a time frame. These suspect policies give Arabs reason to feel suspicious of U.S. policies and intentions as to whether it is officially and actually interested in a termination of the Iraq-Iran war and thus contribute to much-needed regional stability.

The other side is the immigration of Soviet Jews to the occupied Palestinian land. How can we explain the Americans' support and backing for Jewish immigration to the occupied Arab territories, except that the United States does not want peace as it claims and declares? If it really and actually wants peace, the United States would not have encouraged Israel and the aggressive trends in it to adopt such policies, which enhance Israel's capability to commit aggression and carry out expansion. . . .

Therefore, there is no place among the ranks of good Arabs for the faint-hearted who would argue that as a superpower, the United States will be the decisive factor, and others have no choice but to submit. At the same time, there is no place in our midst for those who fail to take note of recent developments that have added to U.S. strength, thus prompting it to the possible commission of follies against the interests and national security of the Arabs—either directly or by fanning and encouraging conflicts detrimental to the Arabs, irrespective of their source. We are thus not out to antagonize or to incite public opinion against the United States on the strength of mere speculation over potential developments. We are only making the point that the Arabs seek peace and justice throughout the world and want to forge relations of friendship with those who show respect to what friendship is all about—be it the United States or any other nation. It is only natural that the Arabs take a realistic approach to the new posture and power of the United States that has led the Soviet Union to abandon its erstwhile position of influence. However, America must respect the Arabs and respect their rights, and should not interfere in their internal affairs under any cover. The United States must not forget that the Arab nation is a great nation that taught humanity things it had been ignorant of. Otherwise, there is no room for unilateral friendship or unilateral respect, and there will be no consideration for the interests and rights of any party unless it is capable of understanding and respecting the Arabs' rights, interests, dignity, options, and pan-Arab security. Against the backdrop of the vital issues related to the substance of national Arab security, the question arises as to what we the Arabs have to do. . . .

Despite all the harm the United States has inflicted upon the Arabs owing to its alliance with Zionism, there remained the fear of communism, the Soviet Union, and the Arab friends and allies of the Soviet Union in the region, in addition to other factors. This continued to prevent the Arabs from taking influential stands toward U.S. policy, with minor exceptions. Their stands became restricted to a mere ineffective rejection or an ineffective silence and acceptance. The United States began not to take Arab stances seriously. The

United States may have the famous red lines beyond which it does not tread concerning the interests of other nations that deal peacefully with it, but its policy so far has no red lines warning beyond them where Arab interests are concerned.

Realizing Arab solidarity on the basis of pan-Arab interests, correctly defining Arab interests, clearly and accurately defining everything that threatens their security and stability, and proceeding from this basis of capability, frankness, and solidarity with the United States, or other countries in general, prevents these countries from exceeding the proper bounds with the Arab nation and thus becoming a threat.

[The principles I have mentioned] might be a realistic basis for the establishment of Arab relations with the United States and other states: . . . mutual respect, noninterference in internal affairs, and respect for the requirements of pan-Arab security and common interests on a legitimate and agreed-upon basis. . . .

The big powers do not become big unless they are influential in small and medium-sized countries. Accordingly, among the means [used] to weaken hostile policies and the harmful influence of those who harm us is weakening the one who harms us inside or outside his national soil. Accordingly, and because interest is the basis of the Soviet Union's new policy, as well as the policy of the East European states, as it has always been the basis of the policy of other states, we are duty bound to ask and answer accurately how we can approach these states in order to weaken our enemies' influence on them or how we can benefit from our common financial, economic, political, informational, and other powers to achieve better results. . . .

The reason the United States stays in the Gulf is that the Gulf has become the most important spot in the region and perhaps the whole world owing to developments in international policy, the oil market, and increasing demands from the United States, Europe, Japan, Eastern Europe, and perhaps the Soviet Union for this product. The country that will have the greatest influence in the region through the Arabian Gulf and its oil will maintain its superiority as a superpower, without an equal to compete with it. This means that if the Gulf people, along with all Arabs, are not careful, the Arabian Gulf region will be governed by the U.S. will. If the Arabs are not alerted and the weakness persists, the situation could develop to the extent desired by the United States; that is, it would fix the amount of oil and gas produced in each country and sold to this or that country in the world. Prices would also be fixed in line with a special perspective benefiting U.S. interests and ignoring the interests of others. . . .

Brothers, the weakness of a big body lies in its bulkiness. All strong men have their Achilles' heel. Therefore, irrespective of our known stand on terror and terrorists, we saw that the United States as a superpower departed Lebanon immediately when some Marines were killed, the very men who are considered to be the most prominent symbol of its arrogance. The whole U.S. administration would have been called into question had the forces that conquered Panama continued to be engaged by the Panamanian armed forces. The United States has been defeated in some combat arenas, for all the forces it possesses, and it has displayed signs of fatigue, frustration, and hesitation when committing aggression on other people's rights and acting from motives of arrogance and hegemony. This is a natural outcome for those who commit aggression against other people's rights. Israel, once dubbed the invincible country, has been defeated by some of the Arabs. The resistance put up by Palestinians and Lebanese militia against Israeli invasion forces in 1982, and before that the heroic Egyptian crossing of the Suez Canal in 1973, have had a more telling psychological and actual impact than all Arab threats. Further, the threat to use Arab oil in 1973 during the October war proved more effective than all political attempts to protest or to beg at the gates of American decision-making centers. The stones in occupied Palestine now turn into a virtual and potentially fatal bullet if additional requirements are made available. It is the best proof of what is possible and indeed gives us cause to hold our heads high.

Just as Israel controls interests to put pressure on the U.S. administration, hundreds of billions invested by the Arabs in the United States and the West may be similarly deployed. Indeed, for instance, some of these investments may be diverted to the USSR and East European countries. It may prove even more profitable than investment in the West, which has grown saturated with its national resources. Such a course of action may yield inestimable benefits for the Arabs and their national causes.

# Indictment against the Khobar Tower Bombers of June 1996 (June 21, 2001)

U.S. DEPARTMENT OF JUSTICE

Nearly five years after a powerful truck bomb ripped through a U.S. military housing complex in Saudi Arabia—killing 19 Americans and wounding 372—terrorism charges have been brought against 13 members of the pro-Iran Saudi Hizballah, or "Party of God." Another, as yet unidentified, person who is linked to the Lebanese Hizballah has also been charged in the attack.

According to the indictment . . . nine of the fourteen are charged with forty-six separate criminal counts including: conspiracy to kill Americans and employees of the United States, to use weapons of mass destruction, and to destroy U.S. property; bombing; and murder. The five others are each charged with five conspiracy counts. The indictment alleges that the conspiracy was driven by the motive to expel Americans from the kingdom of Saudi Arabia. Charged with all counts are: Ahmad al-Mughassil, also known as Abu Omran; Ali al-Houri; Hani al-Sayegh; Ibrahim al-Yacoub; Abd al-Karim al-Nasser; Mustafa al-Qassab; Abdallah al-Jarash; Hussein al-Mughis; and the unidentified Lebanese, listed as "John Doe." The remaining five—Sa'ed al-Bahar, Saleh Ramadan, Ali al-Marhoun, Mustafa al-Mu'alem, and Fadel al-Alawe—are named in the five conspiracy counts. . . .

At about 10:00 P.M. on June 25, 1996, a tanker truck loaded with at least 5,000 pounds of plastic explosives was driven into the parking lot in front of the Khobar Towers residential complex in Dhahran. Moments later a massive explosion sheared the face off of Building 131, an eight-story structure that housed about 100 U.S. Air Force personnel. Although rooftop sentries were immediately suspicious of the truck—parked some eighty feet from the building—and attempted an evacuation, few escaped. Comparable to 20,000 pounds of TNT, the bomb was estimated to be larger than the one that destroyed the federal building in Oklahoma City a year before, and more than twice as powerful as the 1983 bomb used at the Marine barracks in Beirut. . . .

According to the indictment, the Saudi Hizballah, or Hizballah al-Hijaz, was one of a number of related Hizballah terrorist organizations operating in Saudi Arabia, Lebanon, Kuwait, and Bahrain, among other places. The Saudi Hizballah was a terrorist organization that promoted violence against Americans and U.S. property in Saudi Arabia. Since the group was outlawed in Saudi Arabia, its members frequently met in neighboring countries such as Lebanon, Syria, or Iran.

The indictment traces the carefully organized bomb plot back to on or about 1993 when al-Mughassil, under Saudi Hizballah leader al-Nasser, was head of the "military wing" of the Saudi Hizballah. It is alleged that, at that time, al-Mughassil was in charge of directing terrorist attacks against Americans and American interests in Saudi Arabia. Al-Mughassil instructed defendants al-Qassab, al-Yacoub and al-Houri, later joined by al-Sayegh, to begin surveillance of Americans in Saudi Arabia. This operation produced reports that were provided to al-Mughassil, al-Nasser, and officials in Iran. Al-Mughassil carefully reviewed the surveillance reports, according to the indictment.

During the same time, al-Jarash and al-Marhoun conducted surveillance of other sites where Americans lived, worked, or frequented, including the U.S. Embassy in Riyadh and a fish market nearby, according to the charges. Later, in early 1994, al-Qassab began surveillance of locations in the eastern province of Saudi Arabia, an area that includes Khobar. Reports of this operation were provided to al-Nasser and to Iranian officials, the indictment alleges.

In the fall of 1994, defendants al-Marhoun, Ramadan, and al-Mu'alem began watching American sites in eastern Saudi Arabia at al-Mughassil's direction, and al-Bahar looked at other sites at the direction of an Iranian military officer, according to the indictment. It was during this time that al-Marhoun, Ramadan, and al-Mu'alem determined Khobar Towers to be an important American military location and began an effort in the region to locate a storage site for explosives.

In 1995, an Iranian military officer directed al-Bahar and al-Sayegh to conduct surveillance on the Red Sea coast of Saudi Arabia for sites of possible future attacks against Americans. During this time, al-Mughassil told al-Marhoun during a live-fire practice drill in Lebanon that he enjoyed close ties to Iranian officials who were providing financial support to the party, according to the indictment. Al-Mughassil then gave al-Marhoun $2,000 in U.S. currency to support continued efforts to identify American sites.

The indictment alleges that it was in or about June 1995 that al-Marhoun, al-Ramadan, and al-Mu'alem began regular surveillance of Khobar Towers, at the direction of al-Mughassil. By late fall 1995, the three learned that al-Mughassil had decided that Hizballah would attack Khobar Towers with a tanker truck loaded with explosives. According to the indictment, the attack would serve Iran by driving the Americans from the Gulf region.

In early 1996, al-Mughassil instructed al-Marhoun to find places to hide explosives, and in February Ramadan drove a car loaded with explosives from Beirut, Lebanon, to the city of Qatif in the eastern province of Saudi Arabia, the indictment alleges. In March 1996, al-Alawe attempted to drive another explosives-filled car from Lebanon to Saudi Arabia, but he was searched at the Saudi border and arrested. Follow-up Saudi investigation led to the arrests of al-Marhoun, al-Mu'alem, and Ramadan in April 1996.

Meanwhile, according to the indictment, al-Mughassil continued planning for the Khobar attack and sought replacements for those arrested. Joining al-Mughis, al-Mughassil formed a team consisting of al-Jarash, al-Houri, al-Sayegh, and a Lebanese Hizballah member. During this time in 1996, al-Houri and al-Mughis began to hide explosives around the Khobar area.

In early June 1996, according to the indictment, a tanker truck was purchased by the conspirators, who then spent two weeks converting the truck into a truck bomb. The group consisted of al-Mughassil, al-Houri, al-Sayegh, al-Qassab, and John Doe, assisted by al-Mughis and al-Jarash. The indictment alleges that al-Mughassil discussed a plan at this time to bomb the U.S. consulate at nearby Dhahran.

During the first half of June 1996, al-Mughassil, al-Houri, al-Yacoub, al-Sayegh, al-Qassab, and Saudi Hizballah leader al-Nasser discussed the planned bombing. Al-Nasser confirmed that al-Mughassil was in charge of the Khobar attack, according to the indictment.

The indictment details the attack as follows: On the evening of June 25, 1996, al-Mughassil, al-Houri, al-Sayegh, al-Qassab, al-Jarash, and al-Mughis finalized plans for the attack that night. Shortly before 10 P.M., al-Sayegh drove a Datsun, with al-Jarash as his passenger, as a scout vehicle into the public parking lot in the front of Khobar Towers building no. 131. Behind them was the getaway car, a white Chevrolet Caprice that al-Mughis had borrowed. When the Datsun signaled that all was clear by blinking its lights, the bomb truck, driven by al-Mughassil and with al-Houri as a passenger, entered the lot and backed up against a fence in front of building no. 131. Al-Mughassil and al-Houri then exited the truck and entered the back seat of the Caprice for the getaway, driving away followed by the Datsun. In minutes the blast devastated the north side of the building.

Immediately following the terrorist attack, the leaders fled the Khobar area and Saudi Arabia using fake passports. Only al-Jarash and al-Mughis remained behind. Al-Sayegh reached Canada in August 1996, where he was arrested by Canadian authorities seven months later. In May 1997, al-Sayegh requested to meet with American investigators and denied knowledge of the Khobar attack. He also falsely described an estrangement between the Saudi Hizballah and elements of the Iranian government. He was later removed to the United States based on a promise to cooperate. Instead, he reneged on the promise and unsuccessfully sought political asylum in the United States. The indictment charges that the defendants [had] first conspired to kill Americans since at least 1988, when several of the group joined the Saudi Hizballah, and later, in the Khobar attack, carried out the murders of American military personnel who were serving in their official capacity in Saudi Arabia. . . .

# Second Speech to Organization of Islamic Countries Meeting (December 9, 1997)

## ALI AL-HUSSEINI AL-KHAMENE'I*

. . . Since the victory of Islam in Iran, the world has witnessed a powerful effort for the return to the pure source of Islam.

---

* Ali al-Husseini al-Khamene'i is Iran's spiritual guide. This speech was translated by FBIS.

headed by half-witted American leaders usually trapped in their own personal follies! And they wishfully try to throw the honored Iranian people, their honest officials, and their deeply rooted, popular government into a defensive position! Our Muslim brothers and sisters throughout the world should know that the Islamic Republic of Iran is strongly and steadfastly marching along the path illuminated by the teachings of pure Islam. . . .

# The New Barbarism (December 2, 1998)

SAQR ABU FAKHR*

Humanity will remember the twentieth century as the most barbaric and lethal century in human history. In this century the two world wars broke out, the atomic bomb exploded on the Japanese people, and the world witnessed massacres committed by the Nazis, the Fascists, the Jews, the Cambodians, the Serbs, and the Rwandans. This century is the natural result of the barbaric capitalism that gradually rose to rule the world and its markets 500 years ago, carrying with it the destruction of the Indians and the enslavement of the blacks. . . .

However, a new barbarism is threatening us as we prepare ourselves for the twenty-first century. This is the worst kind of contemporary barbarism— the American barbarism committed by the United States in the name of international legitimacy. . . .

---

* Saqr Abu Fakhr is a Palestinian journalist. This article appeared in *al-Hayat al-Jadida*, a newspaper owned by the Palestinian Authority.

# Letter to President Bill Clinton
# (December 3, 1998)

ATALLAH ABU AL-SUBH*

You come to us unwelcomed, carrying your shame and blame, armed with the Jews' spearheads, the Jews' reproach, the Jews' vileness. You come to us to wipe your rotten face with our cloak and wash it with the waters of our Gulf that your fire has inflamed around us. You come to us to exhaust our oil and steal more of our land and give it to those who have stolen our land and existence. You come to us and we see on your hands nothing but the blood of our peoples and [our] downtrodden and miserable.

You have bombed Baghdad, oh master of the world, with more than 250,000 cruise [missiles] to destroy it, [knocking it down] on the heads of its children, women, and elderly. To destroy the playgrounds of its youth and the dolls of its little girls. You had no specific target to bomb and no one you aimed at, [just] a blind, crazy bombing. You come to us with fifty-four Jewish settlers around you holding the top positions in your guided administration, which took upon itself to aid the Jews on our account, which made [then-cabinet member Ariel] Sharon tell the settlers to occupy the peaks of our mountains and build new settlements on them, [while] the fountain of Wye [site of Israeli-Palestinian peace negotiation] turns into whey. What are you thinking of telling us? What?

You are trying to divide us from each other with your dollars so that we forget our names and our memory in order to instill the evil you spread all over our land . . . so that our brother kills our brother, our father, our uncles. So that a son kills his father and his mother. Let me tell you: your hopes will be turned down, it will never happen. . . . We fear [only] Allah, the master of the universe, who has shattered tyrants in times past and will do it [again] in the future.

You come to us with your shame and ignorance. Allah will disgrace you, not welcome nor greet you.

---

* Atallah Abu al-Subh is a Hamas columnist. This article appeared as "Clinton's Visit to Israel and the Palestinian Authority" in *al-Risala* (a Hamas weekly magazine), December 3, 1998.

## An Anti-American Sermon (October 2000)

AHMAD ABU HALABIYA*

. . . We say to Clinton, and we say to all those who supported the Jews and still cooperate with the Jews, we say to them, that this will not shake us, we are the Palestinian people. . . . It will not shake a single hair of ours. Our determination will not sway. We will raise the banner of *jihad*. . . .

This is the truth, O brothers in belief. From here, Allah the Almighty has called upon us not to ally with the Jews or the Christians, not to like them, not to become their partners, not to support them, and not to sign agreements with them. And he who does that is one of them, as Allah said: "O you who believe, do not take the Jews and the Christians as allies, for they are allies of one another. Who from among you takes them as allies will indeed be one of them. . . ."

The Jews are the allies of the Christians, and the Christians are the allies of the Jews, despite the enmity that exists between them. The enmity between the Jews and the Christians is deep, but all of them are in agreement against the monotheists—against those who say, "There is no God but Allah and Muhammad is his messenger," that is—they are against you, O Muslims. . . .

Allah, deal with the Jews, your enemies and the enemies of Islam. Deal with the crusaders, and America, and Europe behind them, O Lord of the worlds. . . .

## Why Attack America (January 2002)

AYMAN AL-ZAWAHIRI**

The Western forces that are hostile to Islam have clearly identified their enemy. They refer to it as Islamic fundamentalism. They are joined in this by their

---

* Ahmad Abu Halabiya is a Palestinian cleric and a member of the Palestinian Authority–appointed Fatwa Council and former acting rector of Islamic University in Gaza. This sermon was delivered in Zayed bin Sultan al-Nahyan mosque and broadcast on Palestinian Authority television. Translated in Middle East Media Research Institute report no. 138, October 14, 2000.
** Ayman al-Zawahiri is an al-Qa'ida leader. This essay is from *Knights under the Prophet's Banner:*

old enemy, Russia. They have adopted a number of tools to fight Islam, including:

1. The United Nations.
2. The friendly rulers of the Muslim peoples.
3. The multinational corporations.
4. The international communications and data exchange systems.
5. The international news agencies and satellite media channels.
6. The international relief agencies, which are being used as a cover for espionage, proselytizing, coup planning, and the transfer of weapons.

In the face of this alliance, a fundamentalist coalition is taking shape. It is made up of the *jihad* movements in the various lands of Islam as well as the two countries that have been liberated in the name of *jihad* for the sake of God (Afghanistan and Chechnya).

If this coalition is still at an early stage, its growth is increasingly and steadily accelerating.

It represents a growing power that is rallying under the banner of *jihad* for the sake of God and operating outside the scope of the new world order. It is free of servitude to the dominating Western empire. It promises destruction and ruin for the new crusades against the lands of Islam. It is ready for revenge against the heads of the world's gathering of infidels, the United States, Russia, and Israel. It is anxious to seek retribution for the blood of the martyrs, the grief of the mothers, the deprivation of the orphans, the suffering of the detainees, and the sores of the tortured people throughout the land of Islam, from eastern Turkestan to Andalusia [the Islamic state in Spain that ended in 1492]. . . .

With the emergence of this new batch of Islamists, who have been missing from the nation for a long time, a new awareness is increasingly developing among the sons of Islam, who are eager to uphold it; namely, that there is no solution without *jihad*. . . .

Tracking down the Americans and the Jews is not impossible. Killing them with a single bullet, a stab, or a device made up of a popular mix of explosives, or hitting them with an iron rod, is not impossible. Burning down their property with Molotov cocktails is not difficult. With the available means, small groups could prove to be a frightening horror for the Americans and the Jews. . . .

The masters in Washington and Tel Aviv are using the regimes to protect their interests and to fight the battle against the Muslims on their behalf. If the

*Meditations on the Jihadist Movement.* Published in *al-Sharq al-Awsat* in eleven installments in January 2002. Translated by FBIS. The analysis by *al-Sharq al-Awsat* says that this portion of the book was written just before the September 11, 2001, attack.

shrapnel from the battle reaches their homes and bodies, they will trade accusations with their agents about who is responsible for this. In that case, they will face one of two bitter choices: Either [they] personally wage the battle against the Muslims, which means that the battle will turn into clear-cut *jihad* against infidels, or they reconsider their plans after acknowledging the failure of the brutal and violent confrontation against Muslims.

Therefore, we must move the battle to the enemy's grounds to burn the hands of those who ignite fire in our countries.

The struggle for the establishment of the Muslim state cannot be launched as a regional struggle:

It is clear from the above that the Jewish-crusader alliance, led by the United States, will not allow any Muslim force to reach power in any of the Islamic countries. It will mobilize all its power to hit it and remove it from power. Toward that end, it will open a battlefront against it that includes the entire world. It will impose sanctions on whoever helps it, if it does not declare war against them altogether. Therefore, to adjust to this new reality we must prepare ourselves for a battle that is not confined to a single region, one that includes the apostate domestic enemy and the Jewish–crusader external enemy. . . .

It is clear from the above that the Jewish–crusader alliance will not give us time to defeat the domestic enemy, then declare war against it thereafter. . . .

## Choosing the Targets and Concentrating on the Martyrdom Operations

. . . . The *mujahid* Islamic movement must escalate its methods of strikes and tools of resisting the enemies to keep up with the tremendous increase in the number of its enemies, the quality of their weapons, their destructive powers, their disregard for all taboos, and [their] disrespect for the customs of wars and conflicts. In this regard, we concentrate on the following:

1. The need to inflict the maximum casualties against the opponent, for this is the language understood by the West, no matter how much time and effort such operations take.
2. The need to concentrate on the method of martyrdom operations as the most successful way of inflicting damage against the opponent and the least costly to the *mujahidin* in terms of casualties.
3. The targets as well as the type and method of weapons used must be chosen to have an impact on the structure of the enemy and deter it enough to stop its brutality, arrogance, and disregard for all taboos and customs. It must restore the struggle to its real size. . . .

# 4

## USAMA BIN LADIN AND

## HIS MOVEMENT

This chapter discusses bin Ladin's self-declared war on America, which culminated in the attack on New York and Washington in September 2001. It shows the evolution of bin Ladin's political and strategic thinking during this period, which is basically consistent but also undergoes a change in priorities.

In August 1996, bin Ladin declared war against the United States with an analysis that would typify his later writings and interviews. The West was engaged in an all-out attack on Muslims everywhere in the world, he claimed, based on a crusader (Christian) and Jewish alliance. Muslims were not practicing their religion properly, in part because they had been misled by *ulama* (clerics) in the pay of regimes. Typical of bin Ladin's earlier period, the critique focused on Saudi Arabia, arguably the Arab world's most Islamically pious state, which he portrayed as having abandoned proper Islam and surrendered to Western control. He justified warfare against the United States and claimed that Muslim youth, eager to fight, would defeat it.

Shortly thereafter he gave an interview to *Nida'ul Islam* magazine, published in the October 1996 issue. The media, security organizations, and even clerics of Saudi Arabia were portrayed as an apparatus that preserves the regime there. What is particularly shocking in Islamic terms, running against traditional mainstream Islam, is his accusation that "some of the leaders are engaging in the major *kufr*"—in other words, abandoning Islam altogether. Also important for his later thinking was the view that two small terrorist operations within Saudi Arabia had achieved tremendous results in turning the people against the regime and Americans, as well as creating quarrels between the United States and Saudi Arabia. Clearly, terrorism is seen by him as a remarkable force, capable of overturning governments, mobilizing Muslims, and overcoming the unfavorable balance of power with the United States.

These conclusions were integrated into the World Islamic Front Statement of February 23, 1998, which called for a "Jihad against Jews and Crusaders." Despite this organization's grand name, it consists only of bin Ladin's own al-Qa'ida group plus four small organizations—two Egyptian, one Pakistani, and one Bangladeshi. This does represent, however, bin Ladin's further diluting of his original anti-Saudi perspective with the vision of a multinational Islamist revolutionary force. Three key issues—the struggle to conquer Saudi Arabia, the sanctions against Iraq, and the battle against Israel—were now given equal weight. The statement unambiguously called "on every Muslim who believes in God and wishes to be rewarded to comply with God's order to kill the Americans and plunder their money wherever and whenever they find it." Not only did the statement explicitly call for murdering civilians in the largest possible numbers, but it also proclaimed that any Muslim who does not participate is not a true Muslim.

In his December 1998 interview, bin Ladin made his fullest autobiographical statement. He claimed that his views represent all Muslims but coyly refused to take responsibility for any specific attacks on Americans.

That al-Qa'ida is engaged in warfare is shown, however, by its internal documents. These include the so-called "Encyclopedia of the Afghan Jihad," which seems to date from 1999 and is often referred to as the "training manual." It is basically an instruction book for waging terrorism and espionage, blending shrewdly sophisticated tradecraft with extremely naive concepts of how spy and underground military organizations function.

Regarding actual operations, the testimony of Jamal Ahmad al-Fadl gives a unique picture of how bin Ladin's headquarters functioned during its years in Sudan. Especially remarkable is the account of how the group tried to go about obtaining the makings of nuclear weapons. The testimony of Ahmad Ressam, another al-Qa'ida member, provides a brief account of the training camps in Afghanistan.

Another critical internal document is the so-called recruitment video, which was widely circulated throughout the Middle East. This translation includes a brilliant analysis by Richard Bulliet and Fawaz A. Gerges, who demonstrate how bin Ladin's sense of showmanship and drama could weave an effective spell over those inclined to accept his message.

# Declaration of War (August 1996)

USAMA BIN LADIN*

The people of Islam had suffered from aggression, iniquity, and injustice imposed on them by the Zionist-crusaders alliance and their collaborators, to the extent that the Muslims' blood became the cheapest and their wealth as loot in the hands of the enemies. Their blood was spilled in Palestine and Iraq. The horrifying pictures of the massacre of Qana, Lebanon, are still fresh in our memory. Massacres in Tajikistan, Burma, Kashmir, Assam [in India], the Philippines, Fatani, Ogadin, Somalia, Eritrea, Chechnya, and Bosnia-Herzegovina took place, massacres that send shivers in the body and shake the conscience. All of this and the world watches and hears, and not only didn't respond to these atrocities, but also, with a clear conspiracy between the United States and its allies and under the cover of the iniquitous United Nations, the dispossessed people were even prevented from obtaining arms to defend themselves.

The people of Islam awakened and realized that they are the main target for the aggression of the Zionist-crusaders alliance. All false claims and propaganda about "human rights" were hammered down and exposed by the massacres that took place against the Muslims in every part of the world.

The latest and the greatest of these aggressions, incurred by the Muslims since the death of the prophet . . . is the occupation of the Land of the Two Holy Places—the foundation of the house of Islam, the place of the revelation, the source of the message, and the place of the noble Kaba [the central Islamic holy site], the *qibla* [direction of prayer] of all Muslims—by the armies of the American crusaders and their allies. (We bemoan this and can only say: "No power and power acquiring except through Allah.")

Under the present circumstances, and under the banner of the blessed awakening that is sweeping the world in general and the Islamic world in particular . . . after a long absence, imposed . . . by the iniquitous crusaders' movement under the leadership of the United States, which fears that . . . the scholars and [those who urge others to follow] Islam will instigate the *umma* [community] of Islam against its enemies as their ancestor scholars—may Allah be pleased with them—as Ibn Taymiyyah [a medieval Islamic theorist popular with contemporary Islamist radicals] and Al'iz Ibn Abdes-Salaam did. And

---

* Published in *al-Quds al-Arabi*, an Iraqi-backed newspaper based in London. Translation from the Defense of Legitimate Rights, a Saudi opposition group.

therefore the Zionist-crusader alliance . . . killed the *mujahid* Sheikh Abdullah Azzam [in Afghanistan], and they arrested the *mujahid* Sheikh Ahmad Yasin [leader of the Palestinian Hamas] and the *mujahid* Sheikh Umar Abd al-Rahman [arrested for involvement in the first World Trade Center bombing].

By order of the United States, they also arrested a large number of scholars and young people—in the land of the two holy places [Saudi Arabia]—among them the prominent Sheikh Salman al-Oud'a and Sheikh Safar al-Hawali and their brothers. . . . We, myself and my group, have suffered some of this injustice ourselves; we have been prevented from addressing the Muslims. We have been pursued in Pakistan, Sudan, and Afghanistan, hence this long absence on my part. But by the grace of Allah, a safe base is now available in the high Hindu Kush mountains in Khurasan [Afghanistan]. . . .

From here, today we begin the work, talking and discussing the ways of correcting what had happened to the Islamic world in general, and the land of the two holy places in particular. We wish to study the means that we could follow to return the situation to its normal path. And to return to the people their own rights, particularly after the large damages and the great aggression on the life and the religion of the people. An injustice that had affected every section and group of the people: civilians, military and security men, government officials and merchants, [and both] the young and the old people, as well as schools and university students. Hundreds of thousands of unemployed graduates, who became the widest section of the society, were also affected.

Injustice had affected the people of . . . industry and agriculture. It affected the people of the rural and urban areas. And almost everybody complain[s] about something. The situation at the land of the two holy places became like a huge volcano at the verge of eruption that would destroy the *kufr* [non-Muslims] and the corruption and its sources. The explosions at Riyadh [the 1995 attack on a Saudi national guard headquarters, in which five Americans were killed] and al-Khobar [the 1996 attack on a U.S. military housing facility in Dhahran, Saudi Arabia, that killed nineteen U.S military personnel] is a warning of this volcanic eruption emerging as a result of the severe oppression, suffering, excessive iniquity, humiliation, and poverty. . . .

Numerous princes share with the people their feelings, privately expressing their concerns and objecting to the corruption, repression, and intimidation taking place in the country. But the competition between influential princes for personal gains and interest had destroyed the country. Through its course of actions the regime has torn [up] its legitimacy:

1. Suspension of the Islamic *Sharia* law and exchanging it [for] man-made civil law. The regime entered into a bloody confrontation with the truthful *ulama* and the righteous youths. . . .

2. The inability of the regime to protect the country, and allowing the enemy of the *umma*—the American crusader forces—to occupy the land for

the longest of years. The crusader forces became the main cause of our disastrous condition, particularly in the economical aspect of it due to the unjustified heavy spending on these forces. As a result of the policy imposed on the country, especially in the . . . oil industry, where production is restricted or expanded and prices are fixed to suit the American economy, ignoring the economy of the country [that produced the oil]. Expensive deals were imposed on the country to purchase arms. People are asking, What is the justification for the very existence of the regime then?

Quick efforts were made by individuals and by different groups of the society to contain the situation and to prevent the danger. They advised the government both privately and openly, they sent letters and poems, reports after reports, reminders after reminders, they explored every avenue and enlisted every influential man in their movement of reform and correction. They wrote in a style of passion, diplomacy, and wisdom asking for corrective measures and repentance from the "great wrongdoings and corruption" that had engulfed even the basic principles of the religion and the legitimate rights of the people. . . .

In spite of the fact that the report was written with soft words and very diplomatic style, reminding of Allah, giving truthful sincere advice, and despite the importance of advice in Islam—being absolutely essential for those in charge of the people—and the large number who signed this document as well as their supporters, all of that was not an intercession for the memorandum. Its content was rejected, and those who signed it and their sympathizers were ridiculed, prevented from travel, punished, and even jailed. . . .

To push the enemy—the greatest *kufr*—out of the country is a prime duty. No other duty after Belief is more important than [this] duty. Utmost effort should be made to prepare and instigate the *umma* against the enemy, the American-Israeli alliance—occupying the country of the two Holy Places . . . to the [al-Aqsa mosque in Jerusalem]. . . .

The regime is fully responsible for what had been incurred by the country and the nation. However, the occupying American enemy is the principal and the main cause of the situation. Therefore efforts should be concentrated on destroying, fighting, and killing the enemy until, by the grace of Allah, it is completely defeated. . . .

It is incredible that our country is the world's largest buyer of arms from the United States and the area's biggest commercial partners of the Americans, who are assisting their Zionist brothers in occupying Palestine and in evicting and killing the Muslims there, by providing arms, men, and financial support.

To deny these occupiers the enormous revenues of their trading with our country is a very important help for our *jihad* against them. To express our anger and hate to them is a very important moral gesture. By doing so we would have taken part in [the process of] cleansing our sanctities from the crusaders and the Zionists and forcing them, by the permission of Allah, to leave disappointed and defeated.

We expect the women of the Land of the Two Holy Places and other countries to carry out their role in boycotting the American goods.

If [economic] boycotting is intertwined with the military operations of the *mujahidin*, then defeating the enemy will be even nearer, by the Permission of Allah. However, if Muslims don't cooperate and support their *mujahidin* brothers, then, in effect, they are supplying the army of the enemy with financial help and extending the war and increasing the suffering of the Muslims. . . .

While some of the well-known individuals had hesitated in their duty of defending Islam and saving themselves and their wealth from the [Saudi government's] injustice, aggression and terror, . . . the youths . . . were forthcoming and raised the banner of *jihad* against the American-Zionist alliance occupying the sanctities of Islam. Others who have been tricked into loving this materialistic world, and those who have been terrorized by the government, choose to give legitimacy to the greatest betrayal, the occupation of the land of the two holy places. . . . Our youths are the best descendants of the best ancestors. . . .

[A] few days ago the news agencies had reported that the defense secretary of the crusading Americans had said that "the explosion at Riyadh and al-Khobar had taught him one lesson: that is not to withdraw when attacked by coward[ly] terrorists."

We say to the defense secretary that his talk can induce a grieving mother to laughter! and shows the fears. . . . Where was this false courage of yours when the explosion in Beirut took place [in] 1983. . . . You were turned into scattered bits and pieces at that time; 241 mainly Marines [and] soldiers were killed. And where was this courage of yours when two explosions made you to leave Aden [after the attack on the USS *Cole*] in less than twenty-four hours!

But your most disgraceful case was in Somalia, where—after vigorous propaganda about the power of the United States and its post–Cold War leadership of the new world order—you moved tens of thousands of international force[s], including 28,000 American soldiers, into Somalia. However, when tens of your solders were killed in minor battles and one American pilot was dragged in the streets of Mogadishu you left the area carrying disappointment, humiliation, defeat, and your dead with you. [President Bill] Clinton appeared in front of the whole world threatening and promising revenge, but these threats were merely a preparation for withdrawal. You have been disgraced by Allah and you withdrew; the extent of your impotence and weaknesses became very clear. It was a pleasure for the "heart" of every Muslim . . . to see you defeated in the three Islamic cities of Beirut, Aden, and Mogadishu. . . .

Since the sons of the land of the two holy places feel and strongly believe that fighting [*jihad*] against the *kufr* in every part of the world is absolutely essential, then they would be even more enthusiastic, more powerful, and larger in number upon fighting on their own land . . . defending the greatest of their [holy places], the noble Kaba. . . . They know that the Muslims of the world will assist and help them to victory. To liberate their [holy places] is the greatest of issues concerning all Muslims; it is the duty of every Muslim in this world.

I say to you [Defense Secretary William Cohen]: These youths love death as you love life. They inherit dignity, pride, courage, generosity, truthfulness, and [pass down dignity . . . from father to son]. They are most delivering and steadfast at war. . . .

Our youths believe in paradise after death. They believe that taking part in fighting will not bring their day nearer, and staying behind will not postpone their day either. . . .

Those youths know that their rewards in fighting you, the United States, is doubling their rewards in fighting someone else not from the people of the book. They have no intention except to enter paradise by killing you. An infidel, and enemy of God like you. . . .

Terrorizing you, while you are carrying arms on our land, is a legitimate and morally demanded duty. It is a legitimate right well known to all humans and other creatures. Your example and our example is like a snake that entered into a house of a man and got killed by him. The coward is the one who lets you walk, while carrying arms, freely on his land and provides you with peace and security.

Those youths are different from your soldiers. Your problem will be how to convince your troops to fight, while our problem will be how to restrain our youths to wait for their turn in fighting and in operations. These youths are commendary [*sic*] and praiseworthy. . . .

The youths hold you responsible for all of the killings and evictions of the Muslims and the violation of the sanctities, carried out by your Zionist brothers in Lebanon, [for] you openly supplied them with arms and finance. More than 600,000 Iraqi children have died due to lack of food and medicine and as a result of the unjustifiable aggression imposed on Iraq and its nation. The children of Iraq are our children. You, the United States, together with the Saudi regime are responsible for the shedding of the blood of these innocent children. Due to all of that, whatever treaty you have with our country is now null and void. . . .

My Muslim Brothers of the World:

Your brothers in Palestine and in the land of the two holy places are calling upon your help and asking you to take part in fighting against the enemy— your enemy and their enemy—the Americans and the Israelis. They are asking you to do whatever you can, with one's own means and ability, to expel the enemy, humiliated and defeated, out of the sanctities of Islam. Exalted be to Allah [who] said in [the Koran]: and if they ask your support, because they are oppressed in their faith, then support them! (Anfaal 8:72). O you horses [soldiers] of Allah ride and march on. This is the time of hardship so be tough. And know that your gathering and cooperation in order to liberate the [holy places] of Islam is the right step toward unifying the word of the *umma* under the banner of "No God but Allah."

From our place we raise our palms humbly to Allah asking him to bestow on us his guidance in every aspect of this issue.

## Interview with Usama bin Ladin (October 1996)*

*Q:* What is the policy that should be adopted by the Islamic movement toward the scholars who defend—intentionally or unintentionally—the likes of the Saudi regime?

*A:* It is not a concealed fact that the police states in the Arab world rely on some foundations in order to protect themselves. Amongst these organizations is the security organization, as they spend generously on it, and its foremost mission is to spy on its own people in order to protect the person of the ruler, even if this was at the expense of the rights of the people and their security, and also the military sector, which is prepared to strike the people if they wish to reject the suppression and to remove oppression and establish truth.

The media sector is in the same category, as it strives to beatify the persons of the leaders, [to make drowsy] the community, and to fulfill the plans of the enemies by keeping the people occupied with minor matters, and to stir their emotions and desires until corruption becomes widespread amongst the believers.

There is also another organization that takes priority with the leaders in the Arab world, and is used to take the people astray, and to open the door wide for the security factions to fulfill their aforementioned objectives. This is the organization of the scholars of the authorities, as the role of this organization is the most dangerous of roles in the entirety of the Arab countries. History is the best witness to this.

* From *Nida'ul Islam*, a magazine based in Australia.

At the same time that some of the leaders are engaging in the major *kufr*, which takes them out of the fold of Islam in broad daylight and in front of all the people, you would find a *fatwa* from their religious organization. In particular, the role of the religious organization in the country of the two sacred mosques is of the most ominous of roles. This is overlooking whether it fulfilled this role intentionally or unintentionally; the harm that eventuated from their efforts is no different from the [result of the] role of the most ardent enemies of the nation.

The regime in the land of the two sacred mosques has given a very high priority to this organization and has been able to enlarge its position in the estimation of the people until it made of it an idol to be worshiped aside from God amongst some of the common people, and without the will of the members of this organization.

However, there continues to be in the land of the two sacred mosques— with gratitude to Allah—a good number of honest scholars and students who work according to their teachings, and those who have taken visible and daring stances against the *kufr* activities [on] which the regime is working.

The regime has strived to keep these scholars in the shadows and then removed them, one way or another, from being effective elements in the lives of the people in the community. At the forefront of these scholars was the Sheikh Abdullah bin Hamid—May Allah bless his soul—who was the mufti [chief religious legal authority] in the Arabian Peninsula [Saudi Arabia], and who headed the supreme council of judges. However, the regime constrained him and tightened their grip on him until he offered his resignation. He has many famous writings in response to the unacceptable laws that the government had introduced instead of the law of Allah; one of these is a treatise dealing with the law of work and workers, which deals with many of the introduced laws that contradict the law of Allah.

At the same time, they promoted some of the scholars who were far below Sheikh Ibn Hamid—may Allah bless his soul—those who have been known to be weak and soft, so they put them forward in a cunning plan that began more than twenty years ago. During the preceding two decades, the regime enlarged the role of Bin Baz [grand mufti of Saudi Arabia] because of what it knows of his weakness and flexibility and the ease of influencing him with the various means that the interior ministry practices through providing him with false information. So, a generation of youth was raised believing that the most pious and knowledgeable of people is Bin Baz, as a result of the media promotion through a well-studied policy that had progressed over twenty years.

After this, the government began to strike with the cane of Bin Baz every corrective program that the honest scholars put forward. Further, it extracted a *fatwa* to hand over Palestine to the Jews, and before this, to permit entry into the country of the two sacred mosques to the modern-day crusaders under the rule of necessity, [and] then it relied on a letter from him to the minister for internal affairs and placed the honest scholars in the jails.

The confidence of the people and the youth in Bin Baz was therefore shaken, however the price was very high, whilst the confidence of the people in the working scholars, particularly those in the prisons, had been increased. . . .

*Q:* How do you evaluate the Saudi regime's foreign policy toward the Muslim world in the past years?

*A:* The external policy of the Saudi regime toward Islamic issues is a policy that is tied to the British outlook from the establishment of Saudi Arabia until [1945]; then it became attached to the American outlook after America gained prominence as a major power in the world after the Second World War.

It is well known that the policies of these two countries bear the greatest enmity toward the Islamic world.

To be taken out of this category is the final phase of the rule of King Faisal, as there was a clear interest in the Muslim issues, in particular al-Quds [Jerusalem] and Palestine.

However, the regime does not cease to cry in the open over the matters affecting the Muslims without making any serious effort to serve the interests of the Muslim community, apart from small efforts in order to confuse people and throw some dust into their eyes.

*Q:* The confrontation between the Islamic movement and the apostate Saudi regime recorded a historical turning point following the latest attacks against the American occupiers' targets. How did these attacks reflect on the internal front, and how did they affect the Saudi-American relations?

*A:* There were important effects of the two explosions in Riyadh on both the internal and external aspects. Most important amongst these is the awareness of the people of the significance of the American occupation of the country of the two sacred mosques, and that the original decrees of the regime are a reflection of the wishes of the American occupiers. So the people became aware that their main problems were caused by the American occupiers and their puppets in the Saudi regime, whether this was from the religious aspect or from other aspects in their everyday lives. The sympathies of the people with the working scholars who had been imprisoned also increased, as has their understanding of their [advice] and guidance, which led the people to support the general rectification [Islamist] movement, which is led by the scholars and the callers to Islam. This movement—with the bounty of Allah—is increasing in power and in supporters day after day at the expense of the regime. The sympathy with these missions at the civil and military levels was great, as [were] also the sympathies of the Muslim world with the struggle against the Americans.

As for the relationship between the regime and the American occupiers, these operations have embarrassed both sides and have led to the exchange of accusations between them. So we have the Americans stating that the causes of the explosions are the bad policies of the regime and the corruption of members of the ruling family, and the regime is accusing the Americans of exceeding their authority by taking advantage of the regime and forcing it to enter into military and civil contracts that are beyond its means, which led to great economic slide that has affected the people. In addition to this is the behavior of the Americans with crudeness and arrogance [toward] the Saudi army and their general behavior with citizens, and the privileges that the Americans enjoy in distinction from the Saudi forces.

These missions also paved the way for the raising of the voices of opposition against the American occupation from within the ruling family and the armed forces; in fact we can say that the remaining Gulf countries have been affected to the same degree, and that the voices of opposition to the American occupation have begun to be heard at the level of the ruling families and the governments of the Cooperative Council of Gulf countries. The differences in outlooks between the Americans and the Gulf states have appeared for the first time since the second Gulf war. This was during the conference of the ministers of external affairs of the Gulf Cooperation Council, which was held in Riyadh to look into the American missile aggression against Iraq. These differences are nothing more than a sign of the strain that has [resulted] in the relationship between America and the countries of the region in the footsteps of the *jihad* missions against the Americans in Riyadh and as a result of the fear of these regimes that their own lands might witness similar *jihad* missions.

*Q:* It was observed that the American and Saudi officials tried to link the latest operations to some foreign countries [i.e., Iran]. What is behind these attempts?

*A:* A result of the increasing reaction of the people against the American occupation and the great sympathy with the *jihad* missions against the Americans is the eagerness of the Americans and the Saudis to propagate false information to disperse these sympathies. This can be witnessed in their statements that some of the countries in the region were behind the *jihad* missions inside the country of the two sacred mosques; however, the people are aware that this is an internal Islamic movement against the American occupation, which is revealing itself in the most clear picture after the killing of the four champions who performed the Riyadh operation, the ones concerning whom, we ask Allah to accept amongst the martyrs.

It has become routine policy for countries . . . facing an internal calamity . . . to lay the responsibility on an external country. Before the [submissiveness] of the Arabic countries to America became plainly obvious, the security sections never hesitated to accuse any rectifying Islamic movement to be a puppet [of] America and Israel.

*Q:* What are the regime's choices with regard to the Muslim uprising, and what are your expectations for the future?

*A:* There are several choices for the regime; one of these is reconciliation with all the different sections of the public, by releasing the scholars, and offering essential changes; the most important of these is to bring back Islamic law, and to practice real *shura* [Islamic version of a legislature]. The regime may resort to this choice after finding itself in the position of a morsel of food for the Americans to take, after the enmity has been stirred with their people. These people today feel that the Americans have exceeded their limits both politically and economically; the regime now knows that the public is aware that its sovereignty is shared. This was particularly evident in the recent period through the American press statements that give justification to the American occupation, which exists only to rob the wealth of the people to the benefit of the Americans. This option is dependent on the agreement of the people who hold the solution and have the ability to effect change; at the forefront of these would be the honest scholars.

As for the other option, this is a very difficult and dangerous one for the regime, and this involves an escalation in the confrontation between the Muslim people and the American occupiers and to confront the economic hemorrhage. Its most important goal would be to change the current regime, with the permission of Allah.

*Q:* As a part of the furious international campaign against the *jihad* movement, you were personally the target of a prejudiced attack, which accused you of financing terrorism and being part of an international terrorist organization. What do you have to say about that?

*A:* After the end of the Cold War, America escalated its campaign against the Muslim world in its entirety, aiming to get rid of Islam itself. Its main focus in this was to target the scholars and the reformers who were enlightening the people to the dangers of the Judeo–American alliance, and they also targeted the *mujahidin.* We also have been hit with some of the traces of this campaign, as we were accused of funding terrorism, and being members of an international terrorist organization. Their aims in making these allegations were to place psychological pressure on the *mujahidin* and their supporters so that they would forsake the obligation of *jihad* and the resistance of oppression and American Israeli occupation of Islamic sacred lands. However, our gratitude to Allah, their campaign was not successful, as terrorizing the American occupiers is a religious and logical obligation. We are grateful to Allah Most Exalted in that he has facilitated *jihad* in his cause for us, against the American-Israeli attacks on the Islamic [holy places].

As for their accusations of terrorizing the innocent, the children, and the women, these are in the category of "accusing others with their own affliction in order to fool the masses." The evidence overwhelmingly shows America and Israel killing the weaker men, women, and children in the Muslim world and elsewhere. A few examples of this are seen in the recent Qana massacre in Lebanon, and the death of more than 600,000 Iraqi children because of the shortage of food and medicine that resulted from the boycotts and sanctions against the Muslim Iraqi people; also their withholding of arms from the Muslims of Bosnia-Herzegovina, leaving them prey to the Christian Serbians, who massacred and raped in a manner not seen in contemporary history. Not to forget the dropping of the H-bombs on cities with their entire populations of children, elderly, and women, on purpose, and in a premeditated manner, as was the case with Hiroshima and Nagasaki. Then, killing hundreds of thousands of children in Iraq, and whose numbers [of dead] continue to increase as a result of the sanctions. Despite the continuing American occupation of the country of the two sacred mosques, America continues to claim that it is upholding the banner of freedom and humanity, whilst these deeds which they did, you would find that the most ravenous of animals would not descend to.

As for what America accuses us of, of killing the innocent people, they have not been able to offer any evidence, despite the magnitude of their expenditure on their intelligence services, [d]espite what our history is witnessing in the Afghan phase of the *jihad*. This was also unstained with any blood of innocent people, despite the inhuman Russian campaign against our women, our children, and our brothers in Afghanistan. . . . Similar is our history with respect to our differences with the Saudi regime; all that has been proved is our joy at the killing of the American soldiers in Riyadh and Khobar, and these are the sentiments of every Muslim. Our encouragement and call to Muslims to enter *jihad* against the American and the Israeli occupiers are actions that we are engaging in as religious obligations. Allah Most High has commanded us in many verses of the Koran to fight in his path and to urge the believers to do so. Of these are his words: "Fight in the path of Allah, you are not charged with the responsibility except for yourself, and urge the believers, lest Allah restrain the might of the rejecters, and Allah is stronger in might and stronger in inflicting punishment." And his words: "And what is it with you that you do not fight in the path of Allah, whilst the weak amongst the men, and the women, and the children who say: our Lord take us out of this town the people of which are oppressive, and make for us from You a protecting friend and make for us from You a succorer." And his words: "So if you meet those who reject, then strike the necks. . . ." We have given an oath to Allah to continue in the struggle as long as we have blood pumping in our veins or a seeing eye, and we beg of Allah to accept and to grant a good ending for us and for all the Muslims.

*Q:* Some media sources mentioned that the Afghan government demanded that you leave the country. How true is this?

*A:* The Afghan government has not asked us to leave the country. . . . All gratitude to Allah, our relationship with our brother *mujahidin* in Afghanistan is a deep and broad relationship where blood and sweat have mixed, as have the links over long years of struggle against the Soviets; it is not a passing relationship, nor one based on personal interests.

They are committed to support the religion approved by Allah, and that country remains as the Muslims have known it, a strong fort for Islam, and its people are amongst the most protective of the religion approved by Allah, and the keenest to fulfill his laws and to establish an Islamic state.

That passing phase of infighting has saddened us as it has saddened all the Muslims; however, we wish to indicate that the picture of events as painted by the international press is grossly distorted, and that this infighting is much smaller and less fierce than what Muslims on the outside may imagine, and that most of the country is living a normal peaceful life; apart from some petty crimes here and there as some elements attempt to create corruption under cover of the disputes amongst some of the groups. We are hoping that Afghanistan would regain very soon—God willing—its Islamic position, which would befit its history of *jihad*.

*Q:* What is the responsibility of the Muslim populations toward the international campaign against Islam?

*A:* What bears no doubt in this fierce Judeo-Christian campaign against the Muslim world, the likes of which has never been seen before, is that the Muslims must prepare all possible might to repel the enemy in the military, economic, missionary, and all other areas. It is crucial for us to be patient and to cooperate in righteousness and piety and to raise awareness of the fact that the highest priority after faith is to repel the incursive enemy, which corrupts the religion and the world, and nothing deserves a higher priority after faith, as the scholars have declared; for this cause it is crucial to overlook many of the issues of bickering in order to unite our ranks so that we can repel the greater *kufr*.

All must move giving life to the words of the Most High: "Indeed this, your community, is one community, and I am your Lord, so worship me," and that they should not be like those whom Allah has described with his words: "Indeed those who have divided their religion and became schisms, you are not of them in any way." It is essential to volunteer and not to bicker, and the Muslim should not belittle righteousness in any way; the messenger (peace and blessings upon him) said: "Whoever believes in Allah and the last day must speak good or not speak at all," and they must heed the words of the messenger (peace and blessings upon him) when they move: "Inform and do not repel, and make it easy and do not make it difficult." . . . And we ask Allah to give this community the guidance to exalt the people who obey him and humiliate those who disobey him, and to give us a rule where decency is commanded and evil is forbidden. . . .

## Statement: Jihad against Jews and Crusaders (February 23, 1998)

WORLD ISLAMIC FRONT

[This statement was signed by Usama bin Ladin; Ayman al-Zawahiri, leader of the Jihad Group in Egypt; Abu-Yasir Rifa'i Ahmad Taha, Egyptian Islamic Group; Sheikh Mir Hamzah, secretary of the Jamiat-ul-Ulema-e-Pakistan; and Fazlul Rahman, leader of the Jihad Movement in Bangladesh.—*Eds.*]

. . . The Arabian Peninsula [Saudi Arabia] has never—since God made it flat, created its desert, and encircled it with seas—been stormed by any forces like the crusader armies spreading in it like locusts, eating its riches and wiping out its plantations. All this is happening at a time in which nations are attacking Muslims like people fighting over a plate of food. In the light of the grave situation and the lack of support, we and you are obliged to discuss current events, and we should all agree on how to settle the matter.

No one argues today about three facts that are known to everyone; we will list them in order to remind everyone:

First, for over seven years the United States has been occupying the lands of Islam in the holiest of places, the Arabian Peninsula, plundering its riches, dictating to its rulers, humiliating its people, terrorizing its neighbors, and turning its bases in the peninsula into a spearhead through which to fight the neighboring Muslim peoples.

If some people have in the past argued about the fact of the occupation, all the people of the peninsula have now acknowledged it. The best proof of this is the Americans' continuing aggression against the Iraqi people using the peninsula as a staging post, even though all its rulers are against their territories being used to that end, but they are helpless.

Second, despite the great devastation inflicted on the Iraqi people by the crusader-Zionist alliance, and despite the huge number of those killed, which has exceeded one million . . . despite all this, the Americans are once again trying to repeat the horrific massacres, as though they are not content with the protracted blockade imposed after the ferocious war or the fragmentation and devastation. So here they come to annihilate what is left of this people and to humiliate their Muslim neighbors.

Third, if the Americans' aims behind these wars are religious and economic, the aim is also to serve the Jews' petty state and divert attention from its occupation of Jerusalem and murder of Muslims there. The best proof of this is their eagerness to destroy Iraq, the strongest neighboring Arab state, and their endeavor to fragment all the states of the region such as Iraq, Saudi Arabia, Egypt, and Sudan into paper statelets and through their disunion and weakness to guarantee Israel's survival and the continuation of the brutal crusader occupation of the peninsula.

All these crimes and sins committed by the Americans are a clear declaration of war on God, his messenger, and Muslims. And *ulama* have throughout Islamic history unanimously agreed that the *jihad* is an individual duty if the enemy destroys the Muslim countries. This was revealed by Imam bin-Qadama in *al-Mughni*, Imam al-Kisa'i in *al-Bada'i*, al-Qurtubi in his interpretation, and the sheikh of al-Islam in his books, where he said: "As for the fighting to repulse [an enemy], it is aimed at defending sanctity and religion, and it is a duty as agreed [by the *ulama*]. Nothing is more sacred than belief except repulsing an enemy who is attacking religion and life."

On that basis, and in compliance with God's order, we issue the following *fatwa* to all Muslims:

The ruling to kill the Americans and their allies—civilians and military—is an individual duty for every Muslim who can do it in any country in which it is possible to do it, in order to liberate the al-Aqsa mosque and the holy mosque [Mecca] from their grip, and in order for their armies to move out of all the lands of Islam, defeated and unable to threaten any Muslim. This is in accordance with the words of Almighty God, "And fight the pagans all together as they fight you all together," and "Fight them until there is no more tumult or oppression, and there prevail justice and faith in God."

This is in addition to the words of Almighty God: "And why should ye not fight in the cause of God and of those who, being weak, are ill-treated (and oppressed)?—women and children, whose cry is: "Our Lord, rescue us from this town, whose people are oppressors; and raise for us from thee one who will help!"

We—with God's help—call on every Muslim who believes in God and wishes to be rewarded to comply with God's order to kill the Americans and plunder their money wherever and whenever they find it. We also call on Muslim *ulama*, leaders, youths, and soldiers to launch the raid on Satan's U.S. troops and the devil's supporters allying with them, and to displace those who are behind them so that they may learn a lesson.

Almighty God said: "O ye who believe, give your response to God and his

Apostle, when he calleth you to that which will give you life. And know that God cometh between a man and his heart, and that it is he to whom ye shall all be gathered."

Almighty God also says: "O ye who believe, what is the matter with you, that when ye are asked to go forth in the cause of God, ye cling so heavily to the earth! Do ye prefer the life of this world to the hereafter? But little is the comfort of this life, as compared with the hereafter. Unless ye go forth, he will punish you with a grievous penalty, and put others in your place; but him ye would not harm in the least. For God hath power over all things."

Almighty God also says: "So lose no heart, nor fall into despair. For ye must gain mastery if ye are true in faith."

# Interview with Usama bin Ladin (December 1998)*

*Usama bin Ladin:* I am Usama bin Muhammad bin Ladin. I was born to Muslim parents in the Arabian peninsula in Riyadh, Malez neighborhood, in 1377 Hijra [the Islamic year: A.D. 1957], and then by the grace of God we went to Medina six months after my birth, where I spent most of my life between Mecca, Jedda, and Medina.

My father, Sheikh Muhammad bin Awad bin Ladin, was born in Hadramout [Yemen], from where he came to Hijaz to work for more than seventy years. God honored him by granting him the tenders to build the mosques of the holy sites where the Kaba is [in Mecca, Saudi Arabia], and at the same time he also built the prophet's holy site.

When my father found out that the Jordanian government had submitted a tender to renovate the Dome [of the Rock, a Muslim religious site in East Jerusalem], he gathered all the engineers and asked them to submit a tender for a cost price only, excluding profits. They told him they could guarantee him winning the bid even if they added on a percentage for profit, but he insisted that it be exclusive of any profit. When they submitted their total figure to him, they were surprised that he (God rest his soul) had then gone ahead and re-

---

* This interview was broadcast on al-Jazira television.

duced the total figure they had submitted for the project even further in an attempt to guarantee their company winning the renovation bid for the building of the holy site and the renovation of this particular one [the Dome of the Rock].

He won the bids and began the work. And on some days he was able to perform three of his daily prayers in three of the holiest sites.

I studied economics at Jedda University and I began working in my father's company and on roads from an early age, even though my father passed away when I was ten. This is the brief history of Usama bin Ladin.

*Q:* What do you seek?

*Bin Ladin:* What I seek is what is right for any living being. We demand that our land be liberated from enemies. That our lands be liberated from the Americans. These living beings have been given an inner sense that rejects any intrusions [of their lands] by outsiders. Let us take an example of poultry. Let us look at a chicken, for example. If an armed person was to enter a chicken's home with the aim of inflicting harm to it, the chicken would automatically fight back.

*Q:* Do you think that the British-American attacks against Iraq will increase the popularity of uprising [by the] people against America, or will such attacks subdue them into desisting from any actions militarily or otherwise against the United States and its interests?

*Bin Ladin:* Our enemies roam and meander in our seas and lands and skies, attack and assault without seeking permission from anyone, in particular on this occasion when America and Britain were unable to muster alliance in this blatant, disgraceful plot. The present [Arab] regimes no longer have the power. Either they are collaborators or have lost the power to do anything against this contemptible occupation. So Muslims should immigrate somewhere where they can raise the symbol of *jihad* and protect their religion and world, otherwise they will lose everything. Are they incapable of appreciating the calamity that befell our brothers in Palestine and forgetting how the Palestinian people, once famous for their activity and agriculture and citrus and also for the making of soap, have become a refugee people, turned into slaves of those colonialist Jews who dictate their movements? The situation is dangerous and if we do not move now, when the ancient holy site of 1.2 billion Muslims has been usurped, then when should people stir? Those who believe that such attacks [against Iraq] will terrorize the Islamic movements are deluding themselves. We Muslims believe that our time of death is fixed. Our fortunes are in the hand of God. Since God created these spirits, granted people fortunes and exchanged them for heaven, why would they [Muslims] refrain from serving their religion?

*Q:* Following last year's attacks against Afghanistan, reports quoted you saying that you will retaliate. So far we have not seen any retaliation. Should there be further attacks against Afghanistan, will there be physical retaliation against the attackers and in what form will it come?

*Bin Ladin:* Our duty is to incite the *jihad* against America, Israel, and their allies. We are following this route. Because of circumstances surrounding us, as well as our inability to move outside Afghanistan to take care of matters closely, we were unable to do so. But, with the grace of God, we have established with a large number of our brothers in the International Islamic Front to confront Jews and the crusaders. We believe that the affairs of many of those are moving in the right direction and have the ability to move widely. We pray to God to grant them victory and revenge on the Jews and Americans.

*Q:* The United States has warned its citizens and interests in the gulf of the possibilities of attacks by your followers. How serious are these threats, and do you target American citizens in general or mainly the American forces in the gulf and other Islamic areas?

*Bin Ladin:* I heard this news [of the U.S. warning] a few days ago, which filled my heart with joy. But how serious the threat is I cannot say. If I knew the person who made the threat I could respond, but unfortunately I have no idea who undertook this blessed effort, and we pray to God to help them, let them be successful, and grant them the body bags of the infidel Americans and others. A target, if made available to Muslims by the grace of God, is every American man. He is an enemy of ours whether he fights us directly or merely pays his taxes. You might have heard those who supported Clinton's attacks against Iraq formed three-quarters of the American population. A people that regards its president in high favor when he kills innocent people is a decadent people with no understanding of morality.

*Q:* The Pentagon has circulated news that you are suffering from a muscular disease, as a result of which you have a life expectancy of five to six years. How true is this report?

*Bin Ladin:* We are continuously thankful to God for I enjoy very excellent health. We here in the mountains endure severe cold weather, as well as extreme hot summers.

My favorite hobby is horseback riding, and I can still ride a horse nonstop for seventy kilometers [forty miles]. These are intentional rumors, perhaps aimed at disheartening some of our Muslim supporters and maybe even to calm the fear of Americans by suggesting that Usama is incapable of doing anything.

The truth is that this issue is not purely tied to Usama, for this is a nation of 1.2 billion Muslims who will never allow the house of God to remain with these tainted arrogant Jews and Christians. We are confident in the knowledge that they will continue the *jihad* and unleash painful strikes against America and its allies. . . .

*Q:* Some newspapers say that you seek to acquire nuclear, chemical, and biological weapons. How true are these reports?

*Bin Ladin:* We are seeking to drive them [the United States] out of our Islamic nations and prevent them from dominating us. We believe that this right to defend oneself is the right of all human beings. At a time when Israel stocks hundreds of nuclear warheads and when the Western crusaders control a large percentage of this [type of] weapon, we do not consider this an accusation but a right, and we reject anyone who accuses us of this. We congratulated the Pakistani people when they achieved this nuclear weapon, and we consider it the right of all Muslims to do so. . . .

*Q:* You were accused of the attacks against the U.S. embassies in Nairobi and Tanzania. What is your true stance with regard to these attacks?

*Bin Ladin:* Those who follow the international news would have worked out how much support there is in the Islamic world for attacks against Americans, even though people were saddened by the deaths of some innocent civilians of those countries. But it was clear that there was huge rejoicing and satisfaction in the Islamic world. So I regard with honor those men who carried out bombing attacks in Riyadh, Khobar, or East Africa. The same applies to the Palestinians, who are teaching the Jews great lessons.

*Q:* But the United States says it has proof of your involvement in these attacks? In the investigation it is said that a person from your group has made confessions relating to your organization and its links to bombings, including the World Trade Center [bombing in 1993]?

*Bin Ladin:* America's allegations are many, but they do not concern us much. Those people are resisting the international infidels who occupied their lands and what angers America most is when people it has abused resist its abuse. Despite this I maintain that its allegations are false, unless it means that I am involved in inciting and goading them, which is very clear and to which I confess at all times. I was one of those who signed an edict calling for *jihad*, and we have incited for several years now and, thank God, many brothers adhered to our calls. Yes, they confessed during some interrogations that they were influenced by some of our statements that we made to people and in which we announced certain edicts about the obligation of Muslims to wage *jihad* against those occupying Americans.

What is wrong with resisting the aggressor? The North Koreans, the Vietnamese, they all resisted the Americans. This is a given right. As I said in the past, we missed a great honor in that we were not involved in the killings of Americans in Riyadh. So these charges are false. If the charges against me are for incitement then they are true. It is I with other Muslim brothers who incite *jihad*.

*Q:* Muhammad Sadeq Howeida [one of those arrested in connection with the East African embassy bombings] claimed that he was trained in your camps and was personally acquainted with you. How true are his confessions?

*Bin Ladin:* In the training camps in Afghanistan more than 15,000 men were trained. As far as reports [that] say I ordered him to carry out these attacks, I believe this is an erroneous American attempt against me. [There is] no evidence. Assuming that brother Howeida did say such things, it would have been under torture during which he was forced to make false confessions.

*Q:* After the air strikes against Afghanistan, the U.S. president called for an economic war against you. Will this cause you major discomfort?

*Bin Ladin:* War is war. You win some days, you lose others. America has created enormous pressures against our activities from an early date, and this did affect us. Certain countries in which we have money and properties ordered us to cease aggression against America, but it is our obligation to goad the *umma* [the community of Muslim people], and thanks to God we continue.

*Q:* Last February you called a *jihad* against the crusaders and the Jews and, in particular, against the Americans. This call came at a time [when] many of the movements that had walked the path of armed struggle started to cease such activities and to start participating in their countries' parliaments. Don't you think that by calling a *jihad* you are going against the trend?

*Bin Ladin:* Those Muslims who say that these are not the times for *jihad* are gravely wrong. Following the absence of *jihad* from our *umma* for such a long time, we acquired a generation of people seeking education who had not experienced the reality of *jihad*, and they have been influenced by the American culture and media invasion that stormed the Muslim countries. Without even participating in a military war, we find this generation has already been psychologically beaten. What is true is that God granted the chance of *jihad* in Afghanistan, Chechnya, and Bosnia, and we are assured that we can wage a *jihad* against the enemies of Islam, in particular against the greater external enemy—the crusader-Jewish alliance.

Those who carried out the *jihad* in Afghanistan did more than was expected of them because with very meager capacities they destroyed the largest military force [the Soviet army] and in doing so removed from our minds this notion of stronger nations. We believe that America is weaker than Russia, and from what we have heard from our brothers who waged *jihad* in Somalia, they found to their greatest surprise the weakness, frailty, and cowardliness of the American soldier. When only eight of them were killed they packed up in the darkness of night and escaped without looking back.

*Q:* A reward of $5 million has been placed for your arrest or information leading to your arrest by the Americans. Are you afraid of being sold by a treacherous party?

*Bin Ladin:* These men left the world and came to these mountains and land, leaving their families, fathers, and mothers. They left their universities and came here under shelling, American missiles, and attacks. Some were killed: six Arabs and one Turk. These men left the world and came for the *jihad.* America, however, which worships money, believes that people here are of this caliber. I swear that we have not had the need to change a single man from his position even after these reports were made. We do not suspect our brothers and accept them for their goodness.

*Q:* What kind of relationship is there between you and the Taliban? Are you part of it or do you function independently but from Afghan territory?

*Bin Ladin:* . . . . Our relationship with the Taliban is very strong, and it is an ideological relationship not based on mere political or financial relationships. Many nations have tried to pressure the Taliban and force them into things, but by the grace of God they have been unyielding in their beliefs. . . .

*Q:* The CIA says there was a relationship with you during the Afghan-Soviet war. . . .

*Bin Ladin:* This is misinformation by the Americans. Every Muslim, the minute he can start differentiating, carries hate toward Americans, Jews, and Christians; this is part of our ideology. Ever since I can recall I felt at war with the Americans and had feelings of animosity and hate toward them. So what they say happened between them and myself is out of the question. It is only because the Americans were occupying the region that they threatened to use military force should the Soviets conduct such an intervention. So the Americans would be lying if they claim they had supported us. We challenge them to provide evidence supporting such claims. They were a burden on us and on the *mujahidin* in Afghanistan, for we were performing our obligations in protecting Islam in Afghanistan even though this obligation of ours was at times serving, though without our consent, interests of America.

When the interests of two sides coincide at times, this does not amount to cooperation. We regard them with animosity, and there are statements going far back with us calling for a boycott of American products, and even the necessity to attack American forces and America's economy. This goes back for over twelve years now. . . .

*Q:* What are your . . . objectives, and what message would you like to make to the Islamic world in general?

*Bin Ladin:* We believe very strongly, and I say this despite the pressures imposed on us by the regimes and media. They want to skin us from our manhood. We believe that we are men, Muslim men, committed to defend the grandest house in the universe. The Holy Kaba is an honor to die and defend. So this is our aim—to liberate the lands of Islam from the sinners. America and some of its agents in the region bargained with me more than ten times to keep quiet and silence this small tongue of mine. "Shut up" and we will return to you your money. They believe that people only live for worldly matters, and they forgot that our lives are meaningless if we do not seek to please the goodwill and pleasure of Allah.

Finally, I advise all Muslims to adhere to the Koran. This is the way out from our present predicament. Our cure is the Koran. When one reads the Koran one wonders: Do they not read the Koran, or do they actually read but not understand as they should?

# Encyclopedia of the Afghan Jihad: Training Manual (December 1999)

AL-QA'IDA*

. . . . The main mission for which the military organization is responsible is:

The overthrow of the godless regimes and their replacement with an Islamic regime. Other missions consist of the following:

1. Gathering information about the enemy, the land, the installations, and the neighbors.

2. Kidnapping enemy personnel, documents, secrets, and arms.

3. Assassinating enemy personnel as well as foreign tourists.

4. Freeing the brothers who are captured by the enemy.

5. Spreading rumors and writing statements that instigate people against the enemy.

6. Blasting and destroying the places of amusement, immorality, and sin; not a vital target.

---

* This 1,000-page terrorism training manual was reportedly seized in Jordan from one of the sixteen men suspected of plotting attacks in Israel and Jordan around the time of the worldwide millennial celebrations. It is believed to have been paid for by Usama bin Ladin and distributed widely by his group.

7. Blasting and destroying the embassies and attacking vital economic centers.

8. Blasting and destroying bridges leading into and out of the cities. . . .

## Second Lesson

### Necessary Qualifications for the Organization's Members

1. Islam: The member of the organization must be Muslim. How can an unbeliever, someone from a revealed religion [Christian or Jew], a secular person, a communist, etc., protect Islam and Muslims and defend their goals and secrets when he does not believe in that religion [Islam]? . . .

2. Commitment to the Organization's Ideology. . . .

3. Maturity: . . . The nature of hard and continuous work in dangerous conditions requires a great deal of psychological, mental, and intellectual fitness, which are not usually found in a minor. . . .

4. Sacrifice: [The member] has to be willing to do the work and undergo martyrdom for the purpose of achieving the goal and establishing the religion of majestic Allah on earth.

5. Listening and Obedience: In the military, this is known today as discipline. It is expressed by how the member obeys the orders given to him. That is what our religion urges. The Glorious says, "O, ye who believe! Obey Allah and obey the messenger and those charged with authority among you." . . .

6. Keeping Secrets and Concealing Information: . . . [Secrecy should be used] even with the closest people, for deceiving the enemies is not easy. Allah's messenger, God bless and keep him, says, "Seek Allah's help in doing your affairs in secrecy." . . .

8. Patience: [The member] . . . should be patient in performing the work, even if it lasts a long time. . . . [The member] should have a calm personality that allows him to endure psychological traumas such as those involving bloodshed, murder, arrest, imprisonment, and reverse psychological traumas such as killing one or all of his organization's comrades. . . .

## Fourth Lesson: Organization Military Bases

### Apartments—Hiding Places

Definition of Bases:

. . . During the initial stages, the military organization usually uses apartments in cities as places for launching assigned missions, such as collecting information, observing members of the ruling regime, etc.

Hiding places and bases in mountains and harsh terrain are used at later stages, from which *jihad* groups are dispatched to execute assassination operations of enemy individuals, bomb their centers, and capture their weapons. In some Arab countries such as Egypt, where there are no mountains or harsh terrain, all stages of *jihad* work would take place in cities. The opposite was true in Afghanistan, where initially *jihad* work was in the cities, then the warriors shifted to mountains and harsh terrain. There, they started battling the communists.

Security Precautions Related to Apartments: Choosing the apartment carefully as far as the location, the size for the work necessary (meetings, storage, arms, fugitives, work preparation). It is preferable to rent apartments on the ground floor to facilitate escape and digging of trenches. Preparing secret locations in the apartment for securing documents, records, arms, and other important items. Preparing ways of vacating the apartment in case of a surprise attack (stands, wooden ladders).

5. Under no circumstances should anyone know about the apartment except those who use it.

6. Providing the necessary cover for the people who frequent the apartment (students, workers, employees, etc.)

7. Avoiding seclusion and isolation from the population and refraining from going to the apartment at suspicious times.

8. It is preferable to rent these apartments using false names, appropriate cover, and non-Muslim appearance.

9. A single brother should not rent more than one apartment in the same area, from the same agent, or using the same rental office.

10. Care should be exercised not to rent apartments that are known to the security apparatus [such as] those used for immoral or prior *jihad* activities.

11. Avoiding police stations and government buildings. Apartments should not be rented near those places.

12. When renting these apartments, one should avoid isolated or deserted locations so the enemy would not be able to catch those living there easily.

13. It is preferable to rent apartments in newly developed areas where people do not know one another. Usually, in older quarters people know one another and strangers are easily identified, especially since these quarters have many informers.

14. Ensuring that there . . . has been no surveillance prior to the members' entering the apartment.

15. Agreement among those living in the apartment on special ways of knocking on the door and special signs prior to entry into the building's main gate to indicate to those who wish to enter that the place is safe and not being monitored. Such signs include hanging out a towel, opening a curtain, placing a cushion in a special way, etc. . . .

18. Apartments used for undercover work should not be visible from higher apartments in order not to expose the nature of the work.

19. In a newer apartment, avoid talking loudly, because prefabricated ceil-

ings and walls [used in the apartments] do not have the same thickness as those in old ones.

20. It is necessary to have at hand documents supporting the undercover [member]. . . .

22. The cover of those who frequent the location should match the cover of that location. For example, a common laborer should not enter a fancy hotel because that would be suspicious and draw attention.

## Fifth Lesson: Means of Communication and Transportation

*Second Means: Meeting in Person*

. . . 2. Finding a proper cover for the meeting: [The cover]

i. should blend well with the nature of the location.

ii. In case they raid the place, the security personnel should believe the cover.

iii. should not arouse the curiosity of those present.

iv. should match the person's appearance and his financial and educational background.

v. should have documents that support it.

vi. provide reasons for the two parties' meeting (for example, one of the two parties should have proof that he is an architect. The other should have documents as proof that he is a landowner. The architect has produced a construction plan for the land). . . .

4. Designating Special Signals between Those Who Meet

If the two individuals meeting know one another's shape and appearance, it is sufficient to use a single safety sign. [In that case,] the sitting and arriving individuals inform each other that there is no enemy surveillance. The sign may be keys, beads, a newspaper, or a scarf. The two parties would agree on moving it in a special way so as not to attract the attention of those present.

If the two individuals do not know one another, they should do the following.

A. The initial sign for becoming acquainted may be that both of them wear a certain type of clothing or carry a certain item. . . .

B. Safety Signal: It is given by the individual sitting in the meeting location to inform the second individual that the place is safe. The second person would reply through signals to inform the first that he is not being monitored. The signals are agreed upon previously and should not cause suspicion.

C. A second signal for getting acquainted is one which the arriving person uses while sitting down. That signal may be a certain clause, a word, a sentence, or a gesture agreed upon previously, and should not cause suspicion for those who hear it or see it. . . .

*Fourth Means: Letters*

This means (letters) may be used as a method of communication between members and the organization provided that the following security measures are taken:

1. It is forbidden to write any secret information in the letter. If one must do so, the writing should be done in general terms.

2. The letter should not be mailed from a post office close to the sender's residence, but from a distant one.

3. The letter should not be sent directly to the receiver's address, but to an inconspicuous location where there are many workers from your country. Afterward, the letter will be forwarded to the intended receiver. (This is regarding the overseas-bound letter).

4. The sender's name and address on the envelope should be fictitious. In case the letters and their contents are discovered, the security apparatus would not be able to determine his [the sender's] name and address.

5. The envelope should not be transparent so as to reveal the letter inside.

6. The enclosed pages should not be many, so as not to raise suspicion.

7. The receiver's address should be written clearly so that the letter would not be returned.

8. Paying the post office box fees should not be forgotten.

*Fifth Means: Facsimile and Wireless*

Considering its modest capabilities and the pursuit by the security apparatus of its members and forces, the Islamic Military Organization cannot obtain theses devices. . . .

## Sixth Lesson: . . . The Trainees

1. Before proceeding to the training place, all security measures connected with an undercover individual should be taken. Meanwhile, during training at the place, personnel safety should be ensured. . . .

3. The trainees should not know one another.

4. The small size of groups that should be together during the training (7–10 individuals). . . .

## Eighth Lesson: Member Safety

. . . The Undercover Member: should . . .

1. Not reveal his true name to the organization's members who are working with him. . . .

2. Have a general appearance that does not indicate Islamic orientation (beard, toothpick, book, [long] shirt, small Koran).

3. Be careful not to mention the brothers' common expressions or show their behaviors (special praying appearance, [saying] "may Allah reward you," "peace be on you," while arriving and departing, etc.).

4. Avoid visiting famous Islamic places (mosques, libraries, Islamic fairs, etc.).

5. Carry falsified personal documents and know all the information they contain. . . .

8. Maintain his family and neighborhood relationships and should not show any changes toward them so that they would not attempt to bring him back [from the organization]. . . .

10. Not speak loudly.

11. Not get involved in advocating good and denouncing evil [i.e., campaigning for proper Islamic behavior] in order not to attract attention to himself.

12. Break the daily routine, especially when performing an undercover mission. For example, changing the departure and return routes, arrival and departure times, and the store where he buys his goods.

13. Not causing any trouble in the neighborhood where he lives or at the place of work.

14. Converse on the telephone using special code so that he does not attract attention.

15. Not contact the overt members except when necessary. Such contacts should be brief.

16. Not fall into the enemy's . . . trap, either through praising or criticizing [the] organization.

17. Perform the exercises to detect surveillance whenever a task is to be performed.

18. Not park in no-parking zones, and not take photographs where it is forbidden. . . .

20. Not undergo a sudden change in his daily routine or any relationships that precede his *jihad* involvement. For example, there should not begin an obvious change in his habits of conversing, movement, presence, or disappearance. Likewise, he should not be hasty to sever his previous relationships.

21. Not meet in places where there are informers, such as coffee shops, and not live in areas close to the residences of important personalities, government establishments, and police stations.

22. Not write down on any media, especially on paper, that could show the traces and words of the pen by rubbing the paper with lead powder.

## Important Note

Married brothers should observe the following:

1. Not talking with their wives about *jihad* work. . . . Members with se-

curity risks should not travel with their wives. A wife with an Islamic appearance (veil) attracts attention.

## Ninth Lesson: Security Plan

An Example of a Security Plan for a Group Mission (assassinating an important person) . . . must take into account the following matters:

A. The Commander: The security apparatus should not know his whereabouts and movements. . . .

B. The Members: . . . During the selection process, members should not know one another. They should not know the original planners of the operation. In case they do, the commander should be notified. He then should modify the plan.

3. They should be distributed as small groups (3 members) in apartments that are not known except to their proprietors. They should also be given field names.

4. During the selection process, consider whether their absence from their families and jobs would clearly attract attention. . . .

C. Method of Operating:

1. The matters of arming and financing should not be known by anyone except the commander.

2. The apartments should not be rented under real names. . . .

3. Prior to executing an operation, falsified documents should be prepared for the participating individuals.

4. The documents related to the operation should be hidden in a secure place and burned immediately after the operation, and traces of the fire should be removed. . . .

6. Prior to the operation, apartments should be prepared to hide the brothers participating in it. These apartments should not be known except to the commander and his soldiers.

7. Reliable transportation means must be made available. It is essential that prior to the operation, these means are checked and properly maintained. . . .

D. Interrogation and Investigation: Prior to executing an operation, the commander should instruct his soldiers on what to say if they are captured. He should explain that more than once, in order to ensure that they have assimilated it. They should, in turn, explain it back to the commander. The commander should also sit with each of them individually [and go over] the agreed-upon matters that would be brought up during the interrogation:

1. The one who conceived, planned, and executed this operation was a brother who [is already known to] the enemy.

2. During the interrogation, each brother would mention a story that suits

his personal status and the province of his residence. The story should be agreed upon with the commander.

## Eleventh Lesson: Espionage . . . Information Gathering Using Public Means

In order to gather enemy information, the military organization can use means such as magazines, publications, periodicals, and official printed matter. Through these means, it is possible to learn about major government events and about the news, meetings, and travel of presidents, ministers, and commanders. Information may be:

1. Names and photographs of important government personalities, police commanders, and security leaders.

2. Published meetings. Through these, one can learn about major decisions and topics being discussed.

3. Future meeting plans.

4. Present and future enemy capabilities through current photographs of projects and strategic sites or through meetings with top officials. . . .

6. Tourism news and the arrival times of foreign tourist groups.

7. Advertisements about apartments for rent, vacant positions, or anything else that is useful.

8. Advertisements about new and used car lots. These [cars] may be used in assassination, kidnapping, and overthrowing the government.

9. Learning the enemy position on current Islamic issues (veil, beard, dedication, *jihad* . . . ).

10. Radio and Television: The military organization can use these important public sources to gather information all day and night. . . .

1. Visual and audible news help the organization to determine its present and future plans.

2. Interviews may help to identify the government policy and its general directives.

3. Spotting the appearance of those who occupy high positions.

4. Learning the prevailing information diplomacy and its position on contemporary issues.

5. Learning about the interior of important government places and establishments during their opening ceremonies or through advertisements.

In addition to the aforementioned, [attention should be given] to newspapers, magazines, and the public's comments and jokes.

## Twelfth Lesson: Espionage

. . . B. Gathering Information through Interrogation: Security personnel in our countries arrest brothers and obtain the needed information through interrogation and torture.

The military organization must do likewise. On one hand, the organization can obtain important information about enemy establishments and personnel. On the other hand, that is a form of necessary punishment.

Information is collected in this method by kidnapping an enemy individual, interrogating him, and torturing him. This source of information is not permanent. Also, caution should be exercised about being deceived by misinformation from enemy individuals. . . .

Gathering Information through Recruitment: Recruiting agents is the most dangerous task that an enlisted brother can perform. Because of this dangerous task, the brother may be killed or imprisoned. Thus, the recruitment task must be performed by special types of members.

There are a number of motives that might entice an uncommitted person to take part in intelligence work. These motives are:

1. Coercion and entanglement
2. Greed and love for money
3. Displaying courage and love of adventure
4. Love of amusement and deviance
5. Mental and political orientation
6. Fear of being harmed

The organization may use motives No. 2, 3, 5, and 6 in recruitment.

Candidates for Recruitment Are:

1. Smugglers
2. Those seeking political asylum
3. Adventurers
4. Workers at coffee shops, restaurants, and hotels
5. People in need
6. Employees at borders, airports, and seaports

Types of Agents Preferred by the American Intelligence Agency (CIA):

1. Foreign officials who are disenchanted with their country's policies and are looking toward the United States for guidance and direction.

2. The ideologue (who is in his county but against his government) is considered a valuable catch and a good candidate for the American Intelligence Agency [CIA].

3. Officials who have a lavish lifestyle and cannot keep up using their regular wages, or those who have weaknesses for women, other men, or alcoholic beverages. The agent who can be bought using the aforementioned means is an easy target, but the agent who considers what he does a noble cause is difficult to recruit by enemy intelligence.

4. For that purpose, students and soldiers in Third World countries are considered valuable targets. Soldiers are the dominating and controlling elements of those countries.

Recruitment Stages: Suppose the Islamic [Military] Organization, with its modest capabilities, wants to obtain information about an important target (important personality, building, camp, agency, ministry). It has to do the following:

1. Finding the Agent: In this stage, the organization picks the suitable person for supplying the information. The organization learns about that person: his financial condition, his family status, his position regarding the government, and his weaknesses and strengths.

2. Evaluating the Agent: In this stage, the agent is placed under continuous observation to learn the times of his departure to and return from work, the places he visits, the individuals he meets, and his social interaction with those whom he meets in coffee shops, clubs, etc.

3. Approaching the Agent: After gathering information about him, a relationship with him is developed under a certain cover, such as: (a) family connection and tribal relations; (b) developing a friendship with him in the club, coffee shop, and workers union. The [recruiting] brother develops the friendship as if it were unpretentious and unplanned. The relationship should develop naturally and gradually in order not to attract the target's attention. . . .

4. Recruiting the Agent: After finding, evaluating, and approaching a target comes the second stage of recruiting him. Recruiting may be direct, that is, telling the agent frankly about working for the organization for a specific and agreed-upon salary. A promise is secured in writing or verbally.

Or recruitment may be indirect, that is, information may be taken from the target without informing him that he is an agent. That may be accomplished by giving him gifts, sharing his joys and sorrows, and attempting to solve his problems.

5. Testing the Agent: In this stage, the agent is assigned certain tasks in order to test his ability, loyalty, and dependability. The agent does not know that the organization already has the information being sought. If the information supplied by the agent does not match the organization's existing information, then the agent may be an unreliable source of information or may be trying to mislead the organization. During the testing stage, the agent should remain under careful observation to spot all his movements.

6. Training the Agent: This stage applies to the recruited agent, that is, the agent who has been recruited directly and is aware that he has been recruited by someone or some organization for money or other things. That agent may be trained in the following:

   a. Work secrecy and means of gathering and hiding information
   b. The method of passing information on to officials
   c. Concealment and disguising
   d. Interrogation and resisting the interrogation

e. Explaining the assigned mission in utmost detail

f. Photography

There might not be any training at all. The agent may be given freedom in his work, relying on his instinct, talents, background, and the capabilities of his superior brother.

7. Treating the Agent: The brother who manages the agent should possess the qualifications of a perfect spy, a psychiatrist, and an interrogator. There are two points of view on treating the agent:

First Point of View: Maintaining a strong personal relationship with the agent. This technique provides the agent with the motivation that entices him to take chances in order to please his friend with the information. However, this technique has disadvantages. The barriers between the agent and his superiors are removed, and the agent may ask for many things that were not agreed upon.

Second Point of View: The person managing the agent treats him roughly and pushes him to the limits for the purpose of getting as much information as possible. This technique uses harshness, cruelty, and threats in order to keep agent constantly active. I believe that the Islamic Military Organization can combine the two techniques. The agent may be treated in a careful Islamic manner, while the managing brother appeals to the agent's conscience and his Islamic association with the work for majestic Allah's religion. He lures the agent with money and gifts, and uses cruelty and kindness when appropriate.

8. Terminating the Agent's Services: That should occur when any of the following take place: (a) the recruitment mission terminates; (b) incapacity to work because of sickness or changes in the job situation; (c) Repeated errors in security measures; (d) The agent requests the termination.

Means for Testing the Recruit: (1) Requesting specific information that the organization knows well; (2) monitoring him while he performs his covert work; (3) overpaying him in order to know his trustworthiness; (4) giving him a chance to tamper with the work documents (unimportant documents).

Important Advice About Dealing with Agents: . . .

1. Do not send sealed packages to the agent or receive them from him. These could be booby traps.

2. Leaving something for the agent should be done as quickly as possible. When transporting and giving an item to the agent at the agreed-upon location, it should not attract attention and lead to the agent's arrest.

3. The financial status of the agent should be controlled so that the agent does not suddenly show great wealth. A portion of the payment should be given to him, while the other should be deposited in his bank account.

4. When wishing to recruit an agent, events should occur naturally. You may agree with a friend that he invite the person to be recruited for dinner, or

something similar. While that intermediary person is talking with him, he notices your arrival at your friend's, greets you, starts to converse with you, and invites you to sit down with the person you want to recruit.

5. When meeting with the agent, make sure neither you nor the meeting place are being monitored. Do not enter a place to meet with an agent before he does. There could be a trap for you.

6. If you wait for your agent at the agreed-upon location, you could be a target for him. Be especially careful if he goes to the bathroom. Once, in Belgium, an Israeli Mossad [intelligence] officer met an Arab agent. A few minutes after they sat down, the Arab agent said that he had to go get something. When he returned, the Israeli intelligence agent was still there. The Arab agent then pulled out a pistol and shot the Mossad agent several times.

7. In order to communicate with the agent, it is necessary to specify locations such as parks, a university campus area, etc.

8. It is necessary to continuously communicate with the agent, to learn about his problems and requests, help him as much as possible, lift his morale, and renew his confidence.

## Eighteenth Lesson: Prisons and Detention Centers

If an indictment is issued and the trial begins, the brother has to pay attention to the following:

1. At the beginning of the trial, once more the brothers must insist on proving that torture was inflicted on them by State Security [investigators] before the judge.

2. Complain [to the court] of mistreatment while in prison. . . .

5. Some brothers may . . . be lured by the state security investigators to testify against the brothers, either by not keeping them together in the same prison during the trials, or by letting them talk to the media. In this case, they have to be treated gently, and should be offered good advice, good treatment, and pray that God may guide them.

6. During the trial, the court has to be notified of any mistreatment of the brothers inside the prison.

7. It is possible to resort to a hunger strike, but it is a tactic that can either succeed or fail.

8. Take advantage of visits to communicate with brothers outside prison and exchange information that may be helpful to them in their work outside prison [according to what occurred during the investigations]. . . .

When the brothers are transported from and to the prison [on their way to the court] they should shout Islamic slogans out loud from inside the prison cars to impress upon the people and their family the need to support Islam.

Inside the prison, the brother should not accept any work that in any way belittles or demeans him or his brothers, such as the cleaning of the prison bathrooms or hallways.

The brothers should create an Islamic program for themselves inside the prison, as well as recreational and educational ones, etc. . . .

# Testimony of Jamal Ahmad al-Fadl (February 6–7, 2001)*

[I joined al-Qa'ida] [at the] end of [19]89 and [start of 19]90. At that time Abu Ayoub al-Iraqi was *emir* [leader and he reported to] our general *emir* [leader], Usama Muhammad al-Wahal bin Ladin. . . . Under the *emir* [is] something called [the] *shura* council. . . . Under [the] *shura* council we have different committee[s]; The military committee focuses [on] training, helping people . . . buy[ing] weapons. . . . We got [a] money and business committee. . . . [al-Qa'ida also had a] *fatwa* committee and Islamic study. . . . We got another committee for media reporting and the newspaper-weekly report about . . . al-Qa'ida and about Islam in the world and *jihad*. . . .

[I traveled to] Egypt and Sudan [for al-Qa'ida]. [I was told], "You have to shave your beard and to wear Western clothes . . . because you need to be [a] normal person. [If] you go with beard and Islamic dress, the intelligence office in Egypt . . . want[s] to ask a lot of questions if you want to go from Pakistan to Egypt. . . . Don't take any magazine or book related to *jihad* or Islamic study. . . . Buy cologne and [a] pack of cigarettes. . . . If somebody in customs, he [sees] the cologne and he see the cigarettes, he is not going to think you [are] in Islamic group." . . . I didn't use my real passport. Under the money committee . . . we got office just [to] work [on] immigration stuff. Like if you want to travel, they give you passport and he gave you name and . . . the ticket. . . .

I remember in a guesthouse for al-Qa'ida . . . members [veterans of the war against the Soviets] start talking: "[I]n Afghanistan we don't have too much work because the Russians . . . left." . . . And they want to make relationship

---

* Jamal Ahmad al-Fadl is a member of al-Qa'ida. This trial transcript is from U.S. District Court, Southern District of New York.

with al-Qa'ida. [If we join and go to its base in Sudan] it's near [the] Arab world. Afghanistan is too far. . . .

[In Khartoum, Sudan] we have some guesthouses and farms and houses for the people, the organization, residential houses. We have office in McNimr [*sic*] Street [with] eight or nine rooms. When you enter the door we have [a] little area for the secretary with [a] table. If somebody want[s] to visit . . . someone, he should . . . give his I.D. card to [the] secretary, [write] his name and [who] he [is] going to visit . . . and he [has] to wait over there until he got permission, or if he got appointment, he check in. . . . When you pass the secretary area it's another hall with other secretaries. After you enter this, sometime[s] you wait to see somebody. . . . In the first office on the left . . . bin Ladin, he got office. . . .

[My salary is] . . . around 100,000 pounds [at] that time. . . . [Salary for the al-Qa'ida members is] around $200 a month . . . [to $300 a month]. . . . Abu Ahmad el-Masry, he gives every month for the al-Qa'ida membership . . . sugar and tea and oil, vegetable oil, and other stuff just to help them because sometimes they busy, they can't go shopping, and also because in Sudan sometimes hard to find sugar anytime or oil and some stuff.

If [an al-Qa'ida member goes to the] doctor or he buy his medicine and he brings a receipt and we pay him the money. Some people, they got more. Some people, they got a little. We have discussion, "why is difference, why not all the same." What I tell [Usama bin Ladin], "Some people complain, because some people, they got high salary, some people, they got a little and they want to know if we all al-Qa'ida membership, why somebody got more than others." . . . [Bin Ladin] say, "some people, they traveling a lot and they do more work and also they got chance to work in the country. Some people, they got citizenship from another country and they go back over there for regular life, they can make more money than in group." And he says that's why he try to make them happy and give them more money. . . .

[Bin Ladin] spend most of his time in the guesthouse. When [members] go over there we do the prayer together and sometime we take dinner together. . . . He liked to sit in the front yard and talk about *jihad* and about Islam and about the al-Qa'ida in general. In the second floor he got big room. It's only for him. . . .

Abu Hajer al-Iraqi [later prosecuted for his involvement in the East African embassy bombings] said that our time now is similar [to the time] of Ibn Taymiyya [a religious thinker often cited by radical Islamists for his harder-line views]. When the Tartars came to wage war [on] Arabic countries [of] that time, he say some Muslims . . . help them. And he says Ibn Taymiyya, he make a *fatwa*. He said [if any Muslim] around the Tartar [buys] something from them and he sell them something, you should kill him. And also, if when you attack the Tartar, if anybody around them [even if he's not a soldier], if you kill him, you don't have to worry about that. If he's a good person, he go to paradise and if he's a bad person, he go to hell. . . . He says it is no guarantee if we fight we [won't] injure innocent people. Also, I remember Abu Hajer say, "If you . . . [blow up] a military building . . . sometimes . . . could be civilian[s] around the building and [if] you don't have any choice. . . . You should do it and you don't have to worry about that." . . .

We have some of our weapons in Afghanistan and want to bring [them] to Sudan. . . . We have Milan and Stinger [rockets]. . . . We use it against tanks. . . . They rent one of the Sudan Airways . . . cargo plane . . . to help them, and . . . we want to take some supplies from Sudan, sugar for Afghani people, and when the cargo come back, we want to bring our supplies, our weapons. . . .

The Egyptian Islamic Group help al-Q'aida . . . and at the same time al-Qaida help the Islamic Group. . . . In early [1990s] Sheikh Umar Abd al-Rahman [was the leader]. . . . I remember I talk one time with Abu Yasir al-Masri because he is *emir* of the Islamic Group. . . . He says he try to make Islamic government in Egypt. I remember I went that time to the guesthouse, and they . . . talk about Sheikh Umar [under arrest by U.S. authorities for involvement in the first bombing of the World Trade Center] and we have to do something. . . . They talk about what we have to do against America because they arrest . . . Rahman. I remember some of the members in al-Qa'ida, they left the group and they say . . . "We [are] not going to stay in group because the group . . . don't want to do anything to help . . . Rahman." . . .

[Among al-Qa'ida's allies are the Armed Islamic Group] from Algeria. . . . We have the Libyan Fight Group. . . . We had Yemeni group. . . . We have people from all groups go . . . help the Chechens [fight against Russia]. . . . [Senior al-Qa'ida official] Abu Fadhl al-Makkee [tells] me, "we open an office in London." . . .

When I was in Khartoum, they told me also, "We need . . . you go to Bosnia, to Zagreb, [Croatia] . . . to study . . . business over there because we learn the government in Croatia has sold some companies and we want to know what kind of companies and how much and how [to do] investments over there." I bring [the report] to Abu Fadhl al-Makkee and I give it to him. . . . They told me we have some money . . . [for the] Abu Ali group. . . . They got separate group [to] work under al-Qa'ida . . . inside Palestine and Jordan. They give me $100,000 cash and they told me when you get to Amman [Jordan] airport, Abu Akram going to help you and give you the money. Abu Fadhl, he bring [the money] from Shamal Bank and he bring it to me. . . . Abu Akram Urdani . . . talks . . . with one of the Custom[s] people and they didn't check my bag. When we went to his car, I give him the money and we went to his farm.

We buy camels to send them to Egypt because we use camels to smuggle

Kalashnikov [automatic weapons] to Egypt. . . . We buy from [the] market for camels over there in Umduhrman City [Sudan] it's near the Nile River . . . around fifty [camels] each trip. . . .

I remember we got meeting with [al-Qa'ida member] Abu Rida al-Suri . . . during [1992]. We talked about bin Ladin and we asked him if we have to make money because the business is very bad in Sudan, because the pounds go down and the dollar is strong. . . . He say, "Our agenda is bigger than business. We not going to make business here, but we need to help the government and the government help our group, and this is our purpose."

[Al-Qa'ida officials] tell me [that we] help group [in the Philippines] to train them and help them against the Philippine[s] government . . . [the group] called Jebba Moro. . . . I remember they send the Azmarai Group on the border of Afghanistan and Tajikistan and they help the *mujahidin* from Tajikistan over there. They train them and they help them to fight.

[Around 1994 or the end of 1993] . . . Abu Fadhl al-Makkee . . . told me, "We hear somebody in Khartoum, he got uranium, and we need you to go and study that, is that true or not." . . . [In a meeting with a contact, Basheer,] he told me, "Are you serious? You want uranium?" I tell him, "Yes. I know people, they very serious, and they want to buy it. . . . They want to know which quality, [what] country make it, and after that we going to talk with you about the price." He say, "I going to give you this information in a paper, and we need $1,500,000. . . . We need the money outside of Sudan." . . . But he [also] need commission for himself, and . . . for Salah Abd al-Mobruk. . . . I went to Ikhlak company in Baraka building in Khartoum City, and I told [Makkee] about the whole information, and he say, "Tell him we have [a Geiger counter]. We going to check the uranium but first we want to see . . . the cylinder and we want . . . information about the quality and which country it [came from]." . . .

We meet Basheer, and [went in his jeep to a town called Bait al-Mal]. . . . They took us inside house . . . and after few minutes they bring a big bag and they open it, and it [is a] cylinder . . . [two to three feet tall]. . . . [I and my colleagues compared the writing on the cylinder to a paper an al-Qa'ida leader had given him.] Abu Rida al-Suri looked to his paper and he looked to the cylinder, and after that he say, "OK. That is good." . . . I remember [the paper said] South Africa and serial number and quality. . . . It's all in English. . . .

We told Basheer, "The people they like to buy the cylinder." And he [asked] me, "How you going to check it?" I told him what Abu Rida al-Suri tell me, "they wait for machine . . . to come from Kenya [probably a Geiger counter]." . . .

After [a] few days Abu Fadl al-Shahideen . . . say, "yes, everything fine, you did great job," and he give me $10,000. He says, "This is for what you did," and he told me . . . "Don't tell anybody, you did great job, we going to check it and everything be fine." . . .

# Testimony of Ahmad Ressam
# (July 3–5, 2001)*

... [The camp] had people from all nationalities who were getting training there, and each group stayed together, those who will have some work to do together later on. Each group was formed depending on the country they came from—Jordanians, Algerians, from Yemen, from Saudi Arabia, from Sweden, from Germany also, French also, Turks also, and Chechens. . . . I received training in light weapons, handguns, and small machine gun and a large one, RPG—it is a small rocket launcher that is used in fighting in the mountains and in cities against tanks. . . . They used to buy [the weapons] from the Taliban—the rulers now in Afghanistan. . . . [Next] I received training in explosives. How to make a charge, the types of explosives, TNT, C4—it's a plastic explosive, and there is another one that was called black plastic. . . . One [type of training] involved the types of explosives and then one is called sabotage. . . . How to blow up the infrastructure of a country . . . such as electric plants, gas plants, airports, railroads, large corporations, gas, gas installations and military installations also [and] . . . hotels, where conferences are held.

[The training] was . . . a month and a few days. I also got training in urban warfare. . . . We learned how to carry out operations in cities, how to block roads, how to assault buildings, and the strategies used in these operations. . . . [We learned] how to assassinate someone. . . . You would first observe him. . . . You watch when he comes in and leaves, and you find where he lives and you find out where his vulnerabilities are. . . . When you go to a place you would wear clothing that would not bring suspicion to yourself—you would wear clothing that tourists wear. You would observe or you would also take pictures. . . . And when you work in a group, each person knows only what he is supposed to do, not more, to preserve your secrets. Avoid the places that are suspicious or will bring suspicion upon you, such as mosques. Avoid wearing clothing that would bring suspicion upon you. When you speak on the phone, speak in a very natural, normal language, or in a foreign language. . . .

---

* Ahmad Ressam is an Algerian member of al-Qa'ida who intended to set off a suitcase bomb at Los Angeles International Airport around January 1, 2000. He testified for the government at the federal trial of an alleged accomplice, fellow Algerian Mokhtar Haouari, who Ressam said lent him money and created a fake driver's license for his mission. The Khaldan camp where he trained was run by al-Qa'ida.

# Al-Qa'ida Recruitment Video (2000)

### USAMA BIN LADIN*

[We have put the description of the video itself in italics and the analysis sections in brackets to set them off from direct quotations of the video.—*Eds.*]

## Prologue Excerpt

*Usama bin Ladin, wearing the plain white head cover of a religious teacher, recites a highly charged, inflammatory poem about the condition of the Muslim* umma *(worldwide community), appalled, mobilized, and seeking vengeance against its enemies. In particular, bin Ladin extols the young men in Najd, Saudi Arabia, who have risen up and joined the* jihad. *He also praises the young men in Aden, Yemen, who demolished the indestructible American destroyer USS* Cole, *directly indicating approval and knowledge of that suicide bombing in Aden.*

[Here, as in several other scenes, bin Ladin is standing in front of a wall-sized map of the world, symbolizing the scope of the problems and solutions he wants his audience to be conscious of. The dagger in his waistband is typical of formal male dress in Yemen and Oman in southern Arabia. This suggests an affinity between bin Ladin, the son of a Yemeni father, and the Yemeni suicide bombers who attacked the USS *Cole*. Visually, an explosion is superimposed over the hole in the hull of the USS *Cole* to convey the sense of watching the attack live.]

## Reel 1: The Situation of the Muslim Community

*Bin Ladin:* "The wounds of the Muslims are deep everywhere. But today our wounds are deeper because the crusaders and the Jews have joined together to invade the heart of Dar al-Islam ('The Abode of Islam': our most sacred places in Saudi Arabia, Mecca and Medina, including the prophet's mosque, and the al-Aqsa mosque and Dome of the Rock in Jerusalem, al-Quds)."

[The term Dar al-Islam comes from an Islamic legal distinction between those lands that observe Islamic law and those that do not, termed Dar al-Harb ("Abode of War"). Labeling this segment "Land of the Two Holy Places" implicitly rejects the legitimacy of Saudi rule in Saudi Arabia. Visually, the scenes of believers engaged in pilgrimage rituals at the Kaba in Mecca, the cubical stone building that Muslims face in prayer, contrast powerfully with scenes of American tanks and soldiers on maneuvers in the Arabian desert. Bin Ladin

---

* Translation and analysis by Richard Bulliet and Fawaz A. Gerges. Reprinted with permission.

reiterates the sacredness of Arabia and details the evils of American presence and the failure of Saudi government to protect Islam.]

*The excerpt begins with interspersed images of American forces in Saudi Arabia: President George Bush in a tank, Secretary of Defense William Cohen meeting King Fahd, Secretary of State Warren Christopher shaking hands with Saudi foreign minister, and Saud bin Faisal and Muslims making the pilgrimage to Mecca. Bin Ladin condemns the Saudi rulers for their failure to protect the holy places by allowing American troops, including Jewish and Christian male and female soldiers, to roam freely on the land where the Prophet Muhammad was born and the Koran descended.*

"This land is exceptional because it is the most beloved by Allah. How could it be that the Americans are permitted to wander freely on the prophet's land? Have Muslim peoples lost their faith? Have they forsaken the prophet's religion? Forgive me, Allah, I wash my hands of these [Arab] rulers!"

[Images suggesting the Saudi's regime subservient, do nothing attitude toward the American presence climaxes with the king awarding a medal to President Bill Clinton. Transition from Arabia to West Bank focuses on al-Aqsa mosque, Ariel Sharon's provocative visit there, and resulting *intifada* (Palestinian uprising)]

*Bin Ladin asks:* "Where is the Muslim *umma* and its one billion believers? The *umma* sees and hears that the Koran is being defamed, burned, and used by the Jews as disposable tissues, yet it stands idly by. Jews in occupied Palestine violate and dishonor defenseless Muslim women and imprison those young, brave cubs who have stood up to defend their religion, while their cowardly Arab presidents and kings betray the prophet's path and way."

[Visually, the transition from "Land of the Two Holy Places" to "Palestine" focuses on images of the al-Aqsa mosque in Jerusalem. Recitation of verses from the Koran mentioning al-Aqsa support this. The issue of Palestine is thus raised without discussing or endorsing the political analyses and demands of any Palestinian organization, to protect Muslim women and children from killing and degradation and to defend Islam]

[A highly charged and emotional poem about Israeli soldiers violating the honor of Palestinian girls and women. The poem appeals to the honor of Arab men and calls on them to protect the sanctity of their sisters and mothers, and of children who are killed in their mother's arms. The poem accuses Muslims of passivity and cowardice in the face of what the Jews have been doing in Palestine in the last fifty years.]

"Muslims are blind and deaf to the suffering of their Palestinian brothers and sisters. O Aqsa! O Aqsa!" [Extensive focus on killing of Palestine boy Muhammad Durra and his father.] [His father was not killed.—*Eds.*].

[This entire excerpt focuses on the well-known and frequently recalled killing of a Palestinian boy and his father caught between Israeli soldiers and

Palestinian gunmen. The video and sound editing expertly intensify the emotion of the scene.] *Poem:* "I am the father of Muhammad trying to no avail to protect him from Israeli fire. I tried in vain to warn Israeli troops to stop firing at my son, but the shooting continued and four shots hit my child, who fell dead." [This powerful poem presents Muhammad's father mourning his baby's death and asking his forgiveness for failing to shield him and protect him. The poem uses the killing of Muhammad to attack what the narrator calls the] "cowardly Arab rulers, thieves and cronies, who betrayed Palestine and the Palestinians and sold them out at the altar of material and political gains. Do not count, Muhammad, on Arabs, for they are no different than your assassins, the Jews." [The death of Muhammad, he continues, also exposed the distortion and corruption of the Arab media, interested mainly in nudity, dance, and in distraction of the Arab mind and consciousness. These denunciations of the Arab governments and media are accompanied by images of cheerful American leaders and a clip subtitled] "The army of the Saudi family dances with Christians and Jews during the al-Aqsa intifada."

*Bin Ladin:* "They [the West] have besieged Iraqi children. More than one million Iraqi children have died, as acknowledged by the Christians themselves. In what religion's name do they besiege these innocent children all these long years? Even if their leader, Saddam Hussein, betrayed Allah and his prophet and took the Ba'th Party [the ruling party in Iraq—*Eds.*] as his God in the same manner in which Arab rulers worship and obey their masters in the White House, why do Iraqi children have to be punished? What is their crime? What is the crime of the peoples of Afghanistan to be besieged and sanctioned by the international infidels and the atheist United Nations of which all Arab and Muslim countries are members?" Bin Ladin, tears in his eyes, accuses oppressive and autocratic Arab rulers of being partners and participants in the crusaders' siege of Iraq and Iraqi children. [This speech, with accompanying images of American leaders receiving and being honored by Arab rulers, is calculated to inflame the passions of Arab and Muslim viewers against the United States and its Muslim allies.]

[By following the clip of an Iraqi soldier paying obeisance to Saddam Hussein with images of Sheikh Jabir, the ruler of Kuwait, and King Fahd of Saudi Arabia honoring President Clinton, bin Ladin symbolically erases the battle lines of the Gulf War. The three rulers are equally guilty of betraying Muslims, and the soldier's subordination to Saddam Hussein is made parallel with King Fahd's implied subordination to President Clinton].

*A speech by one of bin Ladin's associates, Sheikh Abu Hafs, following a portrayal of conflict in Kashmir closes reel 1. It recapitulates the presentation of the Muslim world under attack and repeats the opening emphasis on threats to the Muslim holy places in Arabia and Jerusalem. Abu Hafs decries the fact that infidel nations representing crusaders and Jews have attacked the Muslim* umma *and Mus-*

lim countries, have robbed them of their fortunes and resources, and have destroyed them. More important, the infidel nations have violated and controlled the most sacred places in Islam: Mecca, Medina (particularly the Prophet Muhammad's mosque), and the al-Aqsa mosque and Dome of the Rock in Palestine.

## Reel 2: The Causes

The opening of reel 2, "The Causes," goes directly to bin Ladin speaking in the open air, filmed from below as if the cameraman is among the audience. The voices of children are heard in the background, reinforcing the sense that bin Ladin is telling a group of ordinary people about the problems they face and the reasons behind them. "Muslims must examine Allah's book, the Koran, in order to understand their predicament and the causes of their illnesses so that they may find a way out of their entrapment." [After much reflection and search in the Koran, bin Ladin notes that the main problem facing Muslims lies in the love of this world and hatred of death.] "This is the most fundamental reason for the dismal and shameful conditions of the Muslim umma today." Two other sheikhs convey similar messages. First heard is the voice of the Egyptian Sheikh Umar Abd al-Rahman, who was convicted in New York City of conspiracy to carry out acts of terrorism. The label under his picture says that he is a "prisoner in the prisons of America."

[Then comes a known mentor of bin Ladin, Sheikh Abdullah Azzam, a former professor in Jordan with roots in the Muslim Brotherhood who died in the struggle against the Soviet Union in Afghanistan. Bin Ladin calls on Muslims to give up their fear of death.]

[Bin Ladin also calls on Muslims to stop giving excuses for not fighting on behalf of their religion. He castigates Muslims for putting worldly affairs and obligations over the necessity of preserving the Dar al-Islam (the Islamic community). He reminds the believers that their elders were more pious than they are because they understood well that what matters most is not this life but the afterlife.] The image of a street scene in Saudi Arabia symbolizes the easy life he is asking Muslims to put behind them.

Ayman al-Zawahiri, Abu Yasir, and bin Ladin explain the centrality of America to all of the violence Muslims around the world face.

The speeches from which the clips in this excerpt are drawn took place in a conference setting with the three speakers sitting at a long table before a wall-sized map of the world. The occasion evidently took place during the Clinton administration, probably in 1999.

Ayman al-Zawahiri, the founder of Islamic Jihad in Egypt and believed to be a strong influence on bin Ladin's adoption of a strategy of attacking the United States: "America pursues a hypocritical policy toward the Muslim world. America claims to be the champion and protector of human rights, democracy, and liberties, while at the same time forcing on Muslims oppressive and corrupt political regimes. Egypt is a case in point. As you well know, there are about 60,000 political prisoners in Egyptian jails and dozens of death sentences have been carried out. All this takes place with America's supervision, approval, and orders. America has a CIA station as well as an FBI office and a huge embassy in Egypt, and it closely follows what happens in that country. Therefore, America is responsible for everything that happens in Egypt and responsible for human rights violations there, and in other Arab countries as well."

Sheikh Abu Yasir concurs: "[The late Egyptian President Anwar al-] Sadat said that the Americans control 99 percent of the cards of the political game. After succeeding him, [Egyptian President Husni Mubarak said that 100 percent of the cards are in the Americans hands." *Sheikh Yasir accuses Egypt's leaders of sacrificing the country's national and religious interests on the altar of their own personal interests serving the United States.*

*Bin Ladin:* "The American government is independent in name only. We believe that it represents and is controlled by Israel. If we take a look at the most important ministries in the current government [the Clinton administration], such as the defense department and the state department, and the sensitive intelligence services and others, we find that the Jews have the final say in the American government. The Jews manipulate America and use it to execute their designs in the world, particularly in the Muslim world. The U.S. presence in the land of the two holy places [Saudi Arabia] helps the Jews to consolidate their control over the al-Aqsa mosque [in Jerusalem] and protects their back. Thus the American government endangers the survival of its own citizens. Rational people have no doubts that America will lose its status as a great power in the new millennium."

## Reel 3: The Solution

*Reel 3, "The Solution," like reel 2, opens with bin Ladin giving a lesson from religious history. His topic is the migration from Mecca to Medina that Muhammad and his followers made in 622 to find refuge from persecution by the pagan Meccans.*

*Bin Ladin:* "After we have diagnosed the disease, here is the medicine. And the cure in Allah's Book [the Koran]: migration [*hijra*] and holy war [*jihad*]." Bin Ladin calls on Muslim believers to follow the example of the Prophet Muhammad and his *sahaba* [companions] by migrating and joining in the *jihad*. "There is no other way if a Muslim wants the entire religion to be for Allah."

[Bin Ladin speaks of the historical example of *hijra* in the time of Muhammad and praises the Taliban for establishing an Islamic state in Afghanistan]

*Here bin Ladin appears in a tent wearing a camouflage jacket and a white turban. The turban resembles that worn by Tajiks in western Afghanistan rather than that of the eastern Pashtun region. An assault rifle leans against the wall of the tent.*

*He calls on Muslims, especially the* ulama *[religious scholars], the tribal sheikhs, and businessmen, to follow the historical example of* hijra *[flight from a place of idolatry to a place where Islam can be practiced—Eds.] in the time of the Prophet Muhammad and to mobilize the* umma *to protect and preserve their religion now and forever.*

*Bin Ladin praises the Taliban for establishing an authentic Islamic state in Afghanistan and advises Muslims inside and outside the country to support these students. Literally, the word* taliban *signifies "students." He draws the attention of his audience to the importance of establishing an Islamic state or a bridge, regardless of how tiny it is, to spread the message. He cites the example of the Prophet Muhammad in Mecca and how a few hundred migrants* [muhajirun] *changed the course of Muslim history by defeating the great powers of the day. Accordingly, bin Ladin calls on Muslims to support fully and unconditionally the Islamic state in Afghanistan because it raises the flag of* jihad. *Visually, the reference to the defeat of the great powers is accompanied by a scene of the Taliban capturing Kabul, the Afghan capital, and then of the hanging of President Najib, whom the Soviet Union had installed as ruler.*

Subtitle: "In accordance with Allah's *Sharia*, the Commander of the Faithful (Amir al-Muminin) ordered the destruction of the statues of Buddha in Afghanistan, which are still worshiped in this day and age by godless millions without Allah." [The repeated scenes of the statues being blown up and the jaunty song about destroying idols accompanying them seem designed to create a positive impression of Taliban accomplishments. Ascribing the acts to the Commander of the Faithful emphasizes Mullah Umar Muhammad's role as a warrior for Islam against unbelief. The title Amir al-Muminin is synonymous with the title Caliph, used from Muhammad's death in 632 until the abolition of the office by the Turkish Republic, led by Mustafa Kemal Ataturk, in 1923. The title implies political leadership of the entire Muslim community (*umma*). Several conferences held by Muslim representatives after 1923 failed to reach agreement on how to continue this office in an era of European imperialism. In accepting the Taliban designation of Mullah Muhammad Umar, bin Ladin is supporting a restoration of an institution that many jurists considered necessary for a *jihad* to be legal. This is the only scene in the videotape that tries to characterize Taliban rule, other than the brief glimpses of the taking of Kabul and hanging of President Najib shown in reel 3, excerpt 2.]

*After many clips of volunteers undergoing training in Afghanistan, often accompanied by songs, this scene emphasizes the association of the Koran with the warlike cause. While the song calls on men to rise up and fight, the soldiers display their Korans against raised assault rifles.* . . . [The purpose of these scenes is to reinforce the religious purpose of military training. Military officer speaking to formation of troops.]

[This scene is highly motivational and sheds light on the religious influences used to inspire the foot soldiers.] *The officer exhorting his men speaks with a Saudi accent. The placards display the names of squads honoring the dead heroes mentioned by the officer.* "My brothers and my beloved, Allah has given us a great responsibility. We have left our families, our homes, and our nations to fight for Allah and to spread his message, and also to degrade and humiliate the *umma*'s enemies and its oppressors, the monkeys and pigs [America, the Jews, and Arab rulers]. We want to humiliate them and show them how inconsequential and Insignificant they are. You are following in the footsteps of brothers who have given their lives for Allah's sake. These include heroes like Riyadh al-Hajari, Abd al-Aziz Mutham, Khalid al-Said, and Muslih al-Shumrani, who did not hesitate to sacrifice their lives to please Allah. [They were convicted of bombing the Khobar Towers, a building that housed U.S. military personnel in Saudi Arabia, and were beheaded by the Saudi authorities]. My brothers, my beloved: today we are preparing to avenge them and to humiliate the monkeys and pigs and to humble America and the Jews as well. We are preparing ourselves. Let the world know that we are coming."

*Target practice against projected images, including heads of state, followed by visual and audio intimation that bin Ladin is a hero on horseback.*

*The motivational songs accompanying the target practice deal with the beauty of resistance and standing up to the oppressors of the Muslim* umma. *Like most of the training scenes, the emphasis is on small-scale violence, here the shooting of someone at short range with a handgun. The inclusion of a picture of President Clinton as a target invites the viewer to imagine himself a heroic assassin. This climactic moment is followed by a brief speech by bin Ladin that finishes with a visual and audio intimation that bin Ladin is a hero on horseback leading Muslims against the United States and Israel. This scene is invested with a great deal of religious symbolism: the Islamic dress, the Arabian horses, the desert, and the believers going on* hijra. *The song is in the style of Asir province in southwestern Arabia, near the Yemeni homeland of bin Ladin's family. Boys in "School for Those Who Make the* Hijra" *expressing support for bin Ladin's message.*

*This is the start of a lengthy episode showing little boys undergoing training on the same obstacle course earlier used by soldiers. It begins with the boys in school reciting the Koran and then moves to showing them marching lightheartedly in camouflage suits.*

[Showing young boys in training implies that the struggle will last for many years and suggests to older viewers that they should show similar dedication. This role of young boys reflects bin Ladin's praise of brave young "cubs" in reel 1, excerpt 3, and the later depiction of a heavily armed Israeli soldier fleeing a boy throwing stones in reel 3, excerpt 12.]

*A boy who is apparently bin Ladin's young son recites a poem in which he denounces Zionism for killing Palestinian youngsters. The poem also denounces Muslim governments for being cronies of the West and for their failure to protect Arab and Muslim children.* "These infidel Arab rulers mask their inaction by gathering in conferences without accomplishing anything."

*Accompanying scenes appear to be a meeting of the Arab League.*

[The contrast between idealistic youth and incompetent Arab rulers seems intended to inspire potential recruits to join the struggle for the sake of the younger generation, which has not yet lost its idealism.]

*A speech by bin Ladin opens the final segment of reel 3, entitled "Jihad." It is followed immediately by scenes of Muslim fighters combating Russian troops in Chechnya.*

*Bin Ladin:* "This humiliation and atheism has ruined and blinded the lands and peoples of Islam. The only way to destroy this atheism is by *jihad*, fighting, and bombings that bring martyrdom [i.e., suicide bombings]. Only blood will wipe out the shame and the dishonor inflicted on Muslims. Let us pray that you and we agree on what needs to be done so that when face our Creator, he will bless us and be content with us."

*Bin Ladin, in military costume, begins this excerpt and continues speaking over a scene of a Soviet armored personnel carrier being destroyed by Muslim fighters in Chechnya, illustrating his point that poorly armed but dedicated men can take on better-equipped adversaries. The recitation of a passage from the Koran leads into Bin Ladin resuming his speech.*

*Bin Ladin:* "Using very meager resources and military means, the Afghan *mujahidin* demolished one of the most important human myths in history and the biggest military apparatus. We no longer fear the so-called Great Powers. We believe that America is much weaker than Russia; and our brothers who fought in Somalia told us that they were astonished to observe how weak, impotent, and cowardly the American soldier is. As soon as eighty American troops were killed, they fled in the dark as fast they could, after making a great of noise about the new international order. America's nightmares in Vietnam and Lebanon [referring to the suicide attacks on the U.S. embassy and Marine barracks in the 1980s] will pale by comparison with the forthcoming victory in al-Hijaz."

[Al-Hijaz is the western province of Saudi Arabia where Mecca and Medina are located. He appears to be referring to expelling the U.S. military presence from Arabia, but U.S. forces are normally stationed in the eastern provinces. By specifying al-Hijaz, bin Ladin is misleading naive viewers into thinking that American troops are in physical control of Mecca and Medina.]

[Bin Ladin focuses in this long scene on the United States as a target of his *jihad*. He heaps praise on the martyrs who attacked American targets in Saudi Arabia and East Africa. They exemplify his assertion that America is weak and can be brought down by dedicated fighters with less sophisticated weapons.]

"Do people not believe that the home of the prophet and of his grandchildren is occupied and under American–Jewish control? Thus to fight Americans is fundamental to the Muslim faith and *tawhid* [affirmation of the oneness of God]. We have incited the *umma* against this angry occupier [the Americans] to expel it from the land of the two holy places. Some of the youth [*al-shabab*, an evocative term used for young men who are willing to fight] have responded positively to our incitement. These included Khalid al-Said, Riyadh al-Hajari, Abd al-Aziz Mutham, and Muslih al-Shumrani, who have made us proud and have made us stand tall because they wiped out a large measure of the dishonor inflicted on us as a result of the Saudi government's collusion with the U.S. in allowing the Americans to trample on Allah's lands and the land of the two holy places. We view these *shabab* as great heroes who imitated our prophet. We incited, and they responded. We hope that they are in heaven. The bombings and explosions [against the two U.S. embassies] in East Africa found Muslims all over the world happy and sympathetic to attacking the Americans, as reported by the international media. According to international intelligence reports, the attacks on the U.S. embassies were as painful as the suicide bombing of the Marine barracks in Lebanon [in the early 1980s]. The reason for bombing the U.S. embassy in Nairobi lay in the fact that it organized the brutal American invasion against the Somali people, in which 13,000 of our brothers, sisters, and sons were killed. The U.S. embassy in Nairobi also runs the affairs of that African country and organizes conspiracies to partition Sudan. The embassy has the largest CIA station in East Africa. Thanks to Allah, the attack on that embassy was successful to a large degree. We wanted the Americans to taste what we have tasted in Sabra and Shatila [two Palestinian camps attacked by pro–Israeli right-wing Lebanese elements; 1,800 Palestinian civilians were killed], in Dair Yasin [a Palestinian village subjected to a massacre by Israeli forces during the 1948 war between Israel and the Arabs], in Qana [a village in southern Lebanon bombarded by the Israeli army], in Hebron [the site of an attack on Muslim worshippers by an Israeli settler], and in other areas. It is clear that the wave of celebration and happiness that swept the Muslim world in the aftermath of the attacks on the two U.S. embassies may be explained by the fact that Muslims believe that the Jews and America have overplayed their hand in humiliating, degrading, and punishing them. Muslims have failed to convince their own governments to protect them and defend their religion. These attacks on American targets are legitimate public reactions by the Muslim *shabab*, who are willing to sacrifice their lives to defend their people and Islam. For all these reasons, I view these great men with the utmost respect and humility. They have wiped away the shame from the *umma*'s face."

[Following bin Ladin's speech a brief clip shows his mentor, Sheikh Abdullah Azzam, speaking about terrorism]:

"We are terrorists, and terrorism is our friend and companion. Let the West and East know that we are terrorists and that we are terrifying as well.

We shall do our best in preparing to terrorize Allah's enemy and our own. Thus terrorism is an obligation in Allah's religion."

[The placement of this speech toward the climax of the segment on fighting against America, and of the tape as a whole, implies that the Americans in particular should be fearful of the terrorism Sheikh Azzam is praising.]

[The demonstration of American vulnerability concludes with bin Ladin reciting the poem about the bombing of the USS *Cole* with which the tape began.]

*Scenes from current intifada emphasizing youths with stones putting Israeli soldiers on the run.*

*Bin Ladin:* "To our brothers in Palestine we say that the blood of your children is the same as the blood of our own [children], and your blood is the same as ours. We swear by Almighty Allah that we will not disappoint you until we achieve victory or we meet our creator."

*The following scenes from the* intifada *[Palestinian uprising—Eds.], accompanied by a sprightly song—"Our war is in the streets, with stones and knives"— concentrate on Palestinians fighting in the streets and on Israeli soldiers running away from boys with stones. As a voice intones religious verses, the segment ends with the label "The Intifada Continues."*

[The long and carefully edited scene of an Israeli soldier pursuing a Palestinian boy until he turns and throws a stone lends a strong David-defeating-Goliath quality to this closing episode. The fact that the Israeli soldier is deliberately refraining from shooting the boy and is returning to take shelter behind an armored personnel carrier, as is evident in a later continuation of the scene, does not lessen the impact of the scene as edited. In the overall structure of the tape, these images of Palestinians fighting back, contrasted with the images of Palestinians being attacked and abused shown in reel 1, are intended to give the viewer a feeling of hope that dedication can triumph over seemingly hopeless odds.]

# 5

## AL-QA'IDA'S

## WAR ON AMERICA

This chapter deals with al-Qa'ida attacks prior to September 11, 2001, giving a sense of the organization's structure, some of the main individuals involved, and the tactics used in such operations.

As part of the war against terrorism following the September 11 attacks, the FBI released a special list of the twenty-two most wanted terrorists who had been involved in earlier assaults on American citizens and interests. Most of them were al-Qa'ida members, with Usama bin Ladin in first place, and their names appear in other documents in this chapter regarding specific operations and attacks. Members of other groups, notably Lebanese Hizballah, were wanted in connection with additional attacks, including the 1993 bombing of the World Trade Center and the 1996 bombing of the Khobar Towers in Saudi Arabia.

The most devastating al-Qa'ida attack outside the United States was the August 1998 bombings of the U.S. embassies in Nairobi, Kenya, and Dar es Salaam, Tanzania. The lengthy planning for these attacks is revealed in a letter written by one of the suspects, Haroun Fazul, a full year before they occurred. He discusses the existence of an al-Qa'ida cell in Kenya and expresses fear that cell members are in danger of being discovered by authorities.

But such concerns, tragically, were unfounded. As described by a report from the U.S. Government Accountability Review Board, the bomb in Nairobi killed 213 people, including 12 Americans. The Dar es Salaam attack killed 11 people, and although no Americans were among the fatalities, they were among the 85 injured. The report notes that a number of earlier intelligence reports cited alleged threats against several U.S. diplomatic and other targets, including the U.S. embassy in Nairobi, but that there were no tips immediately before the actual bombing.

Many details of the planning of this attack came out during a court case, *The United States v. bin Ladin*. Some of the al-Qa'ida members among the defendants provided critical evidence for the prosecution. The earlier preparations for the attack are described by Ali A. Muhammad in his testimony of October 2000. The al-Qa'ida member says that in late 1993 bin Ladin asked him to conduct surveillance of American, British, French, and Israeli targets in Nairobi, including the U.S. embassy there.

The events leading up to the actual attack are provided in detail by the testimony of John Michael Anticev, an FBI agent sent to Africa soon after the bombings, who presents his interrogation of one of the defendants, Muhammad Sadeh Odeh. Odeh observed all the preparations for the bombing down to the last detail, although he did not know the actual target until the last minute.

The British Government's report on bin Ladin's involvement in September 11 also provides evidence on the East African attacks, giving a chronology of the plans and execution of the operation.

A major element in the conflict between bin Ladin and the United States was the U.S. attempt to deny him the safe haven and secure base of operations provided by the Taliban government in Afghanistan. In addition, the Taliban's internal policies of repression were also opposed by the United States. On July 6, 1999, President Bill Clinton issued an executive order imposing full economic sanctions on the Taliban. This was followed several months later by UN Security Council Resolution 1267, which imposed mandatory sanctions against Taliban-controlled assets and international airline flights to Afghanistan until bin Ladin was brought to justice. It was believed that such actions would eventually result in the Taliban's downfall, said Karl F. Inderfurth, the deputy assistant secretary of state for South Asian affairs, in his July 20, 2000, testimony on the Taliban: "We believe the Taliban regime has reached its high-water mark. This is a regime which, by its behavior at home and abroad, has isolated itself from almost the entire world, and increasingly from its own people. . . . I believe our strategy of pressure on the Taliban, support for alternative Afghan voices, and concrete cooperation with other countries on these issues can move us closer to that common objective."

One unsuccessful al-Qa'ida operation that showed its growing orientation toward launching attacks in the United States was an attempt to launch assaults during the millennium celebrations. In court testimony of July 2001, Ahmad Ressam, an al-Qa'ida member, describes a plan to bomb the Los Angeles airport. He was arrested with a car full of explosives in Port Angeles, Washington. Although the operation failed, this account shows how small and simple can be the forces needed for a major terrorist attack.

In a report before the September 11 attacks, George J. Tenet, the director of the CIA, described the status of the U.S. counterterrorism program in his February 7, 2001, congressional testimony. The United States and its allies have scored successes against terrorist groups, he says, with "a robust counter terrorism program that has preempted, disrupted, and defeated international terrorists and their activities." Terrorists have been kept off balance, Tenet asserted. But he was wrong.

# Most Wanted (October 10, 2001)

FEDERAL BUREAU OF INVESTIGATION

## 1. Usama Bin Ladin

*Aliases:* Usama bin Muhammad bin Ladin, Sheikh Usama bin Ladin, the Prince, the Emir, Abu Abdallah, Mujahid Sheikh, Hajj, the Director

### Description

Date of Birth Used: 1957     Hair: Brown
Place of Birth: Saudi Arabia     Eyes: Brown
Height: 6'4" to 6'6"     Sex: Male
Weight: Approximately 160 pounds     Complexion: Olive
Build: Thin     Citizenship: Saudi Arabian
Language: Arabic (probably Pashtu)
Scars and Marks: None known

*Remarks:* Bin Ladin is believed to be in Afghanistan. He is left-handed and walks with a cane.

### Caution

Usama bin Ladin is wanted in connection with the August 7, 1998, bombings of the United States embassies in Dar es Salaam, Tanzania, and Nairobi, Kenya. These attacks killed over 200 people. In addition, bin Ladin is a suspect in other terrorist attacks throughout the world.

### Reward

The Rewards For Justice Program, United States Department of State, is offering a reward of up to $25 million for information leading directly to the apprehension or conviction of Usama bin Ladin. An additional $2 million is being offered through a program developed and funded by the Airline Pilots Association and the Air Transport Association. SHOULD BE CONSIDERED ARMED AND DANGEROUS

## 2. Ayman Al-Zawahiri

*Wanted For:* MURDER OF U.S. NATIONALS OUTSIDE THE UNITED STATES; CONSPIRACY TO MURDER U.S. NATIONALS OUTSIDE THE UNITED STATES; ATTACK ON A FEDERAL FACILITY RESULTING IN DEATH

*Aliases:* Abu Muhammad, Abu Fatima, Muhammad Ibrahim, Abu Abdallah, Abu al-Mu'iz, The Doctor, The Teacher, Nur, Ustaz, Abu Mohammed, Abu Mohammed Nur al-Deen, Abdel Muaz, Dr. Ayman al Zawahiri

### Description

Date of Birth Used: June 19, 1951      Hair: Brown/Black
Place of Birth: Egypt      Eyes: Dark
Height: Unknown      Sex: Male
Weight: Unknown      Complexion: Olive
Build: Unknown      Citizenship: Egyptian
Languages: Arabic, French
Scars and Marks: None known

*Remarks:* Al-Zawahiri is a physician and the founder of the Egyptian Islamic Jihad. This organization opposes the secular Egyptian Government and seeks its overthrow through violent means. Al-Zawahiri is believed to now serve as an advisor and doctor to Usama bin Ladin and is currently thought to be in Afghanistan.

### Caution

Ayman al-Zawahiri has been indicted for his alleged role in the August 7, 1998, bombings of the U.S. embassies in Dar es Salaam, Tanzania, and Nairobi, Kenya.

## 3.  Abdelkarim Hussein Mohamed Al-Nasser

*Wanted For:* CONSPIRACY TO KILL U.S. NATIONALS; CONSPIRACY TO MURDER U.S. EMPLOYEES; CONSPIRACY TO USE WEAPONS OF MASS DESTRUCTION AGAINST U.S. NATIONALS; CONSPIRACY TO DESTROY PROPERTY OF THE U.S.; CONSPIRACY TO ATTACK NATIONAL DEFENSE UTILITIES; BOMBING RESULTING IN DEATH; USE OF WEAPONS OF MASS DESTRUCTION AGAINST U.S. NATIONALS; MURDER WHILE USING DESTRUCTIVE DEVICE DURING A CRIME OF VIOLENCE; MURDER OF FEDERAL EMPLOYEES; ATTEMPTED MURDER OF FEDERAL EMPLOYEES

*Aliases:* None known

## Description

Date of Birth Used: Unknown    Hair: Black
Place of Birth: Al Ihsa, Saudi Arabia    Eyes: Brown
Height: 5'8"    Sex: Male
Weight: 170 pounds    Complexion: Olive
Build: Unknown    Citizenship: Saudi Arabian
Languages: Arabic, Farsi
Scars and Marks: None known

*Remarks:* None

## Caution

Abdelkarim Hussein Mohamed al-Nasser has been indicted in the Eastern District of Virginia for the June 25, 1996, bombing of the Khobar Towers military housing complex in Dhahran, Kingdom of Saudi Arabia.

## 4. Abdullah Ahmed Abdullah

*Wanted For:* MURDER OF U.S. NATIONALS OUTSIDE THE UNITED STATES; CONSPIRACY TO MURDER U.S. NATIONALS OUTSIDE THE UNITED STATES; ATTACK ON A FEDERAL FACILITY RESULTING IN DEATH; CONSPIRACY TO KILL U.S. NATIONALS, TO MURDER, TO DESTROY BUILDINGS AND PROPERTY OF THE UNITED STATES, AND TO DESTROY THE NATIONAL DEFENSE UTILITIES OF THE UNITED STATES

*Aliases:* Abu Mohamed Al-Masri, Saleh, Abu Mariam

## Description

Date of Birth Used: Approximately 1963    Hair: Dark
Place of Birth: Egypt    Eyes: Dark
Height: Approximately 5'8"    Sex: Male
Weight: Unknown    Complexion: Olive
Build: Medium    Citizenship: Egyptian
Language: Arabic
Scars and Marks: Abdullah has a scar on the right side of his lower lip.

*Remarks:* Abdullah fled Nairobi, Kenya on August 6, 1998, and went to Karachi, Pakistan. He is believed to currently be in Afghanistan. He may wear a mustache.

*Caution*

Abdullah Ahmed Abdullah has been indicted for his alleged involvement in the August 7, 1998, bombings of the United States embassies in Dar es Salaam, Tanzania, and Nairobi, Kenya.

## 5. Muhsin Musa Matwalli Atwah

*Wanted For:* CONSPIRACY TO KILL UNITED STATES NATIONALS, TO MURDER, TO DESTROY BUILDINGS AND PROPERTY OF THE UNITED STATES, AND TO DESTROY NATIONAL DEFENSE UTILITIES OF THE UNITED STATES

*Aliases:* Abdul Rahman, Abdul Rahman Al-Muhajir, Abdel Rahman, Mohammed K. A. Al-Namer

*Description*

Date of Birth Used: June 19, 1964    Hair: Dark, but graying
Place of Birth: Egypt    Eyes: Dark
Height: Approximately 5'3" to 5'7"    Sex: Male
Weight: Unknown    Complexion: Olive
Build: Medium    Citizenship: Egyptian
Language: Arabic
Scars and Marks: None known

*Remarks:* Atwah is believed to currently be in Afghanistan.

*Caution*

Muhsin Musa Matwalli Atwah is wanted in connection with the August 7, 1998, bombings of the United States embassies in Dar es Salaam, Tanzania, and Nairobi, Kenya.

## 6. Ali Atwa

*Wanted For:* CONSPIRACY TO COMMIT AIRCRAFT PIRACY, TO COMMIT HOSTAGE TAKING, TO COMMIT AIR PIRACY RESULTING IN MURDER, TO INTERFERE WITH A FLIGHT CREW, TO PLACE A DESTRUCTIVE DEVICE ABOARD AN AIRCRAFT, TO HAVE EXPLOSIVE DEVICES ABOUT THE PERSON ON AN AIRCRAFT, AND TO ASSAULT PASSENGERS AND CREW; AIR PIRACY RESULTING IN MURDER; AIR PIRACY; HOSTAGE TAKING; INTERFERENCE WITH FLIGHT CREW; AND PLACING EXPLOSIVES ABOARD AIRCRAFT; PLACING DESTRUCTIVE DEVICES ABOARD AIRCRAFT; ASSAULT ABOARD AIRCRAFT WITH INTENT

TO HIJACK WITH A DANGEROUS WEAPON AND RESULTING IN SERIOUS BODILY INJURY; AIDING AND ABETTING

*Aliases:* Ammar Mansour Bouslim, Hassan Rostom Salim

## Description

Date of Birth Used: Approximately 1960     Hair: Unknown
Place of Birth: Lebanon     Eyes: Brown
Height: 5'8"     Sex: Male
Weight: 150 pounds     Citizenship: Lebanese
Build: Medium
Language: Arabic
Scars and Marks: None known

*Remarks:* Atwa is an alleged member of the terrorist organization Lebanese Hizballah. He is thought to be in Lebanon.

## Caution

Ali Atwa was indicted for his role and participation in the June 14, 1985, hijacking of a commercial airliner [to Beirut] which resulted in the assault on various passengers and crew members, and the murder of one U.S. citizen.

## 7. Anas Al-Liby

*Wanted For:* CONSPIRACY TO KILL U.S. NATIONALS, TO MURDER, TO DESTROY BUILDINGS AND PROPERTY OF THE UNITED STATES, AND TO DESTROY THE NATIONAL DEFENSE UTILITIES OF THE UNITED STATES
*Aliases:* Anas Al-Sabai, Anas Al-Libi, Nazih Al-Raghie, Nazih Abdul Hamed Al-Raghie

## Description

Dates of Birth Used: March 30, 1964; May 14, 1964     Hair: Dark
Place of Birth: Tripoli, Libya     Eyes: Dark
Height: 5'10" to 6'2"     Sex: Male
Weight: Unknown     Complexion: Olive
Build: Medium     Citizenship: Libyan
Languages: Arabic, English
Scars and Marks: Al-Liby has a scar on the left side of his face.

*Remarks:* Al-Liby recently lived in the United Kingdom, where he has political asylum. He is believed to currently be in Afghanistan. Al-Liby usually wears a full beard.

## Caution

Anas al-Liby is wanted in connection with the August 7, 1998, bombings of the United States embassies in Dar es Salaam, Tanzania, and Nairobi, Kenya.

## 8. Ahmed Khalfan Ghailani

*Wanted For:* MURDER OF U.S. NATIONALS OUTSIDE THE UNITED STATES; CONSPIRACY TO MURDER U.S. NATIONALS OUTSIDE THE UNITED STATES; ATTACK ON A FEDERAL FACILITY RESULTING IN DEATH
*Aliases:* Ahmad Khalafan Ghilani, Ahmed Khalfan Ahmed, Abubakar K. Ahmed, Abubakary K. Ahmed, Abubakar Ahmed, Abu Bakr Ahmad, A. Ahmed, Ahmed Khalfan, Ahmed Khalfan Ali, Abubakar Khalfan Ahmed, Ahmed Ghailani, Ahmad Al Tanzani, Abu Khabar, Abu Bakr, Abubakary Khalfan Ahmed Ghailani, Mahafudh Abubakar Ahmed Abdallah Hussein, Shariff Omar Mohammed, "Foopie," "Fupi," "Ahmed the Tanzanian"

## Description

Dates of Birth Used: March 14, 1974; April 13, 1974; April 14, 1974; August 1, 1970     Hair: Black
Place of Birth: Zanzibar, Tanzania     Eyes: Brown
Height: 5'3" to 5'4"     Sex: Male
Weight: 150 pounds     Complexion: Dark
Build: Unknown     Citizenship: Tanzanian
Language: Swahili
Scars and Marks: None known

*Remarks:* None

## Caution

Ahmed Ghailani was indicted in the Southern District of New York, on December 16, 1998, for his alleged involvement in the August 7, 1998, bombings of the United States embassies in Dar es Salaam, Tanzania, and Nairobi, Kenya.

## 9. Hasan Izz-Al-Din

*Wanted For:* CONSPIRACY TO COMMIT AIRCRAFT PIRACY, TO COMMIT HOSTAGE TAKING, TO COMMIT AIR PIRACY RESULTING IN MURDER, TO INTERFERE WITH A FLIGHT

CREW, TO PLACE A DESTRUCTIVE DEVICE ABOARD AN AIRCRAFT, TO HAVE EXPLOSIVE
DEVICES ABOUT THE PERSON ON AN AIRCRAFT, AND TO ASSAULT PASSENGERS AND
CREW; AIR PIRACY RESULTING IN MURDER; AIR PIRACY; HOSTAGE TAKING; INTERFER-
ENCE WITH FLIGHT CREW; AND PLACING EXPLOSIVES ABOARD AIRCRAFT; PLACING
DESTRUCTIVE DEVICES ABOARD AIRCRAFT; ASSAULT ABOARD AIRCRAFT WITH INTENT
TO HIJACK WITH A DANGEROUS WEAPON AND RESULTING IN SERIOUS BODILY INJURY;
AIDING AND ABETTING
*Aliases:* Ahmed Garbaya, Samir Salwwan, Sa-id

## Description

Date of Birth Used: 1963      Hair: Black
Place of Birth: Lebanon      Eyes: Black
Height: 5'9" to 5'11"      Sex: Male
Weight: 145 to 150 pounds      Citizenship: Lebanese
Build: Slender
Language: Arabic
Scars and Marks: None known

*Remarks:* Izz-al-Din is an alleged member of the terrorist organization Lebanese
Hizballah. He is thought to be in Lebanon.

## Caution

Hasan Izz-al-Din was indicted for his role in planning and participation in the
June 14, 1985, hijacking of a commercial airliner which resulted in the assault
on various passengers and crew members, and the murder of one U.S. citizen.

## 10. Ahmed Mohammed Hamed Ali

*Wanted For:* CONSPIRACY TO KILL UNITED STATES NATIONALS, TO MURDER, TO
DESTROY BUILDINGS AND PROPERTY OF THE UNITED STATES, AND TO DESTROY NA-
TIONAL DEFENSE UTILITIES OF THE UNITED STATES
*Aliases:* Shuaib, Abu Islam Al-Surir, Ahmed Ahmed, Ahmed The Egyptian,
Ahmed Hemed, Hamed Ali, Ahmed Shieb, Abu Islam, Ahmed Mohammed
Ali, Ahmed Hamed, Ahmed Mohammed Abdurehman, Abu Khadiijah, Abu
Fatima, Ahmad Al-Masri

## Description

Date of Birth Used: Approximately 1965      Hair: Dark
Place of Birth: Egypt      Eyes: Dark
Height: Approximately 5'6" to 5'8"      Sex: Male

Weight: Unknown    Complexion: Olive
Build: Medium    Citizenship: Egyptian
Language: Arabic
Scars and Marks: None known

*Remarks:* Ali may have formal training in agriculture and may have worked in this field. He lived in Kenya until fleeing that country on August 2, 1998, to Karachi, Pakistan. He is believed to currently be in Afghanistan.

## Caution

Ahmed Mohammed Hamed Ali is wanted in connection with the August 7, 1998, bombings of the United States embassies in Dar es Salaam, Tanzania, and Nairobi, Kenya.

## 11. Fazul Abdullah Mohammed

*Wanted For:* MURDER OF U.S. NATIONALS OUTSIDE THE UNITED STATES; CONSPIRACY TO MURDER U.S. NATIONALS OUTSIDE THE UNITED STATES; ATTACK ON A FEDERAL FACILITY RESULTING IN DEATH
*Aliases:* Abdallah Fazul, Abdalla Fazul, Abdallah Mohammed Fazul, Fazul Abdilahi Mohammed, Fazul Adballah, Fazul Abdalla, Fazul Mohammed, Haroon, Harun, Haroon Fazul, Harun Fazul, Fadil Abdallah Muhamad, Fadhil Haroun, Abu Seif Al Sudani, Abu Aisha, Abu Luqman, Fadel Abdallah Mohammed Ali, Fouad Mohammed

## Description

Dates of Birth Used: August 25, 1972; December 25, 1974; February 25, 1974
Hair: Black
Place of Birth: Moroni, Comoros Islands    Eyes: Brown
Height: 5'3" to 5'5"    Sex: Male
Weight: 120 to 140 pounds    Complexion: Dark
Build: Unknown    Citizenship: Comoros, Kenyan
Languages: French, Swahili, Arabic, English, Comoran
Scars and Marks: None known

*Remarks:* Mohammed likes to wear baseball caps and tends to dress casually. He is very good with computers.

## Caution

Fazul Abdullah Mohammed was indicted on September 17, 1998, in the Southern District of New York, for his alleged involvement in the bombings of the

United States embassies in Dar es Salaam, Tanzania, and Nairobi, Kenya, on August 7, 1998.

## 12. Imad Fayez Mugniyah

*Wanted For:* CONSPIRACY TO COMMIT AIRCRAFT PIRACY, TO COMMIT HOSTAGE TAK-ING, TO COMMIT AIR PIRACY RESULTING IN MURDER, TO INTERFERE WITH A FLIGHT CREW, TO PLACE A DESTRUCTIVE DEVICE ABOARD AN AIRCRAFT, TO HAVE EXPLOSIVE DEVICES ABOUT THE PERSON ON AN AIRCRAFT, AND TO ASSAULT PASSENGERS AND CREW; AIR PIRACY RESULTING IN MURDER; AIR PIRACY; HOSTAGE TAKING; INTERFER-ENCE WITH FLIGHT CREW; AND PLACING EXPLOSIVES ABOARD AIRCRAFT; PLACING DESTRUCTIVE DEVICE ABOARD AIRCRAFT; ASSAULT ABOARD AIRCRAFT WITH INTENT TO HIJACK WITH A DANGEROUS WEAPON AND RESULTING IN SERIOUS BODILY INJURY; AIDING AND ABETTING
*Alias:* Hajj

### Description

Date of Birth Used: 1962      Hair: Brown
Place of Birth: Lebanon       Eyes: Unknown
Height: 5'7"      Sex: Male
Weight: 145 to 150 pounds      Citizenship: Lebanese
Build: Unknown
Language: Arabic
Scars and Marks: None known

*Remarks:* Mugniyah is the alleged head of the security apparatus for the terrorist organization, Lebanese Hizballah. He is thought to be in Lebanon.

### Caution

Imad Fayez Mugniyah was indicted for his role in planning and participation in the June 14, 1985, hijacking of a commercial airliner which resulted in the assault on various passengers and crew members, and the murder of one U.S. citizen.

## 13. Mustafa Mohamed Fadhil

*Wanted For:* MURDER OF U.S. NATIONALS OUTSIDE THE UNITED STATES; CONSPIRACY TO MURDER U.S. NATIONALS OUTSIDE THE UNITED STATES; ATTACK ON A FEDERAL FACILITY RESULTING IN DEATH
*Aliases:* Moustafa Ali Elbishy, Mustafa Mohammed, Mustafa Fazul, Hussein,

Hassan Ali, Mustafa Muhamad Fadil, Abd Al Wakil Al Masri, Abu Anis, Abu Yussrr, Hassan Ali, Nu Man, Khalid, Abu Jihad, Abu Jihad al-Nubi

## Description

Date of Birth Used: June 23, 1976    Hair: Black, short and curly
Place of Birth: Cairo, Egypt    Eyes: Dark
Height: 5'3" to 5'5"    Sex: Male
Weight: 120 to 140 pounds    Complexion: Olive
Build: Unknown    Citizenship: Egyptian, Kenyan
Languages: Arabic, Swahili, reads English
Scars and Marks: None known

*Remarks:* None

## Caution

Khaflan Khamis Mohamed Khaflan Khamis Mohamed was indicted in the Southern District of New York, on December 16, 1998, for his alleged involvement in the August 7, 1998, bombings of the U.S. embassies in Dar es Salaam, Tanzania, and Nairobi, Kenya, and for conspiring to kill U.S. nationals.

## 14. Sheikh Ahmed Salim Swedan

*Wanted For:* MURDER OF U.S. NATIONALS OUTSIDE THE UNITED STATES; CONSPIRACY TO MURDER U.S. NATIONALS OUTSIDE THE UNITED STATES; ATTACK ON A FEDERAL FACILITY RESULTING IN DEATH
*Aliases:* Sheikh Ahmad Salem Suweidan, Sheikh Ahmed Salem Swedan, Sheikh Swedan, Sheikh Bahamadi, Ahmed Ally, Bahamad, Sheik Bahamad, Ahmed the Tall

## Description

Dates of Birth Used: April 9, 1969; April 9, 1960    Hair: Black
Place of Birth: Mombasa, Kenya    Eyes: Brown
Height: 5'8" to 6'0"    Sex: Male
Weight: 175 pounds    Complexion: Dark
Build: Unknown    Citizenship: Kenyan
Languages: Arabic, Swahili, English
Scars and Marks: None known

*Remarks:* Swedan sometimes wears a light beard or moustache and has, in the past, managed a trucking business in Kenya.

## Caution

Sheikh Ahmed Salim Swedan was indicted on December 16, 1998, in the Southern District of New York, for his alleged involvement in the August 7, 1998, bombings of the United States embassies in Dar es Salaam, Tanzania, and Nairobi, Kenya, and for conspiring to kill U.S. nationals.

## 15. Abdul Rahman Yasin

*Wanted For:* DAMAGE BY MEANS OF FIRE OR AN EXPLOSIVE; DAMAGE BY MEANS OF FIRE OR AN EXPLOSIVE TO U.S. PROPERTY; TRANSPORT IN INTERSTATE COMMERCE AN EXPLOSIVE; DESTRUCTION OF MOTOR VEHICLES OR MOTOR VEHICLE FACILITIES; CONSPIRACY TO COMMIT OFFENSE OR DEFRAUD THE U.S.; AIDING AND ABETTING; PENALTY OF DEATH OR LIFE IMPRISONMENT WHEN DEATH RESULTS; ASSAULT OF A FEDERAL OFFICER IN THE LINE OF DUTY; COMMISSION OF A CRIME OF VIOLENCE THROUGH THE USE OF A DEADLY WEAPON OR DEVICE
*Aliases:* Abdul Rahman Said Yasin, Aboud Yasin, Abdul Rahman S. Taha, Abdul Rahman S. Taher

## Description

Date of Birth Used: April 10, 1960    Hair: Black
Place of Birth: Bloomington, Indiana    Eyes: Brown
Height: 5'10"    Sex: Male
Weight: 180 pounds    Complexion: Olive
Build: Unknown    Citizenship: American
Languages: Unknown
Scars and Marks: Yasin possibly has a chemical burn scar on his right thigh.

*Remarks:* Yasin is an epileptic.

## Caution

Abdul Rahman Yasin is wanted for his alleged participation in the terrorist bombing of the World Trade Center, New York City, on February 26, 1993, which resulted in six deaths, the wounding of numerous individuals, and the significant destruction of property and commerce.

## 16. Fahid Mohammed Ally Msalam

*Wanted For:* MURDER OF U.S. NATIONALS OUTSIDE THE UNITED STATES; CONSPIRACY TO MURDER U.S. NATIONALS OUTSIDE THE UNITED STATES; ATTACK ON A FEDERAL FACILITY RESULTING IN DEATH

*Aliases:* Fahid Mohammed Ally, Fahid Mohammed Ali Musalaam, Fahid Mohammed Ali Msalam, Fahid Muhamad Ali Salem, Mohammed Ally Msalam, Usama Al-Kini, Fahad Ally Msalam

## Description

Date of Birth Used: February 19, 1976      Hair: Black, curly
Place of Birth: Mombasa, Kenya      Eyes: Brown
Height: 5'6" to 5'8"      Sex: Male
Weight: 160 to 170 pounds      Complexion: Dark
Build: Unknown      Citizenship: Kenyan
Languages: Arabic, Swahili, English
Scars and Marks: None known

*Remarks:* Msalam sometimes wears a light beard or moustache and has, in the past, worked as a clothing vendor.

## Caution

Fahid Msalam was indicted on December 16, 1998, in the Southern District of New York, for his alleged involvement in the August 7, 1998, bombings of the United States embassies in Dar es Salaam, Tanzania, and Nairobi, Kenya, and for conspiring to kill U.S. nationals.

## 17. Ahmad Ibrahim Al-Mughassil

*Wanted For:* CONSPIRACY TO KILL U.S. NATIONALS; CONSPIRACY TO MURDER U.S. EMPLOYEES; CONSPIRACY TO USE WEAPONS OF MASS DESTRUCTION AGAINST U.S. NATIONALS; CONSPIRACY TO DESTROY PROPERTY OF THE U.S.; CONSPIRACY TO ATTACK NATIONAL DEFENSE UTILITIES; BOMBING RESULTING IN DEATH; USE OF WEAPONS OF MASS DESTRUCTION AGAINST U.S. NATIONALS; MURDER WHILE USING DESTRUCTIVE DEVICE DURING A CRIME OF VIOLENCE; MURDER OF FEDERAL EMPLOYEES; ATTEMPTED MURDER OF FEDERAL EMPLOYEES
*Alias:* Abu Omran

## Description

Date of Birth Used: June 26, 1967      Hair: Black
Place of Birth: Qatif—Bab al-Shamal, Saudi Arabia      Eyes: Brown
Height: 5'4"      Sex: Male
Weight: 145 pounds      Complexion: Olive
Build: Unknown      Citizenship: Saudi Arabian

Languages: Arabic, Farsi
Scars and Marks: None known

*Remarks:* None

## Caution

Ahmad Ibrahim al-Mughassil has been indicted in the Eastern District of Virginia for the June 25, 1996, bombing of the Khobar Towers military housing complex in Dhahran, Kingdom of Saudi Arabia.

## 18. Khalid Shaikh Mohammed

*Wanted For:* CONSPIRACY TO KILL NATIONALS OF THE UNITED STATES
*Aliases:* Ashraf Refaat Nabith Henin, Khalid Adbul Wadood, Salem Ali, Fahd Bin Adballah Bin Khalid

## Description

Dates of Birth Used: April 14, 1965; March 1, 1964        Hair: Black
Place of Birth: Kuwait      Eyes: Brown
Height: Medium      Sex: Male
Weight: Slightly Overweight      Complexion: Olive
Build: Unknown      Citizenship: Kuwaiti
Language: Unknown
Scars and Marks: None known

*Remarks:* Mohammed is known to wear either a full beard or a trimmed beard, or he may be clean shaven. He has been known to wear glasses.

## Caution

Khalid Shaikh Mohammed is wanted for his alleged involvement in a conspiracy plot, based in Manila, The Philippines, to bomb commercial United States airliners flying routes to the United States from Southeast Asia in January of 1995. He was indicted in the Southern District of New York in January of 1996.

## 19. Muhammad Atef

*Wanted For:* MURDER OF U.S. NATIONALS OUTSIDE THE UNITED STATES; CONSPIRACY TO MURDER U.S. NATIONALS OUTSIDE THE UNITED STATES; ATTACK ON A FEDERAL FACILITY RESULTING IN DEATH

*Aliases:* Abu Hafs, Abu Hafs El-Masry El-Khabir, Taysir, Sheikh Taysir Abdullah, Abu Khadijah

## Description

Date of Birth Used: Unknown    Hair: Dark brown/black
Place of Birth: Egypt    Eyes: Dark
Height: 6'4" to 6'6"    Sex: Male
Weight: Unknown    Complexion: Olive
Build: Thin    Citizenship: Egyptian
Language: Arabic
Scars and Marks: None known

*Remarks:* Atef is alleged to be Usama bin Ladin's second-in-command of the terrorist organization al-Qa'ida.

## Caution

Muhammad Atef has been indicted for his alleged involvement with the August 7, 1998, bombings of the United States embassies in Dar es Salaam, Tanzania, and Nairobi, Kenya.

## 20. Ali Saed Bin Ali El-Hoorie

*Wanted For:* CONSPIRACY TO KILL U.S. NATIONALS; CONSPIRACY TO MURDER U.S. EMPLOYEES; CONSPIRACY TO USE WEAPONS OF MASS DESTRUCTION AGAINST U.S. NATIONALS; CONSPIRACY TO DESTROY PROPERTY OF THE U.S.; CONSPIRACY TO ATTACK NATIONAL DEFENSE UTILITIES; BOMBING RESULTING IN DEATH; USE OF WEAPONS OF MASS DESTRUCTION AGAINST U.S. NATIONALS; MURDER WHILE USING DESTRUCTIVE DEVICE DURING A CRIME OF VIOLENCE; MURDER OF FEDERAL EMPLOYEES; ATTEMPTED MURDER OF FEDERAL EMPLOYEES
*Alias:* Ali Saed Bin Ali Al-Houri

## Description

Dates of Birth Used: July 10, 1965; July 11, 1965    Hair: Black
Place of Birth: El Dibabiya, Saudi Arabia    Eyes: Black
Height: 5'2"    Sex: Male
Weight: 130 pounds    Complexion: Olive
Build: Unknown    Citizenship: Saudi Arabian
Language: Arabic
Scars and Marks: El-Hoorie has a mole on his face.

*Remarks:* None

## Caution

Ali Saed bin Ali El-Hoorie has been indicted in the Eastern District of Virginia for the June 25, 1996, bombing of the Khobar Towers military housing complex in Dhahran, Kingdom of Saudi Arabia.

## 21. Saif Al-Adel

*Wanted For:* CONSPIRACY TO KILL U.S. NATIONALS, TO MURDER, TO DESTROY BUILD-INGS AND PROPERTY OF THE UNITED STATES, AND TO DESTROY THE NATIONAL DE-FENSE UTILITIES OF THE UNITED STATES
*Aliases:* Muhamad Ibrahim Makkawi, Seif Al Adel, Ibrahim Al-Madani

## Description

Dates of Birth Used: April 11, 1963; April 11, 1960      Hair: Dark
Place of Birth: Egypt      Eyes: Dark
Height: Unknown      Sex: Male
Weight: Unknown      Complexion: Olive
Build: Unknown      Citizenship: Egyptian
Language: Arabic
Scars and Marks: None known

*Remarks:* Al-Adel is thought to be affiliated with the Egyptian Islamic Jihad (EIJ), and is believed to be a high-ranking member of the al-Qa'ida organization, currently in Afghanistan.

## Caution

Saif Al-Adel is wanted in connection with the August 7, 1998, bombings of the United States embassies in Dar es Salaam, Tanzania, and Nairobi, Kenya.

## 22. Ibrahim Salih Mohammed Al-Yacoub

*Wanted For:* CONSPIRACY TO KILL U.S. NATIONALS; CONSPIRACY TO MURDER U.S. EMPLOYEES; CONSPIRACY TO USE WEAPONS OF MASS DESTRUCTION AGAINST U.S. NATIONALS; CONSPIRACY TO DESTROY PROPERTY OF THE U.S.; CONSPIRACY TO AT-TACK NATIONAL DEFENSE UTILITIES; BOMBING RESULTING IN DEATH; USE OF WEAP-ONS OF MASS DESTRUCTION AGAINST U.S. NATIONALS; MURDER WHILE USING DE-STRUCTIVE DEVICE DURING A CRIME OF VIOLENCE; MURDER OF FEDERAL EMPLOYEES; ATTEMPTED MURDER OF FEDERAL EMPLOYEES

*Description*

Date of Birth Used: October 16, 1966      Hair: Black
Place of Birth: Tarut, Saudi Arabia      Eyes: Brown
Height: 5'4"      Sex: Male
Weight: 150 pounds      Complexion: Olive
Build: Unknown      Citizenship: Saudi Arabian
Language: Arabic

*Caution*

Ibrahim Salih Mohammed Al-Yacoub has been indicted in the Eastern District of Virginia for the June 25, 1996, bombing of the Khobar Towers military housing complex in Dhahran, Kingdom of Saudi Arabia.

# Letter to al-Qa'ida Cell (August 1997)

HAROUN FAZUL*

Brother Sharif,

. . . There are many [r]easons that lead me to believe that the cell members in East Africa are in great danger, which leaves us no choice but to think and work hard to foil the enemy's plans who is working day and night to catch one of us or gather more information about any of us. [This report stems from the basic principle] that anyone who studies security matters seriously will never handle anything carelessly, regardless of how small or great it is, but will take all matters seriously. . . . There is a war on and the situation is dangerous, and . . . anybody who is associated with the Hajj [Usama bin Ladin] regardless of

---

* This letter was found in a raid on the house of Wadih El Hage in Nairobi, Kenya, on his personal computer. El Hage was a top al-Qa'ida member later convicted in the East African embassy bombings. The letter was believed to have been written by Fazul, a member of al-Qa'ida and a suspect in the bombing of the U.S. embassy in Nairobi, who had stayed in el Hage's house. The "Brother Sharif" to whom it is addressed might have been Ahmed Khalfan Ghailani, a leading member of al-Qa'ida's East African cell. The letter is reprinted by permission from *Frontline*, the PBS documentary series; it appeared on *Frontline*'s "Hunting bin Laden" Web site: <*www.pbs. org/frontline/shows/binladen*>.

their position and their nationality are at risk. Also, the American forces carry [out] kidnapping operations against anyone who threatens its [*sic*] national security and its [*sic*] citizens. . . . My recommendation to my brothers in East Africa was to not be complacent regarding security matters, and that they should know that now they have become America's primary target, and that they should know that there is an American-Kenyan-Egyptian intelligence activity in [Na]irobi aiming to identify the names and residences of the members who are associated with the Sheikh [bin Ladin] since America knows well that the youth who lived in Somalia and were members of the Sheikh's cell are the ones who killed the Americans in Somalia. They know that since Kenya was the main gateway for those members, there must be a center in Kenya. . . . Our biggest problem is that our security situation here is very weak. . . . [W]e are convinced 100 percent that Kenyan intelligence is aware of us and that indeed our security situation is extremely bad.

We read in the Kenyan newspaper the "standard" news of the arrest of five terrorists in Kenya. . . . We think there is American pressure on Kenya to search for the Arabs living in the area [country]. Therefore, brother Sharif, please watch out and also let the brother engineers be careful and be advised that anyone of us could fall in the trap. If the engineers come down, it would be better if they did not contact me and God willing, I will try and visit them at their homes.

The last bit of news that almost made me explode [go crazy] and which I consider the primary cause of danger for the East Africa network [concerned] the following. [This was in conjunction with what] we read in one of the British newspapers, the *Daily Telegraph*. . . . The gist of the news is this: "There is an individual from the bin Ladin finance department currently in the hands of the American Central Intelligence Agency 'CIA' and also in the hands on the British intelligence service 'MI6' and is in Saudi Arabia. He was delivered to them through the Saudi intelligence service during the middle of May. Along with him is another individual called 'Jallud' who is an assistant to Usama and who may have cooperated with the Saudi government after he was arrested since May. The newspaper also mentioned that Sidi Tayib [another al-Qa'ida member] had advised the American intelligence service about the scope of distribution of money to various Arab communities who cooperate with the Sheikh in the United States especially in Brooklyn, New Jersey, and Je[r]sey City. This individual was also said to have given details about Usama's financial information in Afghanistan and Pakistan and how much was sent to London and to Detroit in America. . . . We have tried to take some measures here in Nairobi but first we wanted to verify that the man called Sidi Tayib is identifiable wit[h] Abu al-Fadhl, the amputee who is married to [one of] the Sheikh's relatives. In this connection and to the best of my knowledge, there is only one Abu al-Fadhl from Saudi Arabia, who is known as Abu al-Fadhl al-Makki (the Meccan). . . . In t[h]e final analysis we do not care much about verifying the man's nam[e]. What matters is the fact that an important man with close links to the Sheikh seems to have fallen into the enemy's hands, and we have to take all the appropriate security precautions against that. I, along with Tawfiq, have collected all the files that we do not need here a[n]d that might pose a threat against us and have placed them in another location. We did not burn them si[nc]e they belong to engineer Abd al-Sabbur, who may have a different opinion about what we are seeing here, but anyway we are awaiting his return next week. He had called from there to inf[or]m Tawfiq to prepare himself, as they will join the director there after his approval. We tried to leave the house, but we have a problem with cash flow. We also thought that if we were under surveillance, . . . [by moving] this may look very suspicious. . . . [There follows a discussion of possible phone tapping.] The fact of these matters and others leaves us no choice but to ask ourselves, are we ready for that big clandestine battle? Did we take the necessary measures to avoid having one of us fall in the trap? Knowing we were counting on God's blessing with our limited resources.

The second matter is that I would recommend to the good and wise supreme command, which I implore God to keep safe, to work hard to return the caliphate to earth and fight the forces of atheism and dictators who wreaked havoc on earth. We, the East Africa cell members, do not want to know about the operations plans since we are just implementers. We trust our command and appreciate their work and know that they have a lot of problems. But my advice here is for the practical part only, since we started the project for "reestablishing the Muslim state" [as] a collective effort and not an individual one; we are all part of it. So we are asking you, for the sake of organizing the work, to tell us [whether] there is a possible danger that may take place in a while due to a certain decision, so we can prepare ourselves accordingly or [so that] we may go underground for a while, since our presence might foil or complicate your plans that we know no[t]hing of.

As you know, the decision to declare war on America was taken and we only know about it from t[h]e news media, and we should have known about that decision and not the plans so that we could take the necessary precautions and to prevent ca[us]ing any complications or failure in your plans due to our ignorance of them.

As you [know], if one of us fall[s] in the trap due to one of your decisions, God forbid, that will be a loss to the whole cell. We ask you to keep in touch wit[h] us through the Internet from Pakistan, as we get a lot of information now about the Sheikh from that network. Or you can follow Abd al-Sabbur's example, such as when he faxed his family fro[m] the border village next to you. We need to hear your good words, and we are afraid to be in the dark and

[take] any unapproved plans domestically since we do not have the necessary expertise regarding such difficult decisions, decisions which [only you] can undertake. . . . Say a lot of prayers for us so God may grant us success, may God give you his reward.

Your brother,

Salih Suhayb al-Ansari

# Report on the Bomb Attacks in Kenya and Tanzania (January 1999)

## U.S. GOVERNMENT ACCOUNTABILITY REVIEW BOARD

. . . On August 7, 1998, at approximately 10:30 A.M. local time, terrorists driving in a truck detonated a large bomb in the rear parking area, near the ramp to the basement garage, of the American embassy in Nairobi. A total of 213 people were killed, of whom 44 were American embassy employees (12 Americans and 32 Foreign Service National employees). Ten Americans and eleven [local embassy employees] were seriously injured. An estimated 200 Kenyan civilians were killed and 4,000 were injured by the blast in the vicinity of the embassy. . . .

The local-hire contract guards at the rear of the embassy saw the truck pull into the uncontrolled exit lane of the rear parking lot just as they closed the fence gate and the drop bar after a mail van had exited the embassy's garage. (The drop bar paralleled a series of steel bollards which encircled the embassy outside the steel grill fence that surrounds the chancery.) The truck proceeded to the embassy's rear access control area but was blocked by an automobile coming out of the Co-op Bank's underground garage. The blocking auto was forced to back up, allowing the truck to come up to the embassy drop bar.

When one of the two terrorist occupants of the truck demanded that the guards open the gates, they refused. One of the terrorists then began shooting at the chancery and the other tossed a flash grenade at one of the guards. The guards, who were unarmed, ran for cover and tried to raise the Marine Security Guard at the command post on a hand-held radio and by a phone in the nearby guard booth. They were unsuccessful: the embassy's single radio frequency was occupied with other traffic, [and] the telephone was busy. In the several seconds' time lapse between the gunshots/grenade explosion and the detonation of the truck bomb, many embassy employees went to the windows to observe what was happening. Those who did were either killed or seriously injured. . . .

There were no intelligence reports immediately before the bombing to have warned the embassy of the August 7 blast. However, a number of earlier intelligence reports cited alleged threats against several U.S. diplomatic and other targets, including the U.S. embassy in Nairobi. While all of these reports were disseminated to the intelligence community and to appropriate posts abroad, they were largely discounted because of doubts about the sources. Other reporting was imprecise, changing, and nonspecific as to dates, diminishing its usefulness. Additionally, actions taken by intelligence and law enforcement authorities to confront suspect terrorist groups in Nairobi, including the Al-Haramayn non-governmental organization and the Usama bin Ladin organization, were believed to have dissipated the threats. . . .

In March 1998, the Department of State issued a worldwide alert drawing attention to an Usama bin Ladin threat against American military and civilians. However, this alert was not accompanied by any special warning or analysis that embassies in East Africa might be targeted by bin Ladin's group. . . .

According to physical evidence and reports from persons on the scene just prior to the bombing, on the morning of Friday, August 7, 1998, a truck laden with explosives drove up Laibon Road to one of the two vehicular gates of the U.S. embassy in Dar es Salaam. Apparently unable to penetrate the perimeter because it was blocked by an embassy water tanker, the suicide bomber detonated his charge at 10:39 A.M. at a distance of about thirty-five feet from the outer wall of the chancery. The type and quantity of explosives are still under investigation.

The bomb attack killed eleven people; one other is missing and presumed dead. Another eighty-five people were injured. No Americans were among the fatalities, but many were injured, two of them seriously. . . . At the time of the attack, two contract local guards were on duty inside a perimeter guard booth, while two others were in the pedestrian entrance screening area behind the booth and another was in the open area behind the water truck. All five were killed in the blast. The force of the blast propelled the filled water tanker over three stories into the air. It came to rest against the chancery building, having absorbed some of the shock wave that otherwise would have hit the chancery with even greater force. . . .

# Testimony of Ali A. Muhammad
# (October 21, 2000)*

. . . In late 1993 I was asked by bin Ladin to conduct surveillance of American, British, French and Israeli targets in Nairobi. Among the targets I did surveillance for was the American embassy. . . . These targets were selected to retaliate against the United States for its involvement in Somalia. I took pictures, drew diagrams, and wrote a report. Khalid al-Fawwaz [a London-based al-Qa'ida member who was also a defendant in the case—*Eds.*] paid for my expenses and the photo enlarging equipment. He was in Nairobi at this time.

I later went to Khartoum, where my surveillance files and photographs were reviewed by Usama bin Ladin, Abu Hafs [alias of Muhammad Atef, bin Ladin's second-in-command, who was killed in January 2002 by U.S. forces in Afghanistan] and others. Bin Ladin looked at the picture of the American embassy and pointed to where a truck could go as a suicide bomber.

In 1994 bin Ladin sent me to Djibouti to do surveillance on several facilities, including French military bases and the American embassy. In 1994, after an attempt to assassinate bin Ladin, I went to the Sudan . . . to train bin Ladin's bodyguards, [his] security detail. I trained those conducting the security of the interior of his compound and coordinated with the Sudanese intelligence agents who were responsible for the exterior security. . . .

I was aware of certain contacts between al-Qa'ida and [the Egyptian] al-Jihad organization, on one side, and Iran and Hizballah on the other side. I arranged security for a meeting in the Sudan between [Imad Fayez] Mugniyah, Hizballah's chief, and bin Ladin. Hizballah provided explosives training for al-Qa'ida and al-Jihad. Iran supplied Egyptian Jihad with weapons. Iran also used Hizballah to supply explosives that were disguised to look like rocks.

In late 1994 I was in Nairobi. Abu Hafs met another man and me in the back of Wadih el-Hage's house. Abu Hafs told me, along with someone else, to do surveillance for the American, British, French, and Israeli targets in Senegal in West Africa. . . .

At about this time, late 1994, I received a call from an FBI agent who wanted to speak to me about the upcoming trial of *United States v. [Umar] Abd al-Rahman.* [Rahman was tried for the 1993 bombing of the World Trade Center.—*Eds.*] I flew back to the United States [and] spoke to the FBI but didn't disclose everything that I knew.

---

* Preliminary transcript of a hearing in Federal District Court in Manhattan in which Ali A. Muhammad, a member of al-Qa'ida, pled guilty to five charges in connection with a broad terrorism conspiracy.

I reported on my meeting with the FBI to Abu Hafs and was told not to return to Nairobi.

In 1995 I obtained a copy of the co-conspirator list for the Abd al-Rahman trial. I sent the list to el-Hage in Kenya, expecting that it would be forwarded to bin Ladin in Khartoum.

In 1996 I learned from el-Hage that Abu Ubaidah [an al-Qa'ida explosives instructor] had drowned.

In 1998 I received a letter from Ihab Ali [a member of al-Qa'ida] in early January 1998. The letter said that el-Hage had been interviewed by the FBI in Kenya and gave me a contact number for el-Hage. I called the number and then called someone who would pass the message to Fawwaz for bin Ladin.

After the bombing in 1998, I made plans to go to Egypt and later to Afghanistan to meet bin Ladin. Before I could leave, I was subpoenaed to testify before the grand jury in the Southern District of New York. I testified, told some lies, and was then arrested.

[Mr. Muhammad was then questioned by Judge Leonard B. Sand:]

*Judge Sand:* The overall objective of all these activities you described was, what?

*Mr. Muhammad:* . . . I was involved in the Islamic Jihad organization, and the Islamic Jihad organization had a very close link to al-Qa'ida, the organization for bin Ladin. And the objective [was] . . . just to attack any Western target in the Middle East, to force the government of the Western countries just to pull out from the Middle East. . . .

*Judge Sand:* And to achieve that objective, did the conspiracy include killing nationals of the United States?

*Mr. Muhammad:* Yes, sir. Based on the Marine explosion in Beirut . . . and the American pull-out from Beirut, they will be the same method, to force the United States to pull out from Saudi Arabia.

# Testimony of John Michael Anticev
# (February 27–28, 2001)*

[Anticev is testifying regarding his interrogation of Muhammad Sadeh Odeh, a member of al-Qa'ida who is a defendant in the East Africa embassy bombings,

---

* John Michael Anticev is the FBI Agent who investigated the African embassy bombings. This testimony is from *United States of America v. Usama bin Ladin et al.*, U.S. District Court, Southern District of New York, Trial Transcript.

immediately following the attacks in Kenya.] [In 1999] . . . [Muhammad Sadeh Odeh] was approached to join al-Qa'ida . . . and he decided that he wanted to join. . . . He liked al-Qa'ida because it represented the whole Muslim world. He told me that he didn't want to join . . . a Palestinian group or another group based upon one country, one ethnic background, because al-Qa'ida represented all Muslims. . . . He said that compared to the other groups . . . al-Qa'ida was Islamically pure and that the leadership in other groups might do things that are not Islamically correct. . . .

After he took the pledge to al-Qa'ida, he went back to the Jihad Wal camp [in Afghanistan] for just a couple days to get reassigned, and then from there he went back to the Farouq camp. Because he had medical training he went back there to be a medic for a couple of months. . . . After the Farouq camp, he went on to another training camp, called the Sadeek camp, where he took a course in explosives. . . . He learned the more complicated aspects of explosives. He had a trainer there, Abu Ubaidah, that taught him mathematical formulas, the type of explosives to use, how much explosives [*sic*] would be needed to do a certain job. . . .

Saif al-Adel told him that the war in Afghanistan was winding down and that they were going to move the *jihad* to other parts of the world, and he wanted him to go to Somalia via Kenya. . . . He told him [the instructions] were coming from Usama bin Ladin. . . . His job in Somalia was to train one of the tribes. . . . And they picked one particular tribe at that time called the Um Rehan tribe, to give training and other additional support such as food and medical treatments. . . . He provided them training in small arms and medical treatments. . . . That was picked by bin Ladin's group because it had the closest philosophical ties to al-Qa'ida. . . . He said that the tribes were very upset. . . . They felt that [the UN was] controlling the area. They were afraid that if they accepted aid from the United Nations, that they would have to give up their arms in exchange for this aid. . . .

Abu Hafs was sent to Somalia by Usama bin Ladin to not only assist the situation but to make contact with some of the tribal chiefs in Mogadishu and around Somalia also. They were . . . not only fighting amongst [themselves, but also] against the United Nations and the U.S. troops [that] were there. . . . Abu Hafs said that he was going to support them . . . to kick out the United States by military force. . . .

[Later Odeh went to Kenya] . . . to the coastal city of Mombasa. . . . After arriving in Kenya, Abu Hafs came to see him later on, [a] couple of months later in Mombasa, [in] October or November of that year, and he told Odeh that he was going to set him up in a fishing business, and he gave him a fiberglass boat, and he said that he was going to have two employees who were also al-Qa'ida members, and that he could take a small salary for himself just for his own expenses and living, and the other two people would get salaries, and the rest of the profits would remain for al-Qa'ida. . . .

[Odeh] spent a lot of time at [Mercy International Relief, which they were using as an office] . . . and he would type reports for the hierarchy in al-Qa'ida. . . . They were using certain code words to conceal what their true intentions were. . . . For example, the word "working" means "*jihad*." "Tools" mean[s] "weapons." "Potatoes" mean[s] "hand-grenades." . . . And the word "goods" mean[s] fake documents of a particular country, and he gave me an example of "how were the goods from Yemen," which would mean we need fake documents for Yemen . . . travel documents, things of that nature. . . . Once they were typed, [these items would be faxed] to Pakistan, and since there was no electronic communications [*sic*] with the leadership in Afghanistan, it would go by courier to the al-Qa'ida leadership. . . .

In March of [19]98, [Odeh] went to Mombasa to do some furniture business with Omar [an alias of Ahmad Khalfan Ghailani, a member of al-Qa'ida] and [attended an al-Qa'ida meeting there]. . . . In that meeting [Abdallah Ahmad Abdallah, an al-Qa'ida member] indicated that he had just returned from Afghanistan and that he had received word from bin Ladin that he was going to start to get . . . the al-Qa'ida people out of Kenya. . . . About [June] . . . Mustafa [an alias of Muhammad Fadhil, one of the leaders of the cell] came to see him again . . . with another message about "hurry up, get your documents in order, there's an emergency situation and that we have to start getting ready to travel." . . .

Saleh stated . . . he would like to do an operation against the United States in Kenya because he did not like Kenya or Kenyans. And Mustafa had the opposite view. He said he wouldn't want to do an operation in Kenya because he liked Kenya and the Kenyan people. . . . Odeh . . . did not want to do an operation in Kenya. He liked it there and he liked the people. . . .

On August 1st, Ahmad the Egyptian [an alias of Ahmad Mohammed Hamed Ali, a member of al-Qa'ida] Mustafa, and Sheik Bahamad [an alias of Ahmad Salim Swedan, another member of al-Qa'ida] leave for Afghanistan. . . . Odeh is still in Mombasa. . . . He runs into Saleh with Fahad [Msalam, an al-Qa'ida member], and Saleh is extremely upset. . . . Odeh says, he was yelling at me in the middle of the street, [saying] "We have to get out of here, it's an emergency. . . . You have to be out of here by the sixth and you have to get your documents." . . . That night, Fahad and Saleh do come to Omar's house and they give Odeh a . . . Yemeni passport; it's expired, and it has somebody else's picture on it. And they tell him . . . [to] go to immigration authorities and get a picture and get that passport up to date. . . .

[Odeh] . . . arrived in Nairobi . . . August 4. . . . He checked into the hotel. He used that passport given to him by Saleh with the fake name to register, and then he went for a nap. And around noon he said that he woke up and ran into Saleh and Harun. . . . Saleh gave him a razor . . . and told him to shave his beard, and he continued on to Saleh's room and in Saleh's room was

[Muhsin Musa Matwalli Atwah] . . . his trainer in explosives in the Sadeek Camp. . . . He shaved [his beard] so he would conceal himself being a Muslim while traveling. [Saleh and Harun told him] . . . they were going out to do a small job. . . . He knew it was not shopping or something like that, he knew it was to do some al-Qa'ida work. . . .

On the morning of August 6 . . . he said that Saleh was now very happy, not worried, was in good spirits, and that Harun was his normal self. . . . Saleh tells Odeh, "I just got news from Khandahar [Afghanistan]" . . . that all the people have been evacuated. And Odeh says, "What do you mean?" And [Saleh] says, "Well, we're expecting a retaliation by the United States Navy, we're expecting their warplanes to start hitting us and we're expecting missile attacks." . . . Before Saleh left, he gave [money] to each person who was traveling and said that that money was to be used for bribes, if you had to bribe somebody at the border or something, and for personal expenses. . . .

He described during a typical terrorist operation that it's broken down into two cells. . . . One cell . . . gets there ahead of time and they do all the logistics and planning. They observe the building, they do surveillances. If it's difficult to do a really covert surveillance where [you might be spotted], they would maybe set up a food stand or buy or set up some kind of a shop nearby to the target and observe the target and look for weaknesses. They might even send somebody to the target to try to get in, you know, asking questions to see how tough the security was. . . .

The second cell is the actual people who arrive and do the act itself. . . . The best place, he said, was to get the explosive charge inside the building. [The next best alternative] . . . is to get the charge as close to the building as possible. . . .

[Odeh told Anticev he did not know in advance the U.S. embassy in Nairobi was the target. He thought his cell, Saleh and company were responsible] . . . and that . . . Harun and [Muhsin Musa Matwalli Atwah] [built] the bomb at Harun's house. . . . He believed that [Muhsin Musa Matwalli Atwah] could have built [the Tanzania bomb, too]. . . .

He thought [the bombing in Nairobi] was a blunder. He blamed Saleh for making a big mistake. He didn't like the fact that so many civilians and Kenyans were killed. He said that the . . . individuals who . . . drove the truck with the explosives should have got it into the building or died trying. . . . He said that the truck should have been backed into the target closely . . . because the cab in front would act as a diversion for the explosion. . . . What actually happened is, the truck came in nose first, and when the bomb went off, he said, . . . the force of the explosion actually ricocheted for a second off the cab, which diverted the explosion and caused so much more damage in the area. . . .

He stated that the reason he was talking to [the FBI] now was because [his fellow cell members] . . . were pushing him and pushing him and pushing him and they're all gone and he's left [behind in jail] facing big problems.

## Responsibility for the Terrorist Atrocities in the United States, September 11, 2001 (October 4, 2001)

BRITISH GOVERNMENT

. . . 32. Since 1989, Usama bin Ladin has conducted substantial financial and business transactions on behalf of al-Qa'ida and in pursuit of its goals. These include purchasing land for training camps, purchasing warehouses for the storage of items, including explosives, purchasing communications and electronics equipment, and transporting currency and weapons to members of al-Qa'ida and associated terrorist groups in countries throughout the world.

33. Since 1989 Usama bin Ladin has provided training camps and guest houses in Afghanistan, Pakistan, the Sudan, Somalia and Kenya for the use of al-Qa'ida and associated terrorist groups. We know from intelligence that there are currently at least a dozen camps across Afghanistan, of which at least four are used for training terrorists.

34. Since 1989, Usama bin Ladin has established a series of businesses to provide income for al-Qa'ida, and to provide cover for the procurement of explosives, weapons and chemicals, and for the travel of al-Qa'ida operatives. The businesses have included a holding company known as "Wadi Al Aqiq," a construction business known as "Al Hijra," an agricultural business known as "Al Themar al-Mubaraka," and investment companies known as "Ladin International" and "Taba Investments."

### Usama bin Ladin and Previous Attacks

35. In 1992 and 1993 Muhammad Atef traveled to Somalia on several occasions for the purpose of organizing violence against United States and United Nations troops then stationed in Somalia. On each occasion he reported back to Usama bin Ladin, at his base in the Riyadh district of Khartoum.

36. In the spring of 1993 Atef, Saif al-Adel, another senior member of al-

Qa'ida, and other members began to provide military training to Somali tribes for the purpose of fighting the United Nations forces.

37. On 3 and 4 October 1993 operatives of al-Qa'ida participated in the attack on U.S. military personnel serving in Somalia as part of . . . Operation "Restore Hope." Eighteen U.S. military personnel were killed in the attack.

38. From 1993 members of al-Qa'ida began to live in Nairobi and set up businesses there, including Asma Ltd. and Tanzanite King. They were regularly visited there by senior members of al-Qa'ida, in particular by Atef and Abu Ubadiah al-Banshiri.

39. Beginning in the latter part of 1993, members of al-Qa'ida in Kenya began to discuss the possibility of attacking the U.S. embassy in Nairobi in retaliation for U.S. participation in Operation Restore Hope in Somalia. Ali Muhammad, a U.S. citizen and admitted member of al-Qa'ida, surveyed the U.S. embassy as a possible target for a terrorist attack. He took photographs and made sketches, which he presented to Usama bin Ladin while bin Ladin was in Sudan. He also admitted that he had trained terrorists for al-Qa'ida in Afghanistan in the early 1990s, and that those whom he trained included many involved in the East African bombings in August 1998.

40. In June or July 1998, two al-Qa'ida operatives, Fahid Muhammad Ali Msalam and Sheik Ahmad Salim Swedan, purchased a Toyota truck and made various alterations to the back of the truck.

41. In early August 1998, operatives of al-Qa'ida gathered in 43 New Runda Estates, Nairobi, to execute the bombing of the U.S. embassy in Nairobi.

42. On 7 August 1998, Assam, a Saudi national and al-Qa'ida operative, drove the Toyota truck to the U.S. embassy. There was a large bomb in the back of the truck.

43. Also in the truck was Muhammad Rashed Daoud al-Owali, another Saudi. He, by his own confession, was an al-Qa'ida operative, who from about 1996 had been trained in an al-Qa'ida camps in Afghanistan in explosives, hijacking, kidnapping, assassination, and intelligence techniques. With Usama bin Ladin's express permission he fought alongside the Taliban in Afghanistan. He had met Usama bin Ladin personally in 1996 and asked for another "mission." Usama bin Ladin sent him to East Africa after extensive specialized training at camps in Afghanistan.

44. As the truck approached the embassy, al-Owali got out and threw a stun grenade at a security guard. Assam drove the truck up to the rear of the embassy. He got out and then detonated the bomb, which demolished a multistory secretarial college and severely damaged the U.S. embassy, and the Cooperative Bank building. The bomb killed 213 people and injured 4,500. Assam was killed in the explosion.

45. Al-Owali expected the mission to end in his death. He had been willing to die for al-Qa'ida. But at the last minute he ran away from the bomb truck and survived. He had no money, passport, or plan to escape after the mission, because he had expected to die.

46. After a few days, he called a telephone number in Yemen to have money transferred to him in Kenya. The number he rang in Yemen was contacted by Usama bin Ladin's phone on the same day as al-Owali was arranging to get the money.

47. Another person arrested in connection with the Nairobi bombing was Muhammad Sadeh Odeh. He admitted to his involvement. He identified the principal participants in the bombing. He named three other persons, all of whom were al-Qa'ida or Egyptian Islamic Jihad members.

48. In Dar es Salaam the same day, at about the same time, operatives of al-Qa'ida detonated a bomb at the U.S. embassy, killing eleven people. The al-Qa'ida operatives involved included Mustafa Muhammad Fadhil and Khaflan Khamis Muhammad. The bomb was carried in a Nissan Atlas truck, which Ahmad Khalfan Ghailani and Sheikh Ahmad Salim Swedan, two al-Qa'ida operatives, had purchased in July 1998, in Dar es Salaam.

49. Khaflan Khamis Muhammad was arrested for the bombing. He admitted membership of al-Qa'ida and implicated other members of al-Qa'ida in the bombing.

50. On 7 and 8 August 1998, two other members of al-Qa'ida disseminated claims of responsibility for the two bombings by sending faxes to media organizations in Paris, Doha in Qatar, and Dubai in the United Arab Emirates.

51. Additional evidence of the involvement of al-Qa'ida in the East African bombings came from a search conducted in London of several residences and businesses belonging to al-Qa'ida and Egyptian Islamic Jihad members. In those searches a number of documents were found including claims of responsibility for the East African bombings in the name of a fictitious group, "The Islamic Army for the Liberation of the Holy Places."

52. Al-Owali, the would-be suicide bomber, admitted he was told to make a videotape of himself using the name of the same fictitious group.

53. The faxed claims of responsibility were traced to a telephone number, which had been in contact with Usama bin Ladin's cell phone. The claims disseminated to the press were clearly written by someone familiar with the conspiracy. They stated that the bombings had been carried out by two Saudis in Kenya, and one Egyptian in Dar es Salaam. They were probably sent before the bombings had even taken place. They referred to two Saudis dying in the Nairobi attack. In fact, because al-Owali fled at the last minute, only one Saudi died.

54. On 22 December 1998 Usama bin Ladin was asked by *Time* magazine

whether he was responsible for the August 1998 attacks. He replied: "The International Islamic Jihad Front for the *jihad* against the United States and Israel has, by the grace of God, issued a crystal clear *fatwa* calling on the Islamic nation to carry on *jihad* aimed at liberating the holy sites. The nation of Muhammad has responded to this appeal. If instigation for *jihad* against the Jews and the Americans . . . is considered to be a crime, then let history be a witness that I am a criminal. Our job is to instigate and, by the grace of God, we did that, and certain people responded to this instigation." He was asked if he knew the attackers:

". . . . Those who risked their lives to earn the pleasure of God are real men. They managed to rid the Islamic nation of disgrace. We hold them in the highest esteem."

And what the United States could expect of him:

". . . . Any thief or criminal who enters another country to steal should expect to be exposed to murder at any time. . . . The United States knows that I have attacked it, by the grace of God, for more than ten years now. . . . God knows that we have been pleased by the killing of American soldiers [in Somalia in 1993]. This was achieved by the grace of God and the efforts of the *mujahidin*. . . . Hostility toward America is a religious duty and we hope to be rewarded for it by God. I am confident that Muslims will be able to end the legend of the so-called superpower that is America."

55. In December 1999 a terrorist cell linked to al-Qa'ida was discovered trying to carry out attacks inside the United States. An Algerian, Ahmad Ressam, was stopped at the U.S.-Canadian border, and over 100 lbs. of bomb-making material was found in his car. Ressam admitted he was planning to set off a large bomb at Los Angeles International airport on New Year's Day. He said that he had received terrorist training at al-Qa'ida camps in Afghanistan and then been instructed to go abroad and kill U.S. civilians and military personnel.

56. On 3 January 2000, a group of al-Qa'ida members, and other terrorists who had trained in al-Qa'ida camps in Afghanistan, attempted to attack a U.S. destroyer with a small boat loaded with explosives. Their boat sank, aborting the attack.

57. On 12 October 2000, however, the USS *Cole* was struck by an explosive-laden boat while refueling in Aden harbor. Seventeen crew were killed, and forty injured.

58. Several of the perpetrators of the *Cole* attack (mostly Yemenis and Saudis) were trained at Usama bin Ladin's camps in Afghanistan. Al-Owali has identified the two commanders of the attack on the USS *Cole* as having participated in the planning and preparation for the East African embassy bombings.

# Executive Order: Sanctions on the Afghan Taliban (July 6, 1999)

PRESIDENT BILL CLINTON

I, William J. Clinton, President of the United States of America, find that the actions and policies of the Taliban in Afghanistan, in allowing territory under its control in Afghanistan to be used as a safe haven and base of operations for Usama bin Ladin and the al-Qa'ida organization who have committed and threaten to continue to commit acts of violence against the United States and its nationals, constitute an unusual and extraordinary threat to the national security and foreign policy of the United States, and hereby declare a national emergency to deal with that threat. I hereby order . . .

Section 1. . . . (a) all property and interests in property of the Taliban; and (b) all property and interests in property of persons determined by the Secretary of the Treasury, in consultation with the Secretary of State and the Attorney General: (i) to be owned or controlled by, or to act for or on behalf of, the Taliban; or (ii) to provide financial, material, or technological support for, or services in support of, any of the foregoing, that are in the United States, that hereafter come within the United States, or that are or hereafter come within the possession or control of United States persons, are blocked.

Sec. 2. . . . Any contract entered into or any license or permit granted prior to the effective date: (a) any transaction or dealing by United States persons or within the United States in property or interests in property blocked pursuant to this order is prohibited, including the making or receiving of any contribution of funds, goods, or services to or for the benefit of the Taliban or persons designated pursuant to this order; (b) the exportation, reexportation, sale, or supply, directly or indirectly, from the United States, or by a United States person, wherever located, of any goods, software, technology (including technical data), or services to the territory of Afghanistan controlled by the Taliban or to the Taliban or persons designated pursuant to this order is prohibited; (c) the importation into the United States of any goods, software, technology, or services owned or controlled by the Taliban or persons designated pursuant to this order or from the territory of Afghanistan controlled by the Taliban is prohibited. . . .

# Resolution 1267 (October 15, 1999)

UN SECURITY COUNCIL

. . . Reaffirming its strong commitment to the sovereignty, independence, territorial integrity, and national unity of Afghanistan, and its respect for Afghanistan's cultural and historical heritage,

Reiterating its deep concern over the continuing violations of international humanitarian law and of human rights, particularly discrimination against women and girls, and over the significant rise in the illicit production of opium, and stressing that the . . . murder of Iranian diplomats and a journalist in Mazar-e-Sharif constituted flagrant violations of established international law,

Recalling the relevant international counterterrorism conventions and in particular the obligations of parties to those conventions to extradite or prosecute terrorists,

Strongly condemning the continuing use of Afghan territory, especially areas controlled by the Taliban, for the sheltering and training of terrorists and planning of terrorist acts, and reaffirming its conviction that the suppression of international terrorism is essential for the maintenance of international peace and security,

Deploring the fact that the Taliban continues to provide safe haven to Usama bin Ladin and to allow him and others associated with him to operate a network of terrorist training camps from Taliban-controlled territory and to use Afghanistan as a base from which to sponsor international terrorist operations.

Noting the indictment of Usama bin Ladin and his associates by the United States of America for . . . the 7 August 1998 bombings of the United States embassies in Nairobi, Kenya, and Dar es Salaam, Tanzania, and for conspiring to kill American nationals outside the United States, and noting also the request of the United States of America to the Taliban to surrender them for trial . . . Determining that the [action of the] . . . Taliban authorities . . . constitutes a threat to international peace and security . . . the United Nations . . .

1. Insists that the Afghan faction known as the Taliban, which also calls itself the Islamic Emirate of Afghanistan, comply promptly with its previous resolutions and in particular cease the provision of sanctuary and training for international terrorists and their organizations, take appropriate effective measures to ensure that the territory under its control is not used for terrorist installations and camps, or for the preparation or organization of terrorist acts against other States or their citizens, and cooperate with efforts to bring indicted terrorists to justice;

2. Demands that the Taliban turn over Usama bin Ladin without further delay to appropriate authorities in a country where he has been indicted, or to

appropriate authorities in a country where he will be returned to such a country, or to appropriate authorities in a country where he will be arrested and effectively brought to justice; . . .

4. Decides further that, in order to enforce paragraph 2 above, all States shall: (a) Deny permission for any aircraft to take off from or land in their territory if it is owned, leased, or operated by or on behalf of the Taliban . . . unless the particular flight has been approved in advance by the Committee on the grounds of humanitarian need, including religious obligation such as the performance of the Hajj [Muslim pilgrimage to Mecca]; (b) Freeze funds and other financial resources, including funds derived or generated from property owned or controlled directly or indirectly by the Taliban, or by any undertaking owned or controlled by the Taliban . . . except as may be authorized by the Committee on a case-by-case basis on the grounds of humanitarian need;

5. Urges all States to cooperate with efforts to fulfill the demand in paragraph 2 above, and to consider further measures against Usama bin Ladin and his associates. . . .

# Testimony on the Taliban (July 20, 2000)

KARL F. INDERFURTH*

When [the Taliban] swept to power . . . in late 1996, they seemed to have considerable popular acceptance, based on an understandable disgust with protracted civil war and a simple desire for personal security. Since then, while the Taliban have extended their control to cover approximately 85 percent of Afghanistan, their popularity and legitimacy now appear to be in decline. They have failed to end the civil war, and they have failed to offer the Afghan people a better life.

Instead, the Taliban continue to seek a military victory over their opponents in northern Afghanistan, but that objective continues to elude their grasp. . . . We believe the Taliban now have little prospect of completing their goal of gaining control over the 15 percent of the country held by the opposition. . . .

---

* Karl F. Inderfurth was deputy assistant secretary of state for South Asian affairs. He gave this testimony before the Senate Foreign Relations Committee.

We also hear of Taliban difficulty conscripting new recruits for this year's spring and summer offensives, due to serious local resistance and low morale. There are equipment shortages for the Taliban war machine and serious splits within the Taliban movement itself.

It is increasingly clear that many Afghans are giving up whatever hope they had for Taliban rule. Many would surely prefer a more inclusive, more effective, more tolerant, and perhaps above all more peacefully inclined government, if that option were to become available.

What has been the U.S. response? I must emphasize that, contrary to some false and damaging allegations, the United States does not now support and has never supported the Taliban. When they took over the capital of Kabul in 1996, we told them we would look at what they did, and react accordingly. Well, what they have done, in a word, is horrendous. They have chosen to prolong their country's agonizing civil war, while oppressing its numerous ethnic and religious minorities. They have trampled on the human rights of all Afghans, especially women and girls. They have condoned and indeed profited from the deadly trade in narcotics and they have condoned that other scourge of civilized society, namely terrorism, by providing among other things safe haven for Usama bin Ladin and his network. This is the murderer directly responsible for the loss of a dozen American and hundreds of other innocent lives in the East Africa embassy bombings two years ago. We believe Usama bin Ladin continues to this day to plan further acts of international terrorism.

We have consistently and categorically opposed all of these Taliban policies. . . . If anything, the Taliban have moved even further in the wrong direction. On terrorism, not only have they refused to hand over Usama bin Ladin as called for [by] the UN Security Council, but they have aided and abetted other terrorists worldwide, including violent groups in Chechnya and Central Asia. . . .

The Taliban, and some of their supporters, continue to misrepresent our campaign against terrorism as an attack against Islam. Nothing could be further from the truth. We do not oppose Islam. We respect Islam. We do not oppose those who practice their faith in peace. We do not oppose those who have legitimate political concerns they want redressed. But we do oppose those who commit or condone criminal acts, especially those who commit murder and inflict grievous injury against civilians, in the name of any ideology, religion, or cause.

On human rights, though we have publicly recognized occasional local improvements, the central authorities in Kabul have regressed; witness . . . the new edict forbidding females from working even in international humanitarian activities. On narcotics, the Taliban have allowed Afghanistan to acquire, almost overnight, the distinction of [being] the world's largest producer of illicit opium, thereby contributing to the destruction of countless additional lives every year. . . .

Afghanistan has become a gateway country—a gateway for some of the worst evils of drugs and violence—which daily pass through it en route to other parts of the globe. . . .

All of this raises the obvious question: What more can be done to deal with Afghanistan's ongoing tragedy, and with the risks it poses to others? While we have worked hard to develop a united front on Afghanistan with a number of key countries, multilateral diplomacy has had only a limited effect to date. . . .

The strategy that we are pursuing today is two-pronged. First, firm pressure on the Taliban on the issues of greatest concern: terrorism, narcotics, and human rights. On terrorism, President Clinton took the lead last year by issuing Executive Order 13129, imposing unilateral sanctions on the Taliban designed to stop them from deriving any revenue or benefit from economic interaction with the United States. The UN Security Council followed up in October 1999 by unanimously adopting Resolution 1267, which puts in place mandatory sanctions against Taliban-controlled assets and international airline flights until bin Ladin is brought to justice. These sanctions, I want to stress, target only the regime, while providing unimpeded humanitarian access for all the people of Afghanistan.

In April [2000], the [UN] Security Council agreed that further action might be required. We are actively exploring those options, which could include imposition of an arms embargo against the Taliban. We have also let them know, in no uncertain terms, that we will hold them responsible for any terrorist acts undertaken by bin Ladin from Afghanistan. We reserve the right to use military force in self-defense if required. . . .

The second prong of our Afghan strategy is . . . to promote the greatest possible involvement of Afghans in the search for peace in their own country. What is needed, in our view, is a sincere negotiating process among Afghans themselves toward a broad-based, inclusive government which all the Afghan people, first and foremost, and then the United States and the rest of the international community, can accept, and which can take up the cause of rebuilding the country. This will require the involvement of a wide spectrum of Afghans inside and outside the country—more than just the Taliban and the Northern Alliance. For this reason, we are encouraged by the efforts of Afghans around the world to contribute to this search for peace. . . .

This is not, and cannot be, an attempt to impose some kind of outside power *diktat* on the proud people of Afghanistan, which history teaches would be futile. What we seek is not so much confrontation with the Taliban, as common cause with all the other players who wish to contain and ultimately overcome the threats that the Taliban present[s]. . . .

The human crisis in Afghanistan is eloquently summarized in the latest report by UN Secretary General Kofi Annan: "The situation of the Afghan people remains deplorable. Four years after the takeover of Kabul by the Taliban, visitors compare the city to a bombed-out city a few years after the end of the Second World War, except that no reconstruction is in sight and its people have little hope for improvement. There is a growing process of pauperization throughout Afghanistan, exacerbated by the most severe drought in thirty years. Afghanistan remains in a state of acute crisis—its resources depleted, its intelligentsia in exile, its people disfranchised, its traditional political structures shattered, and its human development indices among the lowest in the world." . . .

The Afghani people do not deserve to suffer in this way. That is why the United States continues to lead the world in humanitarian assistance to the Afghan people, totaling around $70 million annually in recent years, rising to a projected $110 million in view of the extraordinary needs this year. . . . It is a sound investment, not only in averting humanitarian tragedy, but in preserving our friendship with the people of Afghanistan, while we and they await a better future. . . .

From both the human and the political standpoints, the situation in Afghanistan remains extremely difficult but not without some hope that conditions may be changing. . . . We believe the Taliban regime has reached its high-water mark. This is a regime which, by its behavior at home and abroad, has isolated itself from almost the entire world, and increasingly from its own people. There is a real sense in which Afghans and the concerned international community want many of the same things: An Afghan government that is representative, that respects human rights, that rejects rather than embraces narcotic traffickers and terrorists. I believe our strategy of pressure on the Taliban, support for alternative Afghan voices, and concrete cooperation with other countries on these issues can move us closer to that common objective. . . . It is my hope that Afghanistan can once again become a gateway nation of a different kind—a gateway for people, commerce, and cultural exchange between different parts of Asia and the world, in the positive sense that we would all desire to see.

## Testimony of Ahmad Ressam (July 3–5, 2001)*

. . . [He describes how in summer 1999 he began thinking of attacking an airport in the United States] . . . because an airport is sensitive politically and econom-

---

* Ahmad Ressam was a member of al-Qa'ida. His testimony is drawn from *The United States of America v. Mokhtar Haouari.*

ically. . . . I bought a map and I also bought a tourist book for North America. I . . . [chose] the airport of Los Angeles . . . because I . . . landed [there] upon my return from Afghanistan in February 1999. . . . I have an idea. . . . I will go to the city of Los Angeles. . . . I will survey the airports until I find . . . a good one, and then I will bring a cart that is used for luggage. I will put the cart in a place that is not suspicious and then I will observe the reaction of security, how long it took them to observe it.

[In September 1999] I started buying electronic equipment and . . . small electronic components that will be used in putting together electronic circuits. . . . I made four [timing devices] . . . in Montreal, at home. . . . In Vancouver, I started collecting chemical materials . . . [including] urea. . . . It is a fertilizer used in agriculture. It is also a component used in explosives. [A]fter I add to it nitric acids. It becomes an explosive substance similar to TNT. I bought also aluminum sulfate. . . . It is used also in agriculture as a fertilizer. . . . [I also collected] nitric acid and sulfuric acid. Those I stole from places that manufactured agricultural fertilizers. . . . I told Mokhtar Haouari [the defendant in the case], "I'm coming to the United States." . . . I asked him to help me with some money. . . . I said: "Mokhtar, I'm not going to America for tourism. I am going on some very important and dangerous business." He said: "There's no problem." . . . [I told him] "I need somebody to help me in America." . . . I did not tell him about the target, for security reasons. . . .

[At the second meeting] we met at his home. He gave me . . . $3,000 Canadian dollars, and he . . . said: "My friend [Dahoumane] Abdelghani will help you." I said: "Mokhtar, did you explain to him well the business in this work?" He said: "Yes, I told him about it. I told him it is a business that has *shteah* in him." . . . *Shteah* basically means "dance," but whenever there's something that involves fear and danger, you say it is something that makes you dance. . . .

I went to Vancouver . . . to get all the chemical materials and to make the explosives. I was . . . preparing to put together the explosives. . . . First, buying some chemical instruments. Also, I went and stole nitric and sulfuric acids and started preparing the chemical materials. . . . Abdelmajid [helped me prepare the chemicals]. I didn't tell [the defendant] very much. . . . I told him: "I'm going to prepare my affairs there and once I do that, I will call you to let you know when to contact your friend to meet me." I took that money and I had already some money myself. I put them together. . . . I used it to buy some chemical instruments and to buy urea. I bought . . . airplane tickets.

At the beginning of December 1999 [I returned to Montreal]. . . . [I met the defendant]. . . . I spoke to him about his friend—that I would want to meet him in a week in Seattle, and tell him, I said to the defendant, that my name would be Reda. And then once I . . . meet him there, I will explain to him precisely what the job is. . . . He gave me the telephone number of his friend. . . . He also showed me a photograph of Abdelghani . . . so that I would recognize him once I met him. . . . I asked him to have his friend bring some money along with him. . . . I left and I immediately called Abdelghani . . . from the Metro station. . . . I said: "In a week, we will meet in Seattle and I will explain to you." . . .

[Between December 6 and December 14] I spent time putting together the explosives. . . . Abdelmajid [helped me]. . . . [On December 14, 1999] we got up, Abdelmajid and I, in the morning. We got all our things out of the hotel. I rented a room for Abdelmajid in a different hotel and I bought him a ticket to leave the next day. . . . And then we went to Victoria . . . [in] a rental car. . . . [I loaded the explosives in the trunk.] . . . the prior evening. . . . I took a ferry . . . from Vancouver to Victoria . . . myself, the car and Abdelmajid. . . . I made reservations at the hotel in Seattle and I bought a ticket for Abdelmajid to return from Victoria to Vancouver. . . . They stopped me [in Port Angeles, Washington]. . . . They asked me: "Where are you going to?" . . . They gave me a form that had information on it. And then they said: "Open the car," and then they started searching. I ran, and they stopped me.

[If I hadn't been arrested] I was to get in touch with Abdelghani so he can help me put the explosives in some suitcases and then . . . return the car to the company and then take a train to Los Angeles. . . . It is a very long way and I was afraid of impact and shock in the car. . . . I had explosives that would be sensitive to impact. . . . I would [then] get a room at the hotel. . . . Then I would go . . . with Abdelghani to get a car, [with] the fake name that Abdelghani had, and check the airport out. . . . [Then I would] return to Montreal . . . to say good-bye to my friends and get a passport . . . from Mokhtar.

# Worldwide Threat 2001: National Security in a Changing World (February 7, 2001)

GEORGE J. TENET*

. . . We have made considerable progress on terrorism against U.S. interests and facilities . . . but it persists. The most dramatic and recent evidence, of course,

---

* George J. Tenet is director of the Central Intelligence Agency. This is from his testimony to the U.S. Senate Select Committee on Intelligence.

is the loss of seventeen of our men and women on the USS *Cole* at the hands of terrorists.

The threat from terrorism is real, it is immediate, and it is evolving. State-sponsored terrorism appears to have declined over the past five years, but transnational groups—with decentralized leadership that makes them harder to identify and disrupt—are emerging. We are seeing fewer centrally controlled operations, and more acts initiated and executed at lower levels.

Terrorists are also becoming more operationally adept and more technically sophisticated in order to defeat counterterrorism measures. For example, as we have increased security around government and military facilities, terrorists are seeking out "softer" targets that provide opportunities for mass casualties. Employing increasingly advanced devices and using strategies such as simultaneous attacks, the number of people killed or injured in international terrorist attacks rose dramatically in the 1990s, despite a general decline in the number of incidents. Approximately one-third of these incidents involved U.S. interests.

Usama bin Ladin and his global network of lieutenants and associates remain the most immediate and serious threat. Since 1998, bin Ladin has declared all U.S. citizens legitimate targets of attack. As shown by the bombing of our embassies in Africa in 1998 and his millennium plots last year, he is capable of planning multiple attacks with little or no warning.

His organization is continuing to place emphasis on developing surrogates to carry out attacks in an effort to avoid detection, blame, and retaliation. As a result it is often difficult to attribute terrorist incidents to his group, al-Qa'ida.

Beyond bin Ladin, the terrorist threat to Israel and to participants in the Middle East peace negotiations has increased in the midst of continuing Palestinian-Israeli violence. Palestinian rejectionists—including Hamas and the Palestine Islamic Jihad (PIJ)—have stepped up violent attacks against Israeli interests since October [2000]. The terrorist threat to U.S. interests, because of our friendship with Israel, has also increased.

At the same time, Islamic militancy is expanding, and the worldwide pool of potential recruits for terrorist networks is growing. In central Asia, the Middle East, and South Asia, Islamic terrorist organizations are trying to attract new recruits, including under the banner of anti-Americanism.

International terrorist networks have used the explosion in information technology to advance their capabilities. The same technologies that allow individual consumers in the United States to search out and buy books in Australia or India also enable terrorists to raise money, spread their dogma, find recruits, and plan operations far afield. Some groups are acquiring rudimentary cyber-attack tools. Terrorist groups are actively searching the Internet to acquire information and capabilities for chemical, biological, radiological, and even nuclear attacks. Many of the twenty-nine officially designated terrorist organizations have an interest in unconventional weapons, and Usama bin Ladin in 1998 even declared their acquisition a "religious duty."

Nevertheless, we and our allies have scored some important successes against terrorist groups and their plans. . . . The intelligence community has designed a robust counterterrorism program that has preempted, disrupted, and defeated international terrorists and their activities. In most instances, we have kept terrorists off balance, forcing them to worry about their own security and degrading their ability to [strike against us]. . . .

The Afghan civil war will continue into the foreseeable future, leaving the country fragmented and unstable. The Taliban remains determined to impose its radical form of Islam on all of Afghanistan, even in the face of resistance from other ethnic groups and the Shia minority. . . .

What we have in Afghanistan is a stark example of the potential dangers of allowing states—even those far from the United States—to fail. The chaos here is providing an incubator for narcotics traffickers and militant Islamic groups operating in such places as Kashmir, Chechnya, and Central Asia. Meanwhile the Taliban shows no sign of relinquishing terrorist Usama bin Ladin, despite strengthened UN sanctions and prospects that bin Ladin's terrorist operations could lead to retaliatory strikes against Afghanistan. The Taliban and bin Ladin have a symbiotic relationship—bin Ladin gets safe haven and in return, he gives the Taliban help in fighting its civil war. . . .

# 6

# SEPTEMBER 11, AL-QA'IDA,

# AND THE TALIBAN

The events of September 11, 2001, were a turning point in American history; they were also a watershed in the history of terrorism for their sheer scope and psychological impact. Nineteen men hijacked four civilian airliners and crashed three of them into the World Trade Center and the Pentagon. This chapter deals with how the terrorists and their leaders planned and justified the attack and how they reacted to its aftermath—the U.S. military attack on al-Qa'ida and the Taliban government in Afghanistan.

The chapter begins with the suicide note of Muhammad Atta, the operation's leader. The note gives an unprecedented view of how a terrorist prepares both mentally and physically for a mission that will result in massive deaths, including his own. It combines both religious fanaticism and cool pragmatism. The road to martyrdom begins the night before by shaving and applying cologne, then comes the brief battle leading directly to the gardens of paradise where beautiful women will call out, "Come hither, friend of God."

While the United States refused to divulge the specific intelligence that led it to conclude bin Ladin was behind the attacks, that information came first instead from Prime Minister Tony Blair of Great Britain, who presented his government's case, "Responsibility for the Terrorist Atrocities in the United States, September 11, 2001." It details the reasons it is clear bin Ladin committed these attacks. The FBI added to the information when it distributed a list of the nineteen hijackers that included their names and many aliases.

Bin Ladin's reaction to the attack is revealed in a remarkable home video made by a visitor, in which he exults that the mission's success was far greater than he had ever expected since he thought only a few floors of the World

Trade Center would be destroyed. He also reveals that most of the nineteen hijackers were ignorant of the operation's details and perhaps their own fates, until just before they boarded the planes.

Support for bin Ladin in Afghanistan is shown in an interview with his close ally, Mullah Umar Muhammad, the Taliban's spiritual guide, who asserts that his government will never turn the terrorist mastermind over to the Americans, because "this is not an issue of Usama bin Ladin. It is an issue of Islam. Islam's prestige is at stake."

As U.S. authorities were trying to hunt him down in Afghanistan, bin Ladin made several television broadcasts whose purpose was to mobilize support throughout the Muslim world and to intimidate the United States by warning of more attacks to come. The battle was between "infidelity and faith," bin Ladin says in the first videotape, made October 7, 2001, as he asks for help that never comes.

The second broadcast is delivered by Suleiman Abu Ghaith, a close aide to bin Ladin, on October 10, three days after American military strikes on Afghanistan had begun, saying that U.S. retaliation for the September 11 attacks was merely the latest of many U.S. assaults against Muslims. Abu Ghaith warns of retaliation: "There are thousands of the Islamic nation's youths who are eager to die just as the Americans are eager to live." In another address three days later, Abu Ghaith charges that the U.S military operation intentionally wiped out entire villages.

Bin Ladin returns with another televised address on November 3, trying to argue that the world is now divided between Muslims, who support the September 11 attacks and oppose the operation in Afghanistan, and those in the United States and its allies, who believe the opposite. He hints in a November 10 interview with a Pakistani journalist that al-Qa'ida has chemical and nuclear weapons at its disposal. But he also insists, in a December 27 interview with al-Jazira television, that the United States will be defeated both in Afghanistan and through attacks on its own territory: "If their economy is destroyed, they will be busy with their own affairs rather than enslaving the weak peoples."

Additional information on the background to the September 11 attacks comes in the U.S. government's indictment of Zacarias Moussaoui, a French citizen of Moroccan origin who had been arrested before September 11 but whose involvement in that operation was discovered afterward. It provides a detailed look at the planning for September 11, which began in 1998 when a group of men, including Muhammad Atta, formed an al-Qa'ida cell in Germany. Three years of traveling to the United States, collecting money, and taking flight lessons eventually culminated in that horrific day.

Abu Ubeid al-Qurashi, a leader of the organization, gives al-Qa'ida's own assessment of September 11, viewing it as a great success both for propaganda and for mobilizing forces for *jihad*. The very extremism of the action—provoking American hostility and minimizing any possibility of compromise—is seen as an advantage that would preserve the movement's military purity and absolutist goals. He compares the operation to the PLO kidnapping and murder of Israeli athletes at the Munich Olympic Games in 1968, which, he says, set off a wave of terrorism throughout the 1970s. He portrays the attack as the real beginning of a war against America.

Before leaving for the United States to participate in the September 11 attack, one of the hijackers, Ahmad al-Haznawi al-Ghamidi, a Saudi citizen, recorded a videotape in Kandahar, Afghanistan, explaining his action. Another videotape, made by bin Ladin aide Ayman al-Zawahiri as bin Ladin sits next to him, also claims responsibility for the attack. Both tapes were apparently made by al-Qa'ida for internal use only and show the organization's direct link with the attack. They were first broadcast in April 2002.

# Suicide Note (September 18, 2001)

MUHAMMAD ATTA*

## The Last Night

1. Make an oath to die and renew your intentions. Shave excess hair from the body and wear cologne. Shower.

2. Make sure you know all aspects of the plan well, and expect the response, or a reaction, from the enemy.

3. Read al-Tawba and Anfal [traditional war chapters from the Koran] and reflect on their meanings and remember all of the things that God has promised for the martyrs.

4. Remind your soul to listen and obey [all divine orders] and remember that you will face decisive situations that might prevent you from 100 percent obedience, so tame your soul, purify it, convince it, make it understand, and incite it. God said: "Obey God and his messenger, and do not fight amongst yourselves or else you will fail. And be patient, for God is with the patient."

5. Pray during the night and be persistent in asking God to give you victory, control and conquest, and that he may make your task easier and not expose us.

6. Remember God frequently, and the best way to do it is to read the Holy Koran, according to all scholars, as far as I know. It is enough for us that it [the Koran] are [sic] the words of the Creator of the Earth and the planets, the One that you will meet [on the Day of Judgment].

7. Purify your soul from all unclean things. Completely forget something called "this world" [or "this life"]. The time for play is over and the serious time is upon us. How much time have we wasted in our lives? Shouldn't we take advantage of these last hours to offer good deeds and obedience?

8. You should feel complete tranquility, because the time between you and your marriage [in heaven] is very short. Afterward begins the happy life, where God is satisfied with you, and eternal bliss "in the company of the prophets, the companions, the martyrs and the good people, who are all good company."

---

* Muhammad Atta was the leader of the September 11 hijackers. This document was discovered by U.S. authorities on September 18, 2001, in Atta's suitcase, which was found in the plane wreckage. This translation was done for the *New York Times* by Capital Communications Group, a Washington-based international consulting firm, and by Imad Musa, a translator for the firm, and is reprinted by permission of the *New York Times* and Capital Communications Group, LLC.

Ask God for his mercy and be optimistic, because [the prophet], peace be upon him, (used to prefer optimism in all his affairs).

9. Keep in mind that, if you fall into hardship, how will you act and how will you remain steadfast and remember that you will return to God and remember that anything that happens to you could never be avoided, and what did not happen to you could never have happened to you. This test from Almighty God is to raise your level [a reference to the levels of heaven] and erase your sins. And be sure that it is a matter of moments, which will then pass, God willing, so blessed are those who win the great reward of God. Almighty God said: "Did you think you could go to heaven before God knows whom [sic] amongst you have fought for Him and are patient?"

10. Remember the words of Almighty God: "You were looking to the battle before you engaged in it, and now you see it with your own two eyes." Remember: "How many small groups beat big groups by the will of God." And his words: "If God gives you victory, no one can beat you. And if he betrays you, who can give you victory without Him? So the faithful put their trust in God."

11. Remind yourself of the supplications and of your brethren and ponder their meanings. [The morning and evening supplications, and the supplications of entering a town, and . . . the supplications said before meeting the enemy.]

12. Bless your body with some verses of the Koran [done by reading verses into one's hands and then rubbing the hands over whatever is to be blessed], the luggage, clothes, the knife, your personal effects, your ID, your passport, and all of your papers.

13. Check your weapon before you leave and long before you leave. (You must make your knife sharp and you must not discomfort your animal during the slaughter.)

14. Tighten your clothes [a reference to one making sure his clothes will cover his private parts at all times], since this is the way of the pious generations after the prophet. They would tighten their clothes before battle. Tighten your shoes well, wear socks so that your feet will be solidly in your shoes. All of these are worldly things [that humans can do to control their fate, although God decrees what will work and what will not] and the rest is left to God, the best One to depend on.

15. Pray the morning prayer in a group and ponder the great rewards of that prayer. Make supplications afterward, and do not leave your apartment unless you have performed ablution before leaving, because (The angels will ask for your forgiveness as long as you are in a state of ablution, and will pray for you). This saying of the prophet was mentioned by [Yaba ibn Sharif] al-Nawawi in his book, *The Best of Supplications*. Read the words of God: "Did you think that We created you for no reason. . . ." from the al-Mu'minun chapter.

## The Second Step

When the taxi takes you to (M) [this initial could stand for *matar*, airport in Arabic] remember God constantly while in the car. (Remember the supplication for entering a car, for entering a town, the supplication of place and other supplications.)

When you have reached (M) and have left the taxi, say a supplication of place ["O Lord, I ask you for the best of this place, and ask you to protect me from its evils"], and everywhere you go say that prayer and smile and be calm, for God is with the believers. And the angels protect you without you feeling anything. Say this supplication: "God is more dear than all of his creation." And say: "O Lord, protect me from them as you wish." And say: "O Lord, take your anger out on them [the enemy] and we ask you to protect us from their evils." And say: "O Lord, block their vision from in front of them, so that they may not see." And say: "God is all we need, he is the best to rely upon." Remember God's words: "Those to whom the people said, 'The people have gathered to get you, so fear them,' but that only increased their faith and they said, God is all we need, he is the best to rely upon." After you say that, you will find . . . as God promised this to his servants who say this supplication:

1. They will come back [from battle] with God's blessings.
2. They were not harmed.
3. And God was satisfied with them.

God says: "They came back with God's blessings, they were not harmed, and God was satisfied with them, and God is ever-blessing."

All of their equipment and gates and technology will not prevent, nor harm, except by God's will. The believers do not fear such things. The only ones that fear it are the allies of Satan, who are the brothers of the devil. They have become their allies, God save us, for fear is a great form of worship, and the only one worthy of it is God. He is the only one who deserves it. He said in the verses: "This is only the Devil scaring his allies" who are fascinated with Western civilization, and have drunk the love [of the West] like they drink water . . . and have become afraid of their weak equipment "so fear them not, and fear Me, if you are believers."

Fear is a great worship. The allies of God do not offer such worship except for the one God, who controls everything . . . with total certainty that God will weaken the schemes of the non-believers. God said: "God will weaken the schemes of the non-believers."

You must remember your brothers with all respect. No one should notice that you are making the supplication, "There is no God but God," because if you say it 1,000 times no one will be able to tell whether you are quiet or remember God. And among its miracles is what the prophet, peace be upon him, said: Whoever says, "There is no God but God," with all his heart, goes to heaven. The prophet, peace be upon him, said: "If you put all the worlds and universes on one side of the balance, and 'No God but God' on the other, 'No God but God' will weigh more heavily." You can repeat these words confidently, and this is just one of the strengths of these words. Whoever thinks deeply about these words will find that they have no dots [in the Arabic letter] and this is just one of its greatnesses, for words that have dots in them carry less weight than those that do not. And it is enough that these are the words of monotheism, which will make you steadfast in battle as the prophet, peace be upon him, and his companions, and those who came after them, God willing, until the Day of Judgment.

Also, do not seem confused or show signs of nervous tension. Be happy, optimistic, calm because you are heading for a deed that God loves and will accept [as a good deed]. It will be the day, God willing, you spend with the women of paradise.

Smile in the face of hardship young man / For you are heading toward eternal paradise.

You must remember to make supplications wherever you go, and anytime you do anything, and God is with his faithful servants, he will protect them and make their tasks easier, and give them success and control, and victory, and everything. . . .

## The Third Phase

When you ride the (T) [probably for *tayyara*, airplane in Arabic], before your foot steps in it, and before you enter it, you make a prayer and supplications. Remember that this is a battle for the sake of God. As the prophet, peace be upon him, said: An action for the sake of God is better than all of what is in this world, or as he said. When you step inside the (T), and sit in your seat, begin with the known supplications that we have mentioned before. Be busy with the constant remembrance of God. God said: "Oh ye faithful, when you find the enemy be steadfast, and remember God constantly so that you may be successful." When the (T) moves, even slightly, toward (Q) [unknown reference], say the supplication of travel. Because you are traveling to Almighty God, so be attentive on this trip. . . .

And then it takes off. This is the moment that both groups come together. So remember God, as he said in his Book: "Oh Lord, pour your patience upon us and make our feet steadfast and give us victory over the infidels." And his words: "And the only thing they said Lord, forgive our sins and excesses and make our feet steadfast and give us victory over the infidels." And his prophet said: "O Lord, you have revealed the book, you move the clouds, you gave us victory over the enemy, conquer them and give us victory over them." Give us victory and make the ground shake under their feet. Pray for yourself and all of your brothers that they may be victorious and hit their targets and [unclear] and ask God to grant you martyrdom facing the enemy, not running away from it, and for him to grant you patience and the feeling that anything that happens to you is for him.

Then every one of you should prepare to carry out his role in a way that would satisfy God. You should clench your teeth, as the pious early generations did.

When the confrontation begins, strike like champions who do not want to go back to this world. Shout, "Allahu Akbar," because this strikes fear in the hearts of the nonbelievers. God said: "Strike above the neck, and strike at all of their extremities." Know that the gardens of paradise are waiting for you in all their beauty, and the women of paradise are waiting, calling out, "Come hither, friend of God." They have dressed in their most beautiful clothing.

If God decrees that any of you are to slaughter, you should dedicate the slaughter to your fathers . . . because you have obligations toward them. Do not disagree, and obey. If you slaughter, do not cause the discomfort of those you are killing, because this is one of the practices of the prophet, peace be upon him. On one condition: that you do not become distracted . . . and neglect what is greater, paying attention to the enemy. That would be treason, and would do more damage than good. If this happens, the deed at hand is more important than doing that, because the deed is an obligation, and [the other thing] is optional. And an obligation has priority over an option.

Do not seek revenge for yourself. Strike for God's sake. One time Ali bin Abi Talib [a companion and close relative of the Prophet Muhammad], may God bless him, fought with a nonbeliever. The nonbeliever spit on Ali, may God bless him. Ali . . . did not strike him. When the battle was over, the companions of the prophet asked him why he had not smitten the nonbeliever. He said, "After he spat at me, I was afraid that I would be striking at him in revenge for myself, so I lifted my sword." After he renewed his intentions, he went back and killed the man. This means that before you do anything, make sure that your soul is prepared to do everything for God only.

Then implement the way of the prophet in taking prisoners. Take prisoners and kill them. As Almighty God said: "No prophet should have prisoners until he has soaked the land with blood. You want the bounties of this world [in exchange for prisoners] and God wants the other world [for you], and God is all-powerful, all-wise."

If everything goes well, every one of you should pat the other on the shoulder in confidence. . . . Remind your brothers that this act is for Almighty God. Do not confuse your brothers or distract them. He should give them glad tidings and make them calm, and remind them [of God] and encourage them. How beautiful it is for one to read God's words, such as: "And those who prefer the afterlife over this world should fight for the sake of God." And his words: "Do not suppose that those who are killed for the sake of God are dead; they are alive. . . ." And others. Or they should sing songs to boost their morale, as the pious first generations did in the throes of battle, to bring calm, tranquility, and joy to the hearts of his brothers.

Do not forget to take a bounty, even if it is a glass of water to quench your thirst or that of your brothers, if possible. When the hour of reality approaches, the zero hour . . . wholeheartedly welcome death for the sake of God. Always be remembering God. Either end your life while praying, seconds before the target, or make your last words: "There is no God but God, Muhammad is his messenger."

Afterward, we will all meet in the highest heaven, God willing.

If you see the enemy as strong, remember the groups [that had formed a coalition to fight the Prophet Muhammad]. They were 10,000. Remember how God gave victory to his faithful servants. God said: "When the faithful saw the [size of the enemy army], they said, this is what God and the prophet promised, they said the truth. It only increased their faith."

And may the peace of the God be upon the prophet.

# Responsibility for the Terrorist Atrocities in the United States, September 11, 2001 (October 4, 2001)

## BRITISH GOVERNMENT

. . . 2. . . . The material in respect of September 11 comes from intelligence and the criminal investigation to date. The details of some aspects cannot be given, but the facts are clear from the intelligence. . . .

59. In the months before the September 11 attacks, propaganda videos were distributed throughout the Middle East and Muslim world by al-Qa'ida, in which Usama bin Ladin and others were shown encouraging Muslims to attack American and Jewish targets.

60. Similar videos, extolling violence against the United States and other targets, were distributed before the East African embassy attacks in August 1998.

61. Nineteen men have been identified as the hijackers from the passenger lists of the four planes hijacked on September 11, 2001. At least three of them have already been positively identified as associates of al-Qa'ida. One has been identified as playing key roles in both the East African embassy attacks and the USS *Cole* attack. Investigations continue into the backgrounds of all the hijackers.

62. From intelligence sources, the following facts have been established subsequent to September 11; for intelligence reasons, the names of associates, though known, are not given.

In the run-up to September 11, bin Ladin was mounting a concerted propaganda campaign amongst like-minded groups of people—including videos and documentation—justifying attacks on Jewish and American targets, and claiming that those who died in the course of them were carrying out God's work.

We have learned, subsequent to September 11, that bin Ladin himself asserted shortly before September 11 that he was preparing a major attack on America.

In August and early September close associates of bin Ladin were warned to return to Afghanistan from other parts of the world by September 10.

Immediately prior to September 11 some known associates of bin Ladin were naming the date for action as on or around September 11.

Since September 11 we have learned that one of bin Ladin's closest and most senior associates was responsible for the detailed planning of the attacks.

There is evidence of a very specific nature relating to the guilt of bin Ladin and his associates that is too sensitive to release.

63. Usama bin Ladin remains in charge, and the mastermind, of al-Qa'ida. In al-Qa'ida, an operation on the scale of the September 11 attacks would have been approved by Usama bin Ladin himself.

64. The modus operandi of September 11 was entirely consistent with previous attacks. Al Qa'ida's record of atrocities is characterized by meticulous long-term planning, a desire to inflict mass casualties, suicide bombers, and multiple simultaneous attacks.

65. The attacks of September 11, 2001 are entirely consistent with the scale and sophistication of the planning which went into the attacks on the East African embassies and the USS *Cole*. No warnings were given for these three attacks, just as there was none on September 11. . . .

67. The operatives involved in the September 11 atrocities attended flight schools, used flight simulators to study the controls of larger aircraft, and placed potential airports and routes under surveillance. . . .

69. No other organization has both the motivation and the capability to carry out attacks like those of September 11—only the al-Qa'ida network under Usama bin Ladin.

## Conclusion

70. The attacks of September 11, 2001, were planned and carried out by al-Qa'ida, an organization whose head is Usama bin Ladin. That organization has the will, and the resources, to execute further attacks of similar scale. Both the United States and its close allies are targets for such attacks. The attack could not have occurred without the alliance between the Taliban and Usama bin Ladin, which allowed bin Ladin to operate freely in Afghanistan, promoting, planning and executing terrorist activity.

# The Hijackers of September 11
# (September 27, 2001)

FEDERAL BUREAU OF INVESTIGATION

[These are the individuals believed to be the hijackers of the four airliners that crashed on September 11, 2001, into the World Trade Center in New York City and the Pentagon in Washington, D.C., and in Stony Creek Township, Pennsylvania.—*Eds.*]

## American Airlines #77, Boeing 757, from Washington, D.C., Bound for Los Angeles

1. Khalid Almihdhar—Possible Saudi national

   • Possible resident of San Diego, California, and New York
   • Alias: Sannan al-Makki; Khalid bin Muhammad; Addallah al-Mihdhar; Khalid Mohammad al-Saqaf

2. Majed Moqed—Possible Saudi national

   • Alias: Majed M. GH Moqed; Majed Mashaan Moqed

3. Nawaf Alhazmi—Possible Saudi national

   • Possible resident of Fort Lee, New Jersey; Wayne, New Jersey; San Diego, California
   • Alias: Nawaf al-Hazmi; Nawaf al-Hazmi; Nawaf M. S. al-Hazmi

4. Salem Alhazmi—Possible Saudi national

   • Possible resident of Fort Lee, New Jersey; Wayne, New Jersey

5. Hani Hanjour—Possible resident of Phoenix, Arizona; and San Diego, California

   • Alias: Hani Saleh Hanjour; Hani Saleh; Hani Saleh H. Hanjour

## American Airlines #11, Boeing 767, from Boston Bound for Los Angeles

1. Satam M. A. al-Suqami—Possible Saudi national

   • Dates of birth used: June 28, 1976; Last known address: United Arab Emirates

2. Waleed M. Alshehri—Possible Saudi national

   • Dates of birth used: September 13, 1974; January 1, 1976; March 3, 1976; July 8, 1977; December 20, 1978; May 11, 1979; November 5, 1979
   • Possible residence(s): Hollywood, Florida; Orlando, Florida; Daytona Beach, Florida
   • Believed to be a pilot

3. Wail M. Alshehri

   • Date of birth used: September 1, 1968
   • Possible residence(s): Hollywood, Florida; Newton, Massachusetts
   • Believed to be a pilot

4. Mohamed Atta—Possible Egyptian national

   • Date of birth used: September 1, 1968
   • Possible residence(s): Hollywood, Florida; Coral Springs, Florida; Hamburg, Germany
   • Believed to be a pilot
   • Alias: Mehan Atta; Mohammad el Amir; Muhammad Atta; Mohamed el Sayed; Mohamed Elsayed; Muhammad Muhammad al-Amir Awag al-Sayyid Atta; Muhammad Muhammad al-Amir Awad al-Sayad

5. Adb al-Aziz Alomari—Possible Saudi national

   • Dates of birth used: December 24, 1972, and May 28, 1979
   • Possible residence(s): Hollywood, Florida
   • Believed to be a pilot

## United Airlines #175, Boeing 767, from Boston Bound for Los Angeles

1. Marwan al-Shehhi

- Date of birth used: May 9, 1978
- Possible residence(s): Hollywood, Florida
- Believed to be a pilot
- Alias: Marwan Yusif Muhammad Rashid al-Shehi; Marwan Yusif Muhammad Rashid Lakrab al-Shihhi; Abu Abdullah

2. Fayez Rashid Ahmad Hassan al Qadi Banihammad

- Possible residence(s): Delray Beach, Florida
- Alias: Fayez Ahmad; Banihammad Fayez Abu Dhabi Banihammad; Fayez Rashid Ahmad; Banihammad Fayez; Rasid Ahmad Hassen Alqadi; Abu Dhabi Banihammad Ahmad Fayez; Faez Ahmad

3. Ahmad Alghamdi [al-Ghamidi]

- Alias: Ahmad Salah Alghamdi

4. Hamza Alghamdi

- Possible residence(s): Delray Beach, Florida
- Alias: Hamza al-Ghamdi; Hamza Ghamdi; Hamzah Alghamdi; Hamza Alghamdi Saleh

5. Mohand Alshehri

- Possible residence(s): Delray Beach, Florida
- Alias: Muhammad Alshehhi; Mohamd Alshehri; Mohald Alshehri

## United Airlines #93, Boeing 757, from Newark Bound for San Francisco

1. Saeed Alghamdi

- Possible residence: Delray Beach, Florida
- Alias: Abdul Rahman Saed Alghamdi; Ali S. Alghamdi; Al-Gamdi; Saad M. S. al-Ghamdi; Sadda al-Ghamdi; Saheed al-Ghamdi; Seed al-Ghamdi

2. Ahmad Ibrahim A. al-Haznawi—Possible Saudi national

- Date of birth used: October 11, 1980
- Possible residence: Delray Beach, Florida
- Alias: Ahmad Alhaznawi

3. Ahmad Alnami

- Possible residence: Delray Beach, Florida
- Alias: Ali Ahmad Alnami; Ahmad A. al-Nami; Ahmad al-Nawi

4. Ziad Samir Jarrah

- Believed to be a pilot

- Alias: Zaid Jarrahi; Zaid Samr Jarrah; Ziad S. Jarrah; Ziad Jarrah Jarrat, Ziad Samir Jarrahi

# Videotape of a Private Meeting (December 13, 2001)

USAMA BIN LADIN*

*Usama bin Ladin:* ... What is the stand of the mosques there [in Saudi Arabia]?

*Sheikh:* Honestly, they are very positive. Sheikh al-Bahrani [a Saudi cleric] gave a good sermon in his class after the sunset prayers. It was videotaped and I was supposed to carry it with me, but unfortunately, I had to leave immediately.

*Bin Ladin:* The day of the events?

*Sheikh:* At the exact time of the attack on America, precisely at the time. He [Bahrani] gave a very impressive sermon. Thanks be to Allah for his blessings. He was the first one to write at wartime.

*Bin Ladin:* Thanks be to Allah.

*Sheikh:* His position is really very encouraging. When I paid him the first visit about a year and half ago, he asked me, "How is Sheikh bin Ladin?" He sends you his special regards.

*Bin Ladin:* Thanks be to Allah.

*Sheikh:* .... [Bahrani] told the youth: "You are asking for martyrdom and wonder where you should go?" Allah was inciting them to go. I asked Allah to grant me to witness the truth in front of the unjust ruler. We ask Allah to protect him and give him the martyrdom, after he issued the first *fatwa*. He was detained for interrogation, as you know. When he was called in and asked to sign, he told them, "Don't waste my time, I have another *fatwa*. If you want me [to], I can sign both at the same time."

---

* On November 9, 2001, Usama bin Ladin spoke to a room of supporters, possibly in Kandahar, Afghanistan, including an unidentified visitor from Saudi Arabia. Translation released by the U.S. government.

*Bin Ladin:* Thanks be to Allah.

*Sheikh:* ... Sheikh Sulayman Ulwan [Saudi cleric] ... gave a beautiful *fatwa*, may Allah bless him. Miraculously, I heard it on the Koran radio station. It was strange because he [Ulwan] sacrificed his position, which is equivalent to a director. It was transcribed word-by-word. The brothers listened to it in detail. I briefly heard it before the noon prayers. [Ulwan] said this was *jihad* and those people [the World Trade Center and Pentagon victims] were not innocent people. He swore to Allah. ...

*Bin Ladin:* ... When people see a strong horse and a weak horse, by nature, they will like the strong horse. This is only one goal; those who want people to worship the lord of the people, without following that doctrine, will be following the doctrine of Muhammad, peace be upon him. [*Bin Ladin quotes several short and incomplete* hadith *verses, as follows*]: "I was ordered to fight the people until they say there is no God but Allah, and his Prophet Muhammad." "Some people may ask: why do you want to fight us?" "There is an association between those who say: I believe in one God and Muhammad is his prophet, and those who don't. ... Those who do not follow the true *fiqh* [behavior]. The *fiqh* of Muhammad, the real *fiqh*. They are just accepting what is being said at face value."

Those youth who conducted the operations did not accept any fight in the popular terms, but they accepted the *fiqh* that the Prophet Muhammad brought. Those young men ... said in deeds, in New York and Washington, speeches that overshadowed all other speeches made everywhere else in the world. The speeches are understood by both Arabs and non-Arabs—even by Chinese. It is above all the media said. Some of them said that in Holland, at one of the centers, the number of people who accepted Islam during the days that followed the operations were more than the people who accepted Islam in the last eleven years. I heard someone on Islamic radio who owns a school in America say: "We don't have time to keep up with the demands of those who are asking about Islamic books to learn about Islam." This event made people think (about true Islam), which benefited Islam greatly.

*Sheikh:* Hundreds of people used to doubt you and few only would follow you until this huge event happened. Now hundreds of people are coming out to join you. I remember a vision by Sheikh Salih al-Shuaybi [a Saudi cleric]. He said: "There will be a great hit and people will go out by hundreds to Afghanistan." I asked him: "To Afghanistan?" He replied, "Yes." According to him, the only ones who stay behind will be the mentally impotent and the liars [hypocrites]. I remembered his saying that hundreds of people will go out to Afghanistan. He had this vision a year ago. This event discriminated between the different types of followers.

*Bin Ladin:* . . . . We calculated in advance the number of casualties from the enemy, who would be killed based on the position of the tower. We calculated that the floors that would be hit would be three or four floors. I was the most optimistic of them all. . . . Due to my experience in this field, I was thinking that the fire from the gas in the plane would melt the iron structure of the building and collapse the area where the plane hit and all the floors above it only. This is all that we had hoped for.

*Sheikh:* Allah be praised.

*Bin Ladin:* We were at [inaudible] when the event took place. We had notification since the previous Thursday that the event would take place that day. We had finished our work that day and had the radio on. It was 5:30 P.M. our time. I was sitting with Dr. Ahmad Abu al-[Khair]. Immediately, we heard the news that a plane had hit the World Trade Center. We turned the radio station to the news from Washington. The news continued and no mention of the attack until the end. At the end of the newscast, they reported that a plane [had] just hit the World Trade Center.

*Sheikh:* Allah be praised.

*Bin Ladin:* After a little while, they announced that another plane had hit the World Trade Center. The brothers who heard the news were overjoyed by it.

*Sheikh:* I listened to the news and I was sitting. We didn't . . . we were not thinking about anything, and all of a sudden, Allah willing, we were talking about how come we didn't hear anything, and all of a sudden the news came and everyone was overjoyed and everyone until the next day, in the morning, was talking about what was happening and we stayed until 4:00, listening to the news every time a little bit different, everyone was very joyous and saying "Allah is great," "Allah is great," "We are thankful to Allah," "Praise Allah." And I was happy for the happiness of my brothers. That day the congratulations were coming on the phone nonstop. The mother was receiving phone calls continuously. . . . No doubt it is a clear victory. Allah has bestowed on us . . . honor on us . . . and he will give us blessing and more victory during this holy month of Ramadan. And this is what everyone is hoping for. Thank Allah America came out of its caves. We hit her the first hit and the next one will hit her with the hands of the believers, the good believers, the strong believers. By Allah it is a great work. Allah prepares for you a great reward for this work. I'm sorry to speak in your presence, but it is just thoughts, just thoughts. By Allah, who there is no God but him. I live in happiness, happiness . . . I have not experienced, or felt, in a long time. I remember the words of al-Rabbani; he said they made a coalition against us in the winter with the infidels like the Turks, and others, and some other Arabs. And they surrounded us like the days . . . in the days of the Prophet Muhammad. Exactly like what's happening right now. But he comforted his followers and said, "This is going to turn and hit them back." And it is a mercy for us. And a blessing to us. . . . By Allah, my sheikh. We congratulate you for the great work. Thank Allah. . . .

*Bin Ladin:* . . . . Abu al-Hasan al-[Masri], who appeared on al-Jazira television a couple of days ago and addressed the Americans saying: "If you are true men, come down here and face us." . . . He told me a year ago: "I saw in a dream, we were playing a soccer game against the Americans. When our team showed up in the field, they were all pilots!" He said: "So I wondered if that was a soccer game or a pilot game? Our players were pilots." He [Abu al-Hasan] didn't know anything about the operation until he heard it on the radio. He said the game went on and we defeated them. That was a good omen for us.

*Sheikh:* May Allah be blessed.

*Unidentified Man Off-Camera:* Abd al-Rahman al-[Ghamri] said he saw a vision, before the operation, [that] a plane crashed into a tall building. He knew nothing about it.

*Sheikh:* May Allah be blessed!

*Suleiman [Abu Ghaith]:* I was sitting with the sheikh in a room, then I left to go to another room where there was a television set. The television broadcast the big event. The scene was showing an Egyptian family sitting in their living room. They exploded with joy. Do you know when there is a soccer game and your team wins, it was the same expression of joy. There was a subtitle that read: "In revenge for the children of al-Aqsa, Usama bin Ladin executes an operation against America." So I went back to the sheikh [bin Ladin] who was sitting in a room with fifty to sixty people. I tried to tell him about what I saw, but he made [a] gesture with his hands, meaning: "I know, I know. . . ."

*Bin Ladin:* He did not know about the operation. Not everybody knew. . . . Muhammad [Atta] from the Egyptian family [meaning al-Qa'ida's ally, the Egyptian Jihad group] was in charge of the group. . . .

*Bin Ladin:* The brothers who conducted the operation, all they knew was that they have a martyrdom operation and we asked each of them to go to America but they didn't know anything about the operation, not even one letter. But they were trained and we did not reveal the operation to them until they are there and just before they boarded the planes. . . . Then he said: Those who were trained to fly didn't know the others. One group of people did not know the other group. . . .

[*Someone in the crowd asks bin Ladin to tell the Sheikh about the dream of Abu-Da'ud.*]

*Bin Ladin:* We were at a camp of one of the brother's guards in Kandahar. This brother belonged to the majority of the group. He came close and told me that he saw, in a dream, a tall building in America. . . . At that point, I was worried that maybe the secret would be revealed if everyone starts seeing it in their dream. So I closed the subject. I told him if he sees another dream, not to tell anybody, because people will be upset with him.

[*Another person's voice can be heard recounting his dream about two planes hitting a big building.*]

*Bin Ladin:* They were overjoyed when the first plane hit the building, so I said to them: be patient.

*Bin Ladin:* The difference between the first and the second plane hitting the towers was twenty minutes. And the difference between the first plane and the plane that hit the Pentagon was one hour.

*Sheikh:* They [the Americans] were terrified thinking there was a coup. . . .

*Bin Ladin [reciting a poem]:*

> I witness that against the sharp blade
> They always faced difficulties and stood together
> When the darkness comes upon us and we are bit by a
> Sharp tooth,
> I say . . . "Our homes are flooded with blood
> and the tyrant is freely wandering in our homes"
> And from the battlefield vanished
> The brightness of swords and the horses
> And over weeping sounds now
> We hear the beats of drums and rhythm
> They are storming his forts
> And shouting: "We will not stop our raids
> Until you free our lands."

# Interview with Mullah Umar Muhammad (September 21, 2001)*

*Question:* Why don't you expel Usama bin Ladin?

*Umar:* This is not an issue of Usama bin Ladin. It is an issue of Islam. Islam's prestige is at stake. So is Afghanistan's tradition.

---

* Mullah Umar Muhammad was the spiritual guide of the Taliban. This interview was broadcast on *Voice of America*.

*Q:* Do you know that the United States has announced a war on terrorism?

*Umar:* I am considering two promises. One is the promise of God, the other is that of Bush. The promise of God is that my land is vast. If you start a journey on God's path, you can reside anywhere on this earth and will be protected. . . . The promise of Bush is that there is no place on earth where you can hide that I cannot find you. We will see which one of these two promises is fulfilled.

*Q:* But aren't you afraid for the people, yourself, the Taliban, your country?

*Umar:* Almighty God . . . is helping the believers and the Muslims. God says he will never be satisfied with the infidels. In terms of worldly affairs, America is very strong. Even if it were twice as strong or twice that, it could not be strong enough to defeat us. We are confident that no one can harm us if God is with us.

*Q:* You are telling me you are not concerned, but Afghans all over the world are concerned.

*Umar:* We are also concerned. Great issues lie ahead. But we depend on God's mercy. Consider our point of view: if we give Usama away today, Muslims who are now pleading to give him up would then be reviling us for giving him up. . . . Everyone is afraid of America and wants to please it. But Americans will not be able to prevent such acts like the one that has just occurred because America has taken Islam hostage. If you look at Islamic countries, the people are in despair. They are complaining that Islam is gone. But people remain firm in their Islamic beliefs. In their pain and frustration, some of them commit suicide acts. They feel they have nothing to lose.

*Q:* What do you mean by saying America has taken the Islamic world hostage?

*Umar:* America controls the governments of the Islamic countries. The people ask to follow Islam, but the governments do not listen because they are in the grip of the United States. If someone follows the path of Islam, the government arrests him, tortures him or kills him. This is the doing of America. If it stops supporting those governments and lets the people deal with them, then such things won't happen. America has created the evil that is attacking it. The evil will not disappear even if I die and Usama dies and others die. The United States should step back and review its policy. It should stop trying to impose its empire on the rest of the world, especially on Islamic countries.

*Q:* So you won't give Usama bin Ladin up?

*Umar:* No. We cannot do that. If we did, it means we are not Muslims . . . that Islam is finished. If we were afraid of attack, we could have surrendered him the last time we were threatened and attacked. So America can hit us again, and this time we don't even have a friend.

*Q:* If you fight America with all your might—can the Taliban do that? Won't America beat you and won't your people suffer even more?

*Umar:* I'm very confident that it won't turn out this way. Please note this: there is nothing more we can do except depend on Almighty God. If a person does, then he is assured that the Almighty will help him, have mercy on him and he will succeed.

# Broadcast by Usama bin Ladin
# (October 7, 2001)*

Praise be to God and we beseech him for help and forgiveness. We seek refuge with the Lord of our bad and evildoing. He whom God guides is rightly guided but he whom God leaves to stray, for him wilt thou find no protector to lead him to the right way.

I witness that there is no God but God and Muhammad is his slave and prophet.

God Almighty hit the United States at its most vulnerable spot. He destroyed its greatest buildings. Praise be to God.

Here is the United States. It was filled with terror from its north to its south and from its east to its west. Praise be to God.

What the United States tastes today is a very small thing compared to what we have tasted for tens of years.

Our nation has been tasting this humiliation and contempt for more than eighty years.

Its sons are being killed, its blood is being shed, its holy places are being attacked, and it is not being ruled according to what God has decreed.

Despite this, nobody cares.

When Almighty God rendered successful a convoy of Muslims, the vanguards of Islam, he allowed them to destroy the United States.

I ask God Almighty to elevate their status and grant them paradise. He is the one who is capable [of doing] so.

---

* Al-Jazira television. Translation by BBC News.

When these defended their oppressed sons, brothers, and sisters in Palestine and in many Islamic countries, the world at large shouted. The infidels shouted, followed by the hypocrites.

One million Iraqi children have thus far died in Iraq, although they did not do anything wrong.

Despite this, we heard no denunciation by anyone in the world or a *fatwa* by the rulers' *ulama* [Muslim scholars].

Israeli tanks and tracked vehicles also enter to wreak havoc in Palestine, in Jenin, Ramallah, Rafah, Beit Jala, and other Islamic areas, and we hear no voices raised or moves made.

But if the sword falls on the United States after eighty years, hypocrisy raises its head, lamenting the deaths of these killers who tampered with the blood, honor, and holy places of the Muslims.

The . . . [best] that one can . . . [say of] these people is that they are morally depraved.

They champion falsehood, support the butcher against the victim, the oppressor against the innocent child.

May God mete them the punishment they deserve.

I say that the matter is clear and explicit.

In the aftermath of this event and now that senior U.S. officials have spoken, beginning with Bush, the head of the world's infidels, and whoever supports him, every Muslim should rush to defend his religion.

They came out in arrogance with their men and horses and instigated even those countries that belong to Islam against us.

They came out to fight this group of people who declared their faith in God and refused to abandon their religion.

They came out to fight Islam in the name of terrorism.

Hundreds of thousands of people, young and old, were killed in the farthest point on earth in Japan.

[For them] this is not a crime, but rather a debatable issue.

They bombed Iraq and considered that a debatable issue.

But when a dozen people of them were killed in Nairobi and Dar es Salaam, Afghanistan and Iraq were bombed and all hypocrite ones stood behind the head of the world's infidelity—behind the *hubal* [an idol worshipped by pagans before the advent of Islam] of the age—namely, America and its supporters.

These incidents divided the entire world into two regions—one of faith, where there is no hypocrisy, and another of infidelity, from which we hope God will protect us.

The winds of faith and change have blown to remove falsehood from the [Arabian] peninsula of Prophet Muhammad, may God's prayers be upon him.

As for the United States, I tell it and its people these few words: I swear by Almighty God, who raised the heavens without pillars, that neither the United States nor he who lives in the United States will enjoy security before we can see it as a reality in Palestine and before all the infidel armies leave the land of Muhammad, may God's peace and blessing be upon him.

God is great and glory to Islam.

May God's peace, mercy, and blessings be upon you.

# Al-Qa'ida Statement (October 10, 2001)

SULEIMAN ABU GHAITH*

We thank Almighty God, who said in his holy book: Ye who believe, take not the Jews and the Christians for your friends and protectors. They are but friends and protectors to each other. And he amongst you that turns to them is of them. Verily God guideth not a people unjustly.

May God's peace and blessings be upon our Prophet Muhammad, his companions, and those who followed his course.

I address this message to the entire Muslim nation to tell them that the confederates have joined forces against the Islamic nation and the crusader war, promised by Bush, has been launched against Afghanistan and against this people who have faith in God.

We now live under this crusader bombardment that targets the entire nation. The Islamic nation should know that we defend a just cause.

The Islamic nation has been groaning in pain for more than eighty years under the yoke of the joint Jewish–crusader aggression. Palestine is living under the yoke of the Jewish occupation and its people groan from this repression and persecution while no one lifts a finger. The Arabian Peninsula is being defiled by the feet of those who came to occupy these lands, usurp these holy places, and plunder these resources.

The Islamic nation must also know that the U.S. version of terrorism is a kind of deception. Is it logical for the United States and its allies to carry out this repression, persecution, plundering, and bloodletting over these long years

---

* BBC translation. Suleiman Abu Ghaith is an al-Qa'ida official.

without this being called terrorism, while when the victim tries to seek justice, he is described as terrorist?

This type of deception can never be accepted in any case whatsoever.

Let the United States know that the Islamic nation will not remain silent after this day on what it is experiencing and what takes place in its land, and that *jihad* for the sake of God today is an obligation on every Muslim in this land if he has no excuse.

God Almighty has said: Then fight in God's cause, thou art held responsible only for thyself and rouse the believers. It may be that God will restrain the fury of the unbelievers, for God is the strongest in might and in punishment.

U.S. interests are spread throughout the world. So every Muslim should carry out his real role to champion his Islamic nation and religion. Carrying out terrorism against the oppressors is one of the tenets of our religion and *Sharia*.

Against them make ready your strength to the utmost of your power, including steeds of war, to strike terror into the hearts of the enemies of God and your enemies.

I would like to touch on one important point in this address. The actions by these young men who destroyed the United States and launched the storm of planes against it have done a good deed.

They transferred the battle into the U.S. heartland. Let the United States know that with God's permission, the battle will continue to be waged on its territory until it leaves our lands, stops its support for the Jews, and lifts the unjust embargo on the Iraqi people, who have lost more than one million children.

The Americans should know that the storm of plane attacks will not abate, with God's permission. There are thousands of the Islamic nation's youths who are eager to die just as the Americans are eager to live.

They should know that with their invasion of the land of Afghanistan, they have started a new phase of enmity and conflict between us and the forces of infidelity. We are confident that we will achieve victory thanks to our material and moral strength and confidence and faith in Almighty God. The Americans have opened a door that will under no circumstances be shut.

I address Muslim youths, men, and women and urge them to shoulder their responsibility. They should know that the land of Afghanistan and the *mujahidin* there are really facing an all-out crusader war that is aimed at eliminating this group, which believes in God and fights on the basis of a creed and religion. Thus, the nation must shoulder its responsibility. It would be a disgrace if the Islamic nation fails to do so.

Finally, I thank Almighty God who enabled us to engage in this *jihad* and fight this battle, which is a decisive one between infidelity and faith. I ask

Almighty God to grant us victory over our enemy, make their machinations backfire on them, and defeat them.

May God's peace, mercy, and blessings be upon you.

# Al-Qa'ida Statement (October 13, 2001)

SULEIMAN ABU GHAITH*

Praise be to God, the Cherisher and Sustainer of the Worlds, and may God's peace and blessings be upon our Prophet Muhammad, may he and all his household and companions be blessed by God.

Based on the questions and queries that we have received regarding how we view the incidents that have taken place over the past five days, we would like to say that the crusade spearheaded by the two crusaders Bush and Blair is continuing on the territory of Muslim Afghanistan and its population, who are demonstrating day in and day out their sacrifices, firmness, and determination to uphold their religion and creed. We pray to the Almighty God to hold their feet firmly, to strengthen their resolve, and to grant them victory over the infidels.

We also would like to declare our full support for this emirate and for the Muslim Afghan people in the face of this ferocious assault, offering all the material and moral resources that we have under the command of Mullah Umar Muhammad, commander of the faithful, may God protect him and grant him certain victory. This holds true regardless of the duration of the war. The issue at hand is the issue of an entire nation that opposes humiliation and subservience under the yoke of U.S. arrogance and Jewish persecution.

The al-Qa'ida organization declares that Bush Sr., Bush Jr., Clinton, Blair, and Sharon are the arch-criminals from among the Zionists and crusaders who committed the most heinous actions and atrocities against the Muslim nation. They perpetrated murders, torture, and displacement. Millions of Muslim men, women, and children died without any fault of their own. Al-Qa'ida stresses that the blood of those killed will not go to waste, God willing, until we punish these criminals.

---

* Broadcast on al-Jazira television. Translation by U.S. Department of Commerce, Foreign Broadcast Information Service (FBIS). Suleiman Abu Ghaith is an al-Qa'ida official.

Bush, in the midst of his arrogance, media frenzy, and the "Enduring Freedom" that he boasts about must not forget the video footage of Muhammad al-Durra [a Palestinian child killed in Israeli-Palestinian crossfire in the early days of the Palestinian *intifada* in the Gaza Strip] and his brothers, Muslim children in Palestine and Iraq.

If he forgot that scene, then we will never forget it. He must know that his "Enduring Freedom" which he boast[s] of has wiped out entire villages in Nangahar near Jalalabad in Afghanistan. Villages were completely wiped out. It was not a mistake but a deliberate action. What mistake is that which is repeated three times? This village was bombed in the beginning of night, in the middle of the night, and before dawn. Those who supported this crusader campaign should realize after things have been clarified that it is a crusader campaign against Islam and the Muslims.

Where will those who supported those criminals go away from Prophet Muhammad, may God's peace and blessings be upon him, who said that the destruction of earth is more tolerable to God than killing a believer without cause. What would they say when their deeds are displayed in front of God, praise be to him. What would they say when the female infant buried alive is questioned [Koranic verse]?

In this regard, we support the religious rulings issued by senior clerics in the kingdom of Saudi Arabia, led by His Eminence Sheikh Humud bin Uqla al-Shuayb, who said that it is impermissible to cooperate with Jews and Christians and that he who cooperates with them and gives them his opinion or take actions in supporting them becomes apostate and revokes his faith in God and his prophet, may God's peace and blessings be upon him.

[The] al-Qa'ida organization orders the Americans and the infidels in the Arabian Peninsula, particularly the Americans and the British, to leave the Arabian Peninsula. If the mothers of these need their sons then they should ask them to leave the Arabian Peninsula, because the land will be set on fire under their feet, God willing. In this regard we greet the *mujahidin* youths who knew their role and the way to respond to the aggression of the unjust and killed them. We also greet the Muslims, both in the East and West, who staged demonstrations rejecting this criminal aggression, repression, and injustice. We say to them that they should continue this pressure, especially since the Islamic countries' foreign ministers announced their support for this unjust campaign. These do not represent the nation in any case. They do not have the legitimacy that qualifies them to dispose of the nation's destiny and resolutions.

As for the decisions made by Bush and the U.S. administration to prevent satellite channels and world news agencies from making our voice heard in the world, then this is clear evidence that the U.S. administration fears the revelation of the truth that led to the Tuesday [September] events.

This truth shows that Bush is an agent of Israel and sacrifices his people and his country's economy for those and helps them occupy the Muslims' land and persecute their sons.

Finally, I address the U.S. secretary of state, who cast doubt about my previous statement and downplayed [it when] we said that there are thousands of Muslim youths who are eager to die and that the aircraft storm will not stop, God willing. Powell and others in the U.S. administration know that if [the] al-Qa'ida organization promises or threatens it fulfills its promise or threat, God willing. Therefore, we tell him tomorrow is not far for [him] who waits for it. What will happen is what you are going to see and not what you hear. And the storms will not calm, especially the aircraft storm. These storms will not calm until you retreat in, defeated in Afghanistan, stop your assistance to the Jews in Palestine, end the siege imposed on the Iraqi people, leave the Arabian Peninsula, and stop your support for the Hindus against the Muslims in Kashmir.

We also say and advise the Muslims in the United States and Britain, the children, and those who reject the unjust U.S. policy not to travel by plane. We also advise them not to live in high-rise buildings and towers.

But honor belongs to God, and his Apostle, and to the believers; but the hypocrites know not [Koranic verse]. Peace and God's blessings be upon you.

# Broadcast by Usama bin Ladin (November 3, 2001)*

We praise God, seek his help, and ask for his forgiveness.

We seek refuge in God from the evils of our souls and our bad deeds.

A person who is guided by God will never be misguided by anyone, and a person who is misguided by God can never be guided by anyone.

I bear witness that there is no God but Allah alone, who has no partner.

Amid the huge developments and in the wake of the great strikes that hit the United States in its most important locations in New York and Washington, a huge media clamor has been raised.

---

* Al-Jazira television. Translation by the BBC.

This clamor is unprecedented. It conveyed the opinions of people on these events.

People were divided into two parts. The first part supported these strikes against U.S. tyranny, while the second denounced them.

Afterward, when the United States launched the unjust campaign against the Islamic emirate in Afghanistan, people also split into two parties.

The first supported these campaigns, while the second denounced and rejected them.

These tremendous incidents, which have split people into two parties, are of great interest to the Muslims, since many of the rulings pertain to them.

These rulings are closely related to Islam and the acts that corrupt a person's Islam.

Therefore, the Muslims must understand the nature and truth of this conflict so that it will be easy for them to determine where they stand.

While talking about the truth of the conflict, opinion polls in the world have shown that a little more than 80 percent of Westerners, of Christians in the United States and elsewhere, have been saddened by the strikes that hit the United States.

The polls showed that the vast majority of the sons of the Islamic world were happy about these strikes because they believe that the strikes were in reaction to the huge criminality practiced by Israel and the United States in Palestine and other Muslim countries.

After the strikes on Afghanistan began, these groups changed positions.

Those who were happy about striking the United States felt sad when Afghanistan was hit, and those who felt sad when the United States was hit were happy when Afghanistan was hit. These groups comprise millions of people.

The entire West, with the exception of a few countries, supports this unfair, barbaric campaign, although there is no evidence of the involvement of the people of Afghanistan in what happened in America.

The people of Afghanistan had nothing to do with this matter. The campaign, however, continues to unjustly annihilate the villagers and civilians, children, women, and innocent people.

The positions of the two sides are very clear. Mass demonstrations have spread from the farthest point in the eastern part of the Islamic world to the farthest point in the western part of the Islamic world, and from Indonesia, the Philippines, Bangladesh, India, [and] Pakistan to the Arab world and Nigeria and Mauritania.

This clearly indicates the nature of this war. This war is fundamentally religious. The people of the East are Muslims. They sympathized with Muslims against the people of the West, who are the crusaders.

Those who try to cover this crystal-clear fact, which the entire world has admitted, are deceiving the Islamic nation.

They are trying to deflect the attention of the Islamic nation from the truth of this conflict.

This fact is proven in the book of God Almighty and in the teachings of our messenger, may God's peace and blessings be upon him.

Under no circumstances should we forget this enmity between us and the infidels. For the enmity is based on creed.

We must be loyal to the believers and those who believe that there is no God but Allah.

We should also renounce the atheists and infidels. It suffices me to seek God's help against them.

God says: "Never will the Jews or the Christians be satisfied with thee unless thou follow their form of religion."

It is a question of faith, not a war against terrorism, as Bush and Blair try to depict it.

Many thieves belonging to this nation were captured in the past. But nobody moved.

The masses that moved in the East and West have not done so for the sake of Usama.

Rather, they moved for the sake of their religion. This is because they know that they are right and that they resist the most ferocious, serious, and violent crusade . . . against Islam ever since the message was revealed to Muhammad, may God's peace and blessings be upon them.

After this has become clear, the Muslim must know and learn where he is standing vis-à-vis this war.

After the U.S. politicians spoke and after the U.S. newspapers and television channels became full of clear crusading hatred in this campaign that aims at mobilizing the West against Islam and Muslims, Bush left no room for doubts or the opinions of journalists, but he openly and clearly said that this war is a crusader war. He said this before the whole world to emphasize this fact.

What can those who allege that this is a war against terrorism say? What terrorism are they speaking about at a time when the Islamic nation has been slaughtered for tens of years without hearing their voices and without seeing any action by them?

But when the victim starts to take revenge for those innocent children in Palestine, Iraq, southern Sudan, Somalia, Kashmir and the Philippines, the rulers' *ulama* [moderate Islamic clerics] and the hypocrites come to defend the clear blasphemy. It suffices me to seek God's help against them.

The common people have understood the issue, but there are those who continue to flatter those who colluded with the unbelievers to anesthetize the

Islamic nation to prevent it from carrying out the duty of *jihad* so that the word of God will be above all words.

The unequivocal truth is that Bush has carried the cross and raised its banner high and stood at the front of the queue.

Anyone who lines up behind Bush in this campaign has committed one of the ten actions that sully one's Islam.

Muslim scholars are unanimous that allegiance to the infidels and support for them against the believers is one of the major acts that sully Islam.

There is no power but in God. Let us investigate whether this war against Afghanistan that broke out a few days ago is a single and unique one or if it is a link to a long series of crusader wars against the Islamic world.

Following World War I, which ended more than eighty-three years ago, the whole Islamic world fell under the crusader banner—under the British, French, and Italian governments.

They divided the whole world, and Palestine was occupied by the British.

Since then, and for more than eighty-three years, our brothers, sons, and sisters in Palestine have been badly tortured.

Hundreds of thousands of them have been killed, and hundreds of thousands of them have been imprisoned or maimed.

Let us examine the recent developments. Take for example the Chechens.

They are a Muslim people who have been attacked by the Russian bear, which embraces the Christian Orthodox faith.

Russians have annihilated the Chechen people in their entirety and forced them to flee to the mountains, where they were assaulted by snow and poverty and disease.

Nonetheless, nobody moved to support them. There is no strength but in God.

This was followed by a war of genocide in Bosnia in sight and hearing of the entire world in the heart of Europe.

For several years our brothers have been killed, our women have been raped, and our children have been massacred in the safe havens of the United Nations and with its knowledge and cooperation.

Those who refer our tragedies today to the United Nations so that they can be resolved are hypocrites who deceive God, his prophet, and the believers.

Are not our tragedies but caused by the United Nations? Who issued the partition resolution on Palestine in 1947 and surrendered the land of Muslims to the Jews? It was the United Nations in its resolution of 1947.

Those who claim that they are the leaders of the Arabs and continue to appeal to the United Nations have disavowed what was revealed to Prophet Muhammad, God's peace and blessings be upon him.

Those who refer things to the international legitimacy have disavowed the legitimacy of the holy book and the tradition of Prophet Muhammad, God's peace and blessings be upon him.

This is the United Nations from which we have suffered greatly. Under no circumstances should any Muslim or sane person resort to the United Nations. The United Nations is nothing but a tool of crime.

We are being massacred everyday, while the United Nations continues to sit idly by.

Our brothers in Kashmir have been subjected to the worst forms of torture for over fifty years. They have been massacred, killed, and raped. Their blood has been shed and their houses have been trespassed upon. Still, the United Nations continues to sit idly by.

Today, and without any evidence, the United Nations passes resolutions supporting unjust and tyrannical America, which oppresses these helpless people who have emerged from a merciless war at the hands of the Soviet Union.

Let us look at the second war in Chechnya, which is still underway. The entire Chechen people are being embattled once again by this Russian bear.

The humanitarian agencies, even the U.S. ones, demanded that President Clinton stop supporting Russia.

However, Clinton said that stopping support for Russia did not serve U.S. interests.

A year ago, [Russian President Vladimir] Putin demanded that the cross and the Jews should stand by him. He told them: You must support us and thank us because we are waging a war against Muslim fundamentalism.

The enemies are speaking very clearly. While this is taking place, the leaders of the region hide and are ashamed to support their brothers.

Let us examine the stand of the West and the United Nations in the developments in Indonesia when they moved to divide the largest country in the Islamic world in terms of population.

This criminal, [UN Secretary General] Kofi Annan, was speaking publicly and putting pressure on the Indonesian government, telling it: You have twenty-four hours to divide and separate East Timor from Indonesia.

Otherwise, we will be forced to send in military forces to separate it by force.

The crusader Australian forces were on Indonesian shores, and in fact they landed to separate East Timor, which is part of the Islamic world.

Therefore, we should view events not as separate links, but as links in a long series of conspiracies, a war of annihilation in the true sense of the word.

In Somalia, on the excuse of restoring hope, 13,000 of our brothers were killed. In southern Sudan, hundreds of thousands were killed.

But when we move to Palestine and Iraq, there can be no bounds to what can be said.

Over one million children were killed in Iraq. The killing is continuing.

As for what is taking place in Palestine these days, I can only say we have no one but God to complain to.

What is taking place cannot be tolerated by any nation. I do not say from the nations of the human race, but from other creatures, from the animals. They would not tolerate what is taking place.

A confidant of mine told me that he saw a butcher slaughtering a camel in front of another camel.

The other camel got agitated while seeing the blood coming out of the other camel. Thus, it burst out with rage and bit the hand of the man and broke it.

How can the weak mothers in Palestine endure the killing of their children in front of their eyes by the unjust Jewish executioners with U.S. support and with U.S. aircraft and tanks?

Those who distinguish between America and Israel are the real enemies of the nation. They are traitors who betrayed God and his prophet, and who betrayed their nation and the trust placed in them. They anesthetize the nation.

These battles cannot be viewed in any case whatsoever as isolated battles, but rather, as part of a chain of the long, fierce, and ugly crusader war.

Every Muslim must stand under the banner of "There is no God but Allah and Muhammad is God's prophet."

I remind you of what our prophet, may God's peace and blessings upon him, told Ibn Abbas, may God be pleased with him.

He told him: Boy, I am going to teach you a few words. Obey God, he will protect you. Obey him, you will find him on your side. If you ask for something, ask God. If you seek help, seek the help of God.

You should know that if all people come together to help you, they will only help you with something that God has already preordained for you.

And if they assemble to harm you, they will only harm you with something that God has already preordained for you. God wrote man's fate and it will never change.

I tell the Muslims who did their utmost during these weeks: you must continue along the same march.

Your support for us will make us stronger and will further support your brothers in Afghanistan.

Exert more efforts in combating this unprecedented war crime. . . .

# *Dawn* Interview with Usama bin Ladin (November 10, 2001)*

*Question:* After [the] American bombing of Afghanistan on October 7, you told al-Jazira television that the September 11 attacks had been carried out by some Muslims. How did you know they were Muslims?

*Bin Ladin:* The Americans themselves released a list of suspects of the September 11 attacks saying that the persons named were involved in the attacks. They were all Muslims, of whom fifteen belonged to Saudi Arabia, two were from the United Arab Emirates, and one from Egypt. . . . [A] *fateha* [funeral] was held for them in their homes. But America said they were hijackers.

*Question:* In your statement of October 7, you expressed satisfaction over the September 11 attacks, although a large number of innocent people perished in them, Hundreds among them were Muslims. Can you justify the killing of innocent men in the light of Islamic teachings?

*Bin Ladin:* This is a major point in jurisprudence. In my view, if an enemy occupies a Muslim territory and uses common people as a human shield, then it is permitted to attack that enemy. For instance, if bandits barge into a home and hold a child hostage, then the child's father can attack the bandits and in that attack even the child may get hurt.

America and its allies are massacring us in Palestine, Chechnya, Kashmir, and Iraq. The Muslims have the right to attack America in reprisal. The Islamic *Sharia* says Muslims should not live in the land of the infidel for long. The September 11 attacks were not targeted at women and children. The real targets were America's icons of military and economic power.

The holy prophet (peace be upon him) was against killing women and children. When he saw a dead woman during a war he asked, Why was she killed? If a child is above thirteen and wields a weapon against Muslims, then it is permitted to kill him.

The American people should remember that they pay taxes to their government, they elect their president, their government manufactures arms and gives them to Israel, and Israel uses them to massacre Palestinians. The American Congress endorses all government measures, and this proves that . . . [all of] America is responsible for the atrocities perpetrated against Muslims. [All of] America because they elect Congress.

I ask the American people to force their government to give up anti-Muslim policies. The American people had risen against their government's war in

---

* *Dawn* is a Pakistani newspaper.

Vietnam. They must do the same today. The American people should stop the massacre of Muslims by their government.

*Question:* Can it be said that you are against the American government, not the American people?

*Bin Ladin:* Yes! We are carrying on the mission of our Prophet Muhammad(peace be upon him). The mission is to spread the word of God, not to indulge in massacring people. We ourselves are the target of killings, destruction, and atrocities. We are only defending ourselves. This is defensive *jihad*. We want to defend our people and our land. That is why I say that if we don't get security, the Americans, too, would not get security.

This is a simple formula that even an American child can understand. This is the formula of live and let live.

*Question:* The head of Egypt's al-Azhar [Islamic university] has issued a *fatwa* against you saying that the views and beliefs of Usama bin Ladin have nothing to do with Islam. What do you have to say about that?

*Bin Ladin:* The *fatwa* of any official *alim* [religious figure] has no value for me. History is full of such *ulama* [clerics] who justify *riba* [economic interest], who justify the occupation of Palestine by the Jews, who justify the presence of American troops around Harmain Sharifain [the Islamic holy places in Saudi Arabia]. These people support the infidels for their personal gain. The true *ulama* support the *jihad* against America. Tell me, if Indian forces invaded Pakistan what would you do? The Israeli forces occupy our land and the American troops are on our territory. We have no other option but to launch *jihad*.

*Question:* Some Western media claim that you are trying to acquire chemical and nuclear weapons. How much truth is there in these reports?

*Bin Ladin:* I heard the speech of [the] American president Bush [on November 7]. He was scaring the European countries that Usama wanted to attack with weapons of mass destruction. I wish to declare that if America used chemical or nuclear weapons against us then we may retort with chemical and nuclear weapons. We have the weapons as a deterrent.

*Question:* Where did you get these weapons from?

*Bin Ladin:* Go to the next question.

*Question:* Demonstrations are being held in many European countries against American attacks on Afghanistan. Thousands of protesters were non-Muslims. What is your opinion about these non-Muslim protesters?

*Bin Ladin:* There are many innocent and good-hearted people in the West. American media instigates them against Muslims. However, some good-hearted people are protesting against American attacks because human nature abhors injustice. The Muslims were massacred under the UN patronage in Bosnia. I am aware that some officers of the state department had resigned in protest. Many years ago the U.S. ambassador in Egypt had resigned in protest against the policies of President Jimmy Carter. Nice and civilized people are everywhere. The Jewish lobby has taken America and the West hostage.

*Question:* Some people say that war is no solution to any issue. Do you think that some political formula could be found to stop the present war?

*Bin Ladin:* You should put this question to those who have started this war. We are only defending ourselves.

*Question:* If America got out of Saudi Arabia and the al-Aqsa mosque was liberated, would you then present yourself for trial in some Muslim country?

*Bin Ladin:* Only Afghanistan is an Islamic country. Pakistan follows the English law. I don't consider Saudi Arabia an Islamic country. If the Americans have charges against me, we too have a charge sheet against them.

*Question:* Pakistan's government decided to cooperate with America after September 11, which you don't consider right. What do you think Pakistan should have done but to cooperate with America?

*Bin Ladin:* The government of Pakistan should have the wishes of the people in view. It should not have surrendered to the unjustified demands of America. America does not have solid proof against us. It just has some surmises. It is unjust to start bombing on the basis of those surmises.

*Question:* Had America decided to attack Pakistan with the help of India and Israel, what would we have done?

*Bin Ladin:* What has America achieved by attacking Afghanistan? We will not leave the Pakistani people and the Pakistani territory at anybody's mercy. We will defend Pakistan. But we have been disappointed by [Pakistan's leader] General Pervez Musharraf. He says that the majority is with him. I say the majority is against him.

Bush has used the word "crusade." This is a crusade declared by Bush. It is no wisdom to barter off blood of Afghan brethren to improve Pakistan's economy. He will be punished by the Pakistani people and Allah.

Right now a great war of Islamic history is being fought in Afghanistan. All the big powers are united against Muslims. It is *sawad* [a good religious deed] to participate in this war. . . .

*Question:* Is it correct that a daughter of Mullah Umar is your wife or your daughter is Mullah Umar's wife?

*Bin Ladin:* [*laughs*] All my wives are Arabs and all my daughters are married to Arab *mujahidin*. I have a spiritual relationship with Mullah Umar. He is a great and brave Muslim of this age. He does not fear anyone but Allah. He is not under any personal relationship or obligation to me. He is only discharging his religious duty. I, too, have not chosen this life out of any personal consideration.

# Interview with Usama bin Ladin
# (December 27, 2001)*

... A person who is guided by God will never be misguided by anyone, and a person who is misguided by God can never be guided by anyone. ...

Three months after the blessed strikes against world infidelity and the head of infidelity, namely America [September 11], and almost two months after the fierce crusade against Islam [began] ... it has become clear that the West in general, led by America, bears an unspeakable crusader grudge against Islam.

Those who lived these months under continuous bombardment by the various kinds of U.S. aircraft are well aware of this. Many villages were wiped out without any guilt. Millions of people were made homeless during this very cold weather. Those oppressed men, women, and children now live in tents in Pakistan. They committed no [crime]. Although it was a mere suspicion, America launched this fierce campaign. Had America had enough evidence that makes it certain that those who carried this action belong to Europe—such as the IRA—it would have had a lot of means to address this problem. Because the matter was a mere suspicion pointing to the Muslim world, the crusade grudges against the Muslim world appeared very clearly. ...

What is going on in Palestine is extremely clear. All of humanity and since the time of Adam, may peace be upon him, are agreed on this. ... What happened in Palestine, and what is happening there today in terms of the deliberate murder of children, is very ugly. This is the highest degree of injustice and aggression that threatens all of humanity. ... It is as if they—Israel, backed by America—have killed all children in the world. What will prevent Israel from killing our children tomorrow in Tabuk, al-Jawf, and other areas [of Saudi Arabia]? What will the rulers do if Israel expands its territories, according to their unjust and false books, and announces that its borders reach Medina?

---

* Broadcast on al-Jazira television. Translation by U.S. Department of Commerce, Foreign Broadcast Information Service (FBIS).

What will the rulers do while they are subservient to this Zionist-American lobby? . . .

The United States is practicing the detestable terrorism in its ugliest forms in Palestine and Iraq. Bush the father . . . was the reason behind the killing of over one million children in Iraq. This is in addition to the men and women. What happened on September 11 is nothing but a reaction to the continuing injustice being done to our children in Palestine, Iraq, Somalia, southern Sudan, and elsewhere, as well as Kashmir and Asia. This thing concerns the nation in its entirety. This is something that requires people to rise from their slumber and rush to find a solution to this disaster, which threatens mankind.

Those who condemned these operations looked at the event as an isolated one. They did not link it with the previous events and the reasons behind it. Therefore, their view is parochial and is neither grounded in *Sharia* nor in reason. They simply saw the people, the United States, and the media criticizing these operations. Therefore, they criticized them.

In doing so, they act just like the wolf, which, upon seeing a lamb, said: You are the one who muddied my water last year. The lamb replied: It was not me who did it. The wolf replied: No, it was you. The lamb then said: I was born only this year. The wolf replied: So, it was your mother who muddied my water. The wolf then ate the lamb. Upon seeing her child being torn under the fangs of this wolf, the poor mother, motivated by the sentiment of motherhood, butted the wolf without causing him any injury. The wolf cried, saying: Look at this terrorist. So, the parrots repeated what the wolf said. They said: Yes, we denounce the butting of the wolf by the ewe.

Where were you when the wolf ate the ewe's lamb? These blessed and successful strikes are reactions to what is happening on our land in Palestine, Iraq, and elsewhere. . . . George Bush the son . . . started his term in office by launching violent air strikes on Iraq to affirm the policy of injustice and aggression and that the blood of Muslims has no value. This led to this blessed reply [of September 11]. . . .

These blessed attacks . . . clearly showed that this arrogant and supercilious power, the *hubal* of the age, America, is fragile and, thanks to Almighty God, collapsed so quickly despite having great economic power.

Those who carried out the act were not nineteen Arab countries. And those who moved were not the armies and ministries of the Arab countries, which have become used to submission and injustice afflicting us in Palestine and elsewhere. Rather, they were nineteen secondary school students; I hope God will accept them [in heaven]. They shook America's throne and struck at the U.S. economy in the heart. They struck the largest military power deep in the heart, thanks to God the Almighty. This is a clear proof that this international usurious, damnable economy—which America uses along with its military power to impose infidelity and humiliation on weak people—can easily collapse.

Thanks to Almighty God, those blessed attacks, as they themselves admitted, have inflicted on the New York and other markets more than a trillion dollars in losses. With small capabilities, they used the planes of the enemy and studied in the schools of the enemy. So they did not need training camps. Rather, God helped them, and they taught those arrogant people, who see freedom as meaningless if not belonging to the white race, a tough lesson. These people believe that other people must be humiliated and enslaved. They do not react, but rather applaud their leaders when they strike us, as was the case before in Iraq.

Despite America's recent show of its military power in Afghanistan, and despite its pouring of anger on the weak people of Afghanistan, we learned, thanks to Almighty God, great and important lessons on how to confront this arrogant power. For example, if the front line with the enemy is 100 kilometers long, the line should be wide. This means we should not be satisfied with a defense line that is 100, 200, or 300 meters wide. Rather, the line should be a few kilometers wide. Trenches should then be dug in breadth and width. The intensity of the U.S. bombing is therefore reduced before completing the destruction of these lines. There should be light and swift forces to move from one line to another and from one defense unit to another defense unit. We learned this following the intensive U.S. bombardment on the north lines and on the Kabul lines. In this way, years will pass and America—God-willing—will not be able to break the lines of the *mujahidin*. . . .

Though the U.S. military power is far from us, and our weapons cannot reach their aircraft, it is possible to absorb these attacks through wide defense lines. There is another way—through hitting the economic structure, which is basic for the military power. If their economy is destroyed, they will be busy with their own affairs rather than enslaving the weak peoples. It is very important to concentrate on hitting the U.S. economy through all possible means. . . .

When the youths—may God accept them as martyrs—detonated in Nairobi less than two tons [of explosives in attacking the U.S. embassy there], America said that this was a terrorist strike with a weapon of mass destruction. However, it did not refrain from dropping two shells each weighing seven million grams. After bombarding entire villages without any justification but with the purpose of terrorizing people only and making them scared of hosting the Arabs or coming close to them, the [U.S.] defense secretary stated that this is our right. It is their right to annihilate people so long as they are Muslims and non-American. . . .

This is the most dangerous, fiercest, and most savage crusade war launched against Islam. God willing, the end of America is imminent. Its end is not dependent on the survival of this slave to God. Regardless if Usama is killed or survives, the awakening has started, praised be God. This was the fruit of these operations.

I beseech God Almighty to accept these young men [the September 11 suicide attackers] as martyrs and to group them together with the prophets, the pious believers, the martyrs, and the virtuous people, and those are the best of companions. These young men have done a great deed, a glorious deed. May God reward them well. We beseech God to make them good assets for their mothers and fathers. They have raised the heads of the Muslims. They gave America a lesson, which it will not forget, God willing. In a previous interview with ABC television, I warned that if it enters into a conflict with the sons of the two holy mosques, America will forget the horrors of Vietnam. This, indeed, was the case; praised be God. What is to come is even greater, God willing. . . .

Those we hear in the media [in Muslim countries] saying that martyrdom-seeking . . . operations are unacceptable are only repeating the whims of tyrants, the whims of America and its agents. A nation of 1.2 billion Muslims is being butchered from east to west every day in Palestine, in Iraq, in Somalia, in southern Sudan, in Kashmir, in the Philippines, in the Bosnia, in Chechnya, and in [India]—and we do not hear anything from them. But if the victim and [the] oppressed rise to sacrifice their soul for [their] religion, then we hear their voices. No one hears the voice of the 1.2 billion Muslims, who are being butchered. But if one man rises to defend those [victims], they rise to repeat the whims of the tyrants. They have no mind and no reason. . . .

I will . . . concentrate on the need to continue the *jihad* action, militarily and economically, against the United States. Praise be to God, the United States has declined. The economic bleeding is continuing to date, but it requires further strikes. The young people should make an effort to look for the key pillars of the U.S. economy. The key pillars of the enemy should be struck, God willing. . . .

The battles that are taking place today in Afghanistan around the clock, especially against the Arab *mujahidin* and the Taliban, have clearly revealed the extent of the powerlessness of the U.S. government, the extent of U.S. weakness, and the fragility of the U.S. soldier. Despite the huge development in military technology, they could not do anything, except by relying on the renegades and the hypocrites [Afghan soldiers]. . . .

# Indictment against Zacarias Moussaoui
# (December 2001)*

... 15. Beginning in and about 1998, Ramzi bin al-Shibh, Muhammad Atta, Marwan al-Shehhi, and Ziad Jarrah, and others formed and maintained an al-Qa'ida terrorist cell in Germany.

16. On or about January 15, 2000, Khalid al-Midhar and Nawaf al-Hazmi traveled from Bangkok, Thailand, to Los Angeles, California.

17. At various times in 2000 and 2001, in Florida, Muhammad Atta made inquiries regarding starting a crop-dusting company.

18. On or about June 3, 2000, Muhammad Atta traveled to the United States from Prague, Czech Republic.

19. In or about early July 2000, Muhammad Atta and Marwan al-Shehhi visited the Airman Flight School in Norman, Oklahoma.

20. Between in or about July 2000 and in or about December 2000, Mohamed Atta and Marwan al-Shehhi attended flight training classes at Huffman Aviation in Venice, Florida.

21. On or about June 29, 2000, $4,790 was wired from the United Arab Emirates (UAE) to Marwan al-Shehhi in Manhattan.

22. On or about July 19, 2000, $9,985 was wired from UAE into a Florida SunTrust bank account in the names of Muhammad Atta and Marwan al-Shehhi.

23. On or about July 26, 2000, in Germany, Ramzi bin al-Shibh wired money to Marwan al-Shehhi in Florida.

24. On or about August 7, 2000, $9,485 was wired from UAE into a Florida SunTrust bank account in the names of Muhammad Atta and Marwan al-Shehhi.

25. On or about August 30, 2000, $19,985 was wired from UAE into a Florida SunTrust bank account in the names of Muhammad Atta and Marwan al-Shehhi.

26. On or about September 18, 2000, $69,985 was wired from UAE into a Florida SunTrust bank account in the names of Muhammad Atta and Marwan al-Shehhi.

27. In or about August 2000, Ziad Jarrah attempted to enroll Ramzi bin al-Shibh in a flight school in Florida.

28. On or about May 17, 2000, in Germany, Ramzi bin al-Shibh applied for a visa to travel to the United States, listing a German telephone number. This visa application was denied.

---

* This material is excerpted from the U.S. government's indictment of Zacarias Moussaoui. Moussaoui is a French citizen of Moroccan orgin who was arrested in the United States before September 11. Authorities believe he was intending to be one of the hijackers.

29. On or about June 15, 2000, in Germany, Ramzi bin al-Shibh applied for a visa to travel to the United States. This visa application was denied.

30. On or about August 14, 2000, in Yemen, Ramzi bin al-Shibh arranged to wire money from his account in Germany to the account of a flight training school in Florida.

31. On or about September 15, 2000, in Yemen, Ramzi bin al-Shibh applied for a visa to travel to the United States, listing a residence in Hamburg, Germany. This visa application was denied in September 2000.

32. On or about October 25, 2000, in Germany, Ramzi bin al-Shibh applied for a visa to travel to the United States. This visa application was denied.

33. On or about September 25, 2000, in Hamburg, Germany, Ramzi bin al-Shibh sent money via wire transfer to Marwan al-Shehhi in Florida.

36. On or about November 5, 2000, Muhammad Atta purchased flight deck videos for the Boeing 747 Model 200, Boeing 757 Model 200, and other items from a pilot store in Ohio ("Ohio Pilot Store"). . . .

39. On or about December 11, 2000, Muhammad Atta purchased flight deck videos for the Boeing 767 Model 300ER and the Airbus A320 Model 200 from the Ohio Pilot Store.

40. Between in or about January 2001 and March 2001, Hani Hanjour attended pilot training courses in Phoenix, Arizona, including at Pan Am International Flight Academy.

41. Between on or about February 1, 2001, and on or about February 15, 2001, Muhammad Atta and Marwan al-Shehhi took a flight check ride around Decatur, Georgia.

42. In or about February 2001, Muhammad Atta and Marwan al-Shehhi attended a health club in Decatur, Georgia.

43. On or about February 7, 2001, ZACARIAS MOUSSAOUI flew from Pakistan to London, England. . . .

46. Between on or about February 26, 2001, and on or about May 29, 2001, ZACARIAS MOUSSAOUI attended the Airman Flight School in Norman, Oklahoma, ending his classes early.

47. On or about March 19, 2001, Nawaf al-Hazmi purchased flight deck videos for the Boeing 747 Model 400, the Boeing 747 Model 200, and the Boeing 777 Model 200, and another video from the Ohio Pilot Store. . . .

51. On or about May 23, 2001, ZACARIAS MOUSSAOUI contacted an office of the Pan Am International Flight Academy in Miami, Florida, via e-mail. . . .

53. In or about June 2001, in Norman, Oklahoma, ZACARIAS MOUSSAOUI made inquiries about starting a crop-dusting company.

54. Between May and July 2001, in Florida, Ziad Jarrah joined a gym and took martial arts lessons, which included instruction in kickboxing and knife fighting.

55. In or about June 2001, in Florida, Waleed al-Shehri, Marwan al-Shehhi, and Satam al-Suqami joined a gym.

56. On or about June 20, 2001, ZACARIAS MOUSSAOUI purchased flight deck videos for the Boeing 747 Model 400 and the Boeing 747 Model 200 from the Ohio Pilot Store.. . . .

59. On or about July 8, 2001, Muhammad Atta purchased a knife in Zurich, Switzerland.

60. On or about July 10 and July 11, 2001, ZACARIAS MOUSSAOUI made credit card payments to the Pan Am International Flight Academy for a simulator course in commercial flight training.

61. On July 18, 2001, Fayez Ahmad gave power of attorney to Mustafa Ahmad al-Hawsawi for Fayez Ahmad's Standard Chartered Bank accounts in UAE.

62. On July 18, 2001, using his power of attorney, al-Hawsawi picked up Fayez Ahmad's Visa and ATM [automated teller machine] cards in UAE.

63. Between July 18 and August 1, 2001, Mustafa Ahmad al-Hawsawi caused Fayez Ahmad's Visa and ATM cards to be shipped from UAE to Fayez Ahmad in Florida. (The Visa card was then used for the first time on August 1, 2001, in Florida.)

64. On or about July 25, 2001, Ziad Jarrah traveled from the United States to Germany. . . .

68. On or about August 3, 2001, ZACARIAS MOUSSAOUI purchased two knives in Oklahoma City, Oklahoma. . . .

71. On or about August 10, 2001, in Minneapolis, Minnesota, ZACARIAS MOUSSAOUI paid approximately $6,300 in cash to the Pan Am International Flight Academy.

72. Between August 13 and August 15, 2001, ZACARIAS MOUSSAOUI attended the Pan Am International Flight Academy in Minneapolis, Minnesota, for simulator training on the Boeing 747 Model 400.

73. On or about August 16, 2001, ZACARIAS MOUSSAOUI possessed, among other things:

- two knives;
- a pair of binoculars;
- flight manuals for the Boeing 747 Model 400;
- a flight simulator computer program;
- fighting gloves and shin guards;
- a piece of paper referring to a handheld Global Positioning System receiver and a camcorder;
- software that could be used to review pilot procedures for the Boeing 747 Model 400;

- a notebook listing German Telephone #1, German Telephone #2, and the name "Ahad Sabet";
- letters indicating that MOUSSAOUI is a marketing consultant in the United States for Infocus Tech;
- a computer disk containing information related to the aerial application of pesticides; and
- a hand-held aviation radio.

74. On or about August 17, 2001, ZACARIAS MOUSSAOUI, while being interviewed by federal agents in Minneapolis, attempted to explain his presence in the United States by falsely stating that he was simply interested in learning to fly.

75. On or about August 17, 2001, Ziad Jarrah undertook a "check ride" at a flight school in Fort Lauderdale, Florida.

76. On or about August 22, 2001, Fayez Ahmad used his Visa card in Florida to obtain approximately $4,900 cash, which had been deposited into his Standard Chartered Bank account in UAE the day before.

77. On or about August 22, 2001, in Miami, Florida, Ziad Jarrah purchased an antenna for a Global Positioning System (GPS), other GPS-related equipment, and schematics for 757 cockpit instrument diagrams. (GPS allows an individual to navigate to a position using coordinates preprogrammed into the GPS unit.)

78. On or about August 25, 2001, Khalid al-Midhar and Majed Moqed purchased with cash tickets for American Airlines Flight 77, from Virginia to Los Angeles, California, scheduled for September 11, 2001.

79. On or about August 26, 2001, Waleed al-Shehri and Wail al-Shehri made reservations on American Airlines Flight 11, from Boston, Massachusetts, to Los Angeles, California, scheduled for September 11, 2001, listing a telephone number in Florida as a contact number.

80. On or about August 27, 2001, reservations for electronic one-way tickets were made for Fayez Ahmad and Mohald al-Shehri for United Airlines Flight 175, from Boston, Massachusetts, to Los Angeles, California, scheduled for September 11, 2001, listing Florida Telephone Number #1 as a contact number.

81. On or about August 27, 2001, Nawaf al-Hazmi and Salem al-Hazmi booked flights on American Airlines Flight 77.

82. On or about August 28, 2001, Satam al-Suqami purchased a ticket with cash for American Airlines Flight 11.

83. On or about August 28, 2001, Muhammad Atta and Adb al-Aziz Alomari reserved two seats on American Airlines Flight 11, listing Florida Telephone #1 as a contact number.

84. On or about August 29, 2001, Ahmad al-Ghamdi and Hamza al-Ghamdi reserved electronic one-way tickets for United Airlines Flight 175.

85. On or about August 29, 2001, Ahmad al-Haznawi purchased a ticket on United Airlines Flight 93 from Newark, New Jersey, to San Francisco, California, scheduled for September 11, 2001.

86. On or about August 30, 2001, Muhammad Atta purchased a utility tool that contained a knife. . . .

97. On September 11, 2001, in UAE, approximately $16,348 was deposited into al-Hawsawi's Standard Chartered Bank account.

98. On September 11, 2001, in UAE, at about 9:22 A.M. local time (the early morning hours of Eastern Daylight Time), Mustafa Ahmad al-Hawsawi moved approximately $6,534 from the $8,055 in Fayez Ahmad's Standard Chartered Bank account into his own account, using a check dated September 10, 2001, and signed by Fayez Ahmad; al-Hawsawi then withdrew approximately $1,361, nearly all the remaining balance in Ahmad's account, by ATM cash withdrawal.

99. On September 11, 2001, in UAE, approximately $40,871 was prepaid to a Visa card connected to al-Hawsawi's Standard Chartered Bank account.

100. On or about September 11, 2001, the hijackers possessed a handwritten set of final instructions for a martyrdom operation on an airplane using knives.

101. On or about September 11, 2001, Muhammad Atta and Adb al-Aziz Alomari flew from Portland, Maine to Boston, Massachusetts.

102. On or about September 11, 2001, Muhammad Atta possessed operating manuals for the Boeing 757 and 767, pepper spray, knives, and German travel visas.

103. On or about September 11, 2001, Ziad Jarrah possessed flight manuals for Boeing 757 and 767 aircraft.

104. On or about September 11, 2001, Muhammad Atta, Abdul Aziz Alomari, Satam al-Suqami, Waleed M. al-Shehri, and Waleed al-Shehri hijacked American Airlines Flight 11, a Boeing 767, which had departed Boston at approximately 7:55 A.M. They flew Flight 11 into the North Tower of the World Trade Center in Manhattan at approximately 8:45 A.M., causing the collapse of the tower and the deaths of thousands of persons.

105. On or about September 11, 2001, Hamza al-Ghamdi, Fayez Ahmad, Mohald al-Shehri, Ahmad al-Ghamdi, and Marwan al-Shehhi hijacked United Airlines Flight 175, a Boeing 767, which had departed from Boston at approximately 8:15 A.M. They flew Flight 175 into the South Tower of the World Trade Center in Manhattan at approximately 9:05 A.M., causing the collapse of the tower and the deaths of thousands of persons.

106. On or about September 11, 2001, Khalid al-Midhar, Majed Moqed, Nawaf al-Hazmi, Salem al-Hazmi, and Hani Hanjour hijacked American Air-

lines Flight 77, a Boeing 757, which had departed from Virginia bound for Los Angeles, at approximately 8:10 A.M. They flew Flight 77 into the Pentagon in Virginia at approximately 9:40 A.M., causing the deaths of 189 persons.

107. On or about September 11, 2001, Saeed al-Ghamdi, Ahmad al-Nami, Ahmad al-Haznawi, and Ziad Jarrah hijacked United Airlines Flight 93, a Boeing 757, which had departed from Newark, New Jersey, bound for San Francisco at approximately 8:00 A.M. After resistance by the passengers, Flight 93 crashed in Somerset County, Pennsylvania at approximately 10:10 A.M., killing all on board.

108. On September 11, 2001, Mustafa Ahmad al-Hawsawi left the UAE for Pakistan.

109. On September 13, 2001, the visa card connected to al-Hawsawi's account was used to make six ATM withdrawals in Karachi, Pakistan. . . .

111. On or about October 7, 2001, in Afghanistan, Usama bin Laden praised the September 11 attack and vowed that the United States would not "enjoy security" before "infidel armies leave" the Saudi Gulf.

112. On or about October 10, 2001, Sulieman Abu Ghaith announced, on behalf of al-Qa'ida, that all Muslims had a duty to attack United States targets around the world.

# September 11 as a Great Success
# (February 27, 2002)

### ABU UBEID AL-QURASHI*

. . . Seemingly, the Munich operation [the PLO attack on the 1972 Olympics games in which nine Israeli athletes were murdered] failed because it did not bring about [the kidnappers' demands] and even cast a shadow of doubt on the justness of the Palestinian cause in world public opinion. But following the operation, and contrary to how it appeared [at first], it was the greatest media

---

* Abu Ubeid al-Qurashi is a leader of al-Qa'ida. This article appeared in that group's online magazine, *al-Ansar*, issue 4. Translation by Middle East Media Research Institute, report no. 353, March 12, 2002.

victory, and the first true proclamation to the entire world of the first of the Palestinian resistance movement. . . .

In truth, the Munich operation was a great propaganda strike. Four thousand journalists and radio personnel and two thousand commentators and television technicians were there to cover the Olympic Games; suddenly, they were broadcasting the suffering of the Palestinian people. Thus, 900 million people in 100 countries were witness to the operation by means of television screens. This meant that at least a quarter of the world knew what was going on the Munich; after this, they could no longer ignore the Palestinian tragedy.

The September 11 [operation] was an even greater propaganda coup. It may be said that it broke a record in propaganda dissemination. . . . With few exceptions, the entire planet heard about it. . . .

America had gained exclusivity in [world] leadership and had, more than at any other time, revealed its tyranny, its contempt of others, and its aspiration to created facts on the ground. . . .

The New York raid was very well planned and accomplished its planners' goals in full. It painfully challenged America and was an unprecedented slap that had, and will still have, ramifications for the entire world. . . . [It] rang the bells of restoring Arab and Islamic glory. . . . They did not aspire to gain Western sympathy; rather, they sought to expose the American lie and deceit to the peoples of the world—and first and foremost to the Islamic peoples.

Al-Qa'ida's and the Taliban's resistance to the crusader campaign . . . will doubtless go down in history as a model of war between unequal sides. . . . Al-Qa'ida can take over the enemy's [technological] means and use them against him, while the enemy cannot do the same. The *mujahidin* can do this because they have come to understand the enemy's mentality and how his society functions; yet the enemy has no way of deterring the believer or influencing his mentality.

After the Munich operation, the Western countries knew how to contain Palestinian rage, at least temporarily: they opened international diplomatic forums to the leaders of the resistance. The best proof of this is Arafat's visit to the UN and his speech to the General Assembly, a mere eighteen months after the Munich operation. The flow of recognition of the PLO increased, and by the late 1970s eighty-six countries had recognized the PLO, as opposed to only seventy-two that recognized Israel.

In contrast, this time it is difficult to contain Islamic rage, because of the high threshold of the goals: completely and comprehensively eliminating Western colonialism in the Islamic region and distancing the West once and for all from regional affairs. . . .

Some may think that the absence of international and regional support for *jihad*, in contrast to past support for the Palestinian resistance, is a weak point [for the *jihad* movement]. Yet the opposite is true. This fact exempts the *mujahidin* from the need to offer any concessions, or to continually lower the threshold of their demands so that it leads to a fall—as happened to many resistance organizations that succumbed to the pitfalls of treachery and subjugation, and lost their principles. . . .

Some commentators maintain that the direct goals of the New York raid were shattering the idols in the mind of the peoples and arousing them from their slumber. This is indeed what happened. From the New York raid, it can be concluded:

No form of surveillance can provide early warning or permit rapid decision making. Even the Echelon satellite surveillance system, which cost billions of dollars, . . . did not manage to stop the nineteen *mujahidin* wielding knives.

The Americans' marketing of the war is totally inefficient. America could not even find an acceptable name for the campaign. Neither Crusader War, Absolute Justice, nor Infinite Justice allowed the American propaganda apparatus to overcome the feelings of hatred for America. They could not even remove internal American qualms.

The Islamic nation is struggling against globalization, and it continued with its negative attitude towards Western rhetoric and explanations. The Westerners' rage increased once it became clear to them that [Muslims] could use the same computers that they did without espousing the same values. Against all their assessments, [Islamic] culture cannot be shattered by technology.

The West ignores the power of faith. Western civilization, which is based on the information revolution, cannot distance the Muslims from the Koran. The book of Allah brings to the hearts of Muslims a faith deeper than all the utopian [alternatives] and than the [lies] of the tyrannical Western propaganda machine.

Symbols never lose their value. [Usama bin Ladin] has become a symbol for the repressed from the four corners of the Earth—even for non-Muslims.

The Western propaganda machine's size did not keep it from being defeated by [bin Ladin] with what resembed a judo move. The aggressive Westerns became accustomed to observing the tragedies of others—but on September 11 the opposite happened. . . .

[As a result of the Munich attack] thousands of young Palestinians were roused to join the *fedayeen* organizations. . . . The number of organizations engaging in international "terror" increased from a mere eleven in 1968 to fifty-five in 1978. Fifty-four percent of these new organizations sought to imitate the success of the Palestinian organization—particularly the publicity the Palestinian cause garnered after Munich.

This increase in "terror" activity after Munich will doubtless recur, particularly if we take into account that the New York raid was a political, economic, and military disaster for America, ten times greater than that of the Munich operation. . . . It will gradually give rise to an all-out struggle against the American crusader campaign, which if it continues to spread, will strike at the heart of America.

# Pre-Attack Videotape (Summer 2001)

### AHMAD AL-HAZNAWI AL-GHAMIDI*

We left our families to send a message, which has the color of blood, to reach the whole world: the friends and enemies, the near and far, the lofty and humiliated, the honest and agent. This message says: O Allah, take from our blood today until you are satisfied. O Allah, do not make a grave for our bodies, nor soil to be buried in, nor a grave to cover them, so that, on the Day of Judgment, they will be blessed with an eternal Paradise—blessed be its Builder. The message says: The time of humiliation and slavery is over. It is time to kill the Americans in their own backyard, among their sons, and near their forces and intelligence. It is time to prove to the whole world that the United States of America has worn a garment which was not originally made for it, when it merely thought about facing or resisting the *mujahidin*. The United States is nothing but propaganda and a huge mass of false statements and exaggeration. The purpose of this propaganda was to make the United States big in the eyes of the world. What it wanted has happened. However, the truth is what you saw. We killed them outside their land, praise be to Allah. Today, we kill them in the midst of their own home.

O Allah, revive an entire nation by our deaths. O Allah, I sacrifice myself for your sake, accept me as a martyr. O Allah, I sacrifice myself for your sake, accept me as a martyr. O Allah, I sacrifice myself for your sake, accept me as a martyr. To the Garden of Eden, our first house. We shall meet in the eternal Paradise with the prophets, honest people, martyrs, and righteous people. They are the best of companions. Praise be to Allah. Allah's peace, mercy, and blessings be upon you.

---

* Ahmad al-Haznawi al-Ghamidi, one of the nineteen September 11 hijackers, was a Saudi citizen and a member of al-Qa'ida. This tape was broadcast by al-Jazira television, April 15, 2002. Translation by FBIS, April 15, 2002.

# Post-Attack Videotape (Fall 2001)

AYMAN AL-ZAWAHIRI*

This great victory [the September 11 attacks] which was achieved is due, in fact, to the grace of Allah alone. It was not due to our skillfulness or superiority, but it is due to Allah's blessing alone. Allah Almighty grants his mercy to whoever He wants. Allah looks into the hearts of his slaves and chooses from them those who are qualified to win His grace, mercy, and blessings. Those nineteen brothers who left [their homes], made efforts, and offered their lives for Allah's cause—Allah has favored them with this conquest, which we are enjoying now.

---

* Ayman al-Zawahiri is an aide to Usama bin Ladin. This tape was broadcast by al-Jazira television, April 15, 2002. Translation by FBIS, April 15, 2002.

# 7

## MIDDLE EAST REACTION

## TO SEPTEMBER 11

Responses to the terrorist attacks of September 11 were an opportunity for much of the world to show revulsion at this act and solidarity with the government and people of the United States. Yet in the Middle East, where the terrorists and their philosophy had originated, the attack provoked mixed reactions from political or religious leaders and journalists writing in state-controlled newspapers.

This chapter organizes the reactions into three categories. First are those who cheered the terrorist attack because it was against a nation they consider guilty of far greater crimes or they doubted that Muslims or Middle Easterners were involved. Second are those who condemned the loss of life but said the U.S. government itself was ultimately to blame for being a bullying superpower and also sharply denounced retaliatory attacks in Afghanistan. A third group denounced the attacks and suggested that they furnished an important occasion and reason for making reforms in the Islamic world.

The chapter begins with those who support the attack. President Saddam Hussein of Iraq was the only Arab leader to issue a public statement endorsing the terrorists. He said on Iraqi television that the attacks were fully warranted for a nation that "exports evil, in terms of corruption and criminality, not only to any place to which its armies travel, but also to anyplace where its movies go." The journalist Ali Yusefpur, in the militantly anti-American state of Iran, writes that the attacks are a sign of the impending decline of the United States as a superpower and further suggests that those responsible were Zionists or domestic foes because the attack's complexity indicated that the terrorists had access to America's most vital areas and high-quality weapons.

Among some, the attacks provoked an almost romantic display of profound glee. Ali Uqleh Ursan, chairman of the Syrian Arab Writers' Association and a cultural commissar for that country's government, describes "breathing in relief, as I had never breathed before," after hearing of the attack, and extols the heroism of one man, apparently bin Ladin, who could defend his people's honor against a superpower. Providing the Islamic justification is Ayman al-Zawahiri, leader of the Egyptian Jihad group and an ally of bin Ladin, who says the terrorists followed the example of the original pious Muslims in the seventh century. Also showing sheer jubilation is Atallah Abu al-Subh, an activist in Hamas, the Palestinian Islamist group, who pens a poetic ode to anthrax, the disease that terrorized the United States, calling upon it to "continue to advance, to permeate, and to spread" into the air, water faucets, and pens of Americans.

The second group of responses acknowledged the lamentable loss of human life in the attack. As Rif'at Sayyid Ahmad, a Lebanese journalist, put it, "One can never gloat about death, and this is what our glorious Islam has taught us," and he points out that some of the victims were Muslims. Yet Ahmad distinguishes between the people and the government of the United States. He believes that the actions of the latter show it to be guilty of arrogance and aggression throughout the world and that this is what prompted the terrorism.

Looking to the U.S. retaliatory campaign in Afghanistan, Fahd al-Fanik, writing in a Jordanian newspaper, says the Arab world should only help the United States if it puts an end to military violence against the Palestinian people, economic violence against the Iraqi people, and propaganda violence against Arabs and Muslims. Makram Muhammad Ahmad, an Egyptian journalist, agrees that if the United States wants Arab nations to stand by it, it must consider the interests of those "subjected to the terrorism of states and government that . . . honor neither legitimacy nor law, and [that] trample the dignity of such peoples."

In an open letter to President George W. Bush, Safar bin Abd al-Rahman al-Hawali, a Saudi cleric, adds that while the United States often inflicts deep wounds and put a small bandage on them, the attack on Afghanistan has violently removed those bandages and opened a wound in the heart of every Muslim. The hatred all Muslims feel for the United States will not dissipate, he adds.

Among the many arrogances of the United States, according to Ibrahim Nafi, editor of *al-Ahram* in Egypt and his country's most important journalist, is its belief that countries throughout the world should blindly support it. The United States must remember that Egypt is a sovereign state with principles, independent positions, and its own views about the international problem. Nafi also accuses the United States of war crimes in Afghanistan, claiming the food supplies it drops there are treated to cause sickness and then dropped in areas full of land mines.

President Pervez Musharraf of Pakistan, who became a key ally of the United States in fighting the Taliban, uses his speech to the UN General Assembly as an opportunity to call for examining the causes of the terrorist attacks, which he defines as the unresolved political disputes in the world that involve Muslims in Bosnia, Kosovo, Palestine, Kashmir and other places.

The third category is those in the region who condemn the attack. Israel, a U.S. ally and the target of many terrorist attacks itself, called September 11 an assault on the civilization of the West and all it represents—liberty, democracy, economic power, and military capability.

Representing the official Saudi view is Salih bin Muhammad al-Luheidan, chairman of the Supreme Judicial Council of Saudi Arabia, who presents a contrast to his fellow Saudi cleric, al-Hawali. Luheidan says categorically that "killing the weak, infants, women, and the elderly, and destroying property, are considered serious crimes in Islam." He calls upon his government "to deplore any criminal and corrupt act, irrespective of whether the perpetrators are Muslims or non-Muslims."

But others say even more steps are needed, including the reform of Arab and Islamic societies. Ahmad Bishara, secretary-general of Kuwait's National Democratic Movement, writes that Islam must be "liberated," the first step being to "disown and discourage fanatical cults and muftis who have hijacked Islam for their own ends." Interpretation of the faith should be institutionalized, and the practice of obscure individuals issuing haphazard *fatwas* on behalf of all Muslims should be banned.

Ilter Turkmen, the former foreign minister of Turkey, a secular Muslim nation that is also a strong U.S. ally, debunks many of the myths about the Islamic world: Arab states have not done much for the Palestinians; Westerners ran to the aid of the Muslims in Bosnia-Herzegovina and Kosovo; and many regional conflicts have shown that there is no solidarity in the Islamic world.

Ahmad al-Baghdadi, a Kuwaiti political science professor, focuses his criticism on the need to change the poor treatment Arab governments give their people. Finally, Abd al-Hamid al-Ansari, a Qatari law professor, points the finger at extremist Islamic clerics, asking, "Who gave the religious parties the right to declare a *jihad* and jeopardize the supreme interests of the nation?"

# Broadcast by Iraqi President Saddam Hussein (September 12, 2001)*

Regardless of the conflicting human feelings about what happened in the United States yesterday, the United States reaps the thorns that its rulers have planted in the world. These thorns have not only caused the feet and hearts of certain people to bleed, but also caused the eyes of people to bleed—those people who wept a lot over their dead. The United States has harvested their lives, not leaving a place without the people there having a symbolic monument indicating the criminal action of the United States against them. This was the case in Japan, which was the first to suffer from the capabilities of nuclear destruction on which the United States prides itself. This also includes what it did in Vietnam and Iraq and what it did against the Russian nuclear submarine. [The *Kursk* actually sank in August 2000 due to an onboard explosion that had nothing to do with the United States.—*Eds.*] Now it carries out criminal acts by supporting criminal and racist Zionism against the women, men, young people, elders, and children of our valiant Palestinian people.

Will the American people save themselves and save the world with them from the evils of their rulers and their terrorist crimes against the world? Or will their rulers, who have become a toy in the hands of criminal world Zionism and its accursed, freak entity, which has usurped the land of Palestine and the land of the Arabs, turn the sentiments of the Americans into new terrorist plans against the world in a way that serves Zionist-Jewish greed for unlawful funds and innocent blood? The American people should remember that, throughout history, no one crossed the Atlantic to come to them, carrying weapons against them. They are the ones who crossed the Atlantic carrying with them death, destruction, and ugly exploitation to the whole world. Despite this, we hope that the people of the United States will remember that the souls that were killed with U.S. weapons and U.S. machinations and plots can rise to God, lord of heavens and earth, to complain about the injustice of the United States. In fact, God, the omnipotent and great, can see. When God strikes, no one can stand in the way of his power.

The one who does not want to reap evil must not plant evil. Those who consider the lives of their people as precious and dear must remember that the

---

* Republic of Iraq Television. Translation by U.S. Department of Commerce, Foreign Broadcast Information Service (FBIS).

lives of people in the world are also precious and dear to their families. The United States exports evil, in terms of corruption and criminality, not only to anyplace to which its armies travel, but also to any place where its movies go. Therefore, the American people should remember all of this. If they remember this, they will save their security and the security of the world from their rulers. However, if what befell the United States is a domestic affair, then the people of the country could diagnose the disease better than others.

# A Blow from Within (September 13, 2001)

### ALI YUSEFPUR*

Several days ago, one of the American writers announced that the superpower America will fall in ten years' time. Of course, in the past twenty years a number of other American scholars and theorists have predicted the fall of the American ruling system within fifty years.

Meanwhile, according to the verses of the Koran, the nations and civilizations that have fallen throughout the history of mankind have had several characteristics:

1. They had reached very high levels from the point of view of advancing in various sciences.
2. They had unparalleled economic, military, and technological power.
3. They had reached the limit from the point of view of oppression and injustice. The dominant ethic group was exploiting and enslaving the weaker underling nations.
4. Moral corruption, promiscuity, and profligacy had proliferated among most of the members of the dominant ethnic group.

According to the noble Koran, the spread of tyranny and injustice and the corrupt moral ways led to the fall of the above-mentioned nations.

Since the Second World War, that is, in the past fifty-seven years, the American ruling system entered world affairs as one of the superpowers of note

---

* Ali Yusefpur is an Iranian journalist. This article appeared in the Tehran newspaper *Siyasat-e Ruz*. Translation by FBIS.

at the global level. Following the disintegration of the Soviet Union, it acts as the undisputed power in the political, economic, cultural, and social arenas of the world. Although this ruling system has achieved great progress in the scientific and technological fields and given certain services to humanity, numerous black marks can be seen in the performance of the American government. The most important of these are as follows:

1. America's atrocities in Latin America, especially the toppling of the popular government of [President Salvador] Allende in Chile and America's support of the [former shah's dynasty in Iran].
2. The nuclear bombing of Hiroshima and Nagasaki in Japan.
3. The slaughter of the Vietnamese people in a long and unequal war.
4. Unquestioned support for the usurper, criminal Israel, in particular, in the past year, which has led to the martyrdom of a number of Palestinian women and children.
5. The promotion of the culture of violence and immorality among the young people throughout the world through the visual and written media.
6. All-round efforts by cartels and trusts and multinational companies to exploit the third world countries, and the accumulation of wealth by a small stratum in America and Europe.
7. The move by the American society toward the fall of its moral and spiritual values. In view of the above, the trend of the fall of America is gathering pace, and this is not hidden from the intellectual and realists in the American community. However, with respect to the recent event, whenever an incident has happened in recent years that has endangered the interests of the West, the finger of accusation has been swiftly pointed at Islamic or Middle Eastern groups by the American and European media. Nevertheless, these incidents have later been found to have been perpetrated by Zionist agents or the agents of certain domestic groups.

The operations that were carried out on [September 11] in America in a complicated methodical, technical, and intelligence plan must have been by a group or organization that has precise intelligence, access to America's vital and sensitive center, access to high-quality weapons and explosives, and infiltrators in those organs. It seems that the following factors have played a role in the incidents in America:

1. Dissident elements in the American community, especially the American military, which played the main role in the explosion at the Oklahoma federal center.
2. Zionist elements, in view of the deadlock in the fight against the Pal-

estinian nation, need to embark on such operations in order to extri-
cate themselves from the deadlock and incite public opinion in the
West against Islamist groups. . . .

# The American Government Had Contaminated
# My Humanity (September 15, 2001)

## ALI UQLEH URSAN*

. . . . The deaths of the innocent pain me; but September 11—the day of the
fall of the symbol of American power—reminded me of the many innocents
whose funerals we attended and whose wounds we treated. . . . I remembered
the funerals that have been held every day in occupied Palestine since 1987.
. . . I remembered Tripoli [Libya] on the day of the American-British aggression, and the attempt to destroy its leader's house as he slept; then, his daughter
was killed under the ruins. . . . I remembered the oppression of the people in
Korea and Vietnam. . . . My soul was inundated with tremendous bitterness,
revulsion, and disgust toward the country that, in the past half-century, has
racked up only a black history of oppression and support for the aggression and
racism of the Nazi Zionists and for apartheid in South Africa.

The American government had contaminated my humanity, and I began
to say to myself, when I saw the masses fleeing in horror in the streets of New
York and Washington, "Let them drink of the cup that their government
has given all the peoples [of the world] to drink from, first and foremost our
people."

When the twin towers collapsed and the New York skyline, which had been
obstructed by them, was revealed to me—I felt deep within me like someone
who had been delivered from the grave; I [felt] that I was being carried in the
air above the corpse of the mythological symbol of arrogant American imperialist power, whose administration had prevented the [American] people from

---

* Ali Uqleh Ursan is chairman of the Syrian Arab Writers' Association. This article appeared in
  *al-Usbu al-Adabi*, the publication of the Syrian Arab Writers' Association. Translation by Middle
  East Media Research Institute, report no. 275 (September 25, 2001).

knowing the crimes it was committing. . . . My lungs filled with air and I breathed in relief, as I had never breathed before.

A few minutes later, I again thought about the people under the ruins, and I began to say to myself: "What sin had these innocents committed?" I was sorry that my humanity had been contaminated by Zionist America and by world Zionism. . . . But a few minutes later, the media informed me of new facts: Arabs and Muslims were blamed and were even threatened with retaliation.

This brought me back to the spiritual tomb, in which I am overwhelmed by the aggression, the arrogance, the racism, and the distortion of facts. Inner strength, which saves me from drowning, has helped me to again breathe above the surface of the grave: we will return, we will live, we will win, and we will realize justice for the world, because we are willing to sacrifice ourselves for rights, justice, and the humanity of the world. . . .

The American people must awake and see the image of [its] policy . . . a filthy policy that dishonors its owners. . . . That hour on September 11 should be significant for the American decision makers; it must lead to a reexamination of [American] ideas, policy, and strategy. It may be that [this event] will also reach the American mind, whose real humanity has been blocked by military and economic might. . . .

The symbolism of penetrating the Pentagon, the destruction of one of its sides [which is] sixty meters long, and the killing of up to a thousand people who were inside it is greater by far than the fact that it continues to exist and continues its aggression against the people and its threats against Afghanistan and bin Ladin. What the [destruction of the Pentagon] means is that the will of one man, who chose to die to defend his honor, his rights, his people, his civilization, and his faith, is enough to realize his goal, even against a superpower and even on its own turf.

[This attack means that] if the people awake, if they have this kind of will and willingness, and if they choose to resist the tyranny, the despots, and the racism that exhale hatred, arrogance and imperialism. . . . What will happen then? . . .

Something collapsed in the United States, and I maintain that this is the beginning of the collapse of the United States as the only dominant superpower in the world. . . . With this collapse will come the building of a new foundation for the victory of the oppressed and wretched peoples. The voice of the nations will rise in a beautiful dawn and say: "Oppression will not survive; every tyrant's end is destruction; power is vanquished by power; there is no limit to the human will when it decides to take on the arrogance of power. . . ."

Nevertheless, I cannot hide my sympathy toward the innocent Americans who fell victim, first and foremost, to the policy of their own government.

I can swear that among the victims in and around the World Trade Center are some who do not deserve mercy, because they belong to the suckers of the blood of the people. But a man cannot rejoice at the misfortune of others, or hate in light of the loss of life. My humanity, which the American and Zionist policy tried to numb and contaminate, ultimately conquers the hatred and enmity and stands by mankind. . . .

# Interview with Ayman al-Zawahiri (October 7, 2001)*

We thank God for supporting the oppressed, the faithful, and the patient. He is the vanquisher of the arrogant.

Muslim nation, this is our call to you at these critical and difficult moments where one differentiates between the sincere and hypocrites. This is our call to you. The nations of infidels assembled against the Muslims, the *mujahidin*, and the steadfast people.

Before addressing you, I would like to ask one question of the people of the U.S. who are being mobilized by their government. O people of the U.S., can you ask yourselves a question: Why all this enmity for the United States and Israel? Why all this hatred in the hearts of the Muslims for the United States? The reply is clear and simple. The United States committed crimes against the Muslim nation that no one can suffer, let alone a *mujahid* Muslim. The United States is the leader of the criminals in the crime of the establishment of Israel. It is a crime that continues to take place and that has been repeating itself for the past fifty years. The Muslim nation cannot accept the continuation of this crime. Your government besieges and kills the children in Iraq. Your government supports the corrupt governments in our countries.

O American people, your government is leading you to a new losing war. O people of the U.S., your government was defeated in Vietnam and fled scared from Lebanon. It fled from Somalia and received a slap in Aden [the attack on

---

* This interview with Ayman al-Zawahiri, an al-Qa'ida leader, was broadcast on al-Jazira television. Translation by FBIS.

the USS *Cole*]. Your government now leads you to a new losing war where you will lose your sons and [your] money. The American people and the world at large should know that we would not accept the recurrence of the Andalusia [the loss of Spain to the Christians in the fifteenth century] tragedy in Palestine. It would be better and easier for us to see the nation perish rather than see al-Aqsa Mosque destroyed or Palestine Judaized and its inhabitants expelled from it.

O Muslims, today is the day of reality and the day of the test. This is your day. We have the new Quraysh [a tribe that became the leaders of Islam in the seventh century] that assembled its forces against the group of patient Muslims as did the old Quraysh with its alliances and tribes against the Muslims in Medina. Act like the companions of the prophet, may God's peace and mercy be upon him. When the believers saw the coalition of tribes [that opposed converting to Islam], they said that God and the prophet had promised us victory over them. Their belief was further enhanced, and they placed their fate in God's hands.

O *mujahid* young people, O sincere *ulama*, O believers who love God and his prophet, this is a new epic of Islam and a new battle of the faithful in which one relives the great battles in Islam's history, like Hittin, Ayn Jalut, and the conquest of Bayt al-Maqdis (Jerusalem) [Muslim victories during the Crusades]. This is the epic that is being relived again. Proceed to win the hereafter. Proceed to join the honor of *jihad*. . . .

# To Anthrax (November 1, 2001)

ATALLAH ABU AL-SUBH*

. . . . O anthrax, despite your wretchedness, you have sown horror in the heart of the lady of arrogance, of tyranny, of boastfulness! Your gentle touch has made the U.S.'s life rough and pointless. You have filled the lady who horrifies and terrorizes the world with fear, and her feet almost fail to bear [her weight] in horror and fear of you. Because of you, she has lost confidence.

* Atallah Abu al-Subh is a Hamas activist. This article appeared in the Palestinian Hamas newspaper, *al-Risala*. Translation by Middle East Media Research Institute, report no. 297 (November 7, 2001).

... You have entered the most fortified of places ... the White House, and they left it like horrified mice. Up until a short time ago this place was the address of the power of brutality, or of the brutality of power! Verily, the owner of that house said, "Woe to any who dare even to glance at it with a hint of rage—but you have turned all this into vanity, weakness, and wretchedness."

By Allah, are you really so deadly? Do you not fear America's intercontinental missiles? Do you not fear the torpedo missiles with nuclear warheads, and cluster bombs? Do you not fear the Swift Sword [Omani-British war games] that Britain drew forth from its scabbard to stab into the heart of our honor in Muscat [Oman's capital], with the agreement of the great sultan, who had no shame in carrying out such a deed? Do you not fear the lady of terror's destroyers that cross the Suez Canal ... ?

The Pentagon was a monster before you entered its corridors. . . . And behold, it now transpires that its men are of paper and its commanders are of cardboard, and they hasten to flee as soon as they see—only see—chalk dust! There are those who think that I exaggerate, but I do not think so. This horror that you have sown ... in the heart of the bloodsucker ... makes me think as I do. . . . They run from you in all directions and their tongues mumble, "My life, my life." Our hearts, repressed, exiled, and oppressed, were filled with belief that Allah is capable of defeating America by means of the weakest of his earthly soldiers, after he used you to sow horror in their hearts. . . .

All [the rulers of Arab and Islamic countries] tell the United States—every time she farts—"Allah bless you." Nevertheless, you have found your way to only eight American breasts so far. . . .

You make the U.S. appease us, and hint to us at a rosy future and a life of ease ... through a [new] Marshall Plan [massive U.S. aid program to rebuild Europe after the Second World War]. Why? Because of our beautiful eyes? Or out of fear that we will turn into anthrax and harm the apple of [the U.S.'s] eye and heart, Tel Aviv ... ? Without permission, you enter the halls of their courthouses, as if you intended to push the symbols of their sovereignty into the mud of worry and fear. . . .

I like you very much. May you continue to advance, to permeate, and to spread. If I may give you a word of advice, enter the air of those symbols, the water faucets from which they drink, and the pens with which they draft their traps and conspiracies against the wretched peoples. . . . Turn the bodies of the tyrants into matches burning slowly and gradually, so that they understand that the truth belongs to Allah and that they should give those entitled to rights their rights. . . .

# Is Usama bin Ladin the Culprit? Has World War III Started? (September 14, 2001)

RIF'AT SAYYID AHMAD*

Tens of thousands of people killed or wounded, several billion dollars in loss, a state of unprecedented panic, a complete closure of airspace, land, and sea, and psychological, political, and universal isolation. This was precisely the status of the world's most powerful nation in the wake of the series of sudden operations that hit New York and Washington the morning of September 11, 2001, according to U.S. time.

What do we read from these events? And what are the implications and future impact on the world and our Arab and Islamic East? First of all, we must affirm that one can never gloat about death, and this is what our glorious Islam has taught us. Islam does not sanction the killing of innocent people, regardless of their beliefs or nationalities (unless they carry out an aggression). What happened in the United States is that the death of these innocent civilians, some of them Muslims, has come as a result of U.S. arrogance, follies, and racism. The joy felt by some ordinary people in Palestine, Korea, or Southeast Asia is nothing but an instinctive expression of hatred of U.S. aggression and arrogance. It must not necessary be interpreted as happiness over the murder of innocent people. It is joy at the humiliation and insulting of the United States more than anything else.

Second, the question now is: Are Usama bin Ladin, the al-Qa'ida organization, [and] the World Front for Resisting the United States and Israel standing behind this incident? And if this is conclusively proved, will this get us into World War III through a retaliatory (perhaps nuclear) U.S. strike against Afghanistan, one that reminds us of the Hiroshima and Nagasaki bombs? . . .

The symbol of the free world and its greatest deity (the little U.S. god) has been broken and its legend has been smashed by the strikes against its three major pillars (globalism, political hegemony, and military hegemony). . . . The strike against the symbol of the free world means that we are facing an injured lion, and it is a foolish lion par excellence. It will attempt to retaliate ferociously to restore its prestige, which came under attack. The lion may strike before it even possesses enough evidence that bin Ladin or others are responsible. It will strike Afghanistan even before this article is published. It will turn the land ablaze in some Arab and Islamic countries even if there is no conclusive evidence that these countries are behind these operations!

---

* Rif'at Sayyid Ahmad is a Lebanese journalist. This article appeared in the Lebanese newspaper *al-Safir*.

Third, this U.S. foolishness, which President George Bush stands for, may lead to fatal negative results. It reminds us of the operations that preceded the First and Second World Wars, which got the world involved in a bloody and merciless furnace. What is going to happen will be a new carbon copy, in a modern and new version, of what happened at the beginning of the First and Second World Wars; . . . the period leading to this major mad event may take longer, but it will come sooner or later. . . .

Fourth, where does Israel stand in all this? This is an extremely important question, particularly since some people suggest that the Israeli intelligence services may be behind these bombings as Israel is the primary beneficiary. Furthermore, the hatred of the Arabs and Muslims and their causes will increase worldwide as a result of these events. Also, these bombings will turn U.S. and world attention away from the *intifada*, thus making it easier for [Israeli Prime Minister Ariel] Sharon to finish it off and continue to exterminate the Palestinians quietly and away from the world's attention. Although I do not subscribe to this theory and believe that this is an intricate and complicated operation that involves several international elements, U.S. local groups, and international intelligence services, judging by the accuracy of the operations and the magnitude of destruction and violence involved, we must not ignore the Israeli political exploitation of these events and its serious impact on the issue of Palestine. We the Arabs must live up to this Israeli exploitation with an Arab political and media counteroffensive that exposes its falsehood and danger and that does not rule out the involvement of the Israeli Mossad in the operation, even if remotely.

By all standards, we are facing a new reality, new facts, and a new era. We must all be prepared for this on the Egyptian, Arab, and Islamic levels. The United States, the arch-Satan, must realize the major significance behind these bombings that struck the heart of the country. It must rethink its policy toward the world in general and the Arabs and Muslims in particular or else learn to live with the outcome of its biases and satanic choices, which will earn it nothing but bitterness and humiliation.

# We Would Help the United States If It Would Help Us (September 17, 2001)

FAHD AL-FANIK*

Jordan has not committed any act of terrorism at any time. On the contrary, it has been the object of various acts of terrorism involving the assassination of two prime ministers, the hijacking of airliners, the killing of diplomats, and other random bombings. There have also been several acts of terrorism that have been foiled thanks to the alertness of the Jordanian security organs. . . .

Jordan, then, is not being accused and has nothing to apologize for. So it does not need to repeat day and night and reaffirm its stand against the terrorism to which the United States has been exposed more than it has done in the case of the terrorism to which several Arab countries, such as Egypt, Algeria, Lebanon, Palestine, Saudi Arabia, Yemen, Syria, and Iraq, have been exposed.

On the other hand, the United States does not consider the incidents to which it has been exposed to be terrorist operations but an act of war. Although the war against international terrorism needs to be tackled through the cooperation of all states, the United States in particular does not lack military power, financial resources, and technological capabilities. The Congress has authorized President [George W.] Bush to use force even before he has demanded this authorization. . . . The United States does not need military or financial backing in its expected attack on the poorest country in the world—namely, Afghanistan.

But it does need an Islamic cover to give it the legality to attack a Muslim country, precisely as it needed an Arab cover ten years ago to give it [legitimacy] to attack Iraq.

The states that gave the cover for the Gulf War against Iraq were not subjected to Iraqi vengeance, because Iraq did not resort to terrorism as an option even in its most difficult circumstances. But the states that would give the cover for the strike against the Taliban could become targets for terrorist commando operations for many years to come.

If a principled and courageous stand calls for international cooperation against terrorism, courage and principle demand that the Arab states, which would take the risk of giving the cover, should make it conditional on putting an end to the terrorism that is practiced by [Ariel] Sharon so openly through

---

* Fahd al-Fanik is a Jordanian writer. This article appeared in the Jordanian newspaper *al-Ra'y*. Translation by FBIS.

political assassinations and besieging and killing civilians and depriving them of their most fundamental human rights prior to their eviction. . . .

We should help the United States on condition that it help us in putting an end to the military violence against the Palestinian people, economic violence against the Iraqi people, and propaganda violence against the Arabs and Muslims.

# A Little Justice to Help Uproot Terrorism (September 21, 2001)

MAKRAM MUHAMMAD AHMAD*

To begin with, we all sympathize with the American people and regret this huge tragedy. . . . The tragedy has showed the serious defects in the powerful U.S. empire. Despite its tremendous capabilities, it came under a legendary overwhelming terrorist attack. Only one person was intelligent enough to defeat all this U.S. high technology.

What happened demonstrates for the thousandth time that force, no matter how great it is, has a certain ceiling and limits. It is not always the ideal solution for a security issue, especially if it grows stubborn, arrogant, and conceited to the point of attacking legitimacy and justice, as we have all seen in the occupied territories.

America plans to attack Afghanistan and smoke out bin Ladin. Nobody will shed any tears if Americans topple the Taliban regime because it is a radical, closed, backward regime.

However, the problem is that thousands of innocent victims might perish in the missile shelling. The death of Usama bin Ladin will spark no sympathy either. If he did actually perpetrate the attacks on the United States, he killed thousands of innocents, distorted the image of Islam, and provided a lying . . . edict [*fatwa*] when he sanctioned the killing of civilians to take revenge against the policies of their countries. He has hurt the interests of tens of thousands of Arab Americans now surrounded by harsh accusations, suspicious looks,

---

* Makram Muhammad Ahmad is an Egyptian journalist. This article was published in the Egyptian newspaper *al-Musawwar*. Translation by FBIS.

snide remarks, harassment, or racist calls to expel them from the United States. Essentially, the problem is not in the Taliban or bin Ladin. The problem is this mysterious war that the United States wants to wage against the unknown, in its quest for an enemy to quench its thirst for revenge and friends to stand by it, without venturing to rationalize its options.

We want Washington to tell us whether Hizballah and Palestinian resistance groups will be considered terrorist, as [Ariel] Sharon and the worldwide Zionist forces want? Nobody can deny these groups the right to resist the most abominable, most racist, repressive, and ugliest form of occupation. . . .

Then what are the differences between terrorism and resistance, which should be very clear and brook no ambiguity if several Arab states are required to become part of this coalition? If Washington wanted everybody to stand by it against the threats of terrorism threatening the free world, Western democracy, free trade, investments, and trends of new globalization, it should also consider the interests of oppressed peoples. These people are subjected to the terrorism of states and government that honor neither legitimacy nor law and trample the dignity of such peoples.

Terrorism is a real threat, but not only to the values of the Western world. Before that, it is a threat to the right of man to life. Undoubtedly, there is urgent need for the world's efforts to combine under a clear plan to resist terrorism, which continues to corrupt many countries that are not all Arab or Islamic, but also Western. London swarms with hubs of terrorism [because it gives refuge to Egyptian government opponents], despite President [Husni] Mubarak's frequent calls on Britain to reconsider its position. . . .

The security of the free world is not only threatened by terrorism. The absence of justice in international relations, neglect of the requirements of legitimacy, double standards, overlooking of abominable crimes against humanity, and blatant bias in favor of Israel in its horrendous aggression on Palestinians are also threats. The great nations have voluntarily relinquished their true mission in maintaining the rights of peoples and preserving international security and peace. They have taken pleasure in inflicting collective punishments on people for no legal or human reason.

These are the real reasons for the widespread hatred and criticism of U.S. policy by many people. They also create a good environment for breeding terrorist groups.

A little justice may help in rooting out terrorism because force alone cannot. . . .

These parties allegedly hate America not because of its inaction and lack of initiative and justice, but merely because it is America! This is wrong.

It could have been true under international polarization, cold war, and ideological divisions. However, today, all, east and west, north and south, are part of one new world order based on respect for individual freedoms, the free market, and acceptance of the standards of globalization. The pace of some might be faster than that of others, but the fact is that they all follow the same path. What reasons therefore would these have to hate America for itself, as the Zionists say?

The only reason is its disgraceful silence vis-à-vis what happens in the occupied territories and its overt and covert encouragement of Sharon's policies.

The best [thing] America could do to eradicate terrorism, other than force and revenge, would be to add a pinch of justice to its positions and lend its policies a human face. It should go back to its true and first beginnings, when it truly stood by the freedom of man and [all] peoples. However, this looks like quite an impossible dream.

# Open Letter to President George W. Bush (October 19, 2001)

## SAFAR BIN ABD AL-RAHMAN AL-HAWALI*

Mr. President:

I am writing this letter to you in the hope that it will be taken into account without regard to the faith of its writer, or the color of his skin, and despite your new division of the children of Adam into the civilized, who support all your views, and the barbarians, who do not.

Perhaps this letter is strange to you, as I write to you as one of the heirs of the prophets, and the prophets, as we know, used to address the tyrants of the earth in the hope that they might repent and fear the Lord of all the worlds. Thus did Moses—peace be upon him—address Pharaoh, Haman, and Karun, and thus did Jesus—peace be upon him—address the Romans and the high priest of the Jews, and thus did Muhammad—peace and blessings be upon him—address Abu Jahl in Mecca, as well as the Roman emperor Heraclius and the Persian emperor Khosraw. . . .

I will not conceal from you that a tremendous wave of joy accompanied

---

* Safar bin Abd al-Rahman al-Hawali is a Saudi cleric. This open letter appeared in *al-Quds al-Arabi*, an Iraqi-backed London newspaper. Translation by FBIS.

the shock that was felt by the Muslim in the street, and whoever tells you otherwise is avoiding the truth.

It is my opinion that America, which believes in freedom and democracy—as you repeat in your speeches—should not become upset by this one-time joy, and should not seize upon the Muslim's spontaneous outpouring of feeling. This nation [Saudi Arabia], which worships God and believes in justice more than any nation on earth, did not do that out of racist enmity or evil intent, but they were joined in this by the entire world: the world that kicked you out of the Organization for Human Rights. Three thousand popular organizations mobilized against you at the Durban conference. More than forty nations suffer from your oppressive boycotts and economic penalties, let alone from your military incursions.

Even the environment has identified you before the world as its greatest enemy.

People's shock at your first speech was greater than their shock at the event itself. It totally equated America with freedom, justice, and noble values, and it contained a harsh threat of vengeance rather than a promise of fair cooperation. We tried to excuse you because of the shock of the events and the need to absorb popular anger, but all of your statements as well as your actions have been of the same mode and have severed any other possibility.

Reckless accusations and hasty revenge are the real tragedy for America, and the true test of its values and civilization. Your security apparatus—which had boasted that it could catch a fly passing over the Pentagon and that it would know about a riot among the Eskimos before it occurred—rushed to the nearest flight school and the nearest hotel and took down the name of every Arab or Muslim student or resident and announced that they are the terrorists! Imagine, Mr. President, if you were sitting among your family or tribe thousands of miles away and heard or saw the news that you had been part of a suicide operation on a plane? Or that it was done by your brother who had died a year ago? Wouldn't you thank God that you were not a citizen of that civilized country or a believer in their so-called values and justice? Especially when your very civilized people answered these calls of yours, your cabinet members, and your security apparatus and started to attack the barbarian invaders in every free and civilized part of your country. . . .

I would like to ask you, Mr. President, if the world chose you to give a prize for the people with the most advanced morals and values and the best treatment of others, to which of the two peoples would you give the prize? To your people or to ours? Does this mean that we bear ill will toward the American people for that we are racist in our treatment of them? No. Never. We believe that the American people in general have such good attributes that they are the closest of all Western peoples to us, and the most deserving of all of them of our desire for them to achieve good in this life and in the hereafter. They are a people the majority of whom believe in the existence of God, and who donate to charitable work more than any other people in the world (and by that we do not mean the evangelization of the Muslims).

The truest proof of the goodness of the American people is that they have embraced Islam more quickly and in greater numbers than other peoples of the world, and have tried to understand it better even after you held the Muslims responsible for the disaster without evidence.

We desire all good and honor for a people like this from the bottom of our hearts, and good and honor are only achieved by any people by . . . embracing God's faith which is alone acceptable to him, the faith of all the prophets: Islam. By doing this Allah grants them both the good of this world and that of the next world. . . .

We say, "We are used to America inflicting deep wounds and then putting a small bandage on them, but your present attack on Afghanistan has violently removed those bandages and opened a wound in the heart of every Muslim. . . . Is it not enough for you to destroy a whole nation because of an unproven accusation against a single person or organization forced to live in that country? Is this hostility, which exceeds all values and morals and shakes every living conscience in the world, only a drop in the sea of your vengeance? . . .

You search with microscopes for so-called terrorist groups in Somalia, which has been destroyed by poverty, or in the Palestinian refugee camps in Lebanon, whose humble dwellings are threatened by Zionist terrorism every day. But you forget that horrible terrorism tangibly dwells among you. It is you, and nothing but you. If you do not believe this then tell me by God, if your best friend comes to congratulate you in ten years on the victory you hope to achieve over the mysterious enemy you have fabricated, what will he be able to congratulate you about? . . .

Mr. President, don't suppose that I want to recount your few faults and forget our own (in your eyes) very many faults. No, I will mention to you a serious fault of us Muslims: we don't forget our tragedies no matter how much time has passed. Imagine, Mr. President, we still weep over Andalusia and remember what Ferdinand and Isabella did there to our religion, culture, and honor! We dream of regaining it. Nor will we forget the destruction of Baghdad, or the fall of Jerusalem at the hands of your Crusader ancestors. That is, we are not (in your opinion) at the level of civilization enjoyed by the Germans and Japanese, who support your hostilities and forget your past treatment of them. Moreover, the African Muslims who embraced Islam after the fall of Andalusia cry along with the Arabs, just as the Indonesians do who only heard recently heard about Andalusia. It may be a problem for us, but who will pay the price after a while? Mr. President, your problem with the Afghans—and the Muslims in general—is that you are stronger than necessary and they are weaker than necessary. Every time you use excessive force, or are excessive in using it, it proves to be a weakness. . . . This is a great divine mystery, which reminds us of what happened to the tyrant pharaoh at the hands of the oppressed children of Israel. . . .

You may say, "We intend to remove anything that will incite hate from sermons, school curricula, newspaper articles and the media." We reply that if that is your democracy, then . . . try as you like, but you should be sure that you will not succeed. We learned to hate oppression and love the truth from our religion and our Koran, and it is stronger than all of your means, and firmer than your mountains. If you refuse everything but the arrogance of force and the insanity of greatness, then there are no means left for you except the extermination of all the Muslims with nuclear or biological weapons. . . . Be sure, there is no Muslim on earth who loves you, even if they donate their blood to you, or set up intelligence-gathering stations for you, or delegate to you setting the curriculum for the education of their people.

Everyone on earth who claims to love you—and no Muslim is able to make that claim—they only love you like frightened prey loves a brutal predator.

You may say, "We will restore the trust of the Islamic peoples by changing their government into tolerant and democratic systems." But we say, you need only cease your evil treatment of us. You destroyed the Iraqi people as well as others by this false promise; . . . we do not want any freedom or democracy that comes from you, and we will not accept it.

The enemy of freedom cannot grant freedom. Mr. President, I advise you and put the fear of God before you, to cease and desist from hostile action. Deal with the problem with fairness and patience, and you will find that we are with you without reservation. Your hostility now, at the beginning of the way, is easier for you and better for the world. If not, easy beginnings are usually followed by extremely difficult ends. For that reason I ask you to think, Mr. President, if you destroy every country on your list of terrorists, will that be the end or only the beginning? Unless you want to be remembered by history for Armageddon, and in that case there will be no history anyway. For this reason I repeat to you: fear God and think hard.

# Egypt Is a Sovereign State (October 19, 2001)

IBRAHIM NAFI*

. . . . The U.S.'s policy . . . aspires to turn governments in most of the countries of the world into dictatorships when it demands that they blindly support American measures while ignoring their own national interests and public opinion. The American government and media ignore one essential fact: Egypt is a sovereign state with principles, independent positions, and highly realistic views about international problems and crises. . . .

Egypt expressed complete sympathy for [the victims of] the disaster in America and strongly condemned the terrorist action. It called on the United States to consider the crisis of September 11 in an objective and balanced manner. Egypt stated that terror should be struck with full force. . . . [At the same time] Egypt emphasized that efforts to strike at terrorism must not lead to damage to innocent civilians, in Afghanistan in particular and in the world in general. Similarly, Egypt maintained that the American war against terrorism need not lead to attacks on any Arab or Islamic countries, which will, if it happens, constitute cruel and stupid aggression that will necessarily serve Israel's interests and necessarily increase the hatred in Arab and Islamic public opinion toward the American policy. . . .

The developments of recent days have proved the justice of Egypt's position and the validity of Egypt's apprehensions, which President Mubarak has been pointing out since the beginning of the crisis. The American military action in Afghanistan has entered a most dangerous phase, after the aerial bombing and the American missiles hit civilians and residential areas in the Afghan capital, and after the bombing continued for a relatively long time and [was] more extensive than initially expected.

The main goal of the American bombing and missile attacks was to achieve what is called air superiority over the arena of events, something for which, it can be assumed, no more than one day, or a few days at most, will suffice, in light of the Taliban movement's and the al-Qa'ida organization's few central military targets in Afghanistan.

This means that American missiles and bombs have nothing to hit in Afghanistan. Instead of cutting this stage short, the American forces have greatly expanded it, and thus many questions have arisen concerning what exactly the

---

* Ibrahim Nafi, Egypt's leading journalist, is editor of *al-Ahram* and has close links to President Husni Mubarak. Nafi wrote in response to articles in the American press pointing out Egypt's lack of support for the American war against terrorism. Translation by Middle East Media Research Institute, Special Dispatch 292, "Jihad and Terrorism Studies" (October 26, 2001).

U.S. forces are bombing. . . . Similarly, it would be expected that the bombings would not hit innocent civilians. . . . This development is evidence that the American-British military actions in Afghanistan have begun to hit civilians, children, and women; it is not limited to the "scarce" military targets, but is expanding into populated areas and causing great damage to civilians.

The United States tries to prove in every way possible that its military campaign is not directed at the Afghan people, but at the Taliban movement and the al-Qaida organization. It has tried to express this in ways considered exceptional in the history of warfare. American planes drop humanitarian aid from the air on Afghan soil, as aid for the starving Afghan people, while American fighter planes, bombs, and missiles crush other regions in Afghanistan. This method poses serious risk . . . for the Afghan people, because [the aid packages are] dropped in areas full of land mines, which cause damage to the Afghan citizens trying to gather them up.

Similarly, there were several reports that the humanitarian materials have been genetically treated with the aim of affecting the health of the Afghan people. If this is true, the United States is committing a crime against humanity by giving the Afghan people hazardous humanitarian products, as was said in those reports. . . .

# Address to the UN General Assembly (November 10, 2001)

### PAKISTANI PRESIDENT PERVEZ MUSHARRAF

Last year, at the Millennium Summit, all of us were looking forward to a renaissance in the new millennium. A renaissance in the hearts and minds of people, for a better world where peace and justice would prevail. Unfortunately, today we gather against the somber backdrop of the terrorist outrage that the world witnessed in shock and horror on that fateful day of September 11. In seconds, images of fire and death reached all of us. Thousands of innocent lives were lost in minutes. Eighty nations lost some of their brightest and their best. Pakistan, like the rest of the world, mourned the colossal loss of innocent lives. The map of the world changed, and the entire globe descended into a deep crisis. At a time of such great turmoil, when there is indeed a need for clear thought and firm action, I come from Pakistan with a message of determination and resolve as well as a message of peace for all peoples.

The General Assembly this year meets under the shadow of a horrendous act of terror perpetrated against the people of the United States, an act for which no grievance or cause can ever be a justification, an act that must be condemned unambiguously and in the strongest words. This was an attack on humanity itself, and we all must therefore unite to fight this scourge.

Mr. President, now that the world has bonded itself to fight against terrorism, it is time for introspection. We owe it to posterity that in this dark hour we shed light on some dangerous and growing trends, misconceptions, and misperceptions which, if not cleared, may lead the world into even greater disorder and disharmony.

The religion of Islam, and Muslims in various parts of the world, are being held responsible for the trials the world is facing. This point of view is totally misplaced. Just as all religions teach peace and love for fellow beings, so does Islam place upon its adherents the obligation to do good, to be generous, merciful, kind, and just to fellow beings. The Muslim greeting *al-salaamu alaikum*, meaning "peace be upon you," symbolizes the very essence of Islamic faith. Islam is a religion of peace, of compassion, and of tolerance. Terrorism is not a Christian, Buddhist, Jewish, or Muslim belief. It is to be condemned no matter who the perpetrator, be it an individual, a group, or a state.

We need to ask ourselves what really causes these extreme acts around the world. To my mind it is the unresolved political disputes the world over, disputes in Bosnia, Kosovo, Palestine, Kashmir, and other places. Unfortunately all these disputes involve Muslims, and more sadly the Muslims happen to be the victims in all, which tends to give a religious tinge to these otherwise political disputes. The lack of progress in resolution of these disputes has created in [Muslims] a sense of deprivation, hopelessness, and powerlessness. The frustration gets even worse when such disputes as Kashmir and Palestine remain unsettled for decades despite the United Nations Security Council resolutions. The question then is whether it is the people asking for their rights in accordance with UN resolutions who are to be called terrorist, or whether it is the countries refusing to implement the UN resolutions who are perpetrators of state terrorism. In Kashmir, Indian occupation forces have killed over 75,000 Kashmiris, attributing these killings to foreign terrorists. It is time India must stop such deceit. UN Security Council Resolutions on Kashmir must be implemented. Media images of the Palestinian child Muhammad al-Durra were etched on the hearts and minds of people all over the world. It is perverse to regard the rape of Kashmiri women as a punishment inflicted in the course of war. The images of that moment when the World Trade Center tower[s] came down will remain definitive for all the agony, disbelief, and loss that people suffer from acts of terror all over the world. All forms of terror must be condemned, prevented, and fought against, but in so doing the world must not trample upon the genuine rights, aspirations, and urges of the people, who are fighting for their liberation and are subjected to state terrorism.

To fight the extremist, deprive him of his motivation. The extremist survives in an environment where millions suffer injustice and indignity. Deprive him of his support by giving the world peace, security, justice, and dignity for all peoples regardless of faith, religion, or creed.

A just and honorable solution for the people of Kashmir [and] an end to the miseries of the people of Palestine are the major burning issues that have to be addressed vigorously, boldly, imaginatively, and urgently. Unless we go to the root causes, cosmetics will only make matters worse. Consider the analogy of a tree. Terrorists are like so many leaves; you take out some, there will be plenty more and an unending growth. Terrorist networks are branches; you prune a few and there will be others and more growth. The only way to go is to go for the roots. Eliminate the roots and there will be no tree. The roots, Mr. President, are the causes, which need to be addressed, tackled, and eliminated, fairly, justly, and honorably.

Give people back their dignity, their self-respect, their honor. In essence, therefore, to tackle the issue of terrorism in its entirety we need to follow a three-pronged strategy of going for individual terrorists, moving against terrorist organizations and addressing disputes around the world in a just manner. After the events of September 11, Pakistan took a deliberate principled decision to join the world coalition in its fight against terrorism. This decision has catapulted us, once again, as a frontline state in the battle against terrorism. While the people of Pakistan have accepted this new reality, they still suffer from a sense of betrayal and abandonment [from] when they were left in the lurch in 1989 after the Soviet withdrawal from Afghanistan. Then, also, we were a frontline state, and what we got in return was three million refugees, a shattered economy, drugs, and Kalashnikov culture, to be faced single-handedly through our limited resources. Pakistan only hopes that the mistakes of the past will not be repeated and [that] Pakistan's legitimate concerns will be addressed. Our economy again faces a crisis of a fallout of the operations in Afghanistan. We need financial and commercial support on an urgent basis and hope that this will be forthcoming.

Mr. President, after September 11 Pakistan had been trying its utmost with the Afghan government ever since Usama bin Ladin and al-Qa'ida became an international issue, till the last moment to avert military action in Afghanistan. Regrettably, we did not meet with success, and the coalition operation against terrorist in Afghanistan continues with no immediate end in sight. Sadly enough, the civilian casualties in this action are getting projected more as an open war against the already poor, suffering, and innocent people of Afghanistan. The world in general and Pakistan in particular mourn the loss of these innocent lives and sympathize with the bereaved. It is desirable that the military operation be as short and accurately targeted as possible. It is also essential that a fallback political strategy be evolved that could attain the same objective as [that] being sought through military application. . . . Dealing with Afghanistan involves a three-pronged strategy—the military, political, and humanitarian *cum* rehabilitation strategies. It must remain the effort of the coalition to prevent a vacuum, [which would] lead to anarchy, after achieving military objectives, through immediate application of political and rehabilitation strategies. . . .

To offset the ill effects of the ongoing military operation, it is imperative that we launch a more coordinated and concerned humanitarian relief effort inside and outside Afghanistan with more generous funding. This will go a long way to alleviate the sufferings of the common Afghan. It is equally important that concurrently we formulate a post-operation rehabilitation program, once peace returns to Afghanistan.

# Editorial in *Ha'aretz* (September 12, 2001)*

The terrible terrorist attack that was unleashed on the United States yesterday was not directed against the American administration, nor against its policies in this or that part of the world. It was an attack planned by people who want to destroy a whole system of values, in effect all that the civilization of "the West" represents—liberty, democracy, economic power, and military capability. . . .

These attacks will not be measured only by the horrific number of casualties, nor the huge amount of damage, nor even by the enormity of the attack on the national symbols of the United States and American prestige. This unprecedented terrorist attack now divides world society into two clear groups—those who promote democracy, progress and development, and human freedoms, and those who wish to destroy those values and advance backward, ignorant ideas. There are also those who stand alongside them who applaud and take joy in the "punishment" of a United States that has become a symbol of evil in their eyes.

* *Ha'aretz* is an Israeli newspaper. Reprinted with permission.

This is not the first time that terror organizations have struck a blow in the United States against what it represents, or from a desire to twist America's arm, or to impose an ideology or policy different than that chosen by America. Such echoes still reverberate from the explosions in the U.S. embassies in Kenya and Tanzania, the attack on the U.S. navy ship off the coast of Yemen, the attack on the U.S. army facilities in Dahran, and further back, the attacks in Lebanon. After each of these, America powerfully and with determination confronted organizations and groups that tried to divert it from its path, and with terrorists who took upon themselves to represent a world bathed in hatred.

Each time, America, both its administration and its people, proved they are not ready to give up—not only their values, but their intention to make the world a more reasonable place. . . . America has paid and pays [a price] for that determination . . . in the name of all freedom-loving countries, including Israel, that are not ready to bow their heads before extremists who enlist God to justify their murderous activities . . .

The citizens of the United States, in any case, are not alone on this terrible day. Those who believe in its values stand by their side to strengthen America in this uncompromising war against terrorism.

# September 11 and Islamic *Sharia* (September 14, 2001)

SALIH BIN MUHAMMAD AL-LUHEIDAN*

Praise be to God Almighty:

In the midst of the catastrophic events that have hit America, questions and queries have been raised as to how such acts are judged and interpreted by Islamic *Sharia*, which encompasses all things and gives clear rulings on every calamity: any calamity that affects humans has its ruling in Islamic *Sharia*.

Many questions have been raised by officials and by the public as to the ruling of Islamic *Sharia* on such acts, and whether it is considered acceptable or permissible by Islamic scholars, who shoulder the responsibility of clarifying rulings and Islam's point of view with respect to disasters.

---

* Salih bin Muhammad al-Luheidan is chairman of the Supreme Judicial Council of Saudi Arabia.

God Almighty, the master of all rulers, has prohibited injustice among humans. Aggression against those who have committed no crime and the killing of innocent people are matters that Islamic *Sharia* has dealt with: these are not permissible even during wars and invasions. Killing the weak, infants, women, and the elderly, and destroying property, are considered serious crimes in Islam. Acts of corruption and even laying waste to the land are forbidden by God and by his prophet. Viewing on the television networks what happened to the twin towers [of the World Trade Center] was like watching doomsday.

Those who commit such crimes are the worst of people. Anyone who thinks that any Islamic scholar will condone such acts is totally wrong.

Aggression, injustice, and gloating over the kind of crime that we have seen are totally unacceptable and forbidden in Islam.

God Almighty says: "And let not the enmity and hatred of others make you avoid justice. Be just, that is nearer to piety." Inflicting a collective punishment is considered by Islam [to be] despicable aggression and perversion. Killing innocent people is by itself a grave crime, quite apart from terrorizing and committing crimes against infants and women. Such acts do no honor to him who commits them, even if he claims to be a Muslim. These sorts of crime are pernicious: in fact, the kingdom's Islamic scholars, at the time when Saudi Arabia was looking into the phenomenon of hijacking planes, resolved to forbid such acts regardless of the religious belief of the passengers, whether Muslims or non-Muslims, since terrorizing any person is forbidden in Islam.

Accordingly, it is incumbent upon the kingdom of Saudi Arabia, as a state governed by the spirit and rulings of Islam, to deplore any criminal and corrupt act, irrespective of whether the perpetrators are Muslims or non-Muslims. Those who are truly versed in the fundamentals and reality of Islam know that such acts are crimes of endless harm.

Considering the numerous questions and queries that arise regarding such acts and our position as a judicial board, from an Islamic perspective, we view them as despicable. It has been said that the perpetrator alone shall carry the burden of his crimes. I have been telling the press that Muslims do not condone such brutal acts, nor should they be held responsible for them, since the creed of Islam urges that no person be responsible for a crime committed by others. This is a prerequisite for justice: "No bearer of burden shall bear the burden of another."

With respect to what has been reported in the media about reactions and how Americans view Arabs and Muslims residing in the United States, I have in the past said that Americans as guardians of democracy cannot deal with Muslims on the basis of crimes committed by a few. Criminals and aggressors cannot be equated with the innocent and the peaceful.

I would like to reiterate that Islam rejects such acts, since it forbids killing of civilians even during times of war, especially if they are not part of the fighting. A religion that views people of the world in such a way cannot in any sense condone such criminal acts, which require that their perpetrators and those who support them are held accountable. As a human community we have to be vigilant and careful to preempt these evils.

Islamic *Sharia* is based on the principle that prevention is better than treatment; one of its goals is looking into causes.

I would like to confirm that the Islamic world and its religious and political leadership cannot condone such acts; and I am convinced that Western and American society cannot deal with Islamic nations and peoples from the basis of the crime committed.

Muslims have to deal in good faith with those who live beside them in all societies, since Islam does not discriminate between humans: for they are all brothers.

This barbaric act is not justified by any sane mindset or any logic, nor by the religion of Islam. This act is pernicious and shameless and evil in the extreme.

I pray to God to guide the devious to the path of righteousness, and to protect us from all evils and from our own bad deeds, and to be gracious to us.

# After Afghanistan: Liberating Islam (September 17, 2001)

AHMAD BISHARA*

Five times a day Muslims the world over pray for Allah, a benevolent and merciful God. Aside from differences in rituals, Muslims in their prayers share a devotion and submission to a mighty deity that is akin to that of Christians, Jews, Sikhs, Buddhists, or any tribal clan in remote areas.

In each of these religious beliefs God is conceived as a force of love, peace, [and] compassion, and a motivating force to the individual.

Enter the bin Ladin factor on the world scene and suddenly the Muslim faith is muddied and dragged into a defused focus like no other faith in history.

Turbaned, shouldering an AK-47, and sporting an offensive beard in front

* Ahmad Bishara is secretary-general of the Kuwaiti National Democratic Movement. This article appeared in the Kuwaiti newspaper *Arab Times* and is reprinted with the author's permission.

of an ancient cave in a remote land called Afghanistan, bin Ladin took Muslims by the neck and wrestled their faith to the ground. The rest of the story, as they say, is now history.

The United States and its allies from nations of the civilized world are rightfully fighting a just war against terror, as exemplified by bin Ladin associates and hosts in Afghanistan. Considering what is at stake and the roots of the conflict, no doubt they will prevail. They will decimate the Taliban, bin Ladin, and his cohorts, and will uproot the bases of terror. Events of the last few days attest to that. Afghanistan will again be free, and its people will pick up the pieces and rebuild their country in ways that will suit them.

But will the war be over?

Far from it. There remains another war that needs no conventional armies and will result in no body counts. This war needs to be undertaken by Muslims to save their faith from within, and from their own folly.

For the responsibility of liberating Islam as a faith and culture and rectifying the damage that has been leveled on it is the responsibility of the faithful. That means all the believers in Muslim faith. No international coalition can or should help in this regard.

The tasks of liberating Islam are mammoth; but they have to be tackled in order to protect our faith and restore its damaged images. A first step in this process is to disown and discourage fanatical cults and muftis who have hijacked Islam for their own ends. Interpretation of the faith should be institutionalized, and the practice of obscure individuals issuing haphazard *fatwas* on behalf of all Muslims should be banned. A body of an enlightened clergy should be created and universally recognized, say, by the Organization of Islamic Countries, as the sole interpreter of the faith.

No respectful religion espouses individual whims as dogmas: Islam should be protected from this archaic and harmful practice.

Concurrently, we need to submit religious education in public schools, pulpits, and Islamic seminaries alike, to a rigorous review by secular and enlightened Islamic scholars. Islam is currently projected as belligerent, prejudiced against women, insensitive to human rights, and intolerant of other faiths and cultures, among other things. School texts, popular books, and public media are brimming with inciting examples.

Many parents constantly express their worry that the educational system overemphasizes religion, and at the expense of other subjects.

Learning is by rote, with questions discouraged. As one scholar put it, religious education "looks innocent—they are just trying to teach religion—but in a subtle way it is a recruiting mechanism for fundamentalist thought, intolerance and hate." We need to stop this irresponsible practice and change it. Islamic education and sermonizing must emphasize the ideals of peace, tolerance, and coexistence if Muslims aspire to fit into a multicultural and multiethnic world.

Governance in Islamic societies, too, needs fundamental restructuring. And here I mean the relationship between the state as a temporal body and religion as a spiritual corpus. From its early beginnings, Islam was conceived as a union of the two. This might have been not only convenient but also required in a primitive seventh-century society and [extending] to some period beyond. However, with the rise of the modern state and its increasing interstate obligations and complexities, religion was increasingly removed from state affairs and relegated to a personal conviction. No society has since succeeded without this model. None will ever, either. Muslim societies cannot continue a self-deception that they are different and exult themselves as an exception. They are not. In fact, it can be argued and extensively corroborated that none of the constituents of a modern society can function properly as long as religion and state are one and the same, be it democratic governance, separation of powers, human rights, or most basic international relations. Muslims and Muslim countries must accommodate themselves to this reality.

These are but some of the basic questions that need deep soul searching, [something that] amounts to a liberation movement from within Islam. Cosmetic changes will not do. Events of September 11 have generated visible interest in the West, especially in the United States, in Islam. Many well-meaning Muslims think Islam is misunderstood in the West. Well, maybe to some extent that is true. But it is the failure of Muslims to understand the fundamental message of their own religion, practice it properly, and accommodate it to the modern world that is at fault. No one can help them in this regard if they do not help themselves.

# Envy and Hate (September 22, 2001)

ILTER TURKMEN*

The gradually integrating, institutionalizing, and globalizing world was anticipating a long-term peace prior to September 11. The terrorist attacks targeting the United States all of a sudden struck a severe blow to these expectations of the civilized world.

---

* Ilter Turkmen was formerly the foreign minister of Turkey. This article appeared in the Turkish daily *Hurriyet*. Translation by FBIS.

It dragged the entire world into an environment of insecurity. Yes, terrorism had struck other countries previously; however, it is obvious that the recent action has a more extensive objective. The incident was realized with a dimension that will shake the balances in the world and perhaps provoke a global struggle. It created financial and economic depression on a global scale. All countries will feel the effects of these. The economic crisis in Turkey has already become worse. . . .

Bin Ladin has never made it a secret that his political philosophy is based on the concept of closing the Islamic world to the West. A characteristic of religious fundamentalism is to perceive the world as an arena of continuous battle and to nourish it with anger and the desire for revenge. Does not even the most moderate political Islam have difficulty in coming to terms with global values?

The most recent terrorist blow has paved the way for the search for an answer to the question of why there is generally a feeling of hate among the Arab people toward the United States. . . . On the one hand, in front of the U.S. consulates there are long lines of people waiting for visas to go to the United States, and there is passion for American popular culture. On the other hand, there were demonstrations of deep resentment and hate and cheering when the United States was struck with a disaster. Naturally, there are concrete reasons for hostility against the United States. In the Arab collective consciousness, the sympathy of the United States with Israel comes before all else.

As a matter of fact, the Arab states have not done much for the Palestinians. They have even been extremely stingy in their humanitarian aid to the Palestinians, but when it comes to making speeches, they have always competed with each other. Even in Egypt and Jordan, which have signed peace agreements with Israel, people's hatred of Israel has not decreased.

All right, could [Samuel] Huntington's prediction of a "conflict of civilizations" be verified after the 11 September disaster? It does not appear to be probable. First of all, the major division in the world today is not along the Christian-Islam axis, it is more along the North–South axis. One of the bloodiest fights after the Second World War occurred between two Muslim countries, Iraq and Iran. In the Balkan wars, the Westerners ran to the aid of the Muslims in Bosnia-Herzegovina and Kosovo. In the Gulf War, many Muslim countries fought against Iraq on the same front with the United States. Let us remember one more thing. Did not a Muslim country [Syria] provide support to the leftist terrorism and then to the PKK [Worker's Party of Kurdistan] terrorism in Turkey for years? Were not the terrorists trained in the Palestinian camps? It is just a daydream to expect solidarity in the Islamic world.

The warnings that the Westerners should not confront Islam in the fight against terrorism are appropriate. In any case, President [George W.] Bush is delivering the necessary messages to the American public on this subject. However, the point one should pay attention to when condemning the attacks against the Muslims is not to give in to a tendency to make any excuses for the September 11 massacre. Especially in a country like Turkey, which is secular and which the West regards as a partner in the area of security. . . . Today, it is time for solidarity with the United States and NATO [North Atlantic Treaty Organization]. . . .

# Sharon Is a Terrorist—And You?
# (November 3, 2001)

AHMAD AL-BAGHDADI*

[Ariel] Sharon was a terrorist from the very first moment of the declaration of the establishment of the Zionist entity; on this there is no dispute. He carries out terrorist assassinations of Palestinians; no doubt about that.

But can anybody prove that Sharon has carried out terrorism against the citizens of Israel who elected him? This has not happened. The Zionist entity does not terrorize and imprison its intellectuals and writers. The Koran orders us to act fairly even to our enemies . . . [thus, it must be acknowledged that] while the prime minister of the Israeli entity rises to power by democratic elections, in the Arab world or the Islamic world there is no such elected prime minister.

The Arabs and the Muslims do not carry out terrorism against [Arabs]. This was a fact up until September 11, the day on which a "group of martyrs" [as bin Ladin said in his first recorded speech after the event] killed 7,000 innocent people! But even before that, and up until that moment, didn't the Arab [rulers] carry out terrorism against their [own] citizens within their [own] countries?

Persecuting intellectuals in the courtrooms [of Arab countries], trials [of intellectuals] for heresy, destruction of families, rulings that marriages must be

---

* Ahmad al-Baghdadi is a Kuwaiti political science professor. This article appeared in the Kuwaiti newspaper *al-Anbaa*. Translation by Middle East Media Research Institute, report no. 302 (November 20, 2001).

broken up [because one spouse is charged with apostasy] all exist only in the Islamic world. Is this not terrorism?

The [Arab] intelligence apparatuses . . . killed hundreds of intellectuals and politicians from the religious stream itself. The Zionist entity has never done [such things] against its citizens. Isn't this terrorism?

The capability of the intelligence apparatus in every Arab and Islamic country to arrest someone and make him disappear . . . does not exist in Israel and in the West. Isn't this terrorism?

Iraq alone is a never-ending story of terrorism of the state against its own citizens and neighbors. Isn't this terrorism?

The Afghans were living a good and healthy life—though they fought each other—until the Muslim Arabs came in and brought them into the hellish circle of terrorism, and now they are paying the price. . . .

The Palestinian Arabs were the first to invent airplane hijacking and the scaring of passengers. Isn't this terrorism?

Arab Muslims have no rivals in this; they are the masters of terrorism toward their citizens, and sometimes their terrorism also reaches the innocent people of the world, with the support of some of the clerics.

Today, the Arabs and the Muslims are paying the price of their terrorism toward their citizens and toward the world. They are persecuted and humiliated across the civilized world. They are rejected in both the West and the East. In restaurants, in airplanes, in buses—everywhere they are spat upon. One cannot complain to the West for what it is doing to them, because the Arab and Muslim world, everyone—governments and peoples—are lying about terrorism.

The Muslims claim that Islam is a religion of peace and brotherhood. Even Saddam Hussein begins his speeches of menace with the words *al-salaamu alaikum*. . . . The Islamic world and the Arab world are the only [places] in which intellectuals—whose only crime was to write—rot in prison. The Arabs and the Muslims claim that their religion is a religion of tolerance, but they show no tolerance for those who oppose their opinions.

For over 500 years, no author or intellectual in the infidel West has been murdered, while religious rulings permitting the blood [of people] in the Arab and Islamic world [are given away for] free. The governments and the people are silent, and this means that they support these criminal rulings.

Now the time has come to pay the price. Nothing comes without a reckoning, and the account is long—longer than all the beards of the Taliban gang together. The West's message to the Arab and Muslim world is clear: mend your ways or else. . . .

# The Fight against Terrorism Must Begin with Curricular, Educational, and Media Reform in the Arab World (November 29, 2001)

ABD AL-HAMID AL-ANSARI*

[Arab] ideological, political, and religious positions on current events remind us of a crucial incident in Islamic history that is connected to the present. I refer to the Khawarij, the "first terrorist organization," which rose up against the Imam Ali [leader of the Muslims in the seventh century]. . . . [They demanded] that Ali either mend his ways or face war. From this, they moved on to accusing the entire society of heresy. They saw anyone with an opinion different from theirs, and anyone who was silent and refrained from joining them, as a heretic. . . .

The Imam Ali and his friends did not hesitate to meet them head on. . . . He . . . fought the Khawarij and thoroughly routed them at al-Naharwan in [659].

But today, we are facing the modern Khawarij, and behold, fortune has smiled on them. They have satellite channels that espouse their ideas, reiterating them tirelessly day and night, and that makes them into popular stars. Host commentators justify and shape their ideas. Religious leaders volunteer to issue religious rulings demanding [that believers] stand by them, and determine that remaining silent or refraining from supporting them is a sin.

[These religious leaders] call for *jihad* against the crusade against Islam, and aspire to incite the Arab public against its governments, who stand by America, the enemy of Islam. Most unfortunately, there are those who believe in this deception, hold demonstrations, and become involved in acts of stupidity against [those] whom they call the enemies of Islam. As a result, they are destroyed, and their families are tragedy stricken. Afterwards, we allow the imams, who pushed them to the edge of the precipice, to continue to live a life of ease, without being held accountable in any way.

The religious and logical question is: *jihad* against whom? For whose sake? Who has the right [to declare a *jihad*]? Will we leave the *jihad* to the hysterical preachers and politicians, who are declaring a war that will destroy everything, or is this a right reserved for the ruler?

Do they have the right to incite the public to become involved in acts of

---

* Abd al-Hamid al-Ansari is a Qatari law professor. This article appeared in the London-based newspaper *al-Hayat*. Translation by Middle East Media Research Institute, report no. 307 (December 4, 2001).

sabotage that victimize innocents and damage state interests? Or should this right be restricted, so that the public interest is unharmed?

Who gave the religious parties the right to declare a *jihad* and jeopardize the supreme interests of the nation? The Saudi clerics fulfilled their duty by declaring that no one had the right to issue a religious ruling calling for *jihad* except the ruler. This is what they taught us, and thus we teach. The clerics must act accordingly. . . .

Do the satellite channels have the right to broadcast terrorist opinions and incitement on the pretext of the "principle of freedom for all," disseminating hatred in the [hearts of] the viewers, who then [carry out] harmful acts of stupidity? Or must the regime intervene and set limits on irresponsible freedoms?

There is a big difference between granting freedom of speech for people who have opposing political opinions [and express them] peacefully . . . and . . . leaving the microphones to [be used by] armed groups that commit murder to advance their ideas. . . . The essential question is: Do they have the right, in the name of freedom, to lead us and their societies over the edge of the precipice?

As a result of this false incitement, 83 percent of the participants in a survey on the Internet site of the al-Jazira satellite [television] channel think that bin Ladin is a *jihad* fighter, not a terrorist, and that his incitement against Western and American interests constitutes a *jihad*. . . .

What is the meaning of all this sympathy for, and defense of, our modern-day Khawarij? Is blind anti-American sentiment . . . enough to account for making terrorists into heroes?

Unfortunately for the Khawarij of the past, they had no satellite channels . . . even though they were more merciful than the Khawarij of our generation, as they permitted the blood of Muslims [to be spilled] but not of the [Jews and Christians] because they wanted to preserve the protection pact given to them. In contrast to them, the Khawarij of our time [the militant Islamists] have permitted the blood of everyone [to be spilled]. . . .

The platforms of the various *jihad* organizations, and of al-Qa'ida, do not include fighting Israel. The ideology of all these organizations establishes a single goal: accusing society and the state of heresy, with the aim of reaching power to set up their false state. When they despaired of their series of criminal acts on Arab land, which have claimed hundreds of victims, Satan told them that the Arab regimes were a product of the West. America, they claimed, was the defender of these regimes. They decided to fight America on its home turf so America would leave Arab lands, thus enabling them to disseminate their corruption.

What are the reasons for the phenomenon of terrorism? In my opinion, the human soul, and primarily the Muslim soul, is repelled by terrorism. But terrorist ideas fall on fertile ground when societies are ruled by a fanatic culture that the people absorb in doses. Opponents are accused of religious heresy; the opposition is accused of political treason. This is a culture of terrorism, which is [easily] absorbed by those who have been exposed to inappropriate education. This culture is rooted in the minds of those who suffered from a closed education that leaves no room for pluralism.

We must examine our curriculum and evaluate our educational methods. We must reexamine our education and our media. This will be the right beginning for the fight against the culture of terrorism.

# 8

# SEPTEMBER 11 AND THE

# WAR AGAINST TERRORISM

$A$fter the worst terrorist attack in history, the U.S. government moved to ensure such an event would not happen again, to punish those responsible, and to unite a shaken nation. It did this with rhetoric, legislation, and military action. President George W. Bush gave several impassioned speeches, as did Prime Minister Tony Blair of Great Britain, while action came from both the executive and legislative branches of the U.S. government and from the United Nations.

On the evening of September 11, 2001, Bush delivered a short address to the nation that showed that the U.S. government was still in control, and to find the good amid the widespread evil of the day. Nine days later he gave his most important speech regarding the attack in an address to a joint session of Congress, in which he defined the terrorists as the new incarnation of fascists and suggests they will follow their predecessors' path to end "in history's un-marked grave of discarded lies." Bush then delivered a blunt ultimatum to the Taliban to hand over bin Ladin or face military attack. He also asserted that the enemies are not "all Muslims," but "a radical network of terrorists and every government that supports them."

After U.S. forces began military attacks on Afghanistan on October 7, Bush delivered another short address, saying that the goals of the attacks were to disrupt the use of that nation as a terrorist base of operations and to destroy the Taliban regime's military capability. His subsequent address at the United Nations, given on November 10, was aimed at an international audience as he stressed that the September 11 victims came from all over the world. There is no such thing as a good terrorist, he further asserted, and all nations must maintain the principle that "no national aspiration, no remembered wrong can ever justify the deliberate murder of the innocent."

Prime Minister Tony Blair's major address to the British public on October 1 is a sober assessment of the evils of the al-Qa'ida network and the Taliban regime and a reassurance that retaliatory attacks are fully justified. As a result of September 11, laws were being changed "not to deny basic liberties but to prevent their abuse and protect the most basic liberty of all: freedom from terror," added Blair.

Several new laws and regulations were enacted in the United States to deter and catch terrorists. The first executive order on September 24 was aimed at undercutting financial backing for terrorists by authorizing the seizure of the property of any individual or organization linked to terrorism. The second executive order, issued on October 8, established the Office of Homeland Security, a governmental office whose mission would be to develop, coordinate, and oversee the national fight against terrorism. The third and most controversial executive order, on November 13, called for establishing military tribunals when needed to try any non-U.S. citizens who were members of terrorist groups. The tribunals would be conducted under a different set of rules from other courts, including conviction and sentencing by concurrence of two-thirds of the commission members rather than unanimously, as is the case in regular courts. Nor may defendants seek appeals in any other U.S. or international court.

On September 28 the U.S. Congress passed a major law to strengthen law enforcement efforts against terrorism, called the Uniting and Strengthening America by Providing Appropriate Tools Required to Intercept and Obstruct Terrorism, or Patriot Act. This law made it easier for law enforcement and intelligence officials to coordinate among themselves, intercept communications, block suspected foreign terrorists from entering the United States, and detain and deport those already present. It authorized the collection of information about foreigners who were in the country on student visas. A section of the bill also opposed any stigma or discrimination against Muslims, Arabs, or other groups.

The United Nations Security Council also passed a resolution September 28 calling on all nations to seize the financial assets of individuals or companies linked to terrorism, not to provide any support—including safe haven—for terrorists, and to cooperate in prosecuting anyone who provides such support.

# Address to the Nation (September 11, 2001)

PRESIDENT GEORGE W. BUSH

Today, our fellow citizens, our way of life, our very freedom came under attack in a series of deliberate and deadly terrorist acts. The victims were in airplanes or in their offices: secretaries, businessmen and -women, military and federal workers, moms and dads, friends and neighbors.

Thousands of lives were suddenly ended by evil, despicable acts of terror. The pictures of airplanes flying into buildings, fires burning, huge structures collapsing have filled us with disbelief, terrible sadness and a quiet, unyielding anger.

These acts of mass murder were intended to frighten our nation into chaos and retreat. But they have failed. Our country is strong. A great people has been moved to defend a great nation.

Terrorist attacks can shake the foundations of our biggest buildings, but they cannot touch the foundation of America. These acts shatter steel, but they cannot dent the steel of American resolve.

America was targeted for attack because we're the brightest beacon for freedom and opportunity in the world. And no one will keep that light from shining.

Today, our nation saw evil, the very worst of human nature, and we responded with the best of America, with the daring of our rescue workers, with the caring for strangers and neighbors who came to give blood and help in any way they could.

Immediately following the first attack, I implemented our government's emergency response plans. Our military is powerful, and it's prepared. Our emergency teams are working in New York City and Washington, D.C., to help with local rescue efforts.

Our first priority is to get help to those who have been injured and to take every precaution to protect our citizens at home and around the world from further attacks.

The functions of our government continue without interruption. Federal agencies in Washington which had to be evacuated today are reopening for essential personnel tonight and will be open for business tomorrow.

Our financial institutions remain strong, and the American economy will be open for business as well.

The search is under way for those who are behind these evil acts. I've directed the full resources for our intelligence and law enforcement communities to find those responsible and bring them to justice. We will make no distinction between the terrorists who committed these acts and those who harbor them.

I appreciate so very much the members of Congress who have joined me in strongly condemning these attacks. And on behalf of the American people, I thank the many world leaders who have called to offer their condolences and assistance.

America and our friends and allies join with all those who want peace and security in the world, and we stand together to win the war against terrorism.

Tonight I ask for your prayers for all those who grieve, for the children whose worlds have been shattered, for all whose sense of safety and security has been threatened. And I pray they will be comforted by a power greater than any of us spoken through the ages in Psalm 23: "Even though I walk through the valley of the shadow of death, I fear no evil for you are with me."

This is a day when all Americans from every walk of life unite in our resolve for justice and peace. America has stood down enemies before, and we will do so this time.

None of us will ever forget this day, yet we go forward to defend freedom and all that is good and just in our world.

Thank you. Good night and God bless America.

# Address to Joint Session of Congress (September 20, 2001)

PRESIDENT GEORGE W. BUSH

In the normal course of events, presidents come to this chamber to report on the state of the union. Tonight, no such report is needed; it has already been delivered by the American people.

We have seen it in the courage of passengers who rushed terrorists to save others on the ground. Passengers like an exceptional man named Todd Beamer [a passenger on one of the hijacked planes who led the resistance to the terrorists]. . . . We have seen the state of our union in the endurance of rescuers working past exhaustion.

We've seen the unfurling of flags, the lighting of candles, the giving of blood, the saying of prayers in English, Hebrew, and Arabic. We have seen the decency of a loving and giving people who have made the grief of strangers their own.

My fellow citizens, for the last nine days, the entire world has seen for itself the state of our union, and it is strong. Tonight, we are a country awakened to danger and called to defend freedom. Our grief has turned to anger and anger to resolution. Whether we bring our enemies to justice or bring justice to our enemies, justice will be done.

I thank the Congress for its leadership at such an important time. All of America was touched on the evening of the tragedy to see Republicans and Democrats joined together on the steps of this Capitol singing "God Bless America." . . . You acted, by delivering $40 billion to rebuild our communities and meet the needs of our military. . . .

And on behalf of the American people, I thank the world for its outpouring of support. America will never forget the sounds of our national anthem playing at Buckingham Palace, on the streets of Paris, and at Berlin's Brandenburg Gate.

We will not forget South Korean children gathering to pray outside our embassy in Seoul, or the prayers of sympathy offered at a mosque in Cairo. We will not forget moments of silence and days of mourning in Australia and Africa and Latin America.

Nor will we forget the citizens of eighty other nations who died with our own. Dozens of Pakistanis, more than 130 Israelis, more than 250 citizens of India, men and women from El Salvador, Iran, Mexico, and Japan, and hundreds of British citizens. America has no truer friend than Great Britain. Once again, we are joined together in a great cause. . . . I'm so honored the British prime minister had crossed an ocean to show his unity with America. Thank you for coming, friend.

On September the 11th, enemies of freedom committed an act of war against our country. Americans have known wars, but [since the American Civil War] they have been wars on foreign soil, except for [the Japanese attack on Pearl Harbor] in 1941. Americans have known the casualties of war, but not at the center of a great city on a peaceful morning. Americans have known surprise attacks, but never before on thousands of civilians. All of this was brought upon us in a single day, and night fell on a different world, a world where freedom itself is under attack.

Americans have many questions tonight. Americans are asking, "Who attacked our country?" The evidence we have gathered all points to a collection of loosely affiliated terrorist organizations known as al-Qa'ida. They are some of the murderers indicted for bombing American embassies in Tanzania and Kenya and responsible for bombing the USS *Cole*.

Al-Qa'ida is to terror what the Mafia is to crime. But its goal is not making money. Its goal is remaking the world and imposing its radical beliefs on people everywhere.

The terrorists practice a fringe form of Islamic extremism that has been rejected by Muslim scholars and the vast majority of Muslim clerics, a fringe movement that perverts the peaceful teachings of Islam.

The terrorists' directive commands them to kill Christians and Jews, to kill all Americans and make no distinctions among military and civilians, including women and children.

This group and its leader, a person named Usama bin Ladin, are linked to many other organizations in different countries, including the Egyptian Islamic Jihad [and] the Islamic Movement of Uzbekistan.

There are thousands of these terrorists in more than sixty countries. They are recruited from their own nations and neighborhoods and brought to camps in places like Afghanistan, where they are trained in the tactics of terror. They are sent back to their homes or sent to hide in countries around the world to plot evil and destruction. The leadership of al Qa'ida has great influence in Afghanistan and supports the Taliban regime in controlling most of that country. In Afghanistan we see al-Qa'ida's vision for the world. Afghanistan's people have been brutalized, many are starving, and many have fled. Women are not allowed to attend school. You can be jailed for owning a television. Religion can be practiced only as their leaders dictate. A man can be jailed in Afghanistan if his beard is not long enough.

The United States respects the people of Afghanistan—after all, we are currently its largest source of humanitarian aid—but we condemn the Taliban regime. It is not only repressing its own people, it is threatening people everywhere by sponsoring and sheltering and supplying terrorists. By aiding and abetting murder, the Taliban regime is committing murder. And tonight the United States of America makes the following demands on the Taliban:

Deliver to United States authorities all of the leaders of al-Qa'ida who hide in your land. Release all foreign nationals, including American citizens, you have unjustly imprisoned. Protect foreign journalists, diplomats, and aid workers in your country. Close immediately and permanently every terrorist training camp in Afghanistan. And hand over every terrorist and every person and their support structure to appropriate authorities. Give the United States full access to terrorist training camps, so we can make sure they are no longer operating. These demands are not open to negotiation or discussion. The Taliban must act and act immediately. They will hand over the terrorists or they will share in their fate.

I also want to speak tonight directly to Muslims throughout the world. We respect your faith. It's practiced freely by many millions of Americans and by millions more in countries that America counts as friends. Its teachings are good and peaceful, and those who commit evil in the name of Allah blaspheme the name of Allah. The terrorists are traitors to their own faith, trying, in effect, to hijack Islam itself.

The enemy of America is not our many Muslim friends. It is not our many Arab friends. Our enemy is a radical network of terrorists and every government that supports them. Our war on terror begins with al-Qa'ida, but it does not end there.

It will not end until every terrorist group of global reach has been found, stopped, and defeated.

Americans are asking, "Why do they hate us?" They hate what they see right here in this chamber: a democratically elected government. Their leaders are self-appointed. They hate our freedoms: our freedom of religion, our freedom of speech, our freedom to vote and assemble and disagree with each other.

They want to overthrow existing governments in many Muslim countries such as Egypt, Saudi Arabia, and Jordan. They want to drive Israel out of the Middle East. They want to drive Christians and Jews out of vast regions of Asia and Africa.

These terrorists kill not merely to end lives, but to disrupt and end a way of life. With every atrocity, they hope that America grows fearful, retreating from the world and forsaking our friends. They stand against us because we stand in their way.

We're not deceived by their pretenses to piety. We have seen their kind before. They're the heirs of all the murderous ideologies of the twentieth century. By sacrificing human life to serve their radical visions, by abandoning every value except the will to power, they follow in the path of fascism, Nazism, and totalitarianism. And they will follow that path all the way to where it ends in history's unmarked grave of discarded lies. Americans are asking, "How will we fight and win this war?"

We will direct every resource at our command—every means of diplomacy, every tool of intelligence, every instrument of law enforcement, every financial influence, and every necessary weapon of war—to the destruction and to the defeat of the global terror network.

Now, this war will not be like the war against Iraq a decade ago, with a decisive liberation of territory and a swift conclusion. It will not look like the air war above Kosovo two years ago, where no ground troops were used and not a single American was lost in combat.

Our response involves far more than instant retaliation and isolated strikes. Americans should not expect one battle, but a lengthy campaign unlike any other we have ever seen. It may include dramatic strikes visible on TV and covert operations secret even in success.

We will starve terrorists of funding, turn them one against another, drive them from place to place until there is no refuge or no rest.

And we will pursue nations that provide aid or safe haven to terrorism. Every nation in every region now has a decision to make: Either you are with us or you are with the terrorists.

From this day forward, any nation that continues to harbor or support terrorism will be regarded by the United States as a hostile regime. Our nation has been put on notice. We're not immune from attack. We will take defensive measures against terrorism to protect Americans.

Today, dozens of federal departments and agencies, as well as state and local governments, have responsibilities affecting homeland security.

These efforts must be coordinated at the highest level. So tonight, I announce the creation of a Cabinet-level position reporting directly to me, the Office of Homeland Security. And tonight, I also announce a distinguished American to lead this effort to strengthen American security: a military veteran, an effective governor, a true patriot, a trusted friend, Pennsylvania's Tom Ridge.

He will lead, oversee, and coordinate a comprehensive national strategy to safeguard our country against terrorism and respond to any attacks that may come.

These measures are essential. The only way to defeat terrorism as a threat to our way of life is to stop it, eliminate it, and destroy it where it grows.

Many will be involved in this effort, from FBI agents, to intelligence operatives, to the reservists we have called to active duty. All deserve our thanks, and all have our prayers.

And tonight, a few miles from the damaged Pentagon, I have a message for our military: Be ready. I have called the armed forces to alert, and there is a reason. The hour is coming when America will act, and you will make us proud. This is not, however, just America's fight. And what is at stake is not just America's freedom.

This is the world's fight. This is civilization's fight. This is the fight of all who believe in progress and pluralism, tolerance and freedom.

We ask every nation to join us.

We will ask and we will need the help of police forces, intelligence services, and banking systems around the world. The United States is grateful that many nations and many international organizations have already responded with sympathy and with support—nations from Latin America to Asia to Africa to Europe to the Islamic world.

Perhaps the NATO charter reflects best the attitude of the world: An attack on one is an attack on all. The civilized world is rallying to America's side.

They understand that if this terror goes unpunished, their own cities, their own citizens may be next. Terror unanswered can not only bring down buildings, it can threaten the stability of legitimate governments.

And you know what? We're not going to allow it.

Americans are asking, "What is expected of us?"

I ask you to live your lives and hug your children.

I know many citizens have fears tonight, and I ask you to be calm and resolute, even in the face of a continuing threat.

I ask you to uphold the values of America and remember why so many have come here.

We're in a fight for our principles, and our first responsibility is to live by them. No one should be singled out for unfair treatment or unkind words because of their ethnic background or religious faith. . . .

I ask [for] your continued participation and confidence in the American economy. Terrorists attacked a symbol of American prosperity; they did not touch its source. America is successful because of the hard work and creativity and enterprise of our people. These were the true strengths of our economy before September 11th, and they are our strengths today.

And finally, please continue praying for the victims of terror and their families, for those in uniform and for our great country. Prayer has comforted us in sorrow and will help strengthen us for the journey ahead. . . .

Tonight we face new and sudden national challenges.

We will come together to improve air safety, to dramatically expand the number of air marshals on domestic flights and take new measures to prevent hijacking.

We will come together to promote stability and keep our airlines flying with direct assistance during this emergency.

We will come together to give law enforcement the additional tools it needs to track down terror here at home.

We will come together to strengthen our intelligence capabilities to know the plans of terrorists before they act and to find them before they strike.

We will come together to take active steps that strengthen America's economy and put our people back to work. . . .

After all that has just passed, all the lives taken and all the possibilities and hopes that died with them, it is natural to wonder if America's future is one of fear. Some speak of an age of terror. I know there are struggles ahead and dangers to face. But this country will define our times, not be defined by them. As long as the United States of America is determined and strong, this will not be an age of terror. This will be an age of liberty here and across the world.

Great harm has been done to us. We have suffered great loss. And in our grief and anger we have found our mission and our moment. Freedom and fear are at war. The advance of human freedom, the great achievement of our time and the great hope of every time, now depends on us.

Our nation, this generation, will lift the dark threat of violence from our people and our future. We will rally the world to this cause by our efforts, by our courage. We will not tire, we will not falter, and we will not fail. It is my hope that in the months and years ahead life will return almost to normal. We'll go back to our lives and routines, and that is good. Even grief recedes with time and grace.

But our resolve must not pass. Each of us will remember what happened that day and to whom it happened. We will remember the moment the news came, where we were and what we were doing. Some will remember an image of a fire or story or rescue. Some will carry memories of a face and a voice gone forever.

And I will carry this: It is the police shield of a man named George Howard who died at the World Trade Center trying to save others. It was given to me by his mom, Arlene, as a proud memorial to her son. It is my reminder of lives that ended and a task that does not end.

I will not forget the wound to our country and those who inflicted it. I will not yield, I will not rest, I will not relent in waging this struggle for freedom and security for the American people.

The course of this conflict is not known, yet its outcome is certain. Freedom and fear, justice and cruelty, have always been at war, and we know that God is not neutral between them.

Fellow citizens, we'll meet violence with patient justice, assured of the rightness of our cause and confident of the victories to come. In all that lies before us, may God grant us wisdom, and may he watch over the United States of America.

# Address to the Nation (October 7, 2001)

PRESIDENT GEORGE W. BUSH

On my orders, the United States military has begun strikes against al-Qa'ida terrorist training camps and military installations of the Taliban regime in Afghanistan. These carefully targeted actions are designed to disrupt the use of Afghanistan as a terrorist base of operations, and to attack the military capability of the Taliban regime.

We are joined in this operation by our staunch friend, Great Britain. Other close friends, including Canada, Australia, Germany, and France, have pledged forces as the operation unfolds. More than forty countries in the Middle East, Africa, Europe, and across Asia have granted air transit or landing rights. Many more have shared intelligence. We are supported by the collective will of the world.

More than two weeks ago, I gave Taliban leaders a series of clear and specific demands: Close terrorist training camps; hand over leaders of the al-Qa'ida network; and return all foreign nationals, including American citizens, unjustly detained in your country. None of these demands were met. And now the Taliban will pay a price. By destroying camps and disrupting communications, we will make it more difficult for the terror network to train new recruits and coordinate their evil plans.

Initially, the terrorists may burrow deeper into caves and other entrenched hiding places. Our military action is also designed to clear the way for sustained, comprehensive, and relentless operations to drive them out and bring them to justice.

At the same time, the oppressed people of Afghanistan will know the generosity of America and our allies. As we strike military targets, we'll also drop food, medicine, and supplies to the starving and suffering men and women and children of Afghanistan.

The United States of America is a friend to the Afghan people, and we are the friends of almost a billion worldwide who practice the Islamic faith. The United States of America is an enemy of those who aid terrorists and of the barbaric criminals who profane a great religion by committing murder in its name.

This military action is a part of our campaign against terrorism, another front in a war that has already been joined through diplomacy, intelligence, the freezing of financial assets, and the arrests of known terrorists by law enforcement agents in thirty-eight countries. Given the nature and reach of our enemies, we will win this conflict by the patient accumulation of successes, by meeting a series of challenges with determination and will and purpose.

Today we focus on Afghanistan, but the battle is broader. Every nation has a choice to make. In this conflict, there is no neutral ground. If any government sponsors the outlaws and killers of innocents, they have become outlaws and murderers themselves. And they will take that lonely path at their own peril.

I'm speaking to you today from the Treaty Room of the White House, a place where American presidents have worked for peace. We're a peaceful nation. Yet, as we have learned, so suddenly and so tragically, there can be no peace in a world of sudden terror. In the face of today's new threat, the only way to pursue peace is to pursue those who threaten it.

We did not ask for this mission, but we will fulfill it. The name of today's military operation is Enduring Freedom. We defend not only our precious freedoms, but also the freedom of people everywhere to live and raise their children free from fear.

I know many Americans feel fear today. And our government is taking strong precautions. All law enforcement and intelligence agencies are working aggressively around America, around the world, and around the clock. At my request, many governors have activated the National Guard to strengthen airport security. We have called up reserves to reinforce our military capability and strengthen the protection of our homeland.

In the months ahead, our patience will be one of our strengths—patience with the long waits that will result from tighter security; patience and understanding that it will take time to achieve our goals; patience in all the sacrifices that may come.

Today, those sacrifices are being made by members of our armed forces who now defend us so far from home, and by their proud and worried families. A commander-in-chief sends America's sons and daughters into a battle in a foreign land only after the greatest care and a lot of prayer. We ask a lot of those who wear our uniform. We ask them to leave their loved ones, to travel great distances, to risk injury, even to be prepared to make the ultimate sacrifice of their lives. They are dedicated, they are honorable; they represent the best of our country. And we are grateful. . . .

The battle is now joined on many fronts. We will not waver; we will not tire; we will not falter; and we will not fail. Peace and freedom will prevail.

## Address to the UN General Assembly (November 10, 2001)

PRESIDENT GEORGE W. BUSH

We meet in a hall devoted to peace, in a city scarred by violence, in a nation awakened to danger, in a world uniting for a long struggle.

Every civilized nation here today is resolved to keep the most basic commitment of civilization. We will defend ourselves and our future against terror and lawless violence.

The United Nations was founded in this cause.

In the Second World War, we learned there is no isolation from evil. We affirmed that some crimes are so terrible they offend humanity itself, and we resolved that the aggressions and ambitions of the wicked must be opposed early, decisively, and collectively before they threaten us all. That evil has returned, and that cause is renewed.

A few miles from here, many thousands still lie in a tomb of rubble. Tomorrow the secretary general, the president of the general assembly, and I will visit that site, where the names of every nation and region that lost citizens will be read aloud.

If we were to read the names of every person who died, it would take more than three hours.

Those names include a citizen of Gambia, whose wife spent their fourth wedding anniversary, September 12, searching in vain for her husband.

Those names include a man who supported his wife in Mexico, sending home money every week.

Those names include a young Pakistani who prayed toward Mecca five times a day and died that day trying to save others.

The suffering of September 11 was inflicted on people of many faiths and many nations. All of the victims, including Muslims, were killed with equal indifference and equal satisfaction by the terrorist leaders.

The terrorists are violating the tenets of every religion, including the one they invoke. Last week, the sheik of al-Azhar University, the world's oldest Islamic institution of higher learning, declared that terrorism is a disease and that Islam prohibits killing innocent civilians.

The terrorists call their cause holy, yet they fund it with drug dealing. They encourage murder and suicide in the name of a great faith that forbids both. They dare to ask God's blessing as they set out to kill innocent men, women, and children. But the God of Isaac and Ishmael would never answer such a prayer.

And a murderer is not a martyr, he is just a murderer. Time is passing. Yet, for the United States of America, there will be no forgetting September 11. We will remember every rescuer who died in honor. We will remember every family that lives in grief. We will remember the fire and ash, the last phone calls, the funerals of the children.

And the people of my country will remember those who have plotted against us. We are learning their names. We are coming to know their faces. There is no corner of the earth distant or dark enough to protect them. However long it takes, their hour of justice will come.

Every nation has a stake in this cause. As we meet, the terrorists are planning more murder, perhaps in my country or perhaps in yours. They kill because they aspire to dominate. They seek to overthrow governments and destabilize entire regions.

Last week, anticipating this meeting of the general assembly, they denounced the United Nations.

They called our secretary general a criminal and condemned all Arab nations here as traitors to Islam.

Few countries meet their exacting standards of brutality and oppression. Every other country is a potential target, and all the world faces the most horrifying prospect of all: These same terrorists are searching for weapons of mass destruction, the tools to turn their hatred into holocaust.

They can be expected to use chemical, biological and nuclear weapons the moment they are capable of doing so. No hint of conscience would prevent it. This threat cannot be ignored. This threat cannot be appeased. Civilization itself, the civilization we share, is threatened.

History will record our response and judge or justify every nation in this hall. The civilized world is now responding. We act to defend ourselves and deliver our children from a future of fear. We choose the dignity of life over a culture of death. We choose lawful change and civil disagreement over coercion, subversion and chaos. These commitments—hope and order, law and life— unite people across cultures and continents. Upon these commitments depend all peace and progress. For these commitments we are determined to fight.

The United Nations has risen to this responsibility. On September 12, these buildings opened for emergency meetings of the general assembly and the security council. Before the sun had set, these attacks on the world stood condemned by the world.

And I want to thank you for this strong and principled stand.

I also thank the Arab and Islamic countries that have condemned terrorist murder. Many of you have seen the destruction of terror in your own lands. The terrorists are increasingly isolated by their own hatred and extremism.

They cannot hide behind Islam. The authors of mass murder and their allies have no place in any culture and no home in any faith.

The conspiracies of terror are being answered by an expanding global coalition. Not every nation will be a part of every action against the enemy, but every nation in our coalition has duties.

These duties can be demanding, as we in America are learning. We have already made adjustments in our laws and in our daily lives. We're taking new measures to investigate terror and to protect against threats. The leaders of all nations must now carefully consider their responsibilities and their future.

Terrorist groups like al-Qa'ida depend upon the aid or indifference of governments. They need the support of a financial infrastructure and safe havens to train and plan and hide.

Some nations want to play their part in the fight against terror but tell us they lack the means to enforce their laws and control their borders. We stand ready to help. Some governments still turn a blind eye to the terrorists, hoping the threat will pass them by. They are mistaken.

And some governments, while pledging to uphold the principles of the

United Nations, have cast their lot with the terrorists. They support them and harbor them, and they will find that their welcomed guests are parasites that will weaken them and eventually consume them.

For every regime that sponsors terror, there is a price to be paid, and it will be paid. The allies of terror are equally guilty of murder and equally accountable to justice. The Taliban are now learning this lesson. That regime and the terrorists who support it are now virtually indistinguishable.

Together, they promote terror abroad and impose a reign of terror on the Afghan people. Women are executed in Kabul's soccer stadium. They can be beaten for wearing socks that are too thin. Men are jailed for missing prayer meetings.

The United States, supported by many nations, is bringing justice to the terrorists in Afghanistan. We're making progress against military targets, and that is our objective. Unlike the enemy, we seek to minimize, not maximize the loss of innocent life.

I'm proud of the honorable conduct of the American military.

And my country grieves for all the suffering the Taliban have brought upon Afghanistan, including the terrible burden of war.

The Afghan people do not deserve their present rulers. Years of Taliban misrule have brought nothing but misery and starvation. Even before this current crisis, 4 million Afghans depended on food from the United States and other nations, and millions of Afghans were refugees from Taliban oppression.

I make this promise to all the victims of that regime: The Taliban's days of harboring terrorists and dealing in heroin and brutalizing women are drawing to a close. And when that regime is gone, the people of Afghanistan will say with the rest of the world, "Good riddance."

I can promise, too, that America will join the world in helping the people of Afghanistan rebuild their country. Many nations, including mine, are sending food and medicine to help Afghans through the winter.

America has airdropped over 1.3 million packages of rations into Afghanistan. Just this week, we airlifted 20,000 blankets and over 200 tons of provisions into the region.

We continue to provide humanitarian aid, even while the Taliban tried to steal the food we sent.

More help eventually will be needed. The United States will work closely with the United Nations and development banks to reconstruct Afghanistan after hostilities there have ceased and the Taliban are no longer in control. And the United States will work with the United Nations to support a post-Taliban government that represents all of the Afghan people.

In this war of terror, each of us must answer for what we have done or what we have left undone.

After tragedy, there is a time for sympathy and condolence. And my country has been very grateful for both. The memorials and vigils around the world will not be forgotten, but the time for sympathy has now passed. The time for action has now arrived.

The most basic obligations in this new conflict have already been defined by the United Nations. On September 28, the security council adopted Resolution 1373. Its requirements are clear. Every United Nations member has a responsibility to crack down on terrorist financing. We must pass all necessary laws in our own countries to allow the confiscation of terrorist assets.

We must apply those laws to every financial institution in every nation. We have a responsibility to share intelligence and coordinate the efforts of law enforcement. If you know something, tell us. If we know something, we'll tell you. And when we find the terrorists, we must work together to bring them to justice.

We have a responsibility to deny any sanctuary, safe haven, or transit to terrorists. Every known terrorist camp must be shut down, its operators apprehended, and evidence of their arrest presented to the United Nations. We have a responsibility to deny weapons to terrorists and to actively prevent private citizens from providing them.

These obligations are urgent, and they are binding on every nation with a place in this chamber. Many governments are taking these obligations seriously, and my country appreciates it.

Yet, even beyond Resolution 1373, more is required and more is expected of our coalition against terror.

We're asking for a comprehensive commitment to this fight.

We must unite in opposing all terrorists, not just some of them.

In this world, there are good causes and bad causes, and we may disagree on where that line is drawn. Yet, there is no such thing as a good terrorist. No national aspiration, no remembered wrong can ever justify the deliberate murder of the innocent. Any government that rejects this principle, trying to pick and choose its terrorist friends, will know the consequences.

We must speak the truth about terror. Let us never tolerate outrageous conspiracy theories concerning the attacks of September 11, malicious lies that attempt to shift the blame away from the terrorists themselves, away from the guilty. To inflame ethnic hatred is to advance the cause of terror.

The war against terror must not serve as an excuse to persecute ethnic and religious minorities in any country. Innocent people must be allowed to live their own lives, by their own customs, under their own religion.

And every nation must have avenues for the peaceful expression of opinion and dissent. When these avenues are closed, the temptation to speak through violence grows.

We must press on with our agenda for peace and prosperity in every land.

My country has pledged to encouraging development and expanding trade. My country had pledged to investing in education and combating AIDS and other infectious diseases around the world.

Following September 11, these pledges are even more important. In our struggle against hateful groups that exploit poverty and despair, we must offer an alternative of opportunity and hope.

The American government also stands by its commitment to a just peace in the Middle East. We are working toward the day when two states—Israel and Palestine—live peacefully together within secure and recognized borders as called for by the security council resolutions. We will do all in our power to bring both parties back into negotiations. But peace will only come when all have sworn off forever incitement, violence, and terror.

And finally, this struggle is a defining moment for the United Nations itself. And the world needs its principled leadership. It undermines the credibility of this great institution, for example, when the Commission on Human Rights offers seats to the world's most persistent violators of human rights. The United Nations depends above all on its moral authority, and that authority must be preserved.

The steps I've described will not be easy. For all nations, they will require effort. For some nations, they will require great courage. Yet, the cost of inaction is far greater. The only alternative to victory is a nightmare world, where every city is a potential killing field.

As I've told the American people, freedom and fear are at war. We face enemies that hate not our policies but our existence, the tolerance of openness and creative culture that defines us. But the outcome of this conflict is certain. There is a current in history, and it runs toward freedom.

Our enemies resent it and dismiss it, but the dreams of mankind are defined by liberty, the natural right to create and build and worship and live in dignity. When men and women are released from oppression and isolation, they find fulfillment and hope, and they leave poverty by the millions.

These aspirations are lifting up the peoples of Europe, Asia, Africa, and the Americas, and they can lift up all of the Islamic world. We stand for the permanent hopes of humanity, and those hopes will not be denied.

We are confident, too, that history has an author who fills time and eternity with his purpose. We know that evil is real, but good will prevail against it. This is the teaching of many faiths.

And in that assurance, we gain strength for a long journey. It is our task, the task of this generation, to provide the response to aggression and terror. We have no other choice, because there is no other peace.

We did not ask for this mission, yet there is honor in history's call. We have a chance to write the story of our times, a story of courage defeating cruelty and light overcoming darkness. This calling is worthy of any life and worthy of every nation.

So let us go forward, confident, determined and unafraid.

# Speech to the Labor Party Conference (October 1, 2001)

BRITISH PRIME MINISTER TONY BLAIR

In retrospect the millennium marked only a moment in time. It was the events of September 11 that marked a turning point in history, where we confront the dangers of the future and assess the choices facing humankind.

It was a tragedy. An act of evil. From this nation go our deepest sympathy and prayers for the victims and our profound solidarity with the American people.

We were with you at the first. We will stay with you to the last. Just two weeks ago, in New York, after the church service I met some of the families of the British victims. . . . And then a middle-aged mother looks you in the eyes and tells you her only son has died, and asks you: Why? . . .

There is no answer. There is no justification for their pain. Their son did nothing wrong. The woman, seven months pregnant, whose child will never know its father, did nothing wrong. They don't want revenge. They want something better in memory of their loved ones.

I believe their memorial can and should be greater than simply the punishment of the guilty. It is that out of the shadow of this evil should emerge lasting good: destruction of the machinery of terrorism wherever it is found; hope amongst all nations of a new beginning where we seek to resolve differences in a calm and ordered way; greater understanding between nations and between faiths; and above all, justice and prosperity for the poor and dispossessed, so that people everywhere can see the chance of a better future through the hard work and creative power of the free citizen, not the violence and savagery of the fanatic.

I know that here in Britain people are anxious, even a little frightened. I understand that. People know we must act, but they worry what might follow. They worry about the economy and talk of recession. And, of course, there are dangers; it is a new situation. But the fundamentals of the U.S., British, and European economies are strong. Every reasonable measure of internal security is being undertaken.

Our way of life is a great deal stronger and will last a great deal longer than the actions of fanatics, small in number and now facing a unified world against them. People should have confidence.

This is a battle with only one outcome: our victory, not theirs.

What happened on September 11 was without parallel in the bloody history of terrorism. Within a few hours, up to 7,000 [*sic*] people were annihilated, the commercial center of New York was reduced to rubble, and in Washington and Pennsylvania further death and horror on an unimaginable scale. Let no one say this was a blow for Islam when the blood of innocent Muslims was shed along with those of the Christian, Jewish, and other faiths around the world.

We know those responsible. In Afghanistan are scores of training camps for the export of terror. Chief amongst the sponsors and organizers is Usama bin Ladin. He is supported, shielded, and given succor by the Taliban regime.

Two days before the September 11 attacks, Masood, the leader of the opposition Northern Alliance, was assassinated by two suicide bombers. Both were linked to bin Ladin. Some may call that coincidence. I call it payment—payment in the currency these people deal in: blood.

Be in no doubt: bin Ladin and his people organized this atrocity. The Taliban aid and abet him. He will not desist from further acts of terror. They will not stop helping him.

Whatever the dangers of the action we take, the dangers of inaction are far, far greater. Look for a moment at the Taliban regime. It is undemocratic. That goes without saying.

There is no sport allowed, or television or photography. No art or culture is permitted. All other faiths, all other interpretations of Islam are ruthlessly suppressed. Those who practice their faith are imprisoned. Women are treated in a way almost too revolting to be credible. First driven out of university, girls [are] not allowed to go to school, [have] no legal rights, [are] unable to go out of doors without a man. Those that disobey are stoned.

There is now no contact permitted with Western agencies, even those delivering food. The people live in abject poverty. It is a regime founded on fear and funded on the drug trade. The biggest drug hoard in the world is in Afghanistan, controlled by the Taliban. Ninety percent of the heroin on British streets originates in Afghanistan.

The arms the Taliban are buying today are paid for with the lives of young British people buying their drugs on British streets. That is another part of their regime that we should seek to destroy.

So what do we do?

"Don't overreact," some say. We aren't. We haven't lashed out. No missiles on the first night just for effect. "Don't kill innocent people." We are not the ones who waged war on the innocent. We seek the guilty.

Look for a diplomatic solution. There is no diplomacy with bin Ladin or the Taliban regime. State an ultimatum and get their response. We stated the ultimatum; they haven't responded.

Understand the causes of terror. Yes, we should try, but let there be no moral ambiguity about this: nothing could ever justify the events of September 11, and it is to turn justice on its head to pretend it could.

The action we take will be proportionate; targeted; we will do all we humanly can to avoid civilian casualties. But understand what we are dealing with. Listen to the calls of those passengers on the planes. Think of the children on them, told they were going to die.

Think of the cruelty beyond our comprehension as amongst the screams and the anguish of the innocent, those hijackers drove at full throttle planes laden with fuel into buildings where tens of thousands worked.

They have no moral inhibition on the slaughter of the innocent. If they could have murdered not 7,000 but 70,000, does anyone doubt they would have done so and rejoiced in it?

There is no compromise possible with such people, no meeting of minds, no point of understanding with such terror. Just a choice: defeat it or be defeated by it. And defeat it we must. Any action taken will be against the terrorist network of bin Ladin.

As for the Taliban, they can surrender the terrorists or face the consequences, and again, in any action the aim will be to eliminate their military hardware, cut off their finances, disrupt their supplies, [and] target their troops, not civilians. We will put a trap around the regime.

I say to the Taliban: Surrender the terrorists; or surrender power. It's your choice. We will take action at every level, national and international, in the United Nations, in G8 [Group of Industrialized Nations], in the EU [European Union], in NATO, in every regional grouping in the world, to strike at international terrorism wherever it exists.

For the first time, the UN Security Council has imposed mandatory obligations on all UN members to cut off terrorist financing and end safe havens for terrorists. Those that finance terror, those who launder their money, those that cover their tracks are every bit as guilty as the fanatic who commits the final act.

Here in this country and in other nations round the world, laws will be changed, not to deny basic liberties but to prevent their abuse and protect the most basic liberty of all: freedom from terror. New extradition laws will be introduced; new rules to ensure asylum is not a front for terrorist entry. This country is proud of its tradition in giving asylum to those fleeing tyranny. We will always do so. But we have a duty to protect the system from abuse. It must be overhauled radically so that from now on, those who abide by the rules get help and those that don't can no longer play the system to gain unfair advantage over others.

Round the world, September 11 is bringing governments and people to reflect, consider, and change. And in this process, amidst all the talk of war and action, there is another dimension appearing. There is a coming together. The power of community is asserting itself. We are realizing how fragile are our frontiers in the face of the world's new challenges.

Today conflicts rarely stay within national boundaries. Today a tremor in one financial market is repeated in the markets of the world. Today confidence is global; either its presence or its absence.

Today the threat is chaos; because for people with work to do, family life to balance, mortgages to pay, careers to further, pensions to provide, the yearning is for order and stability, and if it doesn't exist elsewhere, it is unlikely to exist here. I have long believed this interdependence defines the new world we live in.

People say: we are only acting because it's the United States that was attacked. Double standards, they say. But when [former Yugoslavian President Slobodan] Milosevic embarked on the ethnic cleansing of Muslims in Kosovo, we acted.

The skeptics said it was pointless, we'd make matters worse, we'd make Milosevic stronger; and look what happened: we won, the refugees went home, the policies of ethnic cleansing were reversed, and one of the great dictators of the last century will see justice in this century.

And I tell you if Rwanda happened again today as it did in 1993, when a million people were slaughtered in cold blood, we would have a moral duty to act there also. We were there in Sierra Leone when a murderous group of gangsters threatened its democratically elected government and people. And we as a country should, and I as prime minister do, give thanks for the brilliance, dedication, and sheer professionalism of the British armed forces.

We know this also. The values we believe in should shine through what we do in Afghanistan.

To the Afghan people we make this commitment: The conflict will not be the end. We will not walk away, as the outside world has done so many times before. If the Taliban regime changes, we will work with you to make sure its successor is one that is broad based, that unites all ethnic groups, and that offers some way out of the miserable poverty that is your present existence.

And, more than ever now, with every bit as much thought and planning, we will assemble a humanitarian coalition alongside the military coalition so that inside and outside Afghanistan, the refugees, 4.5 million on the move even before September 11, are given shelter, food, and help during the winter months. The world community must show as much its capacity for compassion as for force.

The critics will say: But how can the world be a community? Nations act in their own self-interest. Of course they do. But what is the lesson of the financial markets, climate change, international terrorism, nuclear proliferation, or world trade? It is that our self-interest and our mutual interests are today inextricably woven together. . . .

When we act to bring to account those that committed the atrocity of September 11, we do so not out of bloodlust. We do so because it is just. We do not act against Islam. The true followers of Islam are our brothers and sisters in this struggle. Bin Ladin is no more obedient to the proper teaching of the Koran than those Crusaders of the twelfth century who pillaged and murdered represented the teaching of the Gospel.

It is time the West confronted its ignorance of Islam. Jews, Muslims, and Christians are all children of Abraham.

This is the moment to bring the faiths closer together in understanding of our common values and heritage, a source of unity and strength.

It is time also for parts of Islam to confront prejudice against America and not only Islam but parts of Western societies too. America has its faults as a society, as we have ours. But I think of the union of America, born out of the defeat of slavery. I think of its constitution, with its inalienable rights granted to every citizen still a model for the world.

I think of a black man, born in poverty, who became chief of their armed forces and is now secretary of state—Colin Powell—and I wonder frankly whether such a thing could have happened here.

I think of the Statue of Liberty and how many refugees, migrants, and . . . impoverished passed its light and felt that if not for them, for their children, a new world could indeed be theirs.

I think of a country where people who do well don't have questions asked about their accent, their class, their beginnings, but have admiration for what they have done and the success they've achieved.

I think of those New Yorkers I met, still in shock, but resolute; the fire-fighters and police, mourning their comrades but still head held high.

I think of all this and I reflect: Yes, America has its faults, but it is a free country, a democracy, it is our ally, and some of the reaction to September 11 betrays a hatred of America that shames those that feel it. So I believe this is a fight for freedom. And I want to make it a fight for justice too.

Justice not only to punish the guilty. But justice to bring those same values of democracy and freedom to people round the world.

And I mean freedom, not only in the narrow sense of personal liberty, but in the broader sense of each individual having the economic and social freedom to develop their potential to the full. That is what community means, founded on the equal worth of all.

The starving, the wretched, the dispossessed, the ignorant, those living in want and squalor from the deserts of northern Africa to the slums of Gaza, to the mountain ranges of Afghanistan: they too are our cause.

This is a moment to seize. . . .

For those people who lost their lives on September 11 and those that mourn them: now is the time for the strength to build that community. Let that be their memorial.

# Executive Order on Blocking Terrorist Financing (September 24, 2001)

PRESIDENT GEORGE W. BUSH

Section 1. . . . All property and interests in property of the following persons that are in the United States or that hereafter come within the United States, or that hereafter come within the possession or control of United States persons are blocked:

(a) foreign persons listed in the Annex to this order;

(b) foreign persons determined by the Secretary of State, in consultation with the Secretary of the Treasury and the Attorney General, to have committed, or to pose a significant risk of committing, acts of terrorism that threaten the security of U.S. nationals or the national security, foreign policy, or economy of the United States;

(c) persons determined by the Secretary of the Treasury, in consultation with the Secretary of State and the Attorney General, to be owned or controlled by, or to act for or on behalf of those persons listed in the Annex to this order. . . .

   (i) to assist in, sponsor, or provide financial, material, or technological support for, or financial or other services to or in support of, such acts of terrorism or those persons listed in the Annex to this order. . . .

   (ii) to be otherwise associated with those persons listed in the Annex to this order. . . .

Sec. 6. The Secretary of State, the Secretary of the Treasury, and other appropriate agencies shall make all relevant efforts to cooperate and coordinate with other countries, including through technical assistance, as well as bilateral and multilateral agreements and arrangements, to achieve the objectives of this order, including the prevention and suppression of acts of terrorism, the denial of financing and financial services to terrorists and terrorist organizations, and the sharing of intelligence about funding activities in support of terrorism. . . .

Sec. 10. For those persons listed in the Annex to this order or determined to be subject to this order who might have a constitutional presence in the United States, I find that because of the ability to transfer funds or assets instantaneously, prior notice to such persons of measures to be taken pursuant to this order would render these measures ineffectual. I therefore determine that for these measures to be effective in addressing the national emergency declared in this order, there need be no prior notice of a listing or determination made pursuant to this order.

[There follows a list of names of eleven terrorist organizations, including al-Qa'ida/Islamic Army, thirteen individuals, including Usama bin Ladin, two charitable organizations, and a company.]

# Executive Order on Establishing the Office of Homeland Security (October 8, 2001)

PRESIDENT GEORGE W. BUSH

Section 1. . . . I hereby establish within the Executive Office of the President an Office of Homeland Security (the "Office") to be headed by the Assistant to the President for Homeland Security.

Sec. 2. . . . The mission of the Office shall be to develop and coordinate the implementation of a comprehensive national strategy to secure the United States from terrorist threats or attacks. . . .

Sec. 3. . . . The functions of the Office shall be to coordinate the executive branch's efforts to detect, prepare for, prevent, protect against, respond to, and recover from terrorist attacks within the United States.

(a) . . . The Office shall work with executive departments and agencies, State and local governments, and private entities to ensure the adequacy of the national strategy for detecting, preparing for, preventing, protecting against, responding to, and recovering from terrorist threats or attacks within the United States and shall periodically review and coordinate revisions to that strategy as necessary.

(b) ... The Office shall identify priorities and coordinate efforts for collection and analysis of information within the United States regarding threats of terrorism against the United States and activities of terrorists or terrorist groups within the United States. The Office also shall identify, in coordination with the Assistant to the President for National Security Affairs, priorities for collection of intelligence outside the United States regarding threats of terrorism within the United States.

## Executive Order on Detention, Treatment, and Trial of Certain Non-Citizens in the War against Terrorism (November 13, 2001)

PRESIDENT GEORGE W. BUSH

... (e) To protect the United States and its citizens, and for the effective conduct of military operations and prevention of terrorist attacks, it is necessary for individuals subject to this order pursuant to section 2 hereof to be detained, and, when tried, to be tried for violations of the laws of war and other applicable laws by military tribunals.

(f) Given the danger to the safety of the United States and the nature of international terrorism, and to the extent provided by and under this order, I find consistent with section 836 of title 10, United States Code, that it is not practicable to apply in military commissions under this order the principles of law and the rules of evidence generally recognized in the trial of criminal cases in the United States district courts.

(g) Having fully considered the magnitude of the potential deaths, injuries, and property destruction that would result from potential acts of terrorism against the United States, and the probability that such acts will occur, I have determined that an extraordinary emergency exists for national defense purposes, that this emergency constitutes an urgent and compelling government interest, and that issuance of this order is necessary to meet the emergency.

Sec. 2. Definition and Policy.

(a) The term "individual subject to this order" shall mean any individual who is not a United States citizen with respect to whom I determine from time to time in writing that: (1) there is reason to believe that such individual, at the relevant times,

  (i) is or was a member of the organization known as al-Qa'ida;
  (ii) has engaged in, aided or abetted, or conspired to commit, acts of international terrorism, or acts in preparation therefore, that have caused, threaten to cause, or have as their aim to cause, injury to or adverse effects on the United States, its citizens, national security, foreign policy, or economy; or
  (iii) has knowingly harbored one or more individuals described in subparagraphs (i) or (ii) of subsection 2(a)(1) of this order; and

    (2) it is in the interest of the United States that such individual be subject to this order. . . .

Sec. 3. Detention Authority of the Secretary of Defense. Any individual subject to this order shall be—

(a) detained at an appropriate location designated by the Secretary of Defense outside or within the United States;
(b) treated humanely, without any adverse distinction based on race, color, religion, gender, birth, wealth, or any similar criteria;
(c) afforded adequate food, drinking water, shelter, clothing, and medical treatment;
(d) allowed the free exercise of religion consistent with the requirements of such detention; and
(e) detained in accordance with such other conditions as the Secretary of Defense may prescribe.

Sec. 4. Authority of the Secretary of Defense Regarding Trials of Individuals Subject to this Order.

(a) Any individual subject to this order shall, when tried, be tried by military commission for any and all offenses triable by military commission that such individual is alleged to have committed, and may be punished in accordance with the penalties provided under applicable law, including life imprisonment or death.
(b) As a military function and in light of the findings in section 1, including subsection (f) thereof, the Secretary of Defense shall issue such orders and regulations, including orders for the appointment of one or more military commissions, as may be necessary to carry out subsection (a) of this section.

(c) Orders and regulations issued under subsection (b) of this section shall include, but not be limited to, rules for the conduct of the proceedings of military commissions, including pretrial, trial, and post-trial procedures, modes of proof, issuance of process, and qualifications of attorneys, which shall at a minimum provide for—

(1) military commissions to sit at any time and any place, consistent with such guidance regarding time and place as the Secretary of Defense may provide;

(2) a full and fair trial, with the military commission sitting as the triers of both fact and law;

(3) admission of such evidence as would, in the opinion of the presiding officer of the military commission (or instead, if any other member of the commission so requests at the time the presiding officer renders that opinion, the opinion of the commission rendered at that time by a majority of the commission), have probative value to a reasonable person. . . .

(5) conduct of the prosecution by one or more attorneys designated by the Secretary of Defense and conduct of the defense by attorneys for the individual subject to this order;

(6) conviction only upon the concurrence of two-thirds of the members of the commission present at the time of the vote, a majority being present;

(7) sentencing only upon the concurrence of two-thirds of the members of the commission present at the time of the vote, a majority being present; and

(8) submission of the record of the trial, including any conviction or sentence, for review and final decision by me or by the Secretary of Defense if so designated by me for that purpose. . . .

(b) With respect to any individual subject to this order—

(1) military tribunals shall have exclusive jurisdiction with respect to offenses by the individual; and

(2) the individual shall not be privileged to seek any remedy or maintain any proceeding, directly or indirectly, or to have any such remedy or proceeding sought on the individual's behalf, in any court of the United States, or any State thereof, (ii) any court of any foreign nation, or (iii) any international tribunal.

# Analysis of U.S. Counterterrorism Legislation (October 25, 2001)

## CONGRESSIONAL RESEARCH SERVICE*

The Uniting and Strengthening America by Providing Appropriate Tools Required to Intercept and Obstruct Terrorism . . . is part of the Congressional response to September 11. The act consists of ten titles which, among other things:

- Give federal law enforcement and intelligence officers greater authority (at least temporarily) to gather and share evidence particularly with respect to wire and electronic communications;
- Amend federal money laundering laws, particularly those involving overseas financial activities;
- Create new federal crimes, increase the ability of federal authorities to prevent foreign terrorists from entering the U.S., to detain foreign terrorist suspects, to deport foreign terrorists, and to mitigate the adverse immigration consequences for the foreign victims of September 11; and
- Authorize appropriations to enhance the capacity of immigration, law enforcement, and intelligence agencies to more effectively respond to the threats of terrorism.

## Title I. Enhancing Domestic Security against Terrorism

. . . Section 102. . . . It is the sense of Congress that the civil rights and civil liberties of all Americans, including Arab Americans, Muslim Americans, and Americans from South Asia, should be protected; that violence and discrimination against any American should be condemned; and that the patriotism of Americans from every ethnic, racial, and religious background should be acknowledged.

Section 106 . . . grants the President emergency economic powers when faced with extraordinary threats to our national security, foreign policy or economic well-being. . . . He may freeze the assets located in this country of a foreign nation or national responsible for the threat. . . .

---

* "Terrorism: Section by Section Analysis of the USA PATRIOT Act," Congressional Research Service Report for Congress, updated December 10, 2001.

## Title II. Enhanced Surveillance Procedures

Section 201 . . . adds several [new] terrorism offenses [to the list of those allowing surveillance]: [use of] chemical weapons . . . use of weapons of mass destruction . . . violent acts of terrorism transcending national borders . . . financial transactions with countries which support terrorism . . . material support of terrorists . . . and material support of terrorist organizations. . . .

Section 206. . . . International terrorists and foreign intelligence officers are trained to thwart surveillance by changing hotels, cell phones, Internet accounts, etc., just prior to important meetings or communications. . . . [This provision] permits the court to issue a generic order that can be presented to the new carrier, landlord, or custodian directing their assistance to assure that the surveillance may be undertaken as soon as technically feasible. . . .

Section 210. Scope of Subpoenas for Records of Electronic Communications. Terrorists and other criminals often use aliases in registering for Internet and telephone services. . . . Permitting investigators to obtain credit card numbers and other payment information by a subpoena . . . will help law enforcement track a suspect and establish his or her true identity.

Section 212. Emergency Disclosure of Electronic Communications to Protect Life and Limb. . . . This section amends [existing law] to authorize electronic communications service providers to disclose the communications (or records relating to such communications) of their customers or subscribers if the provider reasonably believes that an emergency involving immediate danger of death or serious physical injury to any person requires disclosure of the information without delay. . . .

Section 218. Foreign Intelligence Information. The USA PATRIOT Act contemplates a closer working relationship between criminal and intelligence investigators than has previously been the case. . . .

## Title III. International Money Laundering Abatement and Anti-Terrorist Financing Act of 2001

Section 311. Special Measures for Jurisdictions, Financial Institutions, or International Transactions of Primary Money Laundering Concern . . . authorizes the Secretary of Treasury to impose certain regulatory restrictions . . . upon finding that a jurisdiction outside the United States, a financial institution outside the United States, a class of transactions involving a jurisdiction outside the United States, or a type of account, is "of primary money laundering concern."

Section 316. Anti-Terrorist Forfeiture Protection. . . . The new law amends [previous law] to authorize the President, "when the United States is engaged in armed hostilities or has been attacked by a foreign country or foreign nationals," to "confiscate any property, subject to the jurisdiction of the United States, of any foreign person, foreign organizations, or foreign country that he determines has planned, authorized, aided, or engaged in such hostilities or attacks against the United States."

## Title IV. Protecting the Border

. . . Section 402 authorizes appropriations . . . to triple the number of Border Patrol, Custom Service, and the Immigration and Naturalization Service (INS) personnel in each state along the northern border of the United States. . . .

Section 411. Definitions Relating to Terrorism . . . adds to the terrorism-related grounds upon which an alien may be denied admission into the United States. It then recasts the definition of engaging in terrorist activities to include solicitation on behalf of such organizations, or recruiting on their behalf, or providing them with material support. . . . [It] makes representatives of political, social or similar groups, whose public endorsements of terrorist activities undermines our efforts to reduce or eliminate terrorism, inadmissible as well. . . .

An individual who uses his or her place of prominence to endorse, espouse, or advocate support for terrorist activities or terrorist organizations in a manner which the Secretary of State concludes undermine our efforts to reduce or eliminate terrorism becomes inadmissible under section 411. . . .

Finally, any alien, whom the Secretary of State or the Attorney General conclude has associated with terrorist organization and intends to engage in conduct dangerous to the welfare, safety, security of the United States while in their country, is inadmissible. . . .

Section 412 . . . permits the Attorney General to detain alien terrorist suspect for up to seven days. . . . He must certify that he has reasonable grounds to believe that the suspects either are engaged in conduct which threatens the national security of the United States or are inadmissible or deportable on grounds of terrorism, espionage, sabotage, or sedition. Within seven days, the Attorney General must initiate removal or criminal proceedings or release the alien. If the alien is held, the determination must be reexamined every six months to confirm that the alien's release would threaten national security or endanger some individual or the general public. . . .

Section 416. Foreign Student Monitoring Program . . . authorizes appropriations . . . to implement and expand the program for collection of information relating to nonimmigrant foreign students and other exchange program participants. . . . The section adds air flight schools, language training schools, and vocations schools to the list of institutions whose students are to be included in the reporting requirement. . . .

*Subtitle C. Preservation of Immigration Benefits*
*for Victims of Terrorism*

. . . This subtitle endeavors to modify immigration law to provide humanitarian relief to [aliens who were victims in terrorist attacks] and their family members. . . .

## Title V. Removing Obstacles to Investigating Terrorism

Section 501. . . . The USA PATRIOT Act supplies the Attorney General with the power to pay rewards to combat terrorism in any amount and without an aggregate limitation, but for rewards of $250,000 or more it insists on personal approval of the Attorney General or the President and on notification of the Appropriations and Judiciary Committees. . . .

The Act removes the $5 million cap [on rewards the secretary of state can offer] for information concerning the whereabouts of terrorist leaders and facilitating the dissolution of terrorist organizations. . . .

## Title VI. Providing for Victims of Terrorism, Public Safety Officers, and Their Families

[Provides for those involved in combating terrorism and] for supplemental grants to compensate and assist victims of terrorism or mass violence. . . .

## Title VIII. Strengthening the Criminal Law against Terrorism

Section 801 . . . makes terrorist attacks and other acts of violence against mass transportation system federal crimes. . . .

Section 802 Definition of Domestic Terrorism . . . adjusts the definition of international terrorism . . . [to include] domestic terrorism . . . as those criminal acts of violence . . . that appear to be intended to intimidate or coerce a civilian population, or to influence a governmental policy by intimidation or coercion, or to affect the conduct of a government by assassination or kidnapping. . . .

Section 803 instead establishes a separate offense which punishes harboring terrorists by imprisonment for not more than ten years and/or a fine of not more than $250,000.

# Resolution 1373 (September 28, 2001)

UN SECURITY COUNCIL

. . . Decides that all States shall:

  (a) Prevent and suppress the financing of terrorist acts;

  (b) Criminalize the willful provision or collection, by any means, directly or indirectly, of funds by their nationals or in their territories with the intention that the funds should be used, or in the knowledge that they are to be used, in order to carry out terrorist acts;

  (c) Freeze without delay funds and other financial assets or economic resources of persons who commit, or attempt to commit, terrorist acts or participate in or facilitate the commission of terrorist acts; of entities owned or controlled directly or indirectly by such persons; and of persons and entities acting on behalf of, or at the direction of such persons and entities, including funds derived or generated from property owned or controlled directly or indirectly by such persons and associated persons and entities;

  (d) Prohibit their nationals or any persons and entities within their territories from making any funds, financial assets, or economic resources or financial or other related services available, directly or indirectly, for the benefit of persons who commit or attempt to commit or facilitate or participate in the commission of terrorist acts, of entities owned or controlled, directly or indirectly, by such persons and of persons and entities acting on behalf of or at the direction of such persons;

1. Decides also that all States shall:

  (a) Refrain from providing any form of support, active or passive, to entities or persons involved in terrorist acts, including by suppressing recruitment of members of terrorist groups and eliminating the supply of weapons to terrorists;

  (b) Take the necessary steps to prevent the commission of terrorist acts, including by provision of early warning to other States by exchange of information;

  (c) Deny safe haven to those who finance, plan, support, or commit terrorist acts, or provide safe havens;

  (d) Prevent those who finance, plan, facilitate, or commit terrorist acts from using their respective territories for those purposes against other States or their citizens;

  (e) Ensure that any person who participates in the financing, planning, preparation, or perpetration of terrorist acts or in supporting terrorist acts is brought to justice and ensure that, in addition to any other measures against them, such terrorist acts are established as serious criminal offenses in domestic laws and regulations and that the punishment duly reflects the seriousness of such terrorist acts;

(f) Afford one another the greatest measure of assistance in connection with criminal investigations or criminal proceedings relating to the financing or support of terrorist acts, including assistance in obtaining evidence in their possession necessary for the proceedings;

(g) Prevent the movement of terrorists or terrorist groups by effective border controls and controls on issuance of identity papers and travel documents, and through measures for preventing counterfeiting, forgery, or fraudulent use of identity papers and travel documents;

2. Calls upon all States to:

(a) Find ways of intensifying and accelerating the exchange of operational information, especially regarding actions or movements of terrorist persons or networks; forged or falsified travel documents; traffic in arms, explosives, or sensitive materials; use of communications technologies by terrorist groups; and the threat posed by the possession of weapons of mass destruction by terrorist groups;

(b) Exchange information in accordance with international and domestic law and cooperate on administrative and judicial matters to prevent the commission of terrorist acts;

(c) Cooperate, particularly through bilateral and multilateral arrangements and agreements, to prevent and suppress terrorist attacks and take action against perpetrators of such acts;

(d) Become parties as soon as possible to the relevant international conventions and protocols relating to terrorism, including the International Convention for the Suppression of the Financing of Terrorism of December 9, 1999;

(e) Increase cooperation and fully implement the relevant international conventions and protocols relating to terrorism and Security Council resolutions 1269 (1999) and 1368 (2001);

(f) Take appropriate measures in conformity with the relevant provisions of national and international law, including international standards of human rights, before granting refugee status, for the purpose of ensuring that the asylum-seeker has not planned, facilitated, or participated in the commission of terrorist acts;

(g) Ensure, in conformity with international law, that refugee status is not abused by the perpetrators, organizers, or facilitators of terrorist acts, and that claims of political motivation are not recognized as grounds for refusing requests for the extradition of alleged terrorists;

4. Notes with concern the close connection between international terrorism and transnational organized crime, illicit drugs, money laundering, illegal arms trafficking, and illegal movement of nuclear, chemical, biological, and other potentially deadly materials, and in this regard emphasizes the need to enhance coordination of efforts on national, subregional, regional, and international levels in order to strengthen a global response to this serious challenge and threat to international security. . . .

# APPENDIX: CHRONOLOGY OF MIDDLE EAST–CONNECTED TERRORISM AGAINST AMERICANS

## COMPILED BY JUDITH COLP RUBIN AND CAROLINE TAILLANDIER

Note: (+) indicates that Americans were killed or wounded in the described attack, though Americans as such were not the intended target. Cited are only those attacks in which Americans were killed or kidnapped or in which several were wounded.

## 1969

| | |
|---|---|
| +June 17 | Kallia, Israel: Shirley Louise Anderson of Rochester, New York, was killed in a shelling by the Palestine Liberation Organization (PLO) of an Israeli resort town. |
| +December 27 | Hebron, West Bank: Leon Holtz of Brooklyn, New York, was killed during a PLO shooting attack on a bus in Hebron. |

## 1970

| | |
|---|---|
| +February 21 | En route to Israel: Eight Americans were killed during the bombing of an Israeli-bound Swiss airplane |
| +February 23 | Halhoul, West Bank: Barbara Ertle of Granville, Michigan, was killed during a PLO shooting attack on a busload of pilgrims in Halhoul, a village near Hebron. Two other Americans were wounded in the attack. |
| March 28–29 | Beirut, Lebanon: The Popular Front for the Liberation of Palestine (PFLP) fired seven rockets against American targets in Beirut—the U.S. embassy, the American Insurance Company, Bank of America, and the John F. Kennedy Library. The PFLP said the attacks were |

in retaliation "for plans of the United States embassy in Beirut to foment religious strife and create civil massacres in Lebanon aimed at paralyzing the Palestinian resistance movement."

September 14    En route to Amman, Jordan: The PFLP hijacked a TWA flight from Zurich, Switzerland, and forced it to land in Amman, Jordan. During the hijacking, four American citizens were injured.

## 1972

+May 30    Ben Gurion Airport, Israel: Three members of the Japanese Red Army, acting on the PFLP's behalf, carried out a machine-gun and grenade attack at Israel's main airport, killing twenty-six people and wounding seventy-eight. Many of the casualties were from Puerto Rico.

+September 5    Munich, Germany: During the Olympic Games in Munich, Black September, a front for Fatah, took hostage eleven members of the Israeli Olympic team. Nine athletes were killed, including David Berger, an American Israeli weightlifter from Cleveland, Ohio.

## 1973

March 2    Khartoum, Sudan: Cleo A. Noel Jr., the U.S. ambassador to Sudan, and George C. Moore, also a U.S. diplomat, were held hostage and then killed by terrorists at the U.S. embassy in Khartoum. It seems likely that Fatah was responsible for the attack.

+August 15    Athens, Greece: The PLO's Black September unit attacked an Athens airport, killing two Americans and wounding ten.

## 1974

September 9    Greece: Terrorists from the Palestinian Abu Nidal group bombed a TWA jet in the air near Greece, killing eleven Americans.

## 1975

June 29    Beirut, Lebanon: The PFLP kidnapped the U.S. military attaché to Lebanon, Ernest Morgan, and demanded food, clothing, and building materials for indigent residents living near Beirut harbor. The American diplomat was released after an anonymous benefactor provided food to the neighborhood.

+November 21    Ramat Hamagshimim, Israel: Michael Nadler, an American Israeli from Miami Beach, Florida, was killed when ax-wielding terrorists from the Democrat Front for the Liberation of Palestine (DFLP), a PLO faction, attacked students in the Golan Heights.

## 1976

June 16    Beirut, Lebanon: Frances E. Meloy, the U.S. ambassador to Lebanon, and Robert O. Waring, the U.S. economic counselor, were kidnapped by PFLP members as they crossed a militia checkpoint separating the Christian from the Muslim parts of Beirut. They were later shot to death.

+August 11    Istanbul, Turkey: The PFLP launched an attack on the terminal of Israel's major airline, El Al, at the Istanbul airport. Four civilians, including Harold Rosenthal of Philadelphia, Pennsylvania, were killed and twenty injured.

## 1978

+March 11    Tel Aviv, Israel: Gail Rubin, the niece of U.S Senator Abraham Ribicoff, was shot to death by PLO terrorists on an Israeli beach.

+June 2    Jerusalem, Israel: Richard Fishman, a medical student from Maryland, was among six killed in a PLO bus bombing in Jerusalem. Chava Sprecher, another American citizen from Seattle, Washington, was injured.

## 1979

+May 4    Tiberias, Israel: Haim Mark and his wife, Haya, of New Haven, Connecticut, were injured in a PLO bombing attack in northern Israel.

November 4    Teheran, Iran: After President Carter agreed to admit the Shah Reza Pahlavi of Iran into the United States, Iranian radicals seized the U.S. embassy in Tehran and took sixty-six American diplomats hostage. Thirteen hostages were soon freed, but the remaining fifty-three were held until January 20, 1981. On April 25, 1980, a failed rescue mission resulted in the death of eight U.S. soldiers.

## 1980

+May 2    Hebron, West Bank: Eli Haze'ev, an American Israeli from Alexandria, Virginia, was killed in a PLO attack on Jewish worshipers walking home from a synagogue in Hebron.

## 1982

January 18    Paris, France: Lt. Col. Charles Robert Ray, an assistant military attaché, was shot and killed in Paris. The Lebanese Armed Revolutionary Factor claimed responsibility.

+July 2    Bethlehem, West Bank: David Rosenfeld of Philadelphia was killed in a PLO stabbing attack in Bethlehem.

| | |
|---|---|
| July 19 | Beirut, Lebanon: Hizballah members kidnapped David Dodge, acting president of the American University in Beirut (AUB). After a year in captivity, Dodge was released. |
| +August 19 | Paris, France: Two American citizens, Anne Van Zanten and Grace Cutler, were killed when the PLO bombed a Jewish restaurant in Paris. |

## 1983

| | |
|---|---|
| March 16 | Beirut, Lebanon: Five American Marines were wounded in a hand-grenade attack while on patrol north of Beirut International Airport. The Islamic Jihad and Amal, a Shi'ite militia, claimed responsibility for the attack. |
| April 18 | Beirut, Lebanon: A truck bomb detonated by remote control exploded in front of the U.S. embassy in Beirut, killing 63 employees, including the CIA's Middle East director, and wounding 120. Hizballah, with financial backing from Iran, was responsible for the attack. |
| +July 1 | Hebron, Israel: Aharon Gross, a nineteen-year-old American Israeli from New York, was stabbed to death by PLO terrorists in the Hebron marketplace. |
| +September 23 | En route to Abu Dhai: An American was killed when a bomb exploded on an Omani Air flight from Karachi to Abu Dhabi. |
| September 29 | Beirut, Lebanon: Two American Marines were kidnapped by Amal members. They were released after intervention by a Lebanese army officer. |
| October 23 | Beirut, Lebanon: A truck loaded with a bomb crashed into the lobby of the U.S. Marines' headquarters in Beirut, killing 241 soldiers and wounding 81. The attack was carried out by Hizballah with the help of Syrian intelligence and financed by Iran. |
| +December 3 | Jerusalem, Israel: Serena Sussman, a sixty-year-old tourist from Anderson, South Carolina, was wounded after the PLO bombing of a bus in Jerusalem. She died thirteen days later from her injuries. |
| December 12 | Kuwait City, Kuwait: A truck bomb damaged the U.S. and French embassies in Kuwait and a U.S. housing compound. Islamic Jihad claimed responsibility. |

## 1984

| | |
|---|---|
| January 18 | Beirut, Lebanon: Malcolm Kerr, president of the AUB, was killed by two gunmen outside his office. Hizballah said the assassination was part of the organization's plan to "drive all Americans out from Lebanon." |

| February 11 | Beirut, Lebanon: Frank Regier, chairman of AUB's electrical engineering department, was kidnapped. He was freed on April 15 after a raid by Amal militiamen. |
| March 7 | Beirut, Lebanon: Hizballah members kidnapped Jeremy Levin, the Beirut bureau chief of Cable News Network (CNN). Levin was freed eleven months later. |
| March 8 | Beirut, Lebanon: Three Hizballah members kidnapped Reverend Benjamin T. Weir while he was walking with his wife in Beirut's Manara neighborhood. Weir was released after sixteen months of captivity. |
| March 16 | Beirut, Lebanon: Islamic Jihad kidnapped William Buckley, a CIA officer in Beirut, and took him to Iran. On October 4, terrorists said they killed him. His body was dumped in Beirut in 1991. |
| March 26 | Strasburg, France: Robert Oname Homme, the U.S. council general in Strasburg, France, was shot and wounded by a Lebanese Armed Revolutionary Faction gunman. |
| April 12 | Torrejon, Spain: Hizballah bombed a restaurant near a U.S. Air Force base in Torrejon, Spain, killing eighteen servicemen and wounding eighty-three other people. |
| September 20 | Beirut, Lebanon: A suicide bomb attack on the U.S. embassy annex in Beirut killed twenty-three people, including two Americans, and injured seventy-one, among them the American and British ambassadors. The attack was attributed to the Iranian-backed Hizballah group. |
| December 3 | Beirut, Lebanon: Peter Kilburn, a librarian at the American University in Beirut, was taken hostage and killed sixteen months later. The kidnappers said the killing was in retaliation for United States air attacks on Libya. |
| +December 4 | Tehran, Iran: Islamic Jihad terrorists hijacked a Kuwait Airlines plane en route from Dubai, United Emirates, to Karachi, Pakistan. They demanded the release from Kuwaiti jails of members of al-Dawa, a group of Shi'ite extremists serving sentences for attacks on French and American targets on Kuwaiti territory. The terrorists forced the pilot to fly to Tehran, where they murdered two American passengers Charles Hegna and William Stanford, employees of the Agency for International Development. Although the United States thanked Iran after the plane was successfully retaken by an Iranian special unit, it later charged Iran with aiding the terrorists. |

# 1985

| March 16 | Beirut, Lebanon: Terry Anderson, the chief Middle East correspondent with the Associated Press, was taken hostage by Hizballah and freed after more than six years. |

| May 28 | Beirut, Lebanon: David Jacobsen, director of the AUB hospital, was taken hostage by the pro-Iranian terrorists Islamic Jihad and released after sixteen months. |
|---|---|
| June 9 | Beirut, Lebanon: Thomas B. Sutherland, a dean with the AUB, was kidnapped by Hizballah and released six years later. |
| June 15 | Between Athens and Rome: Two Hizballah members hijacked a TWA flight en route to Rome from Athens and forced the pilot to fly to Beirut. The terrorists, believed to belong to Hizballah, asked for the release of members of al-Dawa members in Kuwait and 700 Shi'ite prisoners held in Israeli and South Lebanese prisons. The 8 crewmembers and 145 passengers were held for seventeen days during which one of the hostages—Robert Stethem, a U.S. navy sailor—was murdered. After being flown twice to Algiers, the aircraft returned to Beirut, and the hostages were released. Later on, four Hizballah members were indicted. One of them, the Hizballah senior officer Imad Mughniyah, was later on the U.S list of twenty-two most-wanted terrorists. |
| July 22 | Copenhagen, Denmark: The offices of Northwest Orient Airlines in Copenhagen and a nearby synagogue-nursing home was bombed, killing one and injuring twenty-six. Islamic Jihad in Beirut claimed responsibility. |
| +October 7 | Between Alexandria, Egypt, and Haifa, Israel: A four-member Palestine Liberation Front squad took over the Italian cruise ship *Achille Lauro* as it was sailing from Alexandria, Egypt, to Israel. The squad murdered a disabled U.S. citizen, Leon Klinghoffer. The rest of the passengers were held hostage for two days and later released after the terrorists turned themselves in to Egyptian authorities in return for safe passage. But U.S. navy fighters intercepted the Egyptian aircraft flying the terrorists to Tunis and forced it to land at the NATO airbase in Italy, where the terrorists were arrested. Two of the terrorists were tried in Italy and sentenced to prison. However, the Italian authorities let the two others escape on diplomatic passports. Abu Abbas, who masterminded the hijacking, was later convicted and sentenced to life imprisonment in absentia. |
| +November 23 | Malta: An Egypt Air Jet en route from Athens to Cairo was hijacked and landed in Malta. Scarlett Rogenkamp, a U.S. Air Force civilian employee from Oceanside, California, was killed, along with an Israeli. The hijacker was a member of the Abu Nidal Organization. |
| +December 27 | Rome, Italy: Four terrorists from Abu Nidal's organization attacked El Al offices at the Leonardo di Vinci Airport in Rome. Eighteen people, including five Americans, were killed and seventy-four wounded, among them two Americans. The terrorists had come from Damascus and were supported by the Syrian regime. |

## 1986

| | |
|---|---|
| March 30 | Athens, Greece: A bomb exploded on a TWA flight from Rome as it approached the Athens airport. The attack killed four U.S. citizens who were sucked through a hole made by the blast, although the plane landed safely. The bombing was attributed to the Fatah Special Operations Group's intelligence and security apparatus, headed by Abdullah Abd al-Hamid Labib, alias Colonel Hawari. |
| April 5 | West Berlin, Germany: An explosion at the La Belle, a Berlin nightclub frequented by American soldiers, killed three people—2 U.S. soldiers and a Turkish woman—and wounded 191, including 41 U.S. soldiers. Given evidence of Libyan involvement, the U.S. Air Force later made a retaliatory attack against Libyan targets. Libya refused to hand over five suspects to Germany. Others, however, were tried, including Yassir Shraidi and Musbah Eter, arrested in Rome in August 1997 and extradited; and also Ali Chanaa; his wife, Verena Chanaa; and her sister, Andrea Haeusler. Shraidi, who was accused of masterminding the attack, was sentenced to fourteen years in prison. The Libyan diplomat Musbah Eter and Ali Chanaa were both sentenced to twelve years in prison. Verena Chanaa was sentenced to 14 years in prison. Andrea Haeusler was acquitted. |
| April 15 | Khartoum, Sudan: William Calkins, an American employee with the U.S. embassy in Khartoum, Sudan, was shot and wounded. This was believed to be in retaliation for U.S. air raids in Libya earlier in the day. |
| April 17 | Beirut, Lebanon: Peter Kilburn, a librarian at the American University of Beirut, was among three Westerners taken hostage. He was never seen again. |
| April 17 | Tunis, Tunisia: A firebomb was thrown at the U.S. Marine Guard compound at the U.S. embassy in Tunisia. |
| September 5 | Karachi, Pakistan: Abu Nidal members hijacked a Pan Am flight leaving Karachi, Pakistan, bound for Frankfurt, Germany, and New York with 379 passengers, including 89 Americans. The terrorists forced the plane to land in Larnaca, Cyprus, where they demanded the release of 2 Palestinians and a Briton jailed for the murder of 3 Israelis there in 1985. The terrorists killed 22 of the passengers, including 2 American citizens, and wounded many others. They were caught and sentenced by a Washington, D.C., grand jury in 1991. |
| September 9 | Beirut, Lebanon: Frank Reed, headmaster of the Lebanese International School in Beirut, was kidnapped by the Islamic Jihad organization. He was released forty-four months later. |

| | |
|---|---|
| September 12 | Beirut, Lebanon: Hizballah kidnapped Joseph Cicippio, the acting comptroller at AUB. He was released five years later in December 1991. |
| +October 15 | Jerusalem, Israel: Gali Klein, an American citizen, was killed in a grenade attack by Fatah at the Western Wall in Jerusalem. |
| October 21 | Beirut, Lebanon: Hizballah kidnapped Edward A. Tracy, an American citizen in Beirut. He was released five years later in August 1991. |

## 1987

| | |
|---|---|
| January 24 | Beirut, Lebanon: Gunmen seized three American professors at the U.S.-sponsored Beirut University College. They were held by different organizations and released separately after a number of years. |
| May 26 | Cairo, Egypt: Two U.S. embassy officials were injured in a Cairo suburb. An anonymous caller said a group called "Egypt's Revolution" was responsible. |
| June 17 | Beirut, Lebanon: Charles Glass, an American television journalist, was kidnapped. He escaped from his captors that August. |

## 1988

| | |
|---|---|
| February 17 | Ras-Al-Ein Tyre, Lebanon: Colonel William Higgins, the American chief of the United Nations Truce Supervisory Organization, was abducted by Hizballah while driving from Tyre to Nakura. The hostages demanded the withdrawal of Israeli forces from Lebanon and the release of all Palestinian and Lebanese held prisoners in Israel. The U.S. government refused to answer the request. Hizballah later claimed it killed Higgins. |
| December 21 | Lockerbie, Scotland: Pan Am Flight 103, departing from Frankfurt for New York, was blown up in midair, killing all 259 passengers and another 11 people on the ground in Scotland. Two Libyan agents were found responsible for planting a sophisticated suitcase bomb on board the plane. On November 14, 1991, arrest warrants were issued for al-Amin Khalifa Fahima and Abdel Baset Ali Mohamed al-Megrahi. After Libya refused to extradite the suspects to stand trial, the United Nations leveled sanctions against the country in April 1992, including the freezing of Libyan assets abroad. In 1999 Libya's leader, Muammar Gadhafi, agreed to hand over the two suspects, but only if their trial was held in a neutral country and presided over by a Scottish judge. Al-Megrahi and Fahima were finally extradited and tried in the Netherlands. Megrahi was found guilty and jailed for life, while Fahima was acquitted due to a "lack of evidence" of his involvement. After the extradition, UN sanctions against Libya were automatically lifted. |

## 1989

January 27    Istanbul, Turkey: Two simultaneous bombings were carried out against U.S. business targets—the Turkish-American Businessmen Association and the Economic Development Foundation in Istanbul. The Dev Sol (Revolutionary Left) was held responsible for the attacks.

March 6    Cairo, Egypt: Two explosive devices were safely removed from the grounds of the American and British Cultural Centers in Cairo. Three organizations were believed to be responsible for the attack: The January 15 organization, which had sent a letter bomb to the Israeli ambassador to London in January; the Egyptian Revolutionary Organization, which from out 1984 to 1986 carried out attacks against U.S and Israeli targets; and the Nasserite Organization, which had attacked British and American targets in 1988.

June 12    Istanbul, Turkey: A bomb exploded aboard an unoccupied boat used by U.S. consular staff. The explosion caused extensive damage but no casualties. An organization previously unknown, the Warriors of the June 16th Movement, claimed responsibility for the attack.

+July 6    Between Tel Aviv and Jerusalem, Israel: Rita Levine of Philadelphia, Pennsylvania, was among fifteen killed in an attack by a Hamas terrorist on an Israeli bus between Tel Aviv and Jerusalem.

October 11    Izmir, Turkey: An explosive charge went off outside a U.S. military store. Dev Sol was held responsible for the attack.

## 1991

February 7    Incirlik Air Base, Turkey: Dev Sol members shot and killed a U.S. civilian contractor as he was getting into his car at Incirlik Air Base in Adana, Turkey.

February 28    Izmir, Turkey: Two Dev Sol gunmen shot and wounded a U.S. Air Force officer as he entered his residence in Izmir.

March 28    Jubial, Saudi Arabia: Three U.S. Marines were shot at and injured by an unknown terrorist while driving near Camp Three, Jubial. No organization claimed responsibility for the attack.

October 28    Ankara, Turkey: Victor Marwick, an American soldier serving at the Turkish American base Tuslog, was killed and his wife wounded in a car bomb attack. The Turkish Islamic Jihad claimed responsibility for the attack.

October 28    Istanbul, Turkey: Two car bombings killed a U.S Air Force sergeant and severely wounded an Egyptian diplomat in Istanbul. Turkish Islamic Jihad claimed responsibility.

November 8    Beirut, Lebanon: A 100-kilogram car bomb destroyed the administration building of the AUB, killing one person and wounding at least a dozen.

## 1992

October 12    Umm Qasr, Iraq: A U.S. soldier serving with the United Nations was stabbed and wounded near the port of Umm Qasr. No organization claimed responsibility for the attack.

## 1993

January 25    Virginia, United States: A Pakistani gunman opened fire on Central Intelligence Agency (CIA) employees standing outside of the building. Two agents, Frank Darling and Bennett Lansing, were killed and three others wounded. The assailant was never caught and reportedly fled to Pakistan.

+February 24    Karmei Tzur, West Bank: Hava Wechsberg was killed in an attack on an automobile near Karmei Tzur by Palestinian stone throwers.

+February 26    Cairo, Egypt: A bomb exploded inside a cafe in downtown Cairo, killing three. Among the eighteen wounded were two U.S. citizens. No one claimed responsibility for the attack.

February 26    New York, United States: A massive van bomb exploded in an underground parking garage below the World Trade Center in New York City, killing 6 and wounding 1,042. Four Islamist activists were responsible for the attack. Ramzi Ahmed Yousef, the operation's alleged mastermind, escaped but was later arrested in Pakistan and extradited to the United States. Abd al-Hakim Murad, another suspected conspirator, was arrested by local authorities in the Philippines and handed over to the United States. The two, along with two other terrorists, were tried in the U.S. and sentenced to 240 years.

April 14    Kuwait: The Iraqi intelligence service attempted to assassinate former U.S. President George Bush during a visit to Kuwait. In retaliation, the United States launched a cruise missile attack two months later on the Iraqi capital, Baghdad.

+July 5    Southeast Turkey: In eight separate incidents, the Kurdistan Workers' Party (PKK) kidnapped a total of nineteen Western tourists traveling in southeastern Turkey. The hostages, including one U.S. citizen, Colin Patrick Starger, were released unharmed after spending several weeks in captivity.

+December 1    Jerusalem, Israel: Yitzhak Weinstein of Los Angeles was killed during a Hamas drive-by shooting near Jerusalem.

## 1995

March 8    Karachi, Pakistan: Two unidentified gunmen armed with AK-47 assault rifles opened fire on a U.S. consulate van in Karachi, killing two U.S. diplomats—Jacqueline Keys Van Landingham and Gary C. Durell—and wounding a third, Mark McCloy.

| | |
|---|---|
| +April 9 | Kfar Darom and Netzarim, Gaza Strip: Two suicide attacks were carried out within a few hours of each other in Jewish settlements in the Gaza Strip. In the first attack a suicide bomber crashed an explosive-rigged van into an Israeli bus in Netzarim, killing eight, including a U.S citizen, Alisa Flatow. Over thirty others were injured. In the second attack, a suicide bomber detonated a car bomb in the midst of a convoy of cars in Kfar Darom, injuring twelve. The Palestine Islamic Jihad (PIJ) Shaqaqi Faction claimed responsibility for the attacks. |
| +July 4 | Kashmir, India: In Kashmir, a previously unknown militant group, al-Faran, with suspected links to a Kashmiri separatist group in Pakistan took hostage six tourists, including two U.S citizens. They demanded the release of Muslim militants held in Indian prisons. One of the U.S citizens escaped on July 8, while on August 13 the decapitated body of the Norwegian hostage was found along with a note stating that the other hostages also would be killed if the group's demands were not met. The Indian Government refused. Both Indian and American authorities believe the rest of the hostages were most likely killed in 1996 by their jailers. |
| +August | Istanbul, Turkey: A bombing of Istanbul's popular Taksim Square injured two U.S. citizens. This attack was part of a three-year-old attempt by the PKK to drive foreign tourists away from Turkey by striking at tourist sites. |
| +August 21 | Jerusalem, Israel: A bus bombing in Jerusalem by Hamas killed 4, including an American, Joan Davenny, and wounded more than 100. |
| November 9 | Algiers, Algeria: Islamic extremists set fire to a warehouse belonging to the U.S. embassy, threatened the Algerian security guard because he was working for the United States, and demanded to know whether any U.S. citizens were present. The Armed Islamic Group (GIA) probably carried out the attacks. The group had threatened to strike other foreign targets and especially U.S. objectives in Algeria; the attack's style was similar to past GIA operations against foreign facilities. |
| November 13 | Riyadh, Saudi Arabia: A car bomb exploded in the parking lot outside of the Riyadh headquarters of the Office of the Program Manager/Saudi Arabian National Guard, killing seven persons, five of them U.S citizens, and wounding forty-two. The blast severely damaged the three-story building, which housed a U.S. military advisory group, and several neighboring office buildings. Three groupsthe Islamic Movement for Change, the Tigers of the Gulf, and the Combatant Partisans of God claimed responsibility for the attack. |

## 1996

+February 25    Jerusalem, Israel: A suicide bomber blew up a commuter bus in Jerusalem, killing twenty-six people, including three U.S. citizens, and injuring eighty others, among them another three U.S. citizens. Hamas claimed responsibility for the bombing.

+March 4    Tel Aviv, Israel: A suicide bomber detonated an explosive device outside the Dizengoff Center, Tel Aviv's largest shopping mall, killing twenty persons and injuring seventy-five others, including two U.S. citizens. Both Hamas and the Islamic Jihad claimed responsibility for the bombing.

+May 13    Beit-El, West Bank: Arab gunmen opened fire on a hitchhiking stand near Beit El, wounding three Israelis and killing seventeen-year-old David Boim, an American Israeli from New York. No one claimed responsibility for the attack, although either the Islamic Jihad or Hamas is suspected.

+June 9    Zekharya, West Bank: Yaron Ungar, an American Israeli, and his Israeli wife were killed in a drive-by shooting near their West Bank home. The PFLP is suspected.

June 25    Dhahran, Saudi Arabia: A fuel truck carrying a bomb exploded outside the U.S. military's Khobar Towers housing facility in Dhahran, killing 19 U.S military personnel and wounding 515 persons, including 240 U.S personnel. Several groups claimed responsibility for the attack. In June 2001 a U.S. district court in Alexandria, Virginia, identified Saudi Hizballah as the party responsible for the attack. The court indicated that the members of the organization, banned from Saudi Arabia, "frequently met and were trained in Lebanon, Syria, or Iran" with Libyan help.

+August 17    Mapourdit, Sudan: Sudan People's Liberation Army (SPLA) rebels kidnapped six missionaries in Mapourdit, including a U.S citizen. The SPLA released the hostages on August 28.

+November 1    Sudan: A breakaway group of the Sudanese People's Liberation Army (SPLA) kidnapped three workers of the International Committee of the Red Cross (ICRC), including one U.S citizen. The rebels released the hostages on December 9 in exchange for ICRC supplies and a health survey of their camp.

+December 3    Paris, France: A bomb exploded aboard a Paris subway train, killing four people and injuring eighty-six, including a U.S. citizen. No one claimed responsibility for the attack, but Algerian extremists are suspected.

## 1997

February 23     New York, United States: A Palestinian gunman opened fire on tourists at an observation deck atop the Empire State Building in New York, killing a Danish national and wounding visitors from the United States, Argentina, Switzerland, and France before turning the gun on himself. A handwritten note carried by the gunman claimed this was a punishment attack against the "enemies of Palestine."

+July 30     Jerusalem, Israel: Two bombs detonated in Jerusalem's Mahane Yehuda market, killing 15 persons, including a U.S. citizen, and wounding 168 others, among them Leah Stern of Passiac, New Jersey. The Izz-el-Din al-Qassam Brigades, Hamas's military wing, claimed responsibility for the attack.

+September 4     Jerusalem, Israel: A bombing by Hamas terrorists on a busy street in Jerusalem killed five, including Yael Botwin of Los Angeles, California, and wounded ten other Americans.

October 30     Sanaa, Yemen: Al-Sha'if tribesmen kidnapped a U.S. businessman near Sanaa. The tribesmen sought the release of two fellow tribesmen who were arrested on smuggling charges and several public works projects they claim the government promised them. The hostage was released on November 27.

November 12     Karachi, Pakistan: Two unidentified gunmen shot to death four U.S. auditors from Union Texas Petroleum and their Pakistani driver as they drove away from the Sheraton Hotel in Karachi. Two groups claimed responsibility—the Islamic Inqilabi Council, or Islamic Revolutionary Council, and the Aimal Secret Committee, also known as the Aimal Khufia Action Committee.

+November 25     Aden, Yemen: Yemenite tribesmen kidnapped a U.S citizen, two Italians, and two unspecified Westerners near Aden to protest the eviction of a tribe member from his home. The kidnappers released the five hostages on November 27.

## 1998

+April 19     Maon, Israel: Dov Driben, a twenty-eight-year-old American Israeli farmer, was killed by terrorists near the West Bank town of Maon. One of his assailants, Issa Debavseh, a member of Fatah, was killed on November 7, 2001, by the IDF after being on their wanted list for the murder.

June 21     Beirut, Lebanon: Two hand grenades were thrown at the U.S. embassy in Beirut. No casualties were reported.

| | |
|---|---|
| June 21 | Beirut, Lebanon: Three rocket-propelled grenades attached to a crude detonator exploded near the U.S. embassy compound in Beirut, causing no casualties and little damage. |
| August 7 | Nairobi, Kenya: A car bomb exploded at the rear entrance of the U.S. embassy in Nairobi. The attack killed a total of 292, including 12 U.S. citizens, and injured over 5,000, among them 6 Americans. The perpetrators belonged to al-Qaida, Usama bin Ladin's network. |
| August 7 | Dar es Salaam, Tanzania: A car bomb exploded outside the U.S. embassy in Dar es Salaam, killing eleven and injuring eighty-six. Usama bin Ladin's organization al-Qa'ida was responsible for the attack. Two suspects were arrested. |
| November 21 | Teheran, Iran: Members of Fedayeen Islam, shouting anti-American slogans and wielding stones and iron rods, attacked a group of American tourists in Tehran. Some of the tourists suffered minor injuries from flying glass. |
| December 28 | Mawdiyah, Yemen: Sixteen tourists—twelve Britons, two Americans and two Australians—were taken hostage in the largest kidnapping in Yemen's recent history. The tourists were seized in the Abyan province (some 175 miles south of Sanaa, the capital). One Briton and a Yemeni guide escaped, while the rest were taken to city of Mawdiyah. Four hostages were killed when troops closed in and two were wounded, including an American woman. The kidnappers, members of the Islamic Army of Aden-Abyan, an offshoot of al-Jihad, had demanded the release from jail of their leader, Saleh Haidara al-Atwi. |

## 1999

| | |
|---|---|
| November 12 | Islamabad, Pakistan: Six rockets were fired at the U.S. Information Services cultural center and United Nations offices in Islamabad, injuring a Pakistani guard. |

## 2000

| | |
|---|---|
| +October 8 | Nablus, West Bank: The bullet-ridden body of Hillel Lieberman, a U.S citizen from Brooklyn, New York, living in the Jewish settlement of Elon Moreh, was found at the entrance to the West Bank town of Nablus. Lieberman had headed there after hearing that Palestinians had desecrated Joseph's Tomb, a religious site. No organization claimed responsibility for the murder. |
| October 12 | Aden Harbor, Yemen: A suicide squad rammed the warship the USS *Cole* with an explosives-laden boat, killing thirteen American sailors and injuring thirty-three. The attack was carried out by Usama bin Ladin's al-Qaida organization. |

| | |
|---|---|
| +October 30 | Jerusalem, Israel: Gunmen killed Eish Kodesh Gilmor, a twenty-five-year-old American Israeli on duty as a security guard at the National Insurance Institute in Jerusalem. The "Martyrs of the Al-Aqsa Intifada," a group linked to Fatah, claimed responsibility for the attack. |

## 2001

| | |
|---|---|
| +May 9 | Tekoa, West Bank: Fourteen-year-old Kobi Mandell, an American Israeli, was found stoned to death along with a friend in a cave near the Jewish settlement of Tekoa. Two organizations, the Islamic Jihad and Hizballah-Palestine, claimed responsibility for the attack. |
| +May 29 | Gush Etzion, West Bank: The Fatah Tanzim claimed responsibility for a drive-by shooting of six in the West Bank that killed one American Israeli citizen. |
| +August 9 | Jerusalem, Israel: A suicide bombing at Sbarro's, a pizzeria situated in one of the busiest areas of downtown Jerusalem, killed fifteen people, including a thirty-one-year-old tourist from New Jersey, Shoshana Greenbaum, and wounded more than ninety. Hamas claimed responsibility for the attack. |
| September 11 | New York; Washington, D.C.; and Pennsylvania, United States: During a carefully coordinated attack, 19 hijackers seized four U.S. jetliners and flew three of them to crash into the World Trade Center and the Pentagon. In all, 266 people perished in the four planes, and an estimated 3,000 people were killed on the ground. U.S. investigators determined on the basis of extensive evidence that Usama bin Ladin's al-Qa'ida group was responsible for the attack. The first plane, American Airlines Flight 11, en route from Boston to Los Angeles, crashed into the World Trade Center's north tower at 8:48 A.M. Eighteen minutes later, United Airlines Flight 175, also headed from Boston to Los Angeles, smashed into the World Trade Center's south tower. At 9:40 A.M. a third airplane, an American Airlines Boeing 757 that left Washington's Dulles International Airport for Los Angeles, crashed into the western part of the Pentagon. The fourth plane, United Airlines Flight 93, flying from Newark to San Francisco, crashed near Pittsburgh, Pennsylvania, before it could hit its target. Hundreds of firefighters, police officers, and other rescue workers who arrived at the World Trade Center were killed or injured. |

## 2002

| | |
|---|---|
| January 23 | Karachi, Pakistan: Wall Street Journal correspondent Daniel Pearl was kidnapped by Islamist radicals. He was murdered by them several days later. |

March 15              Sana, Yemen: Two grenades were thrown at the U.S. embassy the
                      day after a visit there by Vice President Dick Cheney.

March 17              Islamabad, Pakistan: Two Americans were among five people killed
                      when grenades were thrown into a Protestant church service near
                      the U.S. embassy. The American victims were Barbara Green, an
                      embassy employee, and her daughter, Kristen Wormsley, a senior
                      at the American School in Islamabad. Ten Americans were among
                      the forty-five injured.

June 14               A suicide attacker, likely with al-Qa'ida, crashed a bomb-laden ve-
                      hicle into a guard post outside the U.S. Consulate in Karachi, Pak-
                      istan. At least eleven people were killed and forty-five injured, in-
                      cluding a U.S. Marine.

## Sources

State Department's Chronology on Terrorist Incidents, 1961–2001
State Department's "Patterns of Terrorism" reports, 1995–2000
Institute for Counter-Terrorism Database, Interdisciplinary Center
Congressional Research Service's "Terrorist Incidents Involving U.S. Citizens or Prop-
    erty," 1981–1989

# GLOSSARY OF TERMS

*aalim:* Plural of *ulama*, a group of Islamic clerics and/or scholars.

*ahl al-kitab:* "People of the book." A term used for Christians and Jews to denote that they have special respect in Islam and certain limited rights—and also restrictions—under its rule. See *dhimmis.*

*Allahu Akbar:* "God is Great," a popular Islamic saying and Islamist battle cry.

*Andalusia:* Muslim name for Spain at the time it was under Muslim rule before the Christian Reconquest of 1492. Since all land ever governed by Islam is supposed to remain under its rule, extreme Islamists include this territory as part of their future empire.

*al-Aqsa:* An important mosque in East Jerusalem which has become a symbol for Islamists of the need to reconquer Jerusalem.

*Dar al-Harb:* See *Dar al-Islam.*

*Dar al-Islam:* The area of the world where an Islamic community predominates. Islamists recall that the Dar al-Islam was traditionally contrasted with the Dar al-Harb, the area where Muslims carry out war against unbelievers. This concept, then, forms a basis for the radical Islamist division of the world into friendly and hostile territories in conflict.

*da'wa:* Proclaiming the message of Islam to the general public. This activity, considered a religious duty, is interpreted by Islamist activists to mean the spreading of propaganda regarding their interpretation of Islam.

*dhimmis:* Jews and Christians living under Islamic rule who are supposed to receive protection in exchange for the political submission and other restrictions.

*emir:* A traditional term for leader; in Islamist politics, the leader of a specific group.

367

*faqih:* An Islamist cleric respected for knowledge of Islamic law and thus able to hand down rulings.

*fatwa:* A religious decision that traditionally could only be issued by clerics.

*fedayeen:* Literally, one who sacrifices himself; a fighter in war.

*fiqh:* Correct behavior under Islam.

*hadith:* A saying of Muhammad, the founder of Islam, that plays an important part in religious law. The reliability of any particular *hadith* depends on the chain of those who passed it down.

*hajj:* The pilgrimage to Mecca and one of the main duties of Islam.

*haram:* Something forbidden by Islam.

*harmain sharifain:* Refers to two holy places—Mecca and Medina—in western Saudi Arabia.

*hijra:* The journey of Muhammad, the founder of Islam, from Mecca to escape persecution there to Medina in 632 C.E. This event marks the beginning of the Islamic calendar.

*hubal:* Idol that was worshipped by pagans before the advent of Islam. Islamists use this to refer to many contemporary ideas and practices that they find pagan.

*hudood:* Islamic penal code.

*imam:* Traditionally, a prayer leader, but can also denote a respected leader in Islam. Ayatollah Ruhollah Khomeini's followers, for example, often refer to him as *imam* to imply his rightful leadership.

*intihar:* Suicide, a forbidden practice in Islam. Islamists want to prove that suicide bombing is not a form of *intihar.*

*Isma'ili:* A sect of Shi'ite Islam which in medieval times produced the Assassins, a long-extinct political-religious group that used terrorism against its enemies.

*istishad:* Martyrdom. In contrast to *intihar,* this is extolled by Islam.

*jahiliyya:* Traditionally understood as the pagan state of ignorance in the times before Islam but reinterpreted by Islamists—a point often credited to Sayyid Qutb—to mean any contemporary system not based on what they consider to be a proper Islamic government and society. This was a very controversial departure from traditional Islam, which, in an effort to ensure stability, opposed declaring fellow Muslims heretics or judging states and societies on their religious acceptability. In the Islamist interpretation, this justifies revolution against governments and terrorism against individual Muslims.

*jahannum:* Hell.

*jahili:* Adjective form of *jahiliyya.*

*janna:* Paradise.

*jihad:* Traditionally in Islam, either a holy war waged against non-Muslims or, in more recent times, a struggle for personal self-improvement. Radical Islamists have focused on the former meaning and interpreted it as requiring all Muslims to wage holy war against non-Muslims and against states with Muslim populations deemed to be in a state of *jahiliyya*.

*jizya:* A special tax that Islamic law decrees must be paid by all non-Muslims who live in Muslim-ruled lands.

*Kaba:* The central Islamic holy site in Mecca, Saudi Arabia.

*kafirs:* A derogatory term for non-Muslims.

*khalifa:* Often written in English as "caliph." Traditionally, the religiously legitimate Muslim ruler over all Muslims. Its original meaning points to this person as a successor in that role to Muhammad, Islam's founder. In practice, however, over the centuries the *khalifa* became a figurehead used by rulers to legitimize their power or was even taken by them as a title. The caliphate was dissolved by the Turkish Republic in 1923. Some radical Islamists, including Usama bin Ladin, want to reestablish a caliphate as a Middle East–wide, or even worldwide, Islamic empire.

*Kharijites (sing. Khariji):* A radical group that launched an unsuccessful seventh-century rebellion against mainstream Islam. Muslim critics of the Islamists see this group as a prototype for today's radical Islamists.

*kufr:* A derogatory word for a nonbeliever in Islam and thus, it is implied, a disbeliever in God. Radical Islamists also use this to describe Muslims whom they deem heretical or hypocritical.

*Land of the Two Holy Places:* A term Usama bin Ladin used for Saudi Arabia, referring to the presence of Mecca and Medina there. Bin Ladin and other Islamists used this term to avoid using the word "Saudi," since they did not recognize the monarchy that ruled that country. Similarly, some Islamists refer to the king of Saudi Arabia by his title "Custodian of the Two Holy Places" to stress his religious duties or to avoid implying that they accept the monarchy.

*marja' al-taqlid:* In Islam, a good example to imitate; the proper source of conduct.

*mihajirun:* Literally, migrants. In Islam, refers to those who accompanied Muhammad, Islam's founder, on his journey from Mecca to Medina; thus, those of exceptional merit who in a sense participated in cofounding Islam.

*mufassala:* In Islam, the process of separating oneself from society to attain spiritual advancement. In mainstream Islam this is a symbolic process, but Islamists have interpreted it as cutting oneself off from society and its practices in a systematic manner.

*mufti:* A chief religious legal authority.

*mujahid (pl. mujahidin):* One who wages *jihad*. In recent years, often used to refer particularly to those who fought the Soviets in Afghanistan.

*mustad'afin:* The oppressed. A term favored by the leader of Iran's Islamist revolution, Ayatollah Ruhollah Khomeini, to refer to the poor and downtrodden people of the world in an Islamist version of class struggle.

*Qadisiyya:* The seventh-century battle where Arabs Muslims defeated and destroyed the

Persian empire, opening Persia for conversion to Islam. Used by President Saddam Hussein of Iraq during the Iran-Iraq war to legitimize his war against non-Arab Iran. Used by Islamists to show that a small group of dedicated Muslims can destroy a seemingly invincible foe.

*al-Qa'ida:* Literally, principle. The name of Usama bin Ladin's group.

*qibla:* The direction of prayer by Muslims toward Mecca.

*al-Quds:* Jerusalem.

*Quraysh:* A seventh-century tribe that became leaders of Islam.

*riba:* Economic interest.

*al-salaamu alaikum:* Traditional Islamic greeting meaning "peace be upon you."

*sawad:* A good religious deed.

*al-shabab:* Literally, young men; used in recent times to indicate those willing to fight.

*sharia:* The body of Islamic law. Islamists say this system of "God-made" laws, and not any laws made by legislatures or rulers, must govern any proper state where Muslims live.

*sheikh:* An honorary term of respect, usually used today for a Muslim cleric.

*Shia:* The version of Islam adhered to by the majority in Iran and large communities elsewhere. Although Islamists insist that all Muslims are united, all of their groups are either Sunni or Shia. Thus, while al-Qa'ida viewed itself as an organization that would bring all Muslims together, it had only Sunni members and followed a Sunni version of Islam. Hizballah, for example, is made up of Shia Islamists, and Ayatollah Khomeini was also a Shia Islamist.

*shirk:* In Islam, the dangerous and heretical practice of associating others with God, implying polytheism.

*shura:* In Islamic sources, says that a ruler should consult with others, which provides the basis for forms of parliamentary government.

*Sunni:* The majority version of Islam. See *Shia.*

*Sunna:* The main tradition of Islam.

*takfir:* The labeling of other Muslims as heretics; a practice traditionally frowned upon by mainstream Muslims.

*tawhid:* The affirmation of the oneness with God, an important Islamic principle.

*ulama:* Religious figures, clerics.

*umma:* The community of Muslims that exists across national borders.

*waqf:* Traditionally, foundation or trust whose assets cannot be touched but used only for some religious or charitable purpose. Islamists argue that Palestine, from the Jordan river to the Mediterranean sea, is a *waqf,* and thus no one can negotiate over its future or cede any of its territory.

# GLOSSARY OF NAMES

*Armed Islamic Group (GIA):* Radical Algerian Islamist organization that fought against the government there using terrorist methods. Worked closely with Usama bin Ladin.

*Atta, Muhammad:* Member of al-Qa'ida who was the leader of the September 11 terrorist attacks. He piloted one of the American Airlines planes into the World Trade Center.

*Azzam, Abdullah:* Palestinian educator and *jihad* fighter who worked in Jordan and eventually played an important part in the building of the Arab Islamist forces fighting in Afghanistan. He is considered by many to be Usama bin Ladin's mentor

*al-Banna, Hasan:* Founder of the Egyptian Muslim Brotherhood.

*Fadlallah, Muhammad Hussein:* Spiritual guide of the Lebanese terrorist group Hizballah.

*Faraj, Abd al-Salam:* Founder and theorist of Egyptian revolutionary Islamist group al-Jihad. His main doctrinal contribution was to stress armed *jihad* as a duty for all Muslims. Executed by the Egyptian government.

*Ghaith, Suleiman Abu:* Member of al-Qa'ida and close aide of Usama bin Ladin.

*Hamas:* Palestinian Islamist movement that uses terrorism to achieve its goal of destroying Israel and establishing a Palestinian Islamist state.

*Hizballah:* Lebanese Islamist movement of Shia Muslims committed both to Israel's destruction and to turning Lebanon into an Islamic republic.

*Hussein, Saddam:* President of Iraq.

*al-Jama'a al-Islamiyya:* Egyptian revolutionary Islamist group.

*al-Jihad:* Egyptian Islamist revolutionary group at one time headed by Ayman al-Zawahiri.

*al-Khamene'i, Ali al-Husseini:* Khomeini's successor as spiritual guide of the Islamic Republic of Iran. Iran's most powerful leader.

*Khomeini, Ayatollah Ruhollah:* Iranian cleric who went into exile during the reign of Shah Reza Pahlavi and returned after the 1979 revolution to become head of Iran and founder of the Islamic republic there.

*bin Ladin, Usama:* Founder and leader of al-Qa'ida who masterminded several terrorist acts against the United States, including the September 11 attacks.

*al-Maqdissy, Sheikh Abu Muhammad:* Jordanian Islamist.

*Ma'soum, Mulla:* Formerly spokesman of Afghan's Taliban government and its ambassador to Pakistan.

*Mawdudi, Abul A'la:* Pakistani who was one of the greatest founding figures and ideologues of the Islamist movement.

*Moussaoui, Zacarias:* French citizen of Moroccan origin who had been arrested before September 11 but whose involvement in that operation was discovered afterward. He was indicted by the U.S. government in December 2001.

*Muhammad, Mullah Umar:* Spiritual guide of the Taliban.

*Muslim Brotherhood:* Egyptian Islamist group that was originally revolutionary but turned to more moderate methods after its leadership was executed or imprisoned in the 1960s.

*Nasser, Gamal Abdel:* Egypt's main leader between 1952 and his death in 1970; the most influential figure in the Arab world and an advocate of pan-Arab nationalism.

*Qutb, Sayyid:* Ideologue of the Egyptian Muslim Brotherhood and perhaps the most important single thinker to shape the contemporary *jihad*-oriented groups, including al-Qa'ida.

*al-Rahman, Umar Abd:* Egyptian cleric who was spiritual guide of the al-Jihad group and a leading figure in the Islamist opposition to the Egyptian government. Immigrated to the United States. He was convicted of being a key figure in the first terror attack on the World Trade Center in 1993 and imprisoned.

*Shariati, Ali:* An influential thinker who helped to shape the Iranian revolution.

*Taha, Rifa'ey Ahmad:* Egyptian Islamist leader.

*Taliban:* Radical Islamist movement that seized power in Afghanistan in 1996 but was deposed by U.S. forces in 2001. It gave safe haven to Usama bin Ladin.

*Tantawi, Sheikh Muhamad Sayyed:* Leader of al-Azhar Islamic university in Cairo and one of the most powerful voices of non-Islamist Islam.

*al-Wahhab, Muhammad Ibn Abd:* Founder of the Wahhabi movement, which later gave birth to the Saudi Arabian state

*Wahhabi movement:* The relatively radical interpretation of Islam prevailing in Saudi Arabia. Saudi-financed movements exported it elsewhere during the 1990s.

*World Islamic Front:* The organization formed by Usama bin Ladin, consisting of al-Qa'ida plus four small organizations, that issued a 1998 "*Jihad* against Jews and Crusaders."

*al-Zawahiri, Ayman:* A leader of the Egyptian group al-Jihad and later of al-Qai'da.

# Index

Printed in the United States
79095LV00004B/21